T5-AFC-870

FIRESIDE

Revised and Enlarged

A TREASURY OF *Great Poems*

ENGLISH AND AMERICAN

Volume Two

from Wordsworth to Dylan Thomas

WITH LIVES OF THE POETS AND HISTORICAL SETTINGS SELECTED AND INTEGRATED

BY

LOUIS UNTERMEYER

A FIRESIDE BOOK PUBLISHED BY

SIMON AND SCHUSTER • NEW YORK

A FIRESIDE BOOK
PUBLISHED BY SIMON AND SCHUSTER
A DIVISION OF GULF & WESTERN CORPORATION
SIMON & SCHUSTER BUILDING
ROCKEFELLER CENTER, 1230 AVE. OF THE AMERICAS
NEW YORK, N.Y. 10020

ISBN 0-671-75021-6
MANUFACTURED IN THE UNITED STATES OF AMERICA

6 7 8 9 10 11 12 13 14 15

CONTENTS

XII

The Spirit of Revolution and Romance

XIII

Faith, Doubt, and Democracy

XIV
Challenge to Tradition

XV

The World of the Twentieth Century

Volume One

Chaucer to Burns

XII

The Spirit of Revolution and Romance

ROMANTICISM has been so variously defined that it has come to mean anything the critic wants it to mean, from Heinrich Heine's "the reawakening of the Middle Ages" to Walter Pater's "the addition of strangeness to beauty." But as the term is commonly used today, romanticism primarily implies a reaction from rationalism. Stressing emotion rather than reason, instinct rather than experience, the romantic writers of the nineteenth century emphasized self and sensibility. Echoing Rousseau, who maintained that man was corrupted by civilized society, they turned the common man into a Noble Savage, glorified Nature as Divine Healer, and struggled to establish liberty in the ever-sharpening conflict between materialism and idealism.

The destruction of the Bastille in 1789 spread the spirit of revolution and romance. Insurgence leaped the Channel, and its challenge was answered by such ardent young men as Coleridge, Southey, Landor, and Hazlitt. Wordsworth, leading them all in enthusiasm, envisioned the rescue of mankind and declared in his FRENCH REVOLUTION:

> Bliss was it in that dawn to be alive,
> But to be young was very heaven!

Poems became battle cries; the inert were aroused; a new dream, gathering strength and swiftness, took on fierce reality. But the reality soon grew too terrible for its disciples; the revolutionary dream became a nightmare of indiscriminate fury and violent excess. Four years after the beginning of the French Revolution, England went to war with France; the dawn of the nineteenth century brought the threat of Napoleon. It was no longer possible to believe in revolt as a liberation, or war as a great catharsis, and the intransigent youths became middle-aged conservatives. Southey lived to be the "turncoat" poet laureate, and Wordsworth, renegade rebel and Tory, was characterized by Browning as "the lost leader."

Nevertheless, it was the flame of revolt that burned out the cynical social doctrines of the eighteenth century and kindled in the younger men a hot hatred of injustice and an even more fiery love of humanity.

WILLIAM WORDSWORTH

[1770–1850]

Champion of the "humble and rustic life" in which "the essential passions of the heart find a better soil," William Wordsworth was born April 7, 1770, at Cockermouth, Cumberland, near the river Derwent in the Lake District. His father was an attorney; his mother, who died when Wordsworth was eight years old, was the daughter of a dry-goods merchant. Five years after his mother's death his father died, and the five children were scattered among schools and guardians. At seventeen Wordsworth was sent to St. John's College, Cambridge, and it was here that he began to connect the images of the countryside with his own thoughts, to celebrate the simple but romantic aspects of nature, and feel:

> A motion and a spirit that impels
> All thinking things, all objects of all thoughts,
> And rolls through all things.

Wordsworth's guardians intended him for the Church, but the young poet put them off with various excuses. After graduating, he convinced them that he needed a year of French, and at twenty-two crossed the Channel, became intimate with members of the French revolutionary party, and lived a year in Blois and Orléans. At Orléans Wordsworth fell in love with Marie-Anne ("Annette") Vallon, four years his senior, who bore him a daughter, Carolyn. It is possible that Wordsworth hoped to marry Annette and settle in France, but the Continental disorders and the war between France and England in 1793 upset any plans which Wordsworth may have made toward this end. Whether or not Wordsworth's double passion for Annette and France had cooled, it is apparent that marriage was no longer considered, although, as G. M. Harper wrote in his remarkable piece of research, WORDSWORTH'S FRENCH DAUGHTER, "Whatever, from a legal point of view, may have been the nature of the connection between Wordsworth and Marie-Anne Vallon, it was openly acknowledged and its consequences were honorably endured." In 1802, when Wordsworth was thirty-two, he returned to France for four weeks and walked by the seashore almost every evening with Annette and Carolyn. One result of these walks on the beach near Calais was the sonnet beginning "It is a beauteous evening, calm and free." Written to his ten-year-old daughter, it is a poem as tranquil in tone as it is moving in spirit.

On the Beach at Calais

It is a beauteous evening, calm and free;
The holy time is quiet as a nun
Breathless with adoration; the broad sun
Is sinking down in its tranquillity;
The gentleness of heaven broods o'er the sea:
Listen! the mighty Being is awake,
And doth with his eternal motion make
A sound like thunder—everlastingly.
Dear child! dear girl! that walkest with me here,
If thou appear untouched by solemn thought,
Thy nature is not therefore less divine:
Thou liest in Abraham's bosom all the year,
And worship'st at the Temple's inner shrine,
God being with thee when we know it not.

The love affair and its consequences, together with his disillusionment in the revolutionary cause, unsettled Wordsworth for years. Unable to live in a fading dream, he found it difficult to adjust himself to the hard world of reality. Even with the coming of April, when "every flower enjoys the air it breathes," he mused unhappily in LINES WRITTEN IN EARLY SPRING:

To her fair works did Nature link
  The human soul that through me ran;
And much it grieved my heart to think
  What man has made of man.

"What man has made of man" continued to trouble Wordsworth. The French Revolution brought hope to millions, particularly to the Negroes in Haiti. But the National Assembly was not ready to extend the "rights of man" to slaves. The Haitian blacks revolted, led by Pierre Dominique Breda, who adopted the sobriquet of Toussaint L'Ouverture. After a struggle of twenty years, the Haitians won their freedom; but, long before independence had been achieved, Toussaint L'Ouverture had been seized and transported to France. When Toussaint was imprisoned, Wordsworth, deeply shaken, addressed one of his most nobly affecting sonnets to the captured liberator.

To Toussaint L'Ouverture

Toussaint, the most unhappy man of men!
Whether the whistling rustic tend his plough
Within thy hearing, or thy head be now
Pillowed in some deep dungeon's earless den—
O miserable Chieftain! where and when
Wilt thou find patience! Yet die not; do thou
Wear rather in thy bonds a cheerful brow:
Though fallen thyself, never to rise again,
Live, and take comfort. Thou hast left behind
Powers that will work for thee; air, earth, and skies
There's not a breathing of the common wind
That will forget thee; thou hast great allies;
Thy friends are exultations, agonies,
And love, and man's unconquerable mind.

Wordsworth wandered about England with his sister Dorothy, whose "exquisite regard for common things" intensified his observation and preserved the poet in him.

She gave me eyes, she gave me ears;
And humble cares, and delicate fears;
A heart, the fountain of sweet tears;
  And love, and thought, and joy.

An influence second only to Dorothy's came into Wordsworth's life in his twenty-sixth year, when he first met Samuel Taylor Coleridge. A few months later William, who had come into a small inheritance, moved with Dorothy to Somerset in order to be near Coleridge. There, visiting daily, collaborating, and continually encouraged by Dorothy, the poets flourished, and the trio became "three persons with one soul."

In September, 1798, Wordsworth and Coleridge published a volume unpretentiously entitled LYRICAL BALLADS, a book which the otherwise restrained ENCYCLOPAEDIA BRITANNICA unreservedly calls "the most important event in the history of English poetry after Milton." Both poets were pledged to the romantic position, but their approach was essentially different. It was agreed that Coleridge was to make incredible romances seem real, while Wordsworth was to reveal the romance of the commonplace. Wordsworth's object was to give "the charm of novelty to things of every day . . . by awakening the mind's attention and directing it to the loveliness and the wonders of the world before us." Thus the LYRICAL BALLADS mingled the "natural" and "supernatural," and revealed them as contrasting marvels of observation and imagination.

The reception accorded to the LYRICAL BALLADS was such as might have discouraged spirits less ardent than Wordsworth's and Coleridge's. Coleridge's major poem, THE RIME OF THE ANCIENT MARINER, one of the chief glories of English poetry, was contemptuously derided, and Wordsworth's magnificent soliloquy, LINES COMPOSED A FEW MILES ABOVE TINTERN ABBEY, was wholly ignored. TINTERN ABBEY justifies Wordsworth's conception of the romantic nature of poetry as "the spontaneous overflow of powerful feelings," a kind of poetry which "takes its origin from emotion recollected in tranquillity." More than most, this is a poem which recollects and confirms, which recalls beloved sights and sensations, and reaffirms their unity. In a beautiful cadence addressed to Dorothy, Wordsworth summons "the still, sad music of humanity" and repeats his faith in Nature, which "never did betray the heart that loved her."

Lines

COMPOSED A FEW MILES ABOVE TINTERN ABBEY, ON REVISITING THE BANKS OF THE WYE DURING A TOUR, JULY 13, 1798

Five years have passed; five summers, with the length
Of five long winters! and again I hear
These waters, rolling from their mountain springs
With a soft inland murmur.—Once again
Do I behold these steep and lofty cliffs,
That on a wild, secluded scene impress
Thoughts of more deep seclusion; and connect
The landscape with the quiet of the sky.
The day is come when I again repose
Here, under this dark sycamore, and view
These plots of cottage-ground, these orchard-tufts,
Which at this season, with their unripe fruits,
Are clad in one green hue, and lose themselves
'Mid groves and copses. Once again I see
These hedge-rows, hardly hedge-rows, little lines
Of sportive wood run wild; these pastoral farms,
Green to the very door; and wreaths of smoke
Sent up, in silence, from among the trees!
With some uncertain notice, as might seem
Of vagrant dwellers in the houseless woods,
Or of some hermit's cave, where by his fire
The hermit sits alone.
These beauteous forms,
Through a long absence, have not been to me
As is a landscape to a blind man's eye;
But oft, in lonely rooms, and 'mid the din
Of towns and cities, I have owed to them
In hours of weariness, sensations sweet,
Felt in the blood, and felt along the heart;
And passing even into my purer mind,
With tranquil restoration:—feelings, too,
Or unremembered pleasure; such, perhaps,
As have no slight or trivial influence
On that best portion of a good man's life,
His little, nameless, unremembered acts
Of kindness and of love. Nor less, I trust,
To them I may have owed another gift,
Of aspect more sublime; that blessed mood,

In which the burthen of the mystery,
In which the heavy and the weary weight
Of all this unintelligible world,
Is lightened—that serene and blessed mood
In which the affections gently lead us on—
Until, the breath of this corporeal frame
And even the motion of our human blood
Almost suspended, we are laid asleep
In body, and become a living soul;
While with an eye made quiet by the power
Of harmony, and the deep power of joy,
We see into the life of things.
If this
Be but a vain belief, yet, oh! how oft—
In darkness and amid the many shapes
Of joyless daylight; when the fretful stir
Unprofitable, and the fever of the world,
Have hung upon the beatings of my heart—
How oft, in spirit, have I turned to thee,
O sylvan Wye! thou wanderer through the woods,
How often has my spirit turned to thee!
And now, with gleams of half-extinguished thought,
With many recognitions dim and faint,
And somewhat of a sad perplexity,
The picture of the mind revives again;
While here I stand, not only with the sense
Of present pleasure, but with pleasing thoughts
That in this moment there is life and food
For future years. And so I dare to hope,
Though changed, no doubt, from what I was when first
I came among these hills; when like a roe
I bounded o'er the mountains, by the sides
Of the deep rivers, and the lonely streams,
Wherever Nature led; more like a man
Flying from something that he dreads, than one
Who sought the thing he loved. For Nature then
(The coarser pleasures of my boyish days,
And their glad animal movements all gone by)
To me was all in all.—I cannot paint
What then I was. The sounding cataract
Haunted me like a passion; the tall rock,
The mountain, and the deep and gloomy wood,
Their colors and their forms, were then to me
An appetite; a feeling and a love,
That had no need of a remoter charm,

By thought supplied, nor any interest
Unborrowed from the eye.—That time is past,
And all its aching joys are now no more,
And all its dizzy raptures. Not for this
Faint I, nor mourn, nor murmur; other gifts
Have followed; for such loss, I would believe,
Abundant recompense. For I have learned
To look on Nature, not as in the hour
Of thoughtless youth; but hearing oftentimes
The still, sad music of humanity,
Nor harsh nor grating, though of ample power
To chasten and subdue. And I have felt
A presence that disturbs me with the joy
Of elevated thoughts; a sense sublime
Of something far more deeply interfused,
Whose dwelling is the light of setting suns,
And the round ocean and the living air,
And the blue sky, and in the mind of man;
A motion and a spirit, that impels
All thinking things, all objects of all thought,
And rolls through all things. Therefore am I still
A lover of the meadows and the woods,
And mountains; and of all that we behold
From this green earth; of all the mighty world
Of eye, and ear—both what they half create,
And what perceive; well pleased to recognize
In Nature and the language of the sense,
The anchor of my purest thoughts, the nurse,
The guide, the guardian of my heart, and soul
Of all my moral being.
                                        Nor perchance,
If I were not thus taught, should I the more
Suffer my genial spirits to decay;
For thou art with me here upon the banks
Of this fair river; thou my dearest Friend,
My dear, dear Friend; and in thy voice I catch
The language of my former heart, and read
My former pleasures in the shooting lights
Of thy wild eyes. Oh! yet a little while
May I behold in thee what I was once,
My dear, dear sister! and this prayer I make,
Knowing that Nature never did betray
The heart that loved her; 'tis her privilege,
Through all the years of this our life, to lead
From joy to joy; for she can so inform

The mind that is within us, so impress
With quietness and beauty, and so feed
With lofty thoughts, that neither evil tongues,
Rash judgments, nor the sneers of selfish men,
Nor greetings where no kindness is, nor all
The dreary intercourse of daily life,
Shall e'er prevail against us, or disturb
Our cheerful faith that all which we behold
Is full of blessings. Therefore let the moon
Shine on thee in thy solitary walk;
And let the misty mountain-winds be free
To blow against thee; and in after years,
When these wild ecstasies shall be matured
Into a sober pleasure; when thy mind
Shall be a mansion for all lovely forms,
Thy memory be as a dwelling-place
For all sweet sounds and harmonies; oh! then,
If solitude, or fear, or pain, or grief,
Should be thy portion, with what healing thoughts
Of tender joy wilt thou remember me,
And these my exhortations! Nor, perchance—
If I should be where I no more can hear
Thy voice, nor catch from thy wild eyes these gleams
Of past existence—wilt thou then forget
That on the banks of this delightful stream
We stood together; and that I, so long
A worshiper of Nature, hither came
Unwearied in that service; rather say
With warmer love—oh! with far deeper zeal
Of holier love. Nor wilt thou then forget
That after many wanderings, many years
Of absence, these steep woods and lofty cliffs,
And this green pastoral landscape, were to me
More dear, both for themselves and for thy sake!

After a trip to Germany with Coleridge, the Wordsworths settled in Grasmere, and there, except for occasional jaunts, they remained the rest of their lives. In his thirty-third year Wordsworth married Mary Hutchinson, a friend of Dorothy's, and the two women devoted themselves to the poet, sharing the housekeeping and the ever-increasing secretarial labors. Three editions of LYRICAL BALLADS were printed before 1805; the second was enriched by a preface which served as the manifesto of the romantic movement. The "advertisement" said that the BALLADS were an experiment to ascertain "how far the language of conversation is adapted for the purposes of poetic pleasure"; and, though many of the poems were flat failures—being as dull and colorless as conversation is likely to be—a new diction had been created. This talk-flavored speech tightened many of Wordsworth's lyrics, and Wordsworth's kinship with natural things gave his domesticated blank verse a quality as different from the sonorous blank verse of Milton as from the pedestrian blank verse of Cowper.

It is in the lyrics that Wordsworth most freely used the "language actually spoken" in contrast to the traditional poetic speech He achieved a frank and often noble simplicity, a plain but penetrating power, by avoiding the artificial elegance of Pope, by shunning inversions, and intensifying "the unassuming commonplace of nature" with "thoughts too deep for tears."

The Solitary Reaper

Behold her, single in the field,
Yon solitary highland lass!
Reaping and singing by herself;
Stop here, or gently pass!
Alone she cuts and binds the grain,
And sings a melancholy strain;
O listen! for the vale profound
Is overflowing with the sound.

No nightingale did ever chaunt
More welcome notes to weary bands
Of travelers in some shady haunt,
Among Arabian sands:
A voice so thrilling ne'er was heard
In spring-time from the cuckoo-bird,
Breaking the silence of the seas
Among the farthest Hebrides.

Will no one tell me what she sings?—
Perhaps the plaintive numbers flow
For old, unhappy, far-off things,
And battles long ago:
Or is it some more humble lay,
Familiar matter of today?

Some natural sorrow, loss, or pain,
That has been, and may be again?

Whate'er the theme, the maiden sang
As if her song could have no ending;
I saw her singing at her work,
And o'er the sickle bending;—
I listened, motionless and still;
And, as I mounted up the hill
The music in my heart I bore,
Long after it was heard no more.

The Daffodils

I wandered lonely as a cloud
That floats on high o'er vales and hills,
When all at once I saw a crowd,
A host of golden daffodils,
Beside the lake, beneath the trees
Fluttering and dancing in the breeze.

Continuous as the stars that shine
And twinkle on the milky way,
They stretched in never-ending line
Along the margin of a bay:
Ten thousand saw I at a glance
Tossing their heads in sprightly dance.

The waves beside them danced, but they
Out-did the sparkling waves in glee:
A poet could not but be gay
In such a jocund company!
I gazed—and gazed—but little thought
What wealth the show to me had brought:

For oft, when on my couch I lie
In vacant or in pensive mood,
They flash upon that inward eye
Which is the bliss of solitude;
And then my heart with pleasure fills,
And dances with the daffodils.

To the Cuckoo

O blithe new-comer! I have heard,
I hear thee and rejoice:
O cuckoo! shall I call thee Bird,
Or but a wandering Voice?

While I am lying on the grass
Thy twofold shout I hear;
From hill to hill it seems to pass,
At once far off and near.

Though babbling only to the vale
Of sunshine and of flowers,
Thou bringest unto me a tale
Of visionary hours.

Thrice welcome, darling of the Spring!
Even yet thou art to me
No bird, but an invisible thing,
A voice, a mystery;

The same whom in my school-boy days
I listened to; that cry
Which made me look a thousand ways
In bush, and tree, and sky.

To seek thee did I often rove
Through woods and on the green;
And thou wert still a hope, a love;
Still longed for, never seen!

And I can listen to thee yet;
Can lie upon the plain
And listen, till I do beget
That golden time again.

O blessèd bird! the earth we pace
Again appears to be
An unsubstantial, faery place,
That is fit home for thee!

To a Skylark

Ethereal minstrel! pilgrim of the sky!
Dost thou despise the earth where cares abound?
Or, while the wings aspire, are heart and eye
Both with thy nest upon the dewy ground?
Thy nest which thou canst drop into at will,
Those quivering wings composed, that music still!

Leave to the nightingale her shady wood;
A privacy of glorious light is thine;
Whence thou dost pour upon the world a flood
Of harmony, with instinct more divine;
Type of the wise who soar, but never roam;
True to the kindred points of Heaven and home!

She Was a Phantom of Delight

She was a phantom of delight
When first she gleamed upon my sight;
A lovely apparition, sent
To be a moment's ornament;
Her eyes as stars of twilight fair;
Like twilight's, too, her dusky hair;
But all things else about her drawn
From May-time and the cheerful dawn;
A dancing shape, an image gay,
To haunt, to startle, and way-lay.

I saw her upon nearer view,
A spirit, yet a woman too!
Her household motions light and free,
And steps of virgin-liberty;
A countenance in which did meet
Sweet records, promises as sweet;
A creature not too bright or good
For human nature's daily food;
For transient sorrows, simple wiles,
Praise, blame, love, kisses, tears, and smiles.

And now I see with eye serene
The very pulse of the machine;
A being breathing thoughtful breath,
A traveller between life and death;
The reason firm, the temperate will,
Endurance, foresight, strength, and skill;
A perfect woman, nobly planned,
To warn, to comfort, and command;
And yet a spirit still, and bright
With something of angelic light.

My Heart Leaps Up When I Behold

My heart leaps up when I behold
    A rainbow in the sky:
So was it when my life began;
So is it now I am a man;
So be it when I shall grow old,
    Or let me die!
The Child is father of the Man;
And I could wish my days to be
Bound each to each by natural piety.

Perhaps the most famous of Wordsworth's simple lyrics are the so-called "Lucy Poems." Written during the poet's sojourn in Germany about an English girl known and lost in boyhood, the sequence is nostalgic in theme and mournful in tone. The plaintive note, however, changes at the end to an uplifted resignation, as Wordsworth reaffirms the unity of all life—and even death—with nature.

Lucy

STRANGE FITS OF PASSION HAVE I KNOWN

Strange fits of passion have I known:
  And I will dare to tell,
But in the Lover's ear alone,
  What once to me befell.

When she I loved looked every day,
  Fresh as a rose in June,
I to her cottage bent my way,
  Beneath an evening moon.

Upon the moon I fixed my eye,
  All over the wide lea;
With quickening pace my horse drew nigh
  Those paths so dear to me.

And now we reached the orchard plot;
  And as we climbed the hill,
The sinking moon to Lucy's cot
  Came near and nearer still.

In one of those sweet dreams I slept,
  Kind Nature's gentlest boon!
And all the while my eyes I kept
  On the descending moon.

My horse moved on; hoof after hoof
  He raised, and never stopped:
When down behind the cottage roof,
  At once, the bright moon dropped.

What fond and wayward thought will slide
  Into a lover's head!—
"Oh, mercy!" to myself I cried,
  "If Lucy should be dead!"

I TRAVELED AMONG UNKNOWN MEN

I traveled among unknown men,
  In lands beyond the sea;
Nor, England! did I know till then
  What love I bore to thee.

'Tis past, that melancholy dream!
  Nor will I quit thy shore
A second time; for still I seem
  To love thee more and more.

Among thy mountains did I feel
  The joy of my desire;
And she I cherished turned her wheel
  Beside an English fire.

Thy mornings showed, thy nights concealed
  The bowers where Lucy played;
And thine too is the last green field
  That Lucy's eyes surveyed.

THREE YEARS SHE GREW IN SUN AND SHOWER

Three years she grew in sun and shower,
Then Nature said, "A lovelier flower
On earth was never sown;
This child I to myself will take;
She shall be mine, and I will make
A lady of my own.

"Myself will to my darling be
Both law and impulse: and with me
The girl, in rock and plain,
In earth and heaven, in glade and bower,
Shall feel an overseeing power
To kindle or restrain.

"She shall be sportive as the fawn
That wild with glee across the lawn,
Or up the mountain springs;
And hers shall be the breathing balm,
And hers the silence and the calm
Of mute insensate things.

"The floating clouds their state shall lend
To her; for her the willow bend;
Nor shall she fail to see
Even in the motions of the storm
Grace that shall mold the maiden's form
By silent sympathy.

"The stars of midnight shall be dear
To her; and she shall lean her ear
In many a secret place
Where rivulets dance their wayward round,
And beauty born of murmuring sound
Shall pass into her face.

"And vital feelings of delight
Shall rear her form to stately height,
Her virgin bosom swell;

Such thoughts to Lucy I will give
While she and I together live
Here in this happy dell."

Thus Nature spake–The work was done–
How soon my Lucy's race was run!
She died, and left to me
This heath, this calm, and quiet scene;
The memory of what has been,
And never more will be.

SHE DWELT AMONG THE UNTRODDEN WAYS

She dwelt among the untrodden ways
  Beside the springs of Dove,
A maid whom there were none to praise
  And very few to love:

A violet by a mossy stone
  Half hidden from the eye.
–Fair as a star, when only one
  Is shining in the sky.

She lived unknown, and few could know
  When Lucy ceased to be;
But she is in her grave, and, oh,
  The difference to me!

A SLUMBER DID MY SPIRIT SEAL

A slumber did my spirit seal;
  I had no human fears:
She seemed a thing that could not feel
  The touch of earthly years.

No motion has she now, no force;
  She neither hears nor sees;
Rolled round in earth's diurnal course,
  With rocks, and stones, and trees.

Approaching forty, Wordsworth published his POEMS IN TWO VOLUMES, which marked him not only as an innovator but as an influence. In an overenthusiastic tribute De Quincey wrote that up to 1820 Wordsworth's name was trampled under foot, from 1820 to 1830 it was militant, and from 1830 to 1835 it was triumphant.

Although this is something of an exaggeration, it is true that Wordsworth made readers reappraise themselves; he taught them to re-estimate their concepts of poetry and regard life itself with new eyes. The sonnets are particularly worthy of the praise showered upon them; they lift to the heights what Wordsworth considered the three great subjects of poetry: "On man, on nature, and on human life." In the sonnets the significance of ordinary experience is enriched and enlarged; they are the autobiography of the spirit as well as a reflection of the times.

Sonnets

THE WORLD IS TOO MUCH WITH US

The world is too much with us; late and soon,
Getting and spending, we lay waste our powers:
Little we see in Nature that is ours;
We have given our hearts away, a sordid boon!
The sea that bares her bosom to the moon;
The winds that will be howling at all hours,
And are up-gathered now like sleeping flowers;
For this, for everything, we are out of tune;
It moves us not.—Great God! I'd rather be
A pagan suckled in a creed outworn.
So might I, standing on this pleasant lea,
Have glimpses that would make me less forlorn;
Have sight of Proteus rising from the sea;
Or hear old Triton blow his wreathed horn.

COMPOSED UPON WESTMINSTER BRIDGE SEPTEMBER 3, 1802

Earth has not anything to show more fair:
Dull would he be of soul who could pass by
A sight so touching in its majesty:
This city now doth, like a garment, wear
The beauty of the morning; silent, bare,
Ships, towers, domes, theaters, and temples lie
Open unto the fields, and to the sky;
All bright and glittering in the smokeless air.
Never did sun more beautifully steep
In his first splendor, valley, rock, or hill;

Ne'er saw I, never felt, a calm so deep!
The river glideth at his own sweet will:
Dear God! the very houses seem asleep;
And all that mighty heart is lying still!

TO MILTON

Milton! thou shouldst be living at this hour:
England hath need of thee: she is a fen
Of stagnant waters: altar, sword, and pen,
Fireside, the heroic wealth of hall and bower,
Have forfeited their ancient English dower
Of inward happiness. We are selfish men;
Oh! raise us up, return to us again;
And give us manners, virtue, freedom, power.
Thy soul was like a star, and dwelt apart:
Thou hadst a voice whose sound was like the sea:
Pure as the naked heavens, majestic, free,
So didst thou travel on life's common way,
In cheerful godliness; and yet thy heart
The lowliest duties on herself did lay.

WRITTEN IN LONDON, SEPTEMBER, 1802

O Friend! [1] I know not which way I must look
For comfort, being, as I am, opprest,
To think that now our life is only drest
For show; mean handy-work of craftsman, cook,
Or groom!—We must run glittering like a brook
In the open sunshine, or we are unblest:
The wealthiest man among us is the best:
No grandeur now in nature or in book
Delights us. Rapine, avarice, expense,
This is idolatry; and these we adore:
Plain living and high thinking are no more:
The homely beauty of the good old cause
Is gone; our peace, our fearful innocence,
And pure religion breathing household laws.

ON THE EXTINCTION OF THE VENETIAN REPUBLIC

Once did she hold the gorgeous east in fee;
And was the safeguard of the west: the worth
Of Venice did not fall below her birth,

[1] *Coleridge.*

Venice, the eldest child of liberty.
She was a maiden city, bright and free;
No guile seduced, no force could violate;
And, when she took unto herself a mate,
She must espouse the everlasting sea.
And what if she had seen those glories fade,
Those titles vanish, and that strength decay;
Yet shall some tribute of regret be paid
When her long life hath reached its final day:
Men are we, and must grieve when even the shade
Of that which once was great, is passed away.

TO SLEEP

A flock of sheep that leisurely pass by,
One after one; the sound of rain, and bees
Murmuring; the fall of rivers, winds and seas,
Smooth fields, white sheets of water, and pure sky;
I have thought of all by turns, and yet do lie
Sleepless! and soon the small birds' melodies
Must hear, first uttered from my orchard trees;
And the first cuckoo's melancholy cry.
Even thus last night, and two nights more, I lay,
And could not win thee, Sleep! by any stealth:
So do not let me wear tonight away:
Without Thee what is all the morning's wealth?
Come, blessed barrier between day and day,
Dear mother of fresh thoughts and joyous health!

THE SONNET

Scorn not the Sonnet; critic, you have frowned,
Mindless of its just honors; with this key
Shakespeare unlocked his heart; the melody
Of this small lute gave ease to Petrarch's wound;
A thousand times this pipe did Tasso sound;
With it Camöens soothed an exile's grief;
The Sonnet glittered a gay myrtle leaf
Amid the cypress with which Dante crowned
His visionary brow: a glow-worm lamp,
It cheered mild Spenser, called from faëryland
To struggle through dark ways; and, when a damp
Fell round the path of Milton, in his hand
The thing became a trumpet; whence he blew
Soul-animating strains—alas, too few!

After his forties Wordsworth's power declined. Influenced by Coleridge, he ceased to be a radical. Although he asserted his continued faith in freedom and the aspirations of youth, he became increasingly conservative. He opposed a free press, and placed "security" above liberty. In 1813 the government gave him a sinecure as distributor of stamps for Westmoreland. In 1818 he helped his patron, Lord Lonsdale, to procure votes by subterfuge; the same year the party of the aristocrats appointed him a justice of the peace. By 1821 he had repudiated all liberalism and had grown into a stubborn Tory. In 1843, when Wordsworth was seventy-three, he succeeded Southey (see page 687) as poet laureate.

Before this, however, his poetry had suffered from attrition. With the loss of convictions, his verse lost strength; it fell into barren platitudes and the inflation of trivialities. Even when it occasionally ascended into emotion, it was emotion too carefully hoarded, the emotion of a pragmatic recluse. Wordsworth died April 23, 1850, shortly after his eightieth birthday.

Wordsworth has often been accused of being both too consciously childlike and too determinedly didactic. Yet in the ODE: INTIMATIONS OF IMMORTALITY, begun in his thirty-third and finished in his thirty-fifth year, Wordsworth combines childlike perceptiveness and didacticism and lifts the combination to one of the peaks of poetry. The poem is a deliberate harking back to "that dreamlike vividness and splendor which invest the objects of sight in childhood." The spirit is that of Vaughan and Traherne. Vaughan's opening lines in THE RETREAT (see page 488):

> Happy those early days when I
> Shined in my Angel-infancy

are echoed in Wordsworth's first lines and in:

> Heaven lies about us in our infancy.

But Wordsworth carries the idea further than Vaughan's idealization of innocence. To the thoughtless acceptance of youth and the impulse to forget, maturity adds a more passionate awareness. Memory is thus neither an escape nor an unhappy disillusion, but to the philosophic mind, a preparation for wisdom.

Ode

INTIMATIONS OF IMMORTALITY FROM RECOLLECTIONS OF EARLY CHILDHOOD

The Child is Father of the Man;
And I could wish my days to be
Bound each to each by natural piety.

There was a time when meadow, grove, and stream,
The earth, and every common sight,
To me did seem
Appareled in celestial light,
The glory and the freshness of a dream.
It is not now as it hath been of yore;—
Turn whereso'er I may,
By night or day,
The things which I have seen I now can see no more.

The rainbow comes and goes,
And lovely is the rose,
The moon doth with delight
Look round her when the heavens are bare,
Waters on a starry night
Are beautiful and fair;
The sunshine is a glorious birth;
But yet I know, where'er I go,
That there hath passed away a glory from the earth.

Now, while the birds thus sing a joyous song,
And while the young lambs bound
As to the tabor's sound,
To me alone there came a thought of grief;
A timely utterance gave that thought relief,
And I again am strong:
The cataracts blow their trumpets from the steep;
No more shall grief of mine the season wrong;
I hear the echoes through the mountains throng;
The winds come to me from the fields of sleep,
And all the earth is gay;
Land and sea
Give themselves up to jollity,
And with the heart of May
Doth every beast keep holiday;—
Thou child of joy,

Shout round me, let me hear thy shouts, thou happy
        shepherd-boy.

Ye blessed Creatures, I have heard the call
    Ye to each other make; I see
The heavens laugh with you in your jubilee;
    My heart is at your festival,
    My head hath its coronal,
The fullness of your bliss, I feel—I feel it all.
    Oh evil day! if I were sullen
    While Earth herself is adorning,
        This sweet May-morning,
    And the children are culling
        On every side,
    In a thousand valleys far and wide,
    Fresh flowers; while the sun shines warm,
And the babe leaps up on his mother's arm:—
    I hear, I hear, with joy I hear!
    —But there's a tree, of many, one,
A single field which I have looked upon,
Both of them speak of something that is gone:
    The pansy at my feet
    Doth the same tale repeat:
Whither is fled the visionary gleam?
Where is it now, the glory of the dream?

Our birth is but a sleep and a forgetting:
The soul that rises with us, our life's star,
    Hath had elsewhere its setting,
        And cometh from afar;
    Not in entire forgetfulness,
    And not in utter nakedness,
But trailing clouds of glory do we come
        From God, who is our home.
Heaven lies about us in our infancy;
Shades of the prison-house begin to close
        Upon the growing boy,
But he beholds the light, and whence it flows.
        He sees it in his joy;
The youth, who daily farther from the east
    Must travel, still is Nature's priest,
        And by the vision splendid
        Is on his way attended;
At length the man perceives it die away,
And fade into the light of common day.

Earth fills her lap with pleasures of her own;
Yearnings she hath in her own natural kind,
And, even with something of a mother's mind,
        And no unworthy aim,
    The homely nurse doth all she can
To make her foster-child, her inmate man,
    Forget the glories he hath known,
And that imperial palace whence he came.

Behold the child among his newborn blisses,
    A six years' darling of a pygmy size!
See, where 'mid work of his own hand he lies,
Fretted by sallies of his mother's kisses,
With light upon him from his father's eyes!
See, at his feet, some little plan or chart,
Some fragment from his dream of human life,
Shaped by himself with newly learned art;
    A wedding or a festival,
    A mourning or a funeral;
        And this hath now his heart,
    And unto this he frames his song:
        Then will he fit his tongue
To dialogues of business, love, or strife;
    But it will not be long
    Ere this be thrown aside,
    And with new joy and pride
The little actor cons another part;
Filling from time to time his "humorous stage"
With all the persons, down to palsied age,
That life brings with her in her equipage;
    As if his whole vocation
    Were endless imitation.

Thou, whose exterior semblance doth belie
    Thy soul's immensity;
Thou best philosopher, who yet dost keep
Thy heritage, thou eye among the blind,
That, deaf and silent, read'st the eternal deep,
Haunted forever by the eternal mind—
    Mighty prophet! seer blest!
    On whom those truths do rest,
Which we are toiling all our lives to find,
In darkness lost, the darkness of the grave;
Thou, over whom thy immortality
Broods like the day, a master o'er a slave,

A presence which is not to be put by;
Thou little Child, yet glorious in the might
Of heaven-born freedom on thy being's height,
Why with such earnest pains dost thou provoke
The years to bring the inevitable yoke,
Thus blindly with thy blessedness at strife?
Full soon thy Soul shall have her earthly freight,
And custom lie upon thee with a weight,
Heavy as frost, and deep almost as life!

O joy! that in our embers
Is something that doth live,
That nature yet remembers
What was so fugitive!

The thought of our past years in me doth breed
Perpetual benediction: not indeed
For that which is most worthy to be blest—
Delight and liberty, the simple creed
Of childhood, whether busy or at rest,
With new-fledged hope still fluttering in his breast:—
Not for these I raise
The song of thanks and praise;
But for those obstinate questionings
Of sense and outward things,
Falling from us, vanishings;
Blank misgivings of a creature
Moving about in worlds not realized,
High instincts before which our mortal nature
Did tremble like a guilty thing surprised:
But for those first affections,
Those shadowy recollections,
Which, be they what they may,
Are yet the fountain-light of all our day,
Are yet a master-light of all our seeing;
Uphold us, cherish, and have power to make
Our noisy years seem moments in the being
Of the eternal silence: truths that wake,
To perish never;
Which neither listlessness, nor mad endeavor,
Nor man nor boy,
Nor all that is at enmity with joy,
Can utterly abolish or destroy!
Hence in a season of calm weather,
Though inland far we be,

Our souls have sight of that immortal sea
Which brought us hither,
Can in a moment travel thither,
And see the children sport upon the shore,
And hear the mighty waters rolling evermore.

Then sing, ye birds! sing, sing a joyous song!
And let the young lambs bound
As to the tabor's sound!
We in thought will join your throng,
Ye that pipe and ye that play,
Ye that through your hearts today
Feel the gladness of the May!
What though the radiance which was once so bright
Be now forever taken from my sight,
Though nothing can bring back the hour
Of splendor in the grass, or glory in the flower;
We will grieve not, rather find
Strength in what remains behind;
In the primal sympathy
Which having been must ever be;
In the soothing thoughts that spring
Out of human suffering;
In the faith that looks through death,
In years that bring the philosophic mind.

And oh, ye fountains, meadows, hills, and groves,
Forebode not any severing of our loves!
Yet in my heart of hearts I feel your might;
I only have relinquished one delight
To live beneath your more habitual sway.
I love the brooks which down their channels fret,
Even more than when I tripped lightly as they;
The innocent brightness of a new-born day
Is lovely yet;
The clouds that gather round the setting sun
Do take a sober coloring from an eye
That hath kept watch o'er man's mortality;
Another race hath been, and other palms are won.
Thanks to the human heart by which we live,
Thanks to its tenderness, its joys, and fears,
To me the meanest flower that blows can give
Thoughts that do often lie too deep for tears.

The fluctuations of Wordsworth's character have been violently condemned and hotly defended. Few appraisers have taken a middle ground, although Wordsworth himself represented the golden mean. Tennyson said that Wordsworth gave us "a sense of the permanent amid the transitory." But it was Shelley who, half proudly, half sadly, weighed the once revolutionary poet of nature in the delicate balance of a sonnet which ends:

> In honored poverty thy voice did weave
> Songs consecrate to truth and liberty—
> Deserting these, thou leavest me to grieve,
> Thus having been, that thou shouldst cease to be.

SIR WALTER SCOTT

[1771–1832]

NO WRITER ever bore a more appropriate surname, for Scott came of an old Border family and was born at Edinburgh, Scotland, August 15, 1771. Author of some of the world's most famous romances, Scott was already acquainted in boyhood with the romantic literature of France and Italy. When he was fifteen, young Walter attended a reception given to honor the poet Burns, and he was the only one of the company who could translate and explain some lines appended to a picture which had attracted Burns's attention. An attack of fever in infancy had crippled him, but, in spite of his lameness, Scott was as robust as he was high-spirited.

Admitted to the bar in his twenty-first year, Scott gradually advanced to the upper circles of his profession; he was clerk of session for twenty-five years. But determined to make a reputation in literature rather than in law, he began with poetry. Inspired by the German ballads he had translated, and stimulated by a study of Percy's RELIQUES OF ANCIENT ENGLISH POETRY, he prepared his own autochthonous collection: MINSTRELSY OF THE SCOTTISH BORDER. The first installment of this compilation was published just after Scott had turned thirty, and the success of the subsequent LAY OF THE LAST MINSTREL, his first important original work, decided Scott's future for him. The subsequent MARMION (1808) and THE LADY OF THE LAKE (1810) were immensely popular. Readers immediately responded to Scott's patriotism, his sense of abounding life, and his glorification of the heroic.

Native Land

Breathes there the man, with soul so dead,
Who never to himself hath said,
This is my own, my native land?
Whose heart hath ne'er within him burned,
As home his footsteps he hath turned
From wandering on a foreign strand?
If such there breathe, go, mark him well;
For him no minstrel raptures swell;
High though his titles, proud his name,
Boundless his wealth as wish can claim—
Despite those titles, power, and pelf,
The wretch, concentred all in self,
Living, shall forfeit fair renown,
And, doubly dying, shall go down
To the vile dust from whence he sprung,
Unwept, unhonored, and unsung.
from THE LAY OF THE LAST MINSTREL

Hunting Song

Waken, lords and ladies gay,
On the mountain dawns the day,
All the jolly chase is here,
With hawk and horse and hunting-spear!
Hounds are in their couples yelling,
Hawks are whistling, horns are knelling,
Merrily, merrily, mingle they,
"Waken, lords and ladies gay."

Waken, lords and ladies gay,
The mist has left the mountain gray,
Springlets in the dawn are steaming,
Diamonds on the brake are gleaming:

And foresters have busy been
To track the buck in thicket green;
Now we come to chant our lay,
"Waken, lords and ladies gay."

Waken, lords and ladies gay,
To the green-wood haste away;
We can show you where he lies,
Fleet of foot and tall of size;
We can show the marks he made,
When 'gainst the oak his antlers frayed;
You shall see him brought to bay,
"Waken, lords and ladies gay."

Louder, louder chant the lay,
Waken, lords and ladies gay!
Tell them youth and mirth and glee
Run a course as well as we;
Time, stern huntsman, who can balk,
Stanch as hound and fleet as hawk?
Think of this and rise with day,
Gentle lords and ladies gay.

from THE LAY OF THE LAST MINSTREL

One Crowded Hour [1]

Sound, sound the clarion, fill the fife!
To all the sensual world proclaim,
One crowded hour of glorious life
Is worth an age without a name.

from OLD MORTALITY

THE LADY OF THE LAKE is liberally interspersed with lyrics of which the world, in spite of changes in poetic taste, has never grown weary. SOLDIER, REST! is a dirge which expresses the spirit of the Highlands but which is universal in its application. CORONACH is a lament in which the images are more "in character." "It is," wrote Scott, "a wild expression of lamentation, poured forth by the mourners over the body of a departed friend."

This poem has sometimes been attributed to Major Thomas Osbert Mordaunt.

Soldier, Rest!

Soldier, rest! thy warfare o'er,
  Sleep the sleep that knows not breaking;
Dream of battled fields no more,
  Days of danger, nights of waking.
In our isle's enchanted hall,
  Hands unseen thy couch are strewing,
Fairy strains of music fall,
  Every sense in slumber dewing.
Soldier, rest! thy warfare o'er,
Dream of fighting fields no more;
Sleep the sleep that knows not breaking,
Morn of toil, nor night of waking.

No rude sound shall reach thine ear,
  Armor's clang of war-steed champing,
Trump nor pibroch summon here
  Mustering clan or squadron tramping.
Yet the lark's shrill fife may come
  At the daybreak from the fallow,
And the bittern sound his drum,
  Booming from the sedgy shallow.
Ruder sounds shall none be near,
Guards nor warders challenge here,
Here's no war-steed's neigh and champing,
Shouting clans or squadrons stamping. . . .

Huntsman, rest! thy chase is done;
  While our slumbrous spells assail ye,
Dream not, with the rising sun,
  Bugles here shall sound reveillé.
Sleep! the deer is in his den;
  Sleep! thy hounds are by thee lying:
Sleep! nor dream in yonder glen
  How thy gallant steed lay dying.
Huntsman, rest! thy chase is done;
Think not of the rising sun,
For at dawning to assail ye
Here no bugles sound reveillé.

from THE LADY OF THE LAKE

Coronach

He is gone on the mountain,
  He is lost to the forest,
Like a summer-dried fountain,
  When our need was the sorest.
The fount, reappearing,
  From the rain-drops shall borrow,
But to us comes no cheering,
  To Duncan no morrow!

The hand of the reaper
  Takes the ears that are hoary,
But the voice of the weeper
  Wails manhood in glory.
The autumn winds rushing
  Waft the leaves that are searest,
But our flower was in flushing,
  When blighting was nearest.

Fleet foot on the correi,[1]
  Sage counsel in cumber,[2]
Red hand in the foray,
  How sound is thy slumber!
Like the dew on the mountain,
  Like the foam on the river,
Like the bubble on the fountain,
  Thou art gone, and forever.

from THE LADY OF THE LAKE

Scott was no less a romantic than Wordsworth. But Wordsworth was intent upon the daily wonder of contemporary life, while Scott devoted himself to the romance of the past. There is no doubt that Scott overloaded his dramatic incidents and overcolored the glamours of history, but there is also no question about the vitality of his characters and situations. He was the father of the modern historical novel. Before he was sixty he had written more than thirty books of fiction, to say nothing of many essays, plays, biographies, and various antiquarian works.

Scott's novels are adorned with verse. THE HEART OF MIDLOTHIAN

[1] *A hollow in the hills.* [2] *Trouble.*

contains one of his most quoted poems; PROUD MAISIE, sung by the demented Madge Wildfire upon her deathbed, is a lyric which is also an extraordinarily condensed ballad.

Proud Maisie

Proud Maisie is in the wood,
Walking so early;
Sweet Robin sits on the bush,
Singing so rarely.

"Tell me, thou bonny bird,
When shall I marry me?"—
"When six braw gentlemen
Kirkward shall carry ye."

"Who makes the bridal bed,
Birdie, say truly?"—
"The gray-headed sexton
That delves the grave duly.

"The glow-worm o'er grave and stone
Shall light thee steady.
The owl from the steeple sing,
'Welcome, proud lady.' "

So successful were his efforts that in 1809 Scott entered into partnership with the publisher John Ballantyne and built the magnificent estate of Abbotsford. When the firm failed, Scott refused to take advantage of the bankruptcy laws; although fifty-six years old and ill, he worked harder than ever and turned over his earnings to the creditors. Thus, without ostentation, he proved as heroic as any of his characters.

Excessive work hastened the end. Scott's health gave way under the strain, and his doctors compelled him to take a long sea voyage. When he realized that he was dying, Scott insisted that he meet death at home. Carried across Europe, he died at Abbotsford, September 21, 1832.

SAMUEL TAYLOR COLERIDGE

[1772–1834]

COLERIDGE's life was a long ambivalence, an alternate acceptance of and struggle with irresolution. Born at his father's vicarage of Ottery St. Mary in Devonshire, the boy was fretful and precocious, morbidly lost in fancies. When his father died, Coleridge at the age of nine was sent to London to live with his uncle; he entered the charity school of Christ's Hospital, and took refuge in books.

Before he was nineteen Coleridge's vacillations had begun. After reading a medical dictionary he planned to be a surgeon. A few months later, he discovered Voltaire and decided to become a philosopher. Means were found so that he could attend Jesus College at Cambridge, but he tired of university life in less than two years. He enlisted in a regiment of dragoons under the grotesque name of Silas Tomkyn Comberback, but a few weeks of discipline convinced him that he was not fitted for military life. He met Southey, who was aflame with the promise of the French Revolution, and immediately became converted to the hope of a government of all by all, a scheme which went by the high-sounding title of Pantisocracy. The two young men determined to migrate to the Promised Land of America, found a utopian colony on the banks of the Susquehanna, and establish an ideal community of brotherly love. Since the young pantisocrats needed wives as well as companions, Southey married Edith Fricker, the daughter of a draper, and Coleridge married her sister Sara. None of them ever reached America. Southey settled in Lisbon, and Coleridge, failing to adjust himself to an unfortunate marriage, immured himself in the English countryside.

Three things reconciled Coleridge to a fitful existence: the use of drugs, a reliance on fantasy, and his friendship with the Wordsworths. An admirer made it possible for Coleridge to write in comparative comfort in a cottage in Somersetshire, and Wordsworth joined him there. Harsh experiences brought the poets closer to each other; Wordsworth's sister Dorothy surrounded them with ministering protectiveness; revolutionary ardors were translated into poetry. A joint volume was discussed, and LYRICAL BALLADS resulted.

The scheme of LYRICAL BALLADS was no mere gathering of scattered poems. The book was to establish the two cardinal points of poetry: "the power of exciting the sympathy of the reader by a faithful adherence to the truth of nature, and the power of giving the interest of novelty to the modifying colors of imagination." Wordsworth, so Coleridge tells us in his BIOGRAPHIA LITERARIA, was to take subjects from ordinary life: "The characters and incidents were to be such as will be found in every village and its vicinity." Coleridge's endeavors were to be directed "to persons and characters supernatural, or at least romantic; yet so as to procure for these shadows of imagination that willing suspension of disbelief for the moment, which constitutes poetic faith."

With this view Coleridge wrote THE RIME OF THE ANCIENT MARINER, a cumulatively exciting poem in the style of an ancient ballad. John Livingston Lowes has traced the sources of this remarkable creation, in THE ROAD TO XANADU, a commentary which is also a masterpiece of deduction. Lowes reveals the intricate web of vision and meditation, of accurate research and unfettered romanticism, spun throughout the work. But the central persuasiveness of this rhymed narrative remains unanalyzable. The employment of archaic words and plain rhythms helps re-create the atmosphere of the old ballads, but the extraordinary power of the poem goes far beyond its rich language and varying movement. Its power is incalculable magic, the magic (as William Hazlitt wrote) "of wild, irregular, overwhelming imagination."

The Rime of the Ancient Mariner

PART I

An ancient Mariner meeteth three Gallants bidden to a wedding-feast, and detaineth one.

It is an ancient Mariner,
And he stoppeth one of three.
"By thy long gray beard and glittering eye,
Now wherefore stopp'st thou me?

The Bridegroom's doors are opened wide,
And I am next of kin;
The guests are met, the feast is set:
May'st hear the merry din."

He holds him with his skinny hand,
"There was a ship," quoth he.
"Hold off! unhand me, gray-beard loon!"
Eftsoons his hand dropt he.

The Wedding-Guest is spellbound by the eye of the old seafaring man, and constrained to hear his tale.

He holds him with his glittering eye—
The Wedding-Guest stood still,
And listens like a three years' child:
The Mariner hath his will.

The Wedding-Guest sat on a stone:
He cannot choose but hear;
And thus spake on that ancient man,
The bright-eyed Mariner.

"The ship was cheered, the harbor cleared,
Merrily did we drop
Below the kirk, below the hill,
Below the lighthouse top.

The Mariner tells how the ship sailed southward with a good wind and fair weather, till it reached the Line.

The sun came up upon the left,
Out of the sea came he!
And he shone bright, and on the right
Went down into the sea.

Higher and higher every day,
Till over the mast at noon—"
The Wedding-Guest here beat his breast,
For he heard the loud bassoon.

The Wedding-Guest heareth the bridal music; but the Mariner continueth his tale.

The bride hath paced into the hall,
Red as a rose is she;
Nodding their heads before her goes
The merry minstrelsy.

The Wedding-Guest he beat his breast,
Yet he cannot choose but hear;
And thus spake on that ancient man,
The bright-eyed Mariner.

The ship driven by a storm toward the south pole.

"And now the storm-blast came, and he
Was tyrannous and strong:
He struck with his o'ertaking wings,
And chased us south along.

With sloping masts and dipping prow,
As who pursued with yell and blow
Still treads the shadow of his foe,
And forward bends his head,
The ship drove fast, loud roared the blast,
And southward aye we fled.

And now there came both mist and snow,
And it grew wondrous cold:
And ice, mast-high, came floating by,
As green as emerald.

The land of ice, and of fearful sounds where no living thing was to be seen.

And through the drifts the snowy clifts
Did send a dismal sheen:
Nor shapes of men nor beasts we ken—
The ice was all between.

The ice was here, the ice was there,
The ice was all around:
It cracked and growled, and roared and howled,
Like noises in a swound!

Till a great sea-bird, called the Albatross, came through the snow-fog, and was received with great joy and hospitality.

At length did cross an Albatross,
Thorough the fog it came;
As if it had been a Christian soul,
We hailed it in God's name.

It ate the food it ne'er had eat,
And round and round it flew.
The ice did split with a thunder-fit;
The helmsman steered us through!

And lo! the Albatross proveth a bird of good omen, and followeth the ship as it returned northward through fog and floating ice.

And a good south wind sprung up behind;
The Albatross did follow,
And every day, for food or play,
Came to the mariners' hollo!

In mist or cloud, on mast or shroud,
It perched for vespers nine;
Whiles all the night, through fog-smoke white,
Glimmered the white moon-shine."

The ancient Mariner inhospitably killeth the pious bird of good omen.

"God save thee, ancient Mariner!
From the fiends, that plague thee thus!—
Why look'st thou so?"—"With my cross-bow
I shot the Albatross.

PART II

"The Sun now rose upon the right:
Out of the sea came he,
Still hid in mist, and on the left
Went down into the sea.

And the good south wind still blew behind,
But no sweet bird did follow,
Nor any day for food or play
Came to the mariners' hollo!

His shipmates cry out against the ancient Mariner, for killing the bird of good luck.

And I had done a hellish thing,
And it would work 'em woe:
For all averred, I had killed the bird
That made the breeze to blow.
'Ah wretch!' said they, 'the bird to slay,
That made the breeze to blow!'

But when the fog cleared off, they justify the same, and thus make themselves accomplices in the crime.

Nor dim nor red, like God's own head,
The glorious Sun uprist:
Then all averred, I had killed the bird
That brought the fog and mist.
' 'Twas right,' said they, 'such birds to slay,
That bring the fog and mist.'

The fair breeze continues; the ship enters the Pacific Ocean, and sails northward, even till it reaches the Line.

The fair breeze blew, the white foam flew,
The furrow followed free;
We were the first that ever burst
Into that silent sea.

The ship hath been suddenly becalmed.

Down dropt the breeze, the sails dropt down,
'Twas sad as sad could be;
And we did speak only to break
The silence of the sea!

All in a hot and copper sky,
The bloody Sun, at noon,
Right up above the mast did stand,
No bigger than the Moon.

Day after day, day after day,
We stuck, nor breath nor motion;
As idle as a painted ship
Upon a painted ocean.

And the Albatross begins to be avenged.

Water, water, everywhere,
And all the boards did shrink;
Water, water, everywhere
Nor any drop to drink.

The very deep did rot: O Christ!
That ever this should be!
Yea, slimy things did crawl with legs
Upon the slimy sea.

About, about, in reel and rout
The death-fires danced at night;
The water, like a witch's oils,
Burnt green, and blue, and white.

A Spirit had followed them; one of the invisible inhabitants of this planet, neither departed souls nor angels; concerning whom the learned Jew, Josephus, and the Platonic Constantinopolitan, Michael Psellus, may be consulted. They are very numerous, and there is no climate or element without one or more.

And some in dreams assured were
Of the Spirit that plagued us so:
Nine fathom deep he had followed us
From the land of mist and snow.

And every tongue, through utter drought,
Was withered at the root;
We could not speak, no more than if
We had been choked with soot.

The ship-mates, in their sore distress, would fain throw the whole guilt on the ancient Mariner: in sign whereof they hang the dead sea-bird round his neck.

Ah! well a-day! what evil looks
Had I from old and young!
Instead of the cross, the Albatross
About my neck was hung.

PART III

The ancient Mariner beholdeth a sign in the element afar off.

"There passed a weary time. Each throat
Was parched, and glazed each eye.
A weary time! a weary time!
How glazed each weary eye,
When looking westward, I beheld
A something in the sky.

At first it seemed a little speck,
And then it seemed a mist;
It moved and moved, and took at last
A certain shape, I wist.

A speck, a mist, a shape, I wist!
And still it neared and neared:
As if it dodged a water-sprite,
It plunged and tacked and veered.

At its nearer approach, it seemeth him to be a ship; and at a dear ransom he freeth his speech from the bonds of thirst.

With throats unslaked, with black lips baked,
We could nor laugh nor wail;
Through utter drought all dumb we stood!
I bit my arm, I sucked the blood,
And cried, 'A sail! a sail!'

With throats unslaked, with black lips baked,
Agape they heard me call;

A flash of joy;

Gramercy! they for joy did grin,
And all at once their breath drew in,
As they were drinking all.

And horror follows. For can it be a ship that comes onward without wind or tide?

'See! see! (I cried) she tacks no more!
Hither to work us weal;
Without a breeze, without a tide,
She steadies with upright keel!'

The western wave was all a-flame;
The day was well nigh done!
Almost upon the western wave
Rested the broad bright Sun;
When that strange shape drove suddenly
Betwixt us and the Sun.

It seemeth him but the skeleton of a ship.

And straight the Sun was flecked with bars
(Heaven's Mother send us grace!)
As if through a dungeon-grate he peered
With broad and burning face.

Alas! (thought I, and my heart beat loud)
How fast she nears and nears!
Are those her sails that glance in the Sun,
Like restless gossameres?

And its ribs are seen as bars on the face of the setting Sun.

Are those her ribs through which the Sun
Did peer, as through a grate?

The Spectre-Woman and her Death-mate, and no other on board the skeleton-ship.

And is that Woman all her crew?
Is that a Death? and are there two?
Is Death that woman's mate?

Like vessel, like crew!

Her lips were red, her looks were free,
Her locks were yellow as gold:
Her skin was as white as leprosy,
The nightmare Life-in-Death was she,
Who thicks man's blood with cold.

Death and Life-in-Death have diced for the ship's crew, and she (the latter) winneth the ancient Mariner.

The naked hulk alongside came,
And the twain were casting dice;
'The game is done! I've won! I've won!'
Quoth she, and whistles thrice.

No twilight within the courts of the Sun.

The Sun's rim dips; the stars rush out:
At one stride comes the dark;
With far-heard whisper, o'er the sea,
Off shot the spectre-bark.

At the rising of the Moon,

We listened and looked sideways up!
Fear at my heart, as at a cup,
My life-blood seemed to sip!
The stars were dim, and thick the night,
The steersman's face by his lamp gleamed white:
From the sails the dew did drip—
Till clomb above the eastern bar
The horned Moon, with one bright star
Within the nether tip.

One after another,

One after one, by the star-dogged Moon,
Too quick for groan or sigh,
Each turned his face with a ghastly pang,
And cursed me with his eye.

His ship-mates drop down dead.

Four times fifty living men
(And I heard nor sigh nor groan)
With heavy thump, a lifeless lump,
They dropped down one by one.

But Life-in-Death begins her work on the ancient Mariner.

The souls did from their bodies fly—
They fled to bliss or woe!
And every soul, it passed me by,
Like the whizz of my cross-bow!"

PART IV

The Wedding-Guest feareth that a Spirit is talking to him;

"I fear thee, ancient Mariner!
I fear thy skinny hand!
And thou art long, and lank, and brown,
As is the ribbed sea-sand.

But the ancient Mariner assureth him of his bodily life, and pro-

I fear thee and thy glittering eye,
And thy skinny hand, so brown."—
"Fear not, fear not, thou Wedding-Guest!
This body dropt not down.

ceedeth to relate his horrible penance.

Alone, alone, all, all alone,
Alone on a wide, wide sea!
And never a saint took pity on
My soul in agony.

He despiseth the creatures of the calm.

The many men, so beautiful!
And they all dead did lie:
And a thousand thousand slimy things
Lived on; and so did I.

And envieth that they should live, and so many lie dead.

I looked upon the rotting sea,
And drew my eyes away;
I looked upon the rotting deck,
And there the dead men lay.

I looked to heaven, and tried to pray;
But or ever a prayer had gusht,
A wicked whisper came, and made
My heart as dry as dust.

I closed my lids, and kept them close,
And the balls like pulses beat;
For the sky and the sea, and the sea and the sky
Lay like a load on my weary eye,
And the dead were at my feet.

But the curse liveth for him in the eye of the dead men.

The cold sweat melted from their limbs,
Nor rot nor reek did they:
The look with which they looked on me
Had never passed away.

An orphan's curse would drag to hell
A spirit from on high;
But oh! more horrible than that
Is the curse in a dead man's eye!
Seven days, seven nights, I saw that curse,
And yet I could not die.

In his loneliness and fixedness he yearneth toward the journeying Moon, and the stars that still sojourn, yet still move onward; and every-

The moving Moon went up the sky,
And nowhere did abide:
Softly she was going up,
And a star or two beside—

where the blue sky belongs to them, and is their appointed rest, and their native country and their own natural homes, which they enter unannounced, as lords that are certainly expected and yet there is a silent joy at their arrival.

Her beams bemocked the sultry main,
Like April hoar-frost spread;
But where the ship's huge shadow lay,
The charmed water burnt alway
A still and awful red.

By the light of the Moon he beholdeth God's creatures of the great calm.

Beyond the shadow of the ship,
I watched the water-snakes:
They moved in tracks of shining white,
And when they reared, the elfish light
Fell off in hoary flakes.

Within the shadow of the ship
I watched their rich attire:
Blue, glossy green, and velvet black,
They coiled and swam; and every track
Was a flash of golden fire.

Their beauty and their happiness.

O happy living things! no tongue
Their beauty might declare:
A spring of love gushed from my heart,
And I blessed them unaware:
Sure my kind saint took pity on me,
And I blessed them unaware.

He blesseth them in his heart.

The spell begins to break.

The selfsame moment I could pray;
And from my neck so free
The Albatross fell off, and sank
Like lead into the sea.

PART V

"Oh sleep! it is a gentle thing,
Beloved from pole to pole!
To Mary Queen the praise be given!
She sent the gentle sleep from Heaven,
That slid into my soul.

By grace of the holy Mother, the ancient Mariner is refreshed with rain.

The silly buckets on the deck,
That had so long remained,
I dreamt that they were filled with dew;
And when I awoke, it rained.

My lips were wet, my throat was cold,
My garments all were dank;
Sure I had drunken in my dreams,
And still my body drank.

I moved, and could not feel my limbs;
I was so light—almost
I thought that I had died in sleep,
And was a blessed ghost.

He heareth sounds and seeth strange sights and commotions in the sky and the element.

And soon I heard a roaring wind:
It did not come anear;
But with its sound it shook the sails,
That were so thin and sere.

The upper air burst into life!
And a hundred fire-flags sheen,
To and fro they were hurried about!
And to and fro, and in and out,
The wan stars danced between.

And the coming wind did roar more loud,
And the sails did sigh like sedge;
And the rain poured down from one black cloud;
The Moon was at its edge.

The thick black cloud was cleft, and still
The Moon was at its side:
Like waters shot from some high crag,
The lightning fell with never a jag,
A river steep and wide.

The loud wind never reached the ship,
Yet now the ship moved on!
Beneath the lightning and the Moon
The dead men gave a groan.

The bodies of the ship's crew are inspired, and the ship moves on:

They groaned, they stirred, they all uprose,
Nor spake, nor moved their eyes;
It had been strange, even in a dream,
To have seen those dead men rise.

The helmsman steered, the ship moved on;
Yet never a breeze up blew;
The mariners all 'gan work the ropes,
Where they were wont to do;
They raised their limbs like lifeless tools—
We were a ghastly crew.

The body of my brother's son
Stood by me, knee to knee:
The body and I pulled at one rope
But he said nought to me."

But not by the souls of the men, nor by daemons of earth or middle air, but by a blessed troop of angelic spirits, sent down by the invocation of the guardian saint.

"I fear thee, ancient Mariner!"
"Be calm, thou Wedding-Guest!
'Twas not those souls that fled in pain,
Which to their corses came again,
But a troop of spirits blest:

For when it dawned—they dropped their arms,
And clustered round the mast;
Sweet sounds rose slowly through their mouths,
And from their bodies passed.

Around, around, flew each sweet sound,
Then darted to the Sun;
Slowly the sounds came back again,
Now mixed, now one by one.

Sometimes a-dropping from the sky
I heard the sky-lark sing;
Sometimes all little birds that are,
How they seemed to fill the sea and air
With their sweet jargoning!

And now 'twas like all instruments,
Now like a lonely flute;
And now it is an angel's song,
That makes the heavens be mute.

It ceased; yet still the sails made on
A pleasant noise till noon,
A noise like of a hidden brook
In the leafy month of June,
That to the sleeping woods all night
Singeth a quiet tune.

Till noon we quietly sailed on,
Yet never a breeze did breathe:
Slowly and smoothly went the ship,
Moved onward from beneath.

The lonesome Spirit from the south pole carries on the ship as far as the Line, in obedience to the angelic troop, but still requireth vengeance.

Under the keel nine fathom deep,
From the land of mist and snow,
The Spirit slid: and it was he
That made the ship to go.
The sails at noon left off their tune,
And the ship stood still also.

The Sun, right up above the mast,
Had fixed her to the ocean:
But in a minute she 'gan stir,
With a short uneasy motion—
Backwards and forwards half her length
With a short uneasy motion.

Then like a pawing horse let go,
She made a sudden bound:
It flung the blood into my head,
And I fell down in a swound.

The Polar Spirit's fellow-daemons, the invisible inhabitants of the element, take part in his wrong; and two of them relate, one to the other, that penance long and heavy for the ancient Mariner hath been accorded to the Polar Spirit, who returneth southward.

How long in that same fit I lay,
I have not to declare;
But ere my living life returned,
I heard and in my soul discerned
Two voices in the air.

'Is it he?' quoth one, 'Is this the man?
By Him who died on cross,
With his cruel bow he laid full low
The harmless Albatross.

The Spirit who bideth by himself
In the land of mist and snow,
He loved the bird that loved the man
Who shot him with his bow.'

The other was a softer voice,
As soft as honey-dew:
Quoth he, 'The man hath penance done,
And penance more will do.'

PART VI

First Voice

"'But tell me, tell me! speak again,
Thy soft response renewing—
What makes that ship drive on so fast?
What is the ocean doing?'

Second Voice

'Still as a slave before his lord,
The ocean hath no blast;
His great bright eye most silently
Up to the Moon is cast—

If he may know which way to go;
For she guides him smooth or grim.
See, brother, see! how graciously
She looketh down on him.'

First Voice

The Mariner hath been cast into a trance; for the angelic power causeth the vessel to drive northward faster than human life could endure.

'But why drives on that ship so fast,
Without or wave or wind?'

Second Voice

'The air is cut away before,
And closes from behind.

Fly, brother, fly! more high, more high!
Or we shall be belated:
For slow and slow that ship will go,
When the Mariner's trance is abated.'

The supernatural motion is retarded; the Mariner awakes, and his penance begins anew.

I woke, and we were sailing on
As in a gentle weather:
'Twas night, calm night, the Moon was high,
The dead men stood together.

All stood together on the deck,
For a charnel-dungeon fitter:
All fixed on me their stony eyes,
That in the Moon did glitter.

The pang, the curse, with which they died,
Had never passed away:
I could not draw my eyes from theirs,
Nor turn them up to pray.

The curse is finally expiated.

And now this spell was snapt: once more
I viewed the ocean green,
And looked far forth, yet little saw
Of what had else been seen–

Like one, that on a lonesome road
Doth walk in fear and dread,
And having once turned round walks on,
And turns no more his head;
Because he knows a frightful fiend
Doth close behind him tread.

But soon there breathed a wind on me,
Nor sound nor motion made:
Its path was not upon the sea,
In ripple or in shade.

It raised my hair, it fanned my cheek
Like a meadow-gale of spring–
It mingled strangely with my fears,
Yet it felt like a welcoming.

Swiftly, swiftly flew the ship,
Yet she sailed softly too:
Sweetly, sweetly blew the breeze–
On me alone it blew.

And the ancient Mariner beholdeth his native country.

Oh! dream of joy! is this indeed
The light-house top I see?
Is this the hill? is this the kirk?
Is this mine our countree?

We drifted o'er the harbor-bar,
And I with sobs did pray–
O let me be awake, my God!
Or let me sleep alway.

The harbor-bay was clear as glass,
So smoothly it was strewn!
And on the bay the moonlight lay,
And the shadow of the Moon.

The rock shone bright, the kirk no less,
That stands above the rock:
The moonlight steeped in silentness
The steady weathercock.

And the bay was white with silent light
Till rising from the same,
Full many shapes, that shadows were,
In crimson colors came.

A little distance from the prow
Those crimson shadows were:
I turned my eyes upon the deck—
Oh, Christ, what saw I there!

The angelic spirits leave the dead bodies,

And appear in their own forms of light.

Each corse lay flat, lifeless and flat,
And, by the holy rood!
A man all light, a seraph-man,
On every corse there stood.

This seraph-band, each waved his hand;
It was a heavenly sight!
They stood as signals to the land,
Each one a lovely light;

This seraph-band, each waved his hand,
No voice did they impart—
No voice; but oh! the silence sank
Like music on my heart.

But soon I heard the dash of oars,
I heard the Pilot's cheer;
My head was turned perforce away,
And I saw a boat appear.

The Pilot and the Pilot's boy,
I heard them coming fast:
Dear Lord in Heaven! it was a joy
The dead men could not blast.

I saw a third—I heard his voice:
It is the Hermit good!
He singeth loud his godly hymns
That he makes in the wood.
He'll shrieve my soul; he'll wash away
The Albatross's blood.

PART VII

The Hermit of the Wood.

"This Hermit good lives in that wood
Which slopes down to the sea.
How loudly his sweet voice he rears!
He loves to talk with marineres
That come from a far countree.

He kneels at morn, and noon, and eve—
He hath a cushion plump:
It is the moss that wholly hides
The rotted old oak-stump.

The skiff-boat neared: I heard them talk,
'Why, this is strange, I trow!
Where are those lights so many and fair,
That signal made but now?'

Approacheth the ship with wonder.

'Strange, by my faith!' the Hermit said—
'And they answered not our cheer!
The planks look warped! and see those sails,
How thin they are and sere!
I never saw aught like to them,
Unless perchance it were

Brown skeletons of leaves that lag
My forest-brook along;
When the ivy-tod is heavy with snow,
And the owlet whoops to the wolf below,
That eats the she-wolf's young.'

'Dear Lord! it hath a fiendish look—
(The Pilot made reply)
I am a-feared'—'Push on, push on!'
Said the Hermit cheerily.

The boat came closer to the ship,
But I nor spake nor stirred;
The boat came close beneath the ship,
And straight a sound was heard.

The ship suddenly sinketh.

Under the water it rumbled on,
Still louder and more dread:
It reached the ship, it split the bay;
The ship went down like lead.

The ancient Mariner is saved in the Pilot's boat.

Stunned by that loud and dreadful sound,
Which sky and ocean smote,
Like one that hath been seven days drowned
My body lay afloat;
But swift as dreams, myself I found
Within the Pilot's boat.

Upon the whirl, where sank the ship,
The boat spun round and round;
And all was still, save that the hill
Was telling of the sound.

I moved my lips—the Pilot shrieked
And fell down in a fit;
The holy Hermit raised his eyes,
And prayed where he did sit.

I took the oars: the Pilot's boy,
Who now doth crazy go,
Laughed loud and long, and all the while
His eyes went to and fro.
'Ha! ha!' quoth he, 'full plain I see,
The Devil knows how to row.'

And now, all in my own countree,
I stood on the firm land!
The Hermit stepped forth from the boat,
And scarcely he could stand.

The ancient Mariner earnestly entreateth the Hermit to shrieve him; and the penance of life falls on him.

'O shrieve me, shrieve me, holy man!'
The Hermit crossed his brow.
'Say quick,' quoth he, 'I bid thee say—
What manner of man art thou?'

Forthwith this frame of mine was wrenched
With a woful agony,
Which forced me to begin my tale;
And then it left me free.

And ever and anon throughout his future life an agony constraineth

Since then, at an uncertain hour,
That agony returns:
And till my ghastly tale is told,
This heart within me burns.

him to travel from land to land,

I pass, like night, from land to land;
I have strange power of speech;
That moment that his face I see,
I know the man that must hear me:
To him my tale I teach.

What loud uproar bursts from that door!
The wedding-guests are there:
But in the garden-bower the bride
And bride-maids singing are:
And hark the little vesper bell
Which biddeth me to prayer!

O Wedding-Guest! this soul hath been
Alone on a wide, wide sea;
So lonely 'twas, that God himself
Scarce seemed there to be.

O sweeter than the marriage-feast,
'Tis sweeter far to me,
To walk together to the kirk
With a goodly company!—

To walk together to the kirk,
And all together pray,
While each to his great Father bends,
Old men, and babes, and loving friends,
And youths and maidens gay!

And to teach, by his own example, love and reverence to all things that God made and loveth.

Farewell, farewell! but this I tell
To thee, thou Wedding-Guest!
He prayeth well, who loveth well
Both man and bird and beast.

He prayeth best, who loveth best
All things both great and small;
For the dear God who loveth us,
He made and loveth all."

The Mariner, whose eye is bright,
Whose beard with age is hoar,
Is gone: and now the Wedding-Guest
Turned from the Bridegroom's door.

He went like one that hath been stunned,
And is of sense forlorn:
A sadder and a wiser man,
He rose the morrow morn.

More than one biographer has declared sadly that Coleridge succumbed to fantasy and laudanum. Yet, if the combination produced a great deal of inane verse, it also made possible some of the strangest and most beautiful pictures in English poetry. Although a man's habits and his creations do not always correspond, the greatest unfinished dream poem ever written sprang indirectly from Coleridge's reading and directly from his addiction to drugs. Coleridge himself explains the composition of KUBLA KHAN in a preface written in the third person. One afternoon in his twenty-fifth year, he took an opiate and fell asleep in a chair at the moment he was reading this sentence in Purchas' PILGRIMAGE: "Here the Khan Kubla commanded a palace to be built, and a stately garden thereunto. And thus ten miles of fertile ground were enclosed with a wall." Coleridge continued for about three hours in a profound sleep, and during that time he had, so he tells us, "the most vivid confidence that he could not have composed less than from two to three hundred lines . . . without any sensation or consciousness of effort. On awaking he appeared to himself to have a distant recollection of the whole, and taking his pen, ink, and paper, instantly and eagerly wrote down the lines that are here preserved. At this moment he was unfortunately called out by a person on business from Porlock and detained by him above an hour, and on return to his room found, to his no small surprise and mortification, that though he still retained some vague recollection of the general purport of the vision, yet with the exception of some eight or ten scattered lines and images, all the rest had passed away."

Lovers of poetry may never be able to forgive the "person from Porlock," but Coleridge was somehow able to put some of the "still surviving recollections" to paper and achieve a miraculous fragment. Vivid yet visionary, KUBLA KHAN paints a terrestrial paradise which, like some Gothic triumph of the imagination, is as wonderful as it is incredible.

Kubla Khan

In Xanadu did Kubla Khan
  A stately pleasure-dome decree:
Where Alph, the sacred river, ran
Through caverns measureless to man
  Down to a sunless sea.
So twice five miles of fertile ground
With walls and towers were girdled round:
And here were gardens bright with sinuous rills,
Where blossomed many an incense-bearing tree,
And here were forests ancient as the hills,
Enfolding sunny spots of greenery.

But oh! that deep romantic chasm which slanted
Down the green hill athwart a cedarn cover!
A savage place; as holy and enchanted
As e'er beneath a waning moon was haunted
By woman wailing for her demon-lover!
And from this chasm, with ceaseless turmoil seething,
As if this earth in fast thick pants were breathing,
A mighty fountain momently was forced,
Amid whose swift half-intermitted burst
Huge fragments vaulted like rebounding hail,
Or chaffy grain beneath the thresher's flail:
And 'mid these dancing rocks at once and ever
It flung up momently the sacred river.
Five miles meandering with a mazy motion
Through wood and dale the sacred river ran,
Then reached the caverns measureless to man,
And sank in tumult to a lifeless ocean:
And 'mid this tumult Kubla heard from far
Ancestral voices prophesying war!

    The shadow of the dome of pleasure
    Floated midway on the waves;
    Where was heard the mingled measure
    From the fountain and the caves.
It was a miracle of rare device,
A sunny pleasure-dome with caves of ice!

    A damsel with a dulcimer
    In a vision once I saw:

It was an Abyssinian maid,
And on her dulcimer she played,
Singing of Mount Abora.
Could I revive within me
Her symphony and song,
To such a deep delight 'twould win me,
That with music loud and long,
I would build that dome in air,
That sunny dome! those caves of ice!
And all who heard should see them there,
And all should cry, Beware! Beware!
His flashing eyes, his floating hair!
Weave a circle round him thrice,
And close your eyes with holy dread,
For he on honey-dew hath fed,
And drunk the milk of Paradise.

Coleridge sank progressively under the spell of opium. He visited Scotland with the Wordsworths, left his family to voyage in the Mediterranean, remained in Malta almost a year, and spent ten months in Naples and Rome. But he could not free himself from his dependence on the drug, if, indeed, he wanted to; it is possible that he left home and friends to indulge himself alone and without reproach. When he returned to England, it was evident that he desperately needed assistance. Friends helped him to obtain work and money; in his early forties he was taken care of by Dr. Gillman, a friendly surgeon whose interests were "other than medical." For the last eighteen years of his life, years that were in many ways his happiest, Coleridge rarely left the Gillman home. He died in his sixty-second year, July 25, 1834.

Coleridge's multiple literary roles have been variously appraised. As a critic he added originality to erudition; his essays, particularly those on Shakespeare, fuse the critical and creative functions. As a thinker, Coleridge let himself drift on the winds of doctrine; he lacked both direction and integration. His mind was, as Hazlitt wrote, "tangential. . . . Hardly a speculation has been left on record from the earliest time, but it is loosely folded up in Mr. Coleridge's memory, like a rich but somewhat tattered piece of tapestry. But," Hazlitt remarked with a malicious nod toward Wordsworth, "Coleridge's discursive reason would not let him trammel himself into a poet laureate or stamp distributor. . . . He could not realize all he knew or thought; other stimulants kept up the intoxicating dream, the fever and the madness of his early impressions."

Two of Coleridge's four children, Hartley and Sara, inherited their father's imaginative gifts. Both wrote poetry and essays which brought them reputations not wholly built upon the family name.

ROBERT SOUTHEY

[1774–1843]

ROBERT SOUTHEY'S collected verse, together with the superfluously explanatory notes, crowds ten volumes. His prose fills about forty. Never before or since has Pegasus been so hobbled; Southey not only put a bridle upon the fiery creature, but relentlessly drove the winged horse to market.

Son of an unsuccessful merchant, Southey was born August 12, 1774, in Bristol. At fourteen he entered Westminster School and was expelled for writing an article against the common practice of flogging. The humiliation aggravated Southey's spirit of protest. At nineteen he wrote an insurrectionary epic poem, JOAN OF ARC; at twenty he espoused the cause of the French Revolution, became the leader of the "pantisocrats" (see page 665), and almost persuaded Coleridge to migrate to America and found a practical utopia by the side of the poetical Susquehanna.

Twenty years later there was no trace left of the revolutionary youth. Southey had not only his own family to support, but Coleridge's. He became a valued contributor to THE QUARTERLY REVIEW, the most prominent Tory sheet of the period. In his fortieth year, Southey was offered the laureateship upon the death of Henry James Pye, the laureate who, it was said, attained the eminence by rescuing the wig of George III while His Majesty was out hunting. (Byron wrote that Pye was prominently respectable in everything but his poetry.) Sir Walter Scott, who had been proposed for the honor, refused it and recommended Southey, who accepted it. Byron, full of republican ardor, attacked Southey and his principles; the mocking opening of DON JUAN (see page 706) excoriated him in "good, simple, savage verse."

Southey continued to avoid a pressing and often hostile world.

He immured himself in a library of some fifteen thousand volumes; Wordsworth remarked that Southey away from his books seemed out of his element. Honors and troubles descended on him simultaneously. He was recovering from the loss of several children when he suffered a new affliction. "I have been parted from my wife by something worse than death," he wrote at sixty. "Forty years she has been the life of my life, and I have left her this day in a lunatic asylum." Three years later his wife died; two years after her death, Southey remarried. His own mind began to fail. He died in his seventieth year, March 21, 1843, and a bust to his memory was placed in the Poets' Corner of Westminster Abbey.

For all their bulk, Southey's fifty volumes of prose and verse give the impression of something never quite completed. Haste and uncertain standards account for much of the sense of disappointment. Of the prose, the best is in his least literary work, his letters. Of the poetry, little survives except a ballad or two, a little didactic verse—chiefly as the butt of ridicule (see page 950)—and the ironic stanzas on the "famous victory" won at Blenheim in 1704.

The Battle of Blenheim

It was a summer evening,
  Old Kaspar's work was done,
And he before his cottage door
  Was sitting in the sun,
And by him sported on the green
His little grandchild Wilhemine.

She saw her brother Peterkin
  Roll something large and round,
Which he beside the rivulet
  In playing there had found;
He came to ask what he had found,
That was so large, and smooth, and round.

Old Kaspar took it from the boy,
  Who stood expectant by;
And then the old man shook his head,
  And with a natural sigh,
" 'Tis some poor fellow's skull," said he,
"Who fell in the great victory.

"I find them in the garden,
  For there's many here about;
And often when I go to plough,
  The ploughshare turns them out!
For many thousand men," said he,
"Were slain in that great victory."

"Now tell us what 'twas all about,"
  Young Peterkin, he cries;
And little Wilhemine looks up
  With wonder-waiting eyes;
"Now tell us all about the war,
And what they fought each other for."

"It was the English," Kaspar cried,
  "Who put the French to rout;
But what they fought each other for,
  I could not well make out;
But everybody said," quoth he,
"That 'twas a famous victory.

"My father lived at Blenheim then,
  Yon little stream hard by;
They burnt his dwelling to the ground,
  And he was forced to fly;
So with his wife and child he fled,
Nor had he where to rest his head.

"With fire and sword the country round
  Was wasted far and wide,
And many a childing mother then,
  And new-born baby died;
But things like that, you know, must be
At every famous victory.

"They say it was a shocking sight
  After the field was won;
For many thousand bodies here
  Lay rotting in the sun;
But things like that, you know, must be
After a famous victory.

"Great praise the Duke of Marlbro' won,
  And our good Prince Eugene."

"Why 'twas a very wicked thing!"
  Said little Wilhemine.
"Nay, nay, my little girl," quoth he,
"It was a famous victory.

"And everybody praised the Duke
  Who this great fight did win."
"But what good came of it at last?"
  Quoth little Peterkin.
"Why that I cannot tell," said he,
"But 'twas a famous victory."

WALTER SAVAGE LANDOR

[1775–1864]

WALTER SAVAGE LANDOR was perpetually in conflict with the world and himself. The poet composed some of the most lucid and restrained poems of the century; the person fulfilled all the implications of his middle name. His almost ninety years were a succession of petty quarrels and public rages, libels and lawsuits, great humiliations and ungratifying triumphs. When he was nineteen, an undergraduate at Trinity College, Oxford, Landor differed politically with a student who refused to share his suddenly espoused republican principles; thereupon he fired a gun at his "enemy." Expelled from college and, later, forgiven, Landor refused to return. He fought with his father, and when, as eldest son, he received his inheritance, he sold the ancestral estate and lost his patrimony. At thirty-three he volunteered in the Spanish army against Napoleon, but, according to his first biographer, "his troop dispersed or melted away, and he came back to England in as great a hurry as he had left." At thirty-six he attended a ball at Bath, and was fascinated by a girl sixteen years his junior. Although he had had several love affairs, he determined to marry the young and penniless Julia Thuillier; before the honeymoon was over it was evident that he had married a little tyrant whose shrewishness was the least of her vices. Landor became more rampant than ever. He wrote seditious articles against the government, and had to leave England. He went to Italy, affronted an official, and was ordered out of Como. It was also in Italy that he threw his cook out of the kitchen window into a flower bed and suddenly shouted, "My God! I forgot about the violets!" Irrepressible and litigious, he had to be prevented from fighting a duel with a neighbor because of the water supply.

Hotheaded in youth, irascible in middle age, Landor was ruined by his temper. At sixty, after twenty-four years of unhappy marriage, he separated from his wife, who impudently housed a lover in the Fiesole villa. He hoped for comfort from his children, whom he had indulged, but they turned against him. He was allowed living expenses only after he had made over his property to the ungrateful family. The friendship of Browning and the admiration of strangers were all that saved him from an embittered old age. He died, within three months of his ninetieth birthday, September 17, 1864.

Landor's work furnishes a proof that a man's art does not parallel his life; nothing could be more dissimilar than Landor's biography and the aesthetics of his craft. There is never anything eccentric or cantankerous in either his balanced verse or the polished prose of his IMAGINARY CONVERSATIONS, a feat of careful reconstruction. The short poems may lack warmth and flexibility, but they are as poised as they are pure. Few English lyrics are more chaste than the poem to Rose Aylmer, daughter of a devoted friend—a brief elegy written when Landor heard the news of her death. Few stanzas are more exquisite than the series of poems to "Ianthe" (Sophia Jane Swift), an early sweetheart who remained the symbol of Landor's unrealized happiness. It is significant that these nostalgic love poems were written between Landor's late fifties and the year before his death. The last of the series was composed in his eighty-eighth year.

Rose Aylmer

Ah, what avails the sceptred race!
  Ah, what the form divine!
What every virtue, every grace!
  Rose Aylmer, all were thine.
Rose Aylmer, whom these wakeful eyes
  May weep, but never see,
A night of memories and sighs
  I consecrate to thee.

Ianthe

FROM YOU, IANTHE

From you, Ianthe, little troubles pass
  Like little ripples down a sunny river;
Your pleasures spring like daisies in the grass,
  Cut down, and up again as blithe as ever.

PAST RUINED ILION

Past ruined Ilion Helen lives;
  Alcestis rises from the shades.
Verse calls them forth; 'tis verse that gives
  Immortal youth to mortal maids.

Soon shall oblivion's deepening veil
  Hide all the peopled hills you see,
The gay, the proud, while lovers hail
  These many summers you and me.

AUTUMN

Mild is the parting year, and sweet
  The odor of the falling spray;
Life passes on more rudely fleet,
  And balmless is its closing day.

I wait its close, I court its gloom,
  But mourn that never must there fall
Or on my breast or on my tomb
  The tear that would have soothed it all.

WELL I REMEMBER

Well I remember how you smiled
  To see me write your name upon
The soft sea-sand. *"O! what a child!
  You think you're writing upon stone!"*
I have since written what no tide
  Shall ever wash away, what men
Unborn shall read o'er ocean wide
  And find Ianthe's name again.

Genially caricatured as the stormy Boythorn in Dickens' BLEAK HOUSE, misread in his day, Landor has been idealized in our own. George Moore and William Butler Yeats hailed him as the embodiment of aesthetic perfection. "The most violent of men," wrote Yeats, "he used his intellect to disengage a visionary image of perfect sanity, seen always in the most serene and classic art imaginable." Never ecstatic, rarely attempting the note of rapture, Landor's voice is low-pitched, cool, almost too well controlled. It is the tone of an old nobility, the marble calm of THE GREEK ANTHOLOGY.

Mother, I Cannot Mind My Wheel

Mother, I cannot mind my wheel;
  My fingers ache, my lips are dry;
O, if you felt the pain I feel!
  But O, who ever felt as I?

No longer could I doubt him true—
  All other men may use deceit.
He always said my eyes were blue,
  And often swore my lips were sweet.

Dirce

Stand close around, ye Stygian set,
  With Dirce in one boat conveyed,
Or Charon, seeing, may forget
  That he is old and she a shade.

Twenty Years Hence

Twenty years hence my eyes may grow
If not quite dim, yet rather so,
Still yours from others they shall know
                Twenty years hence.

Twenty years hence though it may hap
That I be called to take a nap
In a cool cell where thunder-clap
Was never heard,

There breathe but o'er my arch of grass
A not too sadly sighed *Alas,*
And I shall catch, ere you can pass,
That wingéd word.

Very True, the Linnets Sing

Very true, the linnets sing
Sweetest in the leaves of spring;
You have found in all these leaves
That which changes and deceives,
And, to pine by sun or star,
Left them, false ones as they are.
But there be who walk beside
Autumn's, till they all have died,
And who lend a patient ear
To low notes from branches sere.

Nowhere is Landor's serenity more evident than in the quatrains written in his old age. The proudest of these is also the most ironically pathetic; "I strove with none, for none was worth my strife," Landor cries with an arrogance that can deceive no one. This quatrain, ON HIS SEVENTY-FIFTH BIRTHDAY, furnishes a curious contrast to Browning's PROSPICE (page 876) and Tennyson's CROSSING THE BAR (page 838). But ON HIS NINTH DECADE combines truth with poetry. Here style and substance are finally united.

On His Seventy-fifth Birthday

I strove with none, for none was worth my strife.
Nature I loved and, next to Nature, Art;
I warmed both hands before the fire of life;
It sinks, and I am ready to depart.

On Death

Death stands above me, whispering low
  I know not what into my ear;
Of his strange language all I know
  Is, there is not a word of fear.

On His Ninth Decade

To my ninth decade I have tottered on,
  And no soft arm bends now my steps to steady;
She who once led me where she would is gone,
  So when he calls me, Death shall find me ready.

GEORGE GORDON, LORD BYRON

[1788–1824]

THE term "Byronic" has become a characterization which is also a criticism, and Byron's biography is not only more romantic but more readable than his verse. Most of the poems have worn badly, but the legend has never lost its fascination. Born George Gordon Byron in London, January 22, 1788, the boy's inheritance could scarcely have been worse. His father, according to Ernest Hartley Coleridge, one of Byron's early editors, was a "libertine by choice and in an eminent degree." His mother, a descendant of James I of Scotland, was abnormally vain, hysterical, and wholly incapable of dealing with her difficult child. Her father had committed suicide, and it was suspected that she had inherited his neurotic fears.

Lame at birth, Byron was further weakened by infantile paralysis, and his profligacy, the very bravado of his life, was a continued overcompensation for his feeling of physical inferiority. Born only remotely to the title, he suddenly became heir-presumptive at the age of six; the death of his great-uncle brought him the title and the estate in his eleventh year. When Byron entered Cambridge at seventeen, he was already well read in Latin and Greek, and he had fallen deeply in love at least twice. JUVENILE POEMS appeared anonymously when he was an undergraduate of eighteen; a few months later the volume was reissued under his own name as HOURS OF IDLENESS. It was severely criticized by THE EDINBURGH REVIEW, and the article inspired Byron's first characteristically slashing work, a rhymed satire entitled ENGLISH BARDS AND SCOTCH REVIEWERS.

Nervously histrionic, Byron lived in action; he saw to it that events moved rapidly as soon as he came of age. From 1809 to 1811 he traveled in Europe and Asia Minor, swam the Hellespont, made love indiscriminately, contracted malarial fever, and wrote continuously. Upon his return at twenty-three, he took his seat in the House of Lords and published the first two cantos of CHILDE HAROLD'S PILGRIMAGE, an almost undisguised autobiography of the melancholy poet as a distracted pleasure seeker. The work was a success from the very beginning.

Byron literally woke to find himself famous at twenty-four. His first speech in the House of Lords was a passionate defense of workers who had wrecked newly installed machinery that threatened their future. Society, aroused from its boredom, lionized him not only as a "poet of passion" but as a brilliant politician. There were those who already referred to him as a statesman, and Byron did nothing to discourage the adulation. He went from one affair to another. In spite of his clubfoot and spindly legs, he was extraordinarily attractive; his features were both delicate and sensual, and his brow had the pallor which women find irresistible in a poet. He was pursued by the wife of the future Lord Melbourne, Lady Caroline Lamb, who masqueraded as a boy in order to visit him in his rooms and who, when he tired of her, tried to stab herself at a ball which was the talk of London. From Lady Caroline he went to Lady Oxford, who was twice his age, and from Lady Oxford to Lady Frances Webster, whom Byron idealized as "Ginevra" and "Medora." Then he met his half-sister Augusta, who had married her cousin, a Colonel Leigh. The mutual attraction was immediate, and Byron took no pains to conceal the nature of their happiness together.

Too brief for our passion, too long for our peace,
Was that hour—Oh, when can its hope, can its memory cease?

He delighted in open avowals; he repeated the theme boldly:

> We repent, we abjure, we will break from the chain;
> We must part, we must fly—to unite it again.

A few months later Byron married the pretty and capricious Anne Isabella ("Annabella") Milbanke. Within a year, less than a month after the birth of a daughter, his wife returned to her family, charged that Byron was guilty of incest with his half sister, and demanded a separation. Railing at the hypocrisies of society, he thereupon left England, never to return.

In the spring of 1816 Byron joined Shelley, Mary Godwin, and her stepsister Claire Clairmont, who had become Byron's latest mistress and who bore him a daughter, Allegra. But it was impossible for Byron to be faithful to anything but his own wayward impulses. He was, as he assured Thomas Moore, "studious in the day, dissolute in the evening." A list of Byron's inamoratas, besides those already enumerated, would include Marianna Segati, his landlord's wife in Venice; Margarita Cogni, La Fornarina ("the little furnace"), a violent product of the Venetian slums; the twenty-year-old Countess Teresa Guiccioli, who, although married, openly proclaimed herself Byron's mistress and traveled about with him for four years—to say nothing of casual ladies and anonymous chambermaids. "Unnamed and unnumbered," wrote Peter Quennell in BYRON IN ITALY, "his concubines came and went."

Meanwhile Byron's creative faculty was more active than ever. In Europe he composed THE PRISONER OF CHILLON, MANFRED, and MAZEPPA, finished CHILDE HAROLD, and began DON JUAN. The romantic-revolutionary tone of his verse was belittled in England, but on the Continent Byron was hailed as a champion of liberty. An insurrectionary and militant spirit invaded even the love poems; the lyric WE'LL GO NO MORE A-ROVING still surprises us with the second stanza:

> For the sword outwears the sheath,
>   And the soul wears out the breast,
> And the heart must pause to breathe,
>   And Love itself have rest.

But the hater of tyrants was too much an aristocrat to love common humanity. "It is not that I adulate the people," Byron wrote in DON JUAN:

. . . I wish men to be free
As much from mobs as kings . . .

The consequence is, being of no party,
I shall offend all parties:—never mind!
My words, at least, are more sincere and hearty
Than if I sought to sail before the wind.

He satirized the theme in a rough epigram which put a personal edge to his passion for liberty:

When a Man Hath No Freedom to Fight for at Home

When a man hath no freedom to fight for at home,
  Let him combat for that of his neighbors;
Let him think of the glories of Greece and of Rome,
  And get knocked on the head for his labors.

To do good to Mankind is the chivalrous plan,
  And is always as nobly requited;
Then battle for Freedom wherever you can,
  And, if not shot or hanged, you'll get knighted.

Byron's concern with human emancipation found one of its noblest expressions in a long poem and a sonnet to a Swiss patriot, François de Bonnivard, imprisoned for his political opinions. Byron took several liberties with the facts in THE PRISONER OF CHILLON, with whom Byron undoubtedly identified himself; but the sonnet, a far finer poem, is unmarred by false dramatization.

Sonnet on Chillon

Eternal Spirit of the chainless Mind!
  Brightest in dungeons, Liberty! thou art,
  For there thy habitation is the heart—
The heart which love of thee alone can bind;
And when thy sons to fetters are consigned—
  To fetters, and the damp vault's dayless gloom,
  Their country conquers with their martyrdom,
And Freedom's fame finds wings on every wind.

Chillon! thy prison is a holy place,
  And thy sad floor an altar—for 'twas trod,
Until his very steps have left a trace
  Worn, as if thy cold pavement were a sod,
By Bonnivard! May none those marks efface!
  For they appeal from tyranny to God.

In 1821 Byron joined an impending revolution in Italy which came to nothing. In 1823 he again attempted to lead a revolt. He learned that numbers of intransigents were attempting a liberation of Greece, and, after offering money and advice, he joined them. Byron was now eager to find "a soldier's grave." But he was denied that final heroic gesture. The climate and his previous excesses proved too much for him. For months he suffered from fits of dizziness and spasms of pain. His illness increased; he was seized with ague, followed by delirium. He died April 19, 1824, three months more than thirty-six years old. His last words were said to be, "Forward! Courage! Don't be afraid! Follow my example!"

Most of Byron's impulses were in opposition to each other. Byron was a genuinely romantic poet, and a melodramatic poseur; a stern ironist, and a sentimentalist who inflated every protestation; an impassioned rebel with an abstract love of justice, and a nineteenth-century Narcissus whose love for himself was one of the great romances of history. This duality was the core of his creativeness; the period of his greatest debauchery was also the period of his greatest achievements.

When We Two Parted

When we two parted
  In silence and tears,
Half broken-hearted
  To sever for years,
Pale grew thy cheek and cold,
  Colder thy kiss;
Truly that hour foretold
  Sorrow to this.

The dew of the morning
  Sunk chill on my brow—
It felt like the warning
  Of what I feel now.

Thy vows are all broken,
  And light is thy fame;
I hear thy name spoken,
  And share in its shame.

They name thee before me,
  A knell to mine ear;
A shudder comes o'er me—
  Why wert thou so dear?
They know not I knew thee,
  Who knew thee too well:—
Long, long shall I rue thee,
  Too deeply to tell.

In secret we met—
  In silence I grieve
That thy heart could forget,
  Thy spirit deceive.
If I should meet thee
  After long years,
How should I greet thee?—
  With silence and tears.

She Walks in Beauty

She walks in beauty, like the night
Of cloudless climes and starry skies,
And all that's best of dark and bright
Meet in her aspect and her eyes;
Thus mellowed to that tender light
Which heaven to gaudy day denies.

One shade the more, one ray the less,
Had half impaired the nameless grace
Which waves in every raven tress
Or softly lightens o'er her face,
Where thoughts serenely sweet express
How pure, how dear their dwelling-place.

And on that cheek and o'er that brow
So soft, so calm, yet eloquent,

The smiles that win, the tints that glow
But tell of days in goodness spent,
A mind at peace with all below,
A heart whose love is innocent.

We'll Go No More A-Roving

So, we'll go no more a-roving
  So late into the night,
Though the heart be still as loving,
  And the moon be still as bright.

For the sword outwears its sheath,
  And the soul wears out the breast,
And the heart must pause to breathe,
  And love itself have rest.

Though the night was made for loving,
  And the day returns too soon,
Yet we'll go no more a-roving
  By the light of the moon.

Stanzas for Music

There be none of Beauty's daughters
  With a magic like thee;
And like music on the waters
  Is thy sweet voice to me:
When, as if its sound were causing
The charmed Ocean's pausing,
The waves lie still and gleaming,
And the lulled winds seem dreaming:

And the midnight moon is weaving
  Her bright chain o'er the deep;
Whose breast is gently heaving,
  As an infant's asleep:
So the spirit bows before thee,
To listen and adore thee;
With a full but soft emotion,
Like the swell of summer's ocean.

Farewell

Farewell! if ever fondest prayer
  For other's weal availed on high,
Mine will not all be lost in air,
  But waft thy name beyond the sky.
'Twere vain to speak, to weep, to sigh:
  Oh! more than tears of blood can tell,
When wrung from guilt's expiring eye,
  Are in that word—Farewell!—Farewell!

These lips are mute, these eyes are dry;
  But in my breast and in my brain,
Awake the pangs that pass not by,
  The thought that ne'er shall sleep again.
My soul nor deigns nor dares complain,
  Though grief and passion there rebel:
I only know we loved in vain;
  I only feel—Farewell!—Farewell!

As a theory, the romantic movement had nothing but good to recommend it. It was based upon the need of quickened perception, continually aroused imagination, and a broad humanitarian impulse. Its triumphs were many and spectacular, but its dangers were great, and its failures inevitable. The imaginative power, too often overprodded, fell into exaggeration. The humanitarian instinct degenerated into undiscriminating sentiment which, unguarded and uncontrolled, indulged itself in orgies of sentimentality. Following Wordsworth and Coleridge, influenced by Shelley, Byron rode the second wave of romanticism with abandon. He was every one of his heroes—the adventurous Harold, the mocking Beppo, the half-remorseful, half-defiant Manfred, the elegantly pensive Lucifer in CAIN, the piratical Conrad in THE CORSAIR, the cynical and self-infatuated Juan. He was a revolutionary and a rake, a creature of the moment and an exiled "pilgrim of eternity."

Waterloo

There was a sound of revelry by night,
And Belgium's capital had gathered then
Her Beauty and her Chivalry, and bright
The lamps shone o'er fair women and brave men;
A thousand hearts beat happily; and when
Music arose with its voluptuous swell,
Soft eyes looked love to eyes which spake again,
And all went merry as a marriage bell;
But hush! hark! a deep sound strikes like a rising knell!

Did ye not hear it?—No; 'twas but the wind,
Or the car rattling o'er the stony street;
On with the dance! let joy be unconfined;
No sleep till morn, when Youth and Pleasure meet
To chase the glowing Hours with flying feet—
But hark!—that heavy sound breaks in once more,
As if the clouds its echo would repeat;
And nearer, clearer, deadlier than before!
Arm! Arm! it is—it is—the cannon's opening roar!

Within a windowed niche of that high hall
Sat Brunswick's fated chieftain; he did hear
That sound the first amidst the festival,
And caught its tone with Death's prophetic ear;
And when they smiled because he deemed it near,
His heart more truly knew that peal too well
Which stretched his father on a bloody bier,
And roused the vengeance blood alone could quell;
He rushed into the field, and, foremost fighting, fell.

Ah! then and there was hurrying to and fro,
And gathering tears, and tremblings of distress,
And cheeks all pale, which but an hour ago
Blushed at the praise of their own loveliness;
And there were sudden partings, such as press
The life from out young hearts, and choking sighs
Which ne'er might be repeated; who could guess
If ever more should meet those mutual eyes,
Since upon night so sweet such awful morn could rise!

And there was mounting in hot haste—the steed,
The mustering squadron, and the clattering car,
Went pouring forward with impetuous speed,
And swiftly forming in the ranks of war—
And the deep thunder peal on peal afar;
And near, the beat of the alarming drum
Roused up the soldier ere the morning star;
While thronged the citizens with terror dumb,
Or whispering, with white lips—"The foe! they come! they come!"

And wild and high the *Cameron's Gathering* rose!
The war-note of Lochiel, which Albyn's hills
Have heard, and heard, too, have her Saxon foes:—
How in the noon of night that pibroch thrills,
Savage and shrill! But with the breath which fills
Their mountain-pipe, so fill the mountaineers
With the fierce native daring which instills
The stirring memory of a thousand years,
And Evan's—Donald's—fame rings in each clansman's ears!

And Ardennes waves above them her green leaves,
Dewy with Nature's tear-drops as they pass,
Grieving, if aught inanimate e'er grieves,
Over the unreturning brave,—alas!
Ere evening to be trodden like the grass
Which now beneath them, but above shall grow
In its next verdure, when this fiery mass
Of living valor, rolling on the foe
And burning with high hope shall molder cold and low.

Last noon beheld them full of lusty life,
Last eve in Beauty's circle proudly gay,
The midnight brought the signal-sound of strife,
The morn the marshaling in arms,—the day
Battle's magnificently stern array!
The thunder-clouds close o'er it, which when rent
The earth is covered thick with other clay,
Which her own clay shall cover, heaped and pent,
Rider and horse,—friend, foe,—in one red burial blent!

from CHILDE HAROLD'S PILGRIMAGE

Ocean

Roll on, thou deep and dark blue Ocean—roll!
Ten thousand fleets sweep over thee in vain;
Man marks the earth with ruin; his control
Stops with the shore; upon the watery plain
The wrecks are all thy deed, nor doth remain
A shadow of man's ravage, save his own,
When for a moment, like a drop of rain,
He sinks into thy depths with bubbling groan,
Without a grave, unknelled, uncoffined and unknown.

His steps are not upon thy paths—thy fields
Are not a spoil for him—thou dost arise
And shake him from thee; the vile strength he wields
For earth's destruction thou dost all despise,
Spurning him from thy bosom to the skies,
And sendst him, shivering in thy playful spray,
And howling, to his Gods, where haply lies
His petty hope in some near port or bay,
And dashest him again to earth—there let him lay.

The armaments which thunderstrike the walls
Of rock-built cities, bidding nations quake,
And monarchs tremble in their capitals,
The oak leviathans, whose huge ribs make
Their clay creator the vain title take
Of lord of thee, and arbiter of war:—
These are thy toys, and, as the snowy flake,
They melt into thy yeast of waves, which mar
Alike the Armada's pride, or spoils of Trafalgar.

Thy shores are empires, changed in all save thee—
Assyria, Greece, Rome, Carthage, what are they?
Thy waters washed them power while they were free,
And many a tyrant since: their shores obey
The stranger, slave or savage; their decay
Has dried up realms to deserts:—not so thou,
Unchangeable save to thy wild waves' play—
Time writes no wrinkle on thine azure brow—
Such as creation's dawn beheld, thou rollest now.

Thou glorious mirror, where the Almighty's form
Glasses itself in tempests: in all time,
Calm or convulsed—in breeze, or gale, or storm,
Icing the pole, or in the torrid clime
Dark-heaving; boundless, endless, and sublime—
The image of Eternity—the throne
Of the Invisible; even from out thy slime
The monsters of the deep are made; each zone
Obeys thee; thou goest forth, dread, fathomless, alone.

from CHILDE HAROLD'S PILGRIMAGE

Southey and Wordsworth

Bob Southey! You're a poet—Poet laureate,
And representative of all the race;
Although 'tis true that you turned out a Tory at
Last—yours has lately been a common case;
And now, my Epic Renegade! what are ye at?
With all the Lakers,[1] in and out of place?
A nest of tuneful persons, to my eye
Like "four and twenty Blackbirds in a pye; [2]

"Which pye being opened they began to sing"
(This old song and new simile holds good),
"A dainty dish to set before the King,"
Or Regent, who admires such kind of food;—
And Coleridge, too, has lately taken wing,
But like a hawk encumbered with his hood—
Explaining metaphysics to the nation—
I wish he would explain his Explanation.

You, Bob! are rather insolent, you know,
At being disappointed in your wish
To supersede all warblers here below,
And be the only Blackbird in the dish;
And then you overstrain yourself, or so,
And tumble downward like the flying fish
Gasping on deck, because you soar too high, Bob,
And fall for lack of moisture quite a-dry, Bob!

[1] *The Lake School of poets, Coleridge, Southey, and Wordsworth, who lived in the neighborhood of the English lakes.*

[2] *The pun here is directed against Henry James Pye (see page 687), who became laureate in 1790, and who was the target of contemporary derision.*

And Wordsworth, in a rather long "Excursion"
  (I think the quarto holds five hundred pages),
Has given a sample from the vasty version
  Of his new system to perplex the sages;
'Tis poetry—at least by his assertion,
  And may appear so when the dog-star rages—
And he who understands it would be able
To add a story to the Tower of Babel.

You—Gentlemen! by dint of long seclusion
  From better company, have kept your own
At Keswick, and through still continued fusion
  Of one another's minds, at last have grown
To deem as a most logical conclusion,
  That poesy has wreaths for you alone;
There is a narrowness in such a notion,
Which makes me wish you'd change your lakes for ocean.

I would not imitate the petty thought,
  Nor coin my self-love to so base a vice,
For all the glory your conversion brought,
  Since gold alone should not have been its price,
You have your salary; was't for that you wrought?
  And Wordsworth has his place in the Excise.
You're shabby fellows—true—but poets still,
And duly seated on the Immortal Hill.

from DON JUAN

Evening

O Hesperus! thou bringest all good things—
  Home to the weary, to the hungry cheer,
To the young bird the parent's brooding wings,
  The welcome stall to the o'erlabored steer:
Whate'er of peace about our hearthstone clings,
  Whate'er our household gods protect of dear,
Are gathered round us by thy look of rest;
Thou bring'st the child, too, to the mother's breast.

Soft hour! which wakes the wish and melts the heart
  Of those who sail the seas, on the first day
When they from their sweet friends are torn apart;
  Or fills with love the pilgrim on his way

As the far bell of vesper makes him start,
  Seeming to weep the dying day's decay;
Is this a fancy which our reason scorns?
Ah! surely nothing dies but something mourns.

from DON JUAN

Matthew Arnold summed it up for his contemporaries in MEMORIAL VERSES:

When Byron's eyes were shut in death
We bowed our head and held our breath.
He taught us little; but our soul
Had *felt* him like the thunder's roll.

Uncritically overproductive, frankly confessional, Byron shocked and fascinated his generation. The shock has gone out of his work, but the fascination, mixed and somewhat blurred, remains.

JOHN CLARE

[1793–1864]

JOHN CLARE, who failed to support himself as poet and peasant, spent the last twenty-seven years of his life in an insane asylum. As a result most commentators have created legends about him which are as sensational as they are misleading. It was not until about sixty years after Clare's death that Edmund Blunden and Alan Porter re-examined the conflicting evidence, reread his two thousand poems, of which more than two thirds have never been published, and presented a clear picture of the man and his work.

Son of a farm laborer, John Clare was born July 13, 1793, at Helpstone, in a cottage melodramatically described as "a narrow wretched hut, more like a prison than a human dwelling." The boy was put to work at twelve and got what little schooling he received at night. At thirteen, he saw a neighbor thrown from the top of a hay wagon and break his neck; the sight so affected Clare that his mind was temporarily unbalanced. At sixteen he fell in love with Mary Joyce, daughter of a well-to-do farmer, who forbade their meetings. Clare never quite recovered from this early hurt; the wound grew worse with age. In his imagination he was wedded to Mary; long after she had died and Clare had married Patty Turner, he held long conversations with Mary under the delusion that she was alive and his wife.

From his sixteenth to his twenty-fourth year Clare worked as a gardener, enlisted in the militia, and was employed in a limekiln. At twenty-four he met his wife-to-be, and issued a PROPOSAL FOR PUBLISHING BY SUBSCRIPTION A COLLECTION OF ORIGINAL TRIFLES ON MISCELLANEOUS SUBJECTS IN VERSE. Only seven subscribers responded to the appeal. Worse, Clare was discharged from the limekiln for distributing his prospectus during working hours, and at twenty-five had to ask for parish relief. A bookseller named Drury, who had seen Clare's circular, interested John Taylor, publisher of Keats and Shelley; after an anxious wait of nearly two years, Taylor published Clare's POEMS DESCRIPTIVE OF RURAL LIFE AND SCENERY.

Clare's first volume was an immediate success. Three editions were sold in as many months. The London intelligentsia made Clare the season's fashion much as the Edinburgh coteries had feted Burns. He was hailed as "The Northamptonshire Peasant Poet." Lord Milton entertained him—in the servants' hall—and Lady Milton offered to give him any book that was his favorite, but Clare was confused and could think of nothing. "Lord Fitzwilliam, and Lady Fitzwilliam, too, talked to me and noticed me kindly, and his Lordship gave me some advice which I had done well to have noticed better than I have. He bade me beware of booksellers and warned me not to be fed with promises." Besides the advice, Lord Fitzwilliam presented Clare with seventeen pounds, on the strength of which Clare married Patty Turner shortly before the birth of their first child.

Lord Fitzwilliam's warnings were unhappily justified. Drury, the bookseller, and Taylor, the publisher, saw to it that Clare's royalties were absorbed in "advertising," "commissions," "deductions to agents," and the all-covering "sundries." They suspected that Clare was regarded as a novelty, a bucolic ten days' wonder in the metropolis, and they were right. Although Taylor published THE VILLAGE MINSTREL AND OTHER POEMS in two volumes a year after the publication of Clare's first book, the critics were no longer interested. In 1820 Clare had been trotted from one drawing room to another and had been besieged by visitors eager to drink his health at the tavern. Now he was alone except for a growing family. Continuing to work in the fields, Clare offered to sell his entire output for five years to Taylor for two hundred pounds; but the cautious Taylor rejected the offer with evasive generalities and advised Clare not to be "ambitious but remain in the state in which God had placed him."

Clare began to suffer from overwork and illness. Farmers refused to employ him. He drank to escape his worries, and worried himself into spells of drinking. Two more volumes were published reluctantly and unprofitably, and Clare had premonitions intensified by ominous dreams. He hawked his poems from house to house, dragging a sack of unsold books as much as thirty miles in one day. There were nine people dependent upon him when, in his forty-fourth year, he was placed in a private asylum. A few years later he was committed to the Northampton County Asylum, and it was here that he wrote some of his most lucid verse.

I Am

WRITTEN IN NORTHAMPTON COUNTY ASYLUM

I am: yet what I am none cares or knows,
  My friends forsake me like a memory lost;
I am the self-consumer of my woes,
  They rise and vanish in oblivious host,
Like shades in love and death's oblivion lost;
And yet I am, and live with shadows tost.

Into the nothingness of scorn and noise,
  Into the living sea of waking dreams,
Where there is neither sense of life nor joys,
  But the vast shipwreck of my life's esteems;
And e'en the dearest—that I loved the best—
Are strange—nay, rather stranger than the rest.

I long for scenes where man has never trod;
  A place where woman never smiled or wept;
There to abide with my Creator, God,
  And sleep as I in childhood sweetly slept:
Untroubling and untroubled where I lie;
The grass below—above the vaulted sky.

Clare continued to write to the end, and the words of the "harmless lunatic" were never more precise and expressive than in his last phase. He died quietly May 20, 1864.

Considered as a curiosity by his contemporaries, forgotten for almost a century, Clare has been appreciated only in the last twenty years. He has been compared in some quarters to Blake, and, although the comparison may be excessive, there is no doubt about Clare's fresh vision and clear spontaneity.

Secret Love

I hid my love when young till I
Couldn't bear the buzzing of a fly;
I hid my love to my despite
Till I could not bear to look at light:
I dare not gaze upon her face
But left her memory in each place;
Where'er I saw a wild flower lie
I kissed and bade my love good-bye.

I met her in the greenest dells
Where dewdrops pearl the wood blue-bells
The lost breeze kissed her bright blue eye,
The bee kissed and went singing by,
A sunbeam found a passage there,
A gold chain round her neck so fair;
As secret as the wild bee's song
She lay there all the summer long.

I hid my love in field and town
Till e'en the breeze would knock me down,
The bees seemed singing ballads o'er,
The fly's bass turned a lion's roar;
And even silence found a tongue,
To haunt me all the summer long;
The riddle nature could not prove
Was nothing else but secret love.

The Dying Child

He could not die when trees were green,
For he loved the time too well.
His little hands, when flowers were seen,
Were held for the bluebell,
As he was carried o'er the green.

His eye glanced at the white-nosed bee;
He knew those children of the Spring:
When he was well and on the lea
He held one in his hands to sing,
Which filled his heart with glee.

Infants, the children of the Spring!
How can an infant die
When butterflies are on the wing,
Green grass, and such a sky?
How can they die at Spring?

He held his hands for daisies white,
And then for violets blue,
And took them all to bed at night
That in the green fields grew,
As childhood's sweet delight.

And then he shut his little eyes,
And flowers would notice not;
Birds' nests and eggs caused no surprise,
He now no blossoms got:
They met with plaintive sighs.

When Winter came and blasts did sigh,
And bare were plain and tree,
As he for ease in bed did lie
His soul seemed with the free,
He died so quietly.

Clare's spell is his own. His scenes are familiar, but they are never commonplace; his language is simple but seldom trite. Every detail is recorded as sharply as though it had never before been observed. "There is," wrote Edmund Blunden, "no poet who in his nature poetry so completely subdues self and mood, and deals with the topic for its own sake." If Clare's charm is limited because of its bucolic setting, it is unsurpassed in its purity.

Young Lambs

The spring is coming by a many signs;
The trays are up, the hedges broken down
That fenced the haystack, and the remnant shines
Like some old antique fragment weathered brown.
And where suns peep, in every sheltered place,
The little early buttercups unfold
A glittering star or two—till many trace
The edges of the blackthorn clumps in gold.
And then a little lamb bolts up behind
The hill, and wags his tail to meet the yoe;
And then another, sheltered from the wind,
Lies all his length as dead—and lets me go
Close by, and never stirs, but basking lies,
With legs stretched out as though he could not rise.

Firwood

The fir trees taper into twigs and wear
The rich blue green of summer all the year,
Softening the roughest tempest almost calm
And offering shelter ever still and warm
To the small path that towels underneath,
Where loudest winds—almost as summer's breath—
Scarce fan the weed that lingers green below,
When others out of doors are lost in frost and snow.
And sweet the music trembles on the ear
As the wind suthers through each tiny spear,
Makeshifts for leaves; and yet, so rich they show,
Winter is almost summer where they grow.

Evening Primrose

When once the sun sinks in the west,
And dew-drops pearl the evening's breast,
Almost as pale as moonbeams are,
Or its companionable star,

The evening primrose opes anew
Its delicate blossoms to the dew;
And, shunning-hermit of the light,
Wastes its fair bloom upon the night,
Who, blindfold to its fond caresses,
Knows not the beauty he possesses.
Thus it blooms on till night is by
And day looks out with open eye,
Abashed at the gaze it cannot shun,
It faints and withers, and is done.

Clock-o'-Clay

In the cowslip pips I lie,
Hidden from the buzzing fly,
While green grass beneath me lies,
Pearled with dew like fishes' eyes,
Here I lie, a clock-o'-clay,
Waiting for the time o' day.

While the forest quakes surprise,
And the wild wind sobs and sighs,
My home rocks as like to fall,
On its pillar green and tall;
When the pattering rain drives by
Clock-o'-clay keeps warm and dry.

Day by day and night by night,
All the week I hide from sight;
In the cowslip pips I lie,
In the rain still warm and dry;
Day and night, and night and day,
Red, black-spotted clock-o'-clay.

My home shakes in wind and showers,
Pale green pillar topped with flowers,
Bending at the wild wind's breath,
Till I touch the grass beneath;
Here I live, lone clock-o'-clay,
Watching for the time of day.

PERCY BYSSHE SHELLEY

[1792–1822]

Two beings fought it out in the body of Percy Bysshe Shelley. One was an uncompromising zealot, a passionate seeker after truth. The other was a victim of illusions, "a beautiful and ineffectual angel, beating in the void his luminous wings in vain."

Born at Field Place, near the little Sussex village of Horsham, on August 4, 1792, Percy was the son of Timothy Shelley. The poet's grandfather, Sir Bysshe Shelley, was the son of an emigrant and had been born in Newark, New Jersey. Returning to England, he married successively two heiresses, built up a fortune, and, according to William Michael Rossetti, "lived in sullen and penurious retirement." Even as a child Shelley was brilliant and hypersensitive, resentful of all authority, and, when hurt, quick to become hysterical. These characteristics, together with his physical beauty, made him unpopular among his fellows. His schooling at Eton and Oxford was a long misery. He was cruelly mocked by the younger boys, badgered and bullied by the older students. As a result Shelley became so nonconformist that he refused to accept any form of discipline. When an Eton master found Shelley's room full of blue chemical flames, the young scientist explained, "Sir, I am trying to call up the Devil." Turning away from the brute world to the necromancy of a dream, he heartened himself with Godwin's anarchical POLITICAL JUSTICE, and was dubbed "mad Shelley." At nineteen he was expelled from Oxford for having published, anonymously, THE NECESSITY OF ATHEISM.

Returning home to an angry father, supported by pocket money supplied by his sisters, Shelley met Harriet Westbrook, daughter of a hotelkeeper. Harriet was sixteen, and when Shelley learned that her father insisted on her returning to school, he determined to rescue her from "persecution." Shelley had not yet recovered from a love affair with his cousin Harriet Grove, who was alarmed at his efforts to convert her to his "heresies." But the young crusader, roused with new zeal, ran away with Harriet Westbrook, married her at Edinburgh—although he still objected to the despotic institution of marriage—and spent his honeymoon in Ireland, distributing copies of a pamphlet, DECLARATION OF RIGHTS, by hand, from balloons, and in bottles set adrift.

Upon his return to England Shelley became a father at twenty-one, engaged in a warm but platonic intimacy with Elizabeth Hitchener, a schoolmistress, and published his first important poem, QUEEN MAB, which denounced religion and aggressively criticized the structure of human society. A few months later, Shelley began corresponding with Godwin, met his daughter, Mary Wollstonecraft Godwin, and immediately fell in love with her. She was seventeen, a radical like her father, and, like Shelley, a philosophic anarchist. In July, 1814, the two eloped to Switzerland.

Shelley's life became increasingly complicated with the Godwin family, which was, in itself, a fine study in complication. Mary was Godwin's daughter by his first wife, author of THE RIGHTS OF WOMEN. Before her marriage, the first Mrs. Godwin had borne a daughter to Gilbert Imlay, an American in Paris; this daughter, Fanny, committed suicide in 1816, and it was rumored that her death was due to a hopeless love of Shelley. Godwin's second wife was a Mrs. Clairmont, whose daughter by her first marriage was Clara Mary Jane ("Claire") Clairmont, who became Byron's mistress and bore him a daughter, Allegra. Claire insisted upon accompanying Shelley and Mary to the Continent. When they returned in 1815 Shelley found that he had again become a father—Harriet having given birth to a son—and that he had inherited property worth six thousand pounds a year from his grandfather. Shelley assigned two hundred pounds a year to his wife Harriet and invited her to share his establishment with Mary, an invitation Harriet declined. Shelley and Mary spent the next summer in Switzerland—again accompanied by Claire—and their return to England was followed by the suicides of Fanny and Harriet. Shelley's wife had always threatened self-destruction, but Shelley believed that she had talked herself out of the act; the discovery of her body in the Serpentine was a shock from which he never fully recovered.

Shelley married Miss Godwin in December, 1816, but their peace was shattered by Harriet's father, who demanded the custody of his two grandchildren on the charges that Shelley had deserted his wife and that, because of his antisocial principles, he was morally unfit to bring up the children. Lord Chancellor Eldon affirmed the charges and appointed a Dr. Hume as guardian; whereupon the baffled poet countered with a set of furious verses beginning, "Thy country's curse is on thee!"

Shelley received the Lord Chancellor's verdict as a kind of excommunication and sentence of exile. In 1818, like Byron before him, he left England for Italy, and, like Byron, never returned. Soon after his departure, he wrote a sonnet which, though flawed in form, is a perfect expression of Shelley's feeling for his fatherland, his humiliation and grief, and his ineradicable hope.

England in 1819

An old, mad, blind, despised, and dying king—[1]
Princes, the dregs of their dull race, who flow
Through public scorn—mud from a muddy spring;
Rulers, who neither see, nor feel, nor know,
But leech-like to their fainting country cling,
Till they drop, blind in blood, without a blow;
A people starved and stabbed in the untilled field—
An army, which liberticide and prey
Makes as a two-edged sword to all who wield—
Golden and sanguine laws which tempt and slay—
Religion Christless, Godless—a book sealed;
A Senate—Time's worst statute unrepealed—
Are graves, from which a glorious Phantom may
Burst, to illumine our tempestuous day.

In Italy Byron and Shelley became close companions, and the last phase of Shelley's life was a period of full creativeness as well as the time of his greatest intellectual growth. Besides his attachment for Byron, whom he idolized and influenced, he became infatuated with Emilia Viviani and Mrs. Jane Williams, both of whom inspired some of Shelley's most famous love poems. But he maintained his emotional equilibrium. "I think one is always in love with something or other," he wrote. "The error consists in seeking in a mortal image the likeness of what is perhaps eternal."

Shelley found the "likeness of what is perhaps eternal" not only in "mortal images" but in the immortal imagery of the poems written in his late twenties: THE CENCI, that marvelous poetic drama; PROMETHEUS UNBOUND, the triumphant vision of a perfect future; HELLAS, a glorification of the Greek revolt; EPIPSYCHIDION, a hymn

[1] *George III.*

to abstract beauty and spiritual love inspired by Emilia Viviani; and ADONAIS, that magnificent elegy in which Shelley, vindicating all poets in his defense of Keats, "in another's fate now wept his own."

In the late spring of 1821 the Shelleys moved to a villa on the Gulf of Spezia. Their friend Lieutenant Edward Williams had designed a small boat, which was speedy but none too safe. On July 1, 1822, Shelley and Williams sailed over to Leghorn to greet Byron and Leigh Hunt, who had just arrived in Italy. On July 8 they started to return, but never reached home. Just what happened is unknown. It has never been determined whether the boat capsized, collided with some larger vessel, or was run down by pirates. Two weeks later the two bodies were washed ashore; a volume of Keats was found in Shelley's pocket. Since the Italian laws required complete destruction because of the plague, the bodies were buried in quicklime. But Trelawny and other friends dug them up and burned the corpses on the beach; at the last moment, Trelawny snatched the poet's heart from the pyre. Shelley's ashes were collected and buried in the Protestant Cemetery in Rome, where the body of Keats had already been interred. Had he lived another month, Shelley would have been thirty years old.

"Poets," wrote Shelley at the conclusion of THE DEFENSE OF POETRY, "are the unacknowledged legislators of the world." As a legislator, Shelley would have been a severe and stubborn insurrectionary. Misjudged as a licentious pagan by a self-righteous world, he was essentially a passionate believer in universal goodness, even in human perfectibility. A dedicated poet of protest, he always had, as he wrote in his preface to PROMETHEUS UNBOUND, "a passion for reforming the world."

Two extremes of Shelley's protesting spirit are manifest in the SONG TO THE MEN OF ENGLAND and the Final Chorus from HELLAS. Here condemnation turns to affirmation, and scorn ascends to prophecy.

Song to the Men of England

Men of England, wherefore plough
For the lords who lay ye low?
Wherefore weave with toil and care
The rich robes your tyrants wear?

Wherefore feed, and clothe, and save,
From the cradle to the grave,
Those ungrateful drones who would
Drain your sweat—nay, drink your blood!

Wherefore, Bees of England, forge
Many a weapon, chain, and scourge,
That these stingless drones may spoil
The forced produce of your toil?

Have ye leisure, comfort, calm,
Shelter, food, love's gentle balm?
Or what is it ye buy so dear
With your pain and with your fear?

The seed ye sow, another reaps;
The wealth ye find, another keeps;
The robes ye weave, another wears;
The arms ye forge, another bears.

Sow seed—but let no tyrant reap;
Find wealth—let no impostor heap;
Weave robes—let not the idle wear;
Forge arms—in your defence to bear.

Shrink to your cellars, holes, and cells;
In halls ye deck, another dwells.
Why shake the chains ye wrought? Ye see
The steel ye tempered glance on ye.

With plough and spade, and hoe and loom,
Trace your grave, and build your tomb,
And weave your winding-sheet, till fair
England be your sepulchre.

A New World

The world's great age begins anew,
  The golden years return,
The earth doth like a snake renew
  Her winter weeds outworn:
Heaven smiles, and faiths and empires gleam,
Like wrecks of a dissolving dream.

A brighter Hellas rears its mountains
  From waves serener far;
A new Peneus rolls his fountains
  Against the morning star.
Where fairer Tempes bloom, there sleep
Young Cyclads on a sunnier deep.

A loftier Argo cleaves the main,
  Fraught with a later prize;
Another Orpheus sings again,
  And loves, and weeps, and dies.
A new Ulysses leaves once more
Calypso for his native shore.

Oh! write no more the tale of Troy,
  If earth death's scroll must be!
Nor mix with Laian rage the joy
  Which dawns upon the free,
Altho' a subtler Sphinx renew
Riddles of death Thebes never knew.

Another Athens shall arise,
  And to remoter time
Bequeath, like sunset to the skies,
  The splendor of its prime;
And leave, if naught so bright may live,
All earth can take or heaven can give.

Saturn and Love their long repose
  Shall burst, more bright and good
Than all who fell, than One who rose,
  Than many unsubdued:
Not gold, not blood, their altar dowers,
But votive tears and symbol flowers.

Oh, cease! must hate and death return?
  Cease! must men kill and die?
Cease! drain not to its dregs the urn
  Of bitter prophecy.
The world is weary of the past.
Oh, might it die or rest at last!

Final Chorus: HELLAS

Although the idea of revolution burns through Shelley's pages, it is doubtful that most readers are drawn to the poet because of his message. It is the music, the ardent imagination, which first arrest and then hold the reader; it is the power of communicating acute emotion, of intense yearning which is all the more cherished because it cannot be consummated. Shelley may be admired for his insurgent and iconoclastic spirit, but he is loved for his sheer effluence, the overbrimming lyricism, the ever-fertile fancy, the profound hypnotic power.

To a Skylark

Hail to thee, blithe Spirit!
  Bird thou never wert,
That from Heaven, or near it,
  Pourest thy full heart
In profuse strains of unpremeditated art.

Higher still and higher
  From the earth thou springest
Like a cloud of fire;
  The blue deep thou wingest,
And singing still dost soar, and soaring ever singest.

In the golden lightning
  Of the sunken sun
O'er which clouds are bright'ning,
  Thou dost float and run,
Like an unbodied joy whose race is just begun.

The pale purple even
  Melts around thy flight;
Like a star of Heaven
  In the broad daylight
Thou art unseen, but yet I hear thy shrill delight:

Keen as are the arrows
  Of that silver sphere,
Whose intense lamp narrows
  In the white dawn clear
Until we hardly see—we feel that it is there.

All the earth and air
  With thy voice is loud,
As, when night is bare,
  From one lonely cloud
The moon rains out her beams, and heaven is overflowed.

What thou art we know not;
  What is most like thee?
From rainbow clouds there flow not
  Drops so bright to see
As from thy presence showers a rain of melody.

Like a poet hidden
  In the light of thought,
Singing hymns unbidden,
  Till the world is wrought
To sympathy with hopes and fears it heeded not:

Like a high-born maiden
  In a palace tower,
Soothing her love-laden
  Soul in secret hour
With music sweet as love, which overflows her bower:

Like a glow-worm golden
  In a dell of dew,
Scattering unbeholden
  Its aerial hue
Among the flowers and grass, which screen it from the view:

Like a rose embowered
  In its own green leaves,
By warm winds deflowered,
  Till the scent it gives
Makes faint with too much sweet these heavy-winged thieves.

Sound of vernal showers
  On the twinkling grass,
Rain-awakened flowers,
  All that ever was
Joyous, and clear, and fresh, thy music doth surpass.

Teach us, sprite or bird,
  What sweet thoughts are thine:
I have never heard
  Praise of love or wine
That panted forth a flood of rapture so divine.

Chorus hymeneal
  Or triumphal chaunt
Matched with thine, would be all
  But an empty vaunt—
A thing wherein we feel there is some hidden want.

What objects are the fountains
  Of thy happy strain?
What fields, or waves, or mountains?
  What shapes of sky or plain?
What love of thine own kind? what ignorance of pain?

With thy clear keen joyance
  Languor cannot be:
Shadow of annoyance
  Never came near thee:
Thou lovest, but ne'er knew love's sad satiety.

Waking or asleep,
  Thou of death must deem
Things more true and deep
  Than we mortals dream,
Or how could thy notes flow in such a crystal stream?

We look before and after,
  And pine for what is not:
Our sincerest laughter
  With some pain is fraught;
Our sweetest songs are those that tell of saddest thought.

Yet if we could scorn
  Hate, and pride, and fear;
If we were things born
  Not to shed a tear,
I know not how thy joy we ever should come near.

Better than all measures
  Of delightful sound,
Better than all treasures
  That in books are found,
Thy skill to poet were, thou scorner of the ground!

Teach me half the gladness
  That thy brain must know,
Such harmonious madness
  From my lips would flow
The world should listen then, as I am listening now!

To Night

Swiftly walk o'er the western wave,
    Spirit of Night!
Out of the misty eastern cave,
Where, all the long and lone daylight,
Thou wovest dreams of joy and fear,
Which make thee terrible and dear–
    Swift be thy flight!

Wrap thy form in a mantle gray,
    Star-inwrought!
Blind with thine hair the eyes of day;
Kiss her until she be wearied out,
Then wander o'er city, and sea, and land,
Touching all with thine opiate wand–
    Come, long-sought!

When I arose and saw the dawn,
    I sighed for thee;
When light rode high, and the dew was gone,
And noon lay heavy on flower and tree,
And the weary day turned to his rest,
Lingering like an unloved guest,
    I sighed for thee.

Thy brother Death came, and cried,
    Wouldst thou me?
Thy sweet child Sleep, the filmy-eyed,
Murmured like a noontide bee,
Shall I nestle near thy side?
Wouldst thou me?–And I replied,
    No, not thee!

Death will come when thou art dead,
    Soon, too soon–
Sleep will come when thou art fled;
Of neither would I ask the boon
I ask of thee, beloved Night–
Swift be thine approaching flight,
    Come soon, soon!

The Waning Moon

And like a dying lady, lean and pale,
Who totters forth, wrapped in a gauzy veil,
Out of her chamber, led by the insane
And feeble wanderings of her fading brain,
The moon arose up in the murky East,
A white and shapeless mass.

To the Moon

Art thou pale for weariness
Of climbing heaven and gazing on the earth,
Wandering companionless
Among the stars that have a different birth—
And ever changing, like a joyless eye
That finds no object worth its constancy?

Love's Philosophy

The fountains mingle with the river
And the rivers with the Ocean,
The winds of Heaven mix for ever
With a sweet emotion;
Nothing in the world is single;
All things by a law divine
In one spirit meet and mingle.
Why not I with thine?—

See the mountains kiss high Heaven
And the waves clasp one another;
No sister-flower would be forgiven
If it disdained its brother;
And the sunlight clasps the earth
And the moonbeams kiss the sea:
What is all this sweet work worth
If thou kiss not me?

Music, When Soft Voices Die

Music, when soft voices die,
Vibrates in the memory—
Odors, when sweet violets sicken,
Live within the sense they quicken.

Rose leaves, when the rose is dead,
Are heaped for the beloved's bed;
And so thy thoughts, when thou art gone,
Love itself shall slumber on.

To ——[1]

THE DESIRE OF THE MOTH

One word is too often profaned
  For me to profane it,
One feeling too falsely disdained
  For thee to disdain it;
One hope is too like despair
  For prudence to smother,
And pity from thee more dear
  Than that from another.

I can give not what men call love,
  But wilt thou accept not
The worship the heart lifts above
  And the Heavens reject not,—
The desire of the moth for the star,
  Of the night for the morrow,
The devotion to something afar
  From the sphere of our sorrow?

The Indian Serenade

I arise from dreams of thee
In the first sweet sleep of night,
When the winds are breathing low,
And the stars are shining bright

[1] *Jane Williams, see page 717.*

I arise from dreams of thee,
And a spirit in my feet
Hath led me—who knows how?
To thy chamber window, Sweet!

The wandering airs they faint
On the dark, the silent stream—
The champak odors fail
Like sweet thoughts in a dream;
The nightingale's complaint,
It dies upon her heart;
As I must on thine,
Oh, beloved as thou art!

O lift me from the grass!
I die! I faint! I fail!
Let thy love in kisses rain
On my lips and eyelids pale.
My cheek is cold and white, alas!
My heart beats loud and fast;—
Oh! press it to thine own again,
Where it will break at last.

When the Lamp Is Shattered

  When the lamp is shattered,
The light in the dust lies dead;
  When the cloud is scattered,
The rainbow's glory is shed;
  When the lute is broken,
Sweet tones are remembered not;
  When the lips have spoken,
Loved accents are soon forgot.

  As music and splendor
Survive not the lamp and the lute,
  The heart's echoes render
No song when the spirit is mute:—
  No song but sad dirges,
Like the wind through a ruined cell,
  Or the mournful surges
That ring the dead seaman's knell.

When hearts have once mingled,
Love first leaves the well-built nest;
The weak one is singled
To endure what it once possessed.
O Love! who bewailest
The frailty of all things here,
Why choose you the frailest
For your cradle, your home, and your bier?

Its passions will rock thee,
As the storms rock the ravens on high;
Bright reason will mock thee,
Like the sun from a wintry sky.
From thy nest every rafter
Will rot, and thine eagle home
Leave thee naked to laughter,
When leaves fall and cold winds come.

Song

Rarely, rarely comest thou,
Spirit of Delight!
Wherefore hast thou left me now
Many a day and night?
Many a weary night and day
'Tis since thou art fled away.

How shall ever one like me
Win thee back again?
With the joyous and the free
Thou wilt scoff at pain.
Spirit false! thou hast forgot
All but those who need thee not.

As a lizard with the shade
Of a trembling leaf,
Thou with sorrow art dismayed;
Even the sighs of grief
Reproach thee, that thou art not near,
And reproach thou wilt not hear.

Let me set my mournful ditty
To a merry measure;—

Thou wilt never come for pity,
  Thou wilt come for pleasure;
Pity then will cut away
Those cruel wings, and thou wilt stay.

I love all that thou lovest,
  Spirit of Delight!
The fresh Earth in new leaves dressed,
  And the starry night;
Autumn evening, and the morn
When the golden mists are born.

I love snow and all the forms
  Of the radiant frost;
I love waves, and winds, and storms,
  Everything almost
Which is Nature's, and may be
Untainted by man's misery.

I love tranquil solitude,
  And such society
As is quiet, wise, and good;
  Between thee and me
What difference? but thou dost possess
The things I seek, not love them less.

I love Love—though he has wings,
  And like light can flee,
But above all other things,
  Spirit, I love thee—
Thou art love and life! O come!
Make once more my heart thy home!

The superb ODE TO THE WEST WIND was conceived and chiefly written, so Shelley tells us, "in a wood that skirts the Arno, near Florence, on a day when the tempestuous wind, whose temperature is at once mild and animating, was collecting the vapors which pour down the autumnal rains." Apart from the force of the swiftly changing images, the poem is technically exciting for the way the rise and fall of the wind is suggested by the long-rolling sentences, and the manner in which the autumnal music is suspended through the interlocking *terza rima,* the linked "third rhyme" employed so differently by Dante.

Ode to the West Wind

I

O wild West Wind, thou breath of Autumn's being,
Thou, from whose unseen presence the leaves dead
Are driven, like ghosts from an enchanter fleeing,

Yellow, and black, and pale, and hectic red,
Pestilence-stricken multitudes: O thou,
Who chariotest to their dark wintry bed

The wingèd seeds, where they lie cold and low,
Each like a corpse within its grave, until
Thine azure sister of the Spring shall blow

Her clarion o'er the dreaming earth, and fill
(Driving sweet buds like flocks to feed in air)
With living hues and odors plain and hill:

Wild Spirit, which art moving everywhere;
Destroyer and preserver; hear, oh, hear!

II

Thou on whose stream, 'mid the steep sky's commotion,
Loose clouds like earth's decaying leaves are shed,
Shook from the tangled boughs of Heaven and Ocean,

Angels of rain and lightning: there are spread
On the blue surface of thine aery surge,
Like the bright hair uplifted from the head

Of some fierce Maenad, even from the dim verge
Of the horizon to the zenith's height,
The locks of the approaching storm. Thou dirge

Of the dying year, to which this closing night
Will be the dome of a vast sepulchre,
Vaulted with all thy congregated might

Of vapors, from whose solid atmosphere
Black rain, and fire, and hail will burst: oh, hear!

III

Thou who didst waken from his summer dreams
The blue Mediterranean, where he lay,
Lulled by the coil of his crystàlline streams,

Beside a pumice isle in Baiae's bay,
And saw in sleep old palaces and towers
Quivering within the wave's intenser day,

All overgrown with azure moss and flowers
So sweet, the sense faints picturing them! Thou
For whose path the Atlantic's level powers

Cleave themselves into chasms, while far below
The sea-blooms and the oozy woods which wear
The sapless foliage of the ocean, know

Thy voice, and suddenly grow gray with fear,
And tremble and despoil themselves: oh, hear!

IV

If I were a dead leaf thou mightest bear;
If I were a swift cloud to fly with thee;
A wave to pant beneath thy power, and share

The impulse of thy strength, only less free
Than thou, O uncontrollable! If even
I were as in my boyhood, and could be

The comrade of thy wanderings over Heaven,
As then, when to outstrip thy skiey speed
Scarce seemed a vision; I would ne'er have striven

As thus with thee in prayer in my sore need.
Oh, lift me as a wave, a leaf, a cloud!
I fall upon the thorns of life! I bleed!

A heavy weight of hours has chained and bowed
One too like thee: tameless, and swift, and proud.

V

Make me thy lyre, even as the forest is:
What if my leaves are falling like its own!
The tumult of thy mighty harmonies

Will take from both a deep, autumnal tone,
Sweet though in sadness. Be thou, Spirit fierce,
My spirit! Be thou me, impetuous one!

Drive my dead thoughts over the universe
Like withered leaves to quicken a new birth!
And, by the incantation of this verse,

Scatter, as from an unextinguished hearth
Ashes and sparks, my words among mankind!
Be through my lips to unawakened earth

The trumpet of a prophecy! O Wind,
If Winter comes, can Spring be far behind?

Although Shelley is ranked among the great ones, his fame was wholly posthumous. Rarely praised for his work during his lifetime, he felt that the world had refused to consider him as a poet. It was inevitable that, when he composed ADONAIS, he should identify himself with Keats, whom he knew only slightly, but who seemed to Shelley to be another rejected poet, victim of oppression. ADONAIS, like Milton's LYCIDAS (see page 447), is an elegy in the antique form of a memorial idyl: the invocation, the personification of a grief-stricken Nature, the pastoral procession of mourning fellow poets, and the concluding consolation. But, although the classic mold is never broken, the poem is a personal outcry, a Shelleyan succession of verbal melodies and subtly modulated images.

Adonais

I weep for Adonais—he is dead!
Oh, weep for Adonais! though our tears
Thaw not the frost which binds so dear a head!
And thou, sad Hour, selected from all years
To mourn our loss, rouse thy obscure compeers,

And teach them thine own sorrow! Say: "With me
Died Adonais; till the Future dares
Forget the Past, his fate and fame shall be
An echo and a light unto eternity."

Where wert thou, mighty Mother, when he lay,
When thy son lay, pierced by the shaft which flies
In darkness? Where was lorn Urania
When Adonais died? With veiled eyes,
'Mid listening Echoes, in her Paradise
She sate, while one, with soft enamored breath,
Rekindled all the fading melodies,
With which, like flowers that mock the corse beneath,
He had adorned and hid the coming bulk of death.

Oh, weep for Adonais—he is dead!
Wake, melancholy Mother, wake and weep!
Yet wherefore? Quench within their burning bed
Thy fiery tears, and let thy loud heart keep,
Like his, a mute and uncomplaining sleep;
For he is gone, where all things wise and fair
Descend—oh, dream not that the amorous Deep
Will yet restore him to the vital air;
Death feeds on his mute voice, and laughs at our despair.

Most musical of mourners, weep again!
Lament anew, Urania!—He [1] died—
Who was the Sire of an immortal strain,
Blind, old, and lonely, when his country's pride,
The priest, the slave, and the liberticide,
Trampled and mocked with many a loathed rite
Of lust and blood; he went, unterrified,
Into the gulf of death; but his clear Sprite
Yet reigns o'er earth—the third among the sons of light.

Most musical of mourners, weep anew!
Not all to that bright station dared to climb;
And happier they their happiness who knew,
Whose tapers yet burn through that night of time
In which suns perished; others more sublime,
Struck by the envious wrath of man or god,
Have sunk, extinct in their refulgent prime;
And some yet live, treading the thorny road,
Which leads, through toil and hate, to Fame's serene abode.

[1] *Milton.*

But now, thy youngest, dearest one has perished,
The nursling of thy widowhood, who grew,
Like a pale flower by some sad maiden cherished,
And fed with true-love tears, instead of dew;
Most musical of mourners, weep anew!
Thy extreme hope, the loveliest and the last,
The bloom, whose petals, nipped before they blew,
Died on the promise of the fruit, is waste;
The broken lily lies—the storm is overpast.

To that high Capital,[2] where kingly Death
Keeps his pale court in beauty and decay,
He came; and bought, with price of purest breath,
A grave among the eternal.—Come away!
Haste, while the vault of blue Italian day
Is yet his fitting charnel-roof! while still
He lies, as if in dewy sleep he lay;
Awake him not! surely he takes his fill
Of deep and liquid rest, forgetful of all ill.

He will awake no more, oh, never more!—
Within the twilight chamber spreads apace
The shadow of white Death, and at the door
Invisible Corruption waits to trace
His extreme way to her dim dwelling-place;
The eternal Hunger sits, but pity and awe
Soothe her pale rage, nor dares she to deface
So fair a prey, till darkness and the law
Of change shall o'er his sleep the mortal curtain draw.

Oh, weep for Adonais!—The quick Dreams,
The passion-wingèd Ministers of thought,
Who were his flocks, whom near the living streams
Of his young spirit he fed, and whom he taught
The love which was its music, wander not—
Wander no more, from kindling brain to brain,
But droop there, whence they sprung; and mourn their lot
Round the cold heart, where, after their sweet pain,
They ne'er will gather strength, or find a home again.

And one with trembling hands clasps his cold head,
And fans him with her moonlight wings, and cries:
"Our love, our hope, our sorrow, is not dead;
See, on the silken fringe of his faint eyes,

[2] *Rome, where Keats died and was buried.*

Like dew upon a sleeping flower, there lies
A tear some Dream has loosened from his brain."
Lost Angel of a ruined Paradise!
She knew not 'twas her own; as with no stain
She faded, like a cloud which had outwept its rain.

One from a lucid urn of starry dew
Washed his light limbs as if embalming them;
Another clipped her profuse locks, and threw
The wreath upon him, like an anadem,
Which frozen tears instead of pearls begem;
Another in her willful grief would break
Her bow and winged reeds, as if to stem
A greater loss with one which was more weak;
And dull the barbed fire against his frozen cheek.

Another Splendor on his mouth alit,
That mouth, whence it was wont to draw the breath
Which gave it strength to pierce the guarded wit,
And pass into the panting heart beneath
With lightning and with music; the damp death
Quenched its caress upon his icy lips;
And, as a dying meteor stains a wreath
Of moonlight vapor, which the cold night clips,
It flushed through his pale limbs, and passed to its eclipse.

And others came—Desires and Adorations,
Winged Persuasions and veiled Destinies,
Splendors, and Glooms, and glimmering Incarnations
Of hopes and fears, and twilight Phantasies;
And Sorrow, with her family of Sighs,
And Pleasure, blind with tears, led by the gleam
Of her own dying smile instead of eyes,
Came in slow pomp—the moving pomp might seem
Like pageantry of mist on an autumnal stream.

All he had loved, and molded into thought
From shape, and hue, and odor, and sweet sound,
Lamented Adonais. Morning sought
Her eastern watchtower, and her hair unbound,
Wet with the tears which should adorn the ground,
Dimmed the aërial eyes that kindle day;
Afar the melancholy thunder moaned,
Pale Ocean in unquiet slumber lay,
And the wild winds flew round, sobbing in their dismay.

Lost Echo sits amid the voiceless mountains,
And feeds her grief with his remembered lay,
And will no more reply to winds or fountains,
Or amorous birds perched on the young green spray,
Or herdsman's horn, or bell at closing day;
Since she can mimic not his lips, more dear
Than those for whose disdain she pined away
Into a shadow of all sounds—a drear
Murmur, between their songs, is all the woodmen hear.

Grief made the young Spring wild, and she threw down
Her kindling buds, as if she Autumn were,
Or they dead leaves; since her delight is flown,
For whom should she have waked the sullen year?
To Phoebus was not Hyacinth so dear
Nor to himself Narcissus, as to both
Thou, Adonais. Wan they stand and sere
Amid the faint companions of their youth,
With dew all turned to tears; odor, to sighing ruth.

Thy spirit's sister, the lorn nightingale,
Mourns not her mate with such melodious pain;
Not so the eagle, who like thee could scale
Heaven, and could nourish in the sun's domain
Her mighty youth with morning, doth complain,
Soaring and screaming round her empty nest,
As Albion wails for thee. The curse of Cain
Light on his head who pierced thy innocent breast,
And scared the angel soul that was its earthly guest!

Ah, woe is me! Winter is come and gone,
But grief returns with the revolving year;
The airs and streams renew their joyous tone;
The ants, the bees, the swallows reappear;
Fresh leaves and flowers deck the dead Seasons' bier;
The amorous birds now pair in every brake,
And build their mossy homes in field and brere;
And the green lizard, and the golden snake,
Like unimprisoned flames, out of their trance awake.

Through wood and stream and field and hill and ocean
A quickening life from the earth's heart has burst,
As it has ever done, with change and motion,
From the great morning of the world when first
God dawned on Chaos; in its stream immersed,

The lamps of heaven flash with a softer light;
All baser things pant with life's sacred thirst,
Diffuse themselves, and spend in love's delight
The beauty and the joy of their renewèd might.

The leprous corpse, touched by this spirit tender,
Exhales itself in flowers of gentle breath;
Like incarnations of the stars, when splendor
Is changed to fragrance, they illumine death
And mock the merry worm that wakes beneath;
Naught we know, dies. Shall that alone which knows
Be as a sword consumed before the sheath
By sightless lightning?—the intense atom glows
A moment, then is quenched in a most cold repose.

Alas! that all we loved of him should be,
But for our grief, as if it had not been,
And grief itself be mortal! Woe is me!
Whence are we, and why are we? Of what scene
The actors or spectators? Great and mean
Meet massed in death, who lends what life must borrow.
As long as skies are blue, and fields are green,
Evening must usher night, night urge the morrow,
Month follow month with woe, and year wake year to sorrow.

He will awake no more, oh, never more!
"Wake thou," cried Misery, "childless Mother, rise
Out of thy sleep, and slake, in thy heart's core,
A wound more fierce than his with tears and sighs."
And all the Dreams that watched Urania's eyes,
And all the Echoes whom their sister's song
Had held in holy silence, cried: "Arise!"
Swift as a Thought by the snake Memory stung,
From her ambrosial rest the fading Splendor sprung.

She rose like an autumnal Night, that springs
Out of the East, and follows wild and drear
The golden Day, which, on eternal wings,
Even as a ghost abandoning a bier,
Had left the earth a corpse. Sorrow and fear
So struck, so roused, so rapt Urania;
So saddened round her like an atmosphere
Of stormy mist; so swept her on her way
Even to the mournful place where Adonais lay.

Out of her secret Paradise she sped,
Through camps and cities rough with stone, and steel,
And human hearts, which to her aëry tread
Yielding not, wounded the invisible
Palms of her tender feet where'er they fell;
And barbed tongues, and thoughts more sharp than they,
Rent the soft Form they never could repel,
Whose sacred blood, like the young tears of May,
Paved with eternal flowers that undeserving way.

In the death chamber for a moment Death,
Shamed by the presence of that living Might,
Blushed to annihilation, and the breath
Revisited those lips, and life's pale light
Flashed through those limbs, so late her dear delight.
"Leave me not wild and drear and comfortless,
As silent lightning leaves the starless night!
Leave me not!" cried Urania. Her distress
Roused Death; Death rose and smiled, and met her vain caress.

"Stay yet awhile! speak to me once again;
Kiss me, so long but as a kiss may live;
And in my heartless breast and burning brain
That word, that kiss, shall all thoughts else survive,
With food of saddest memory kept alive,
Now thou art dead, as if it were a part
Of thee, my Adonais! I would give
All that I am to be as thou now art!
But I am chained to Time, and cannot thence depart!

"O gentle child, beautiful as thou wert,
Why didst thou leave the trodden paths of men
Too soon, and with weak hands though mighty heart
Dare the unpastured dragon in his den?
Defenseless as thou wert, oh, where was then
Wisdom the mirrored shield, or scorn the spear?
Or hadst thou waited the full cycle, when
Thy spirit should have filled its crescent sphere,
The monsters of life's waste had fled from thee like deer.

"The herded wolves, bold only to pursue;
The obscene ravens, clamorous o'er the dead;
The vultures to the conqueror's banner true,
Who feed where Desolation first has fed,

And whose wings rain contagion—how they fled,
When like Apollo, from his golden bow,
The Pythian of the age,[3] one arrow sped
And smiled!—The spoilers tempt no second blow;
They fawn on the proud feet that spurn them lying low.

"The Sun comes forth, and many reptiles spawn;
He sets, and each ephemeral insect then
Is gathered into death without a dawn,
And the immortal stars awake again;
So is it in the world of living men:
A godlike mind soars forth, in its delight
Making earth bare and veiling heaven, and when
It sinks, the swarms that dimmed or shared its light
Leave to its kindred lamps the spirit's awful night."

Thus ceased she; and the mountain shepherds came,
Their garlands sere, their magic mantles rent;
The Pilgrim of Eternity,[4] whose fame
Over his living head like heaven is bent,
An early but enduring monument,
Came, veiling all the lightnings of his song
In sorrow; from her wilds Ierne[5] sent
The sweetest lyrist of her saddest wrong,[6]
And love taught grief to fall like music from his tongue.

Midst others of less note, came one frail Form,[7]
A phantom among men, companionless
As the last cloud of an expiring storm
Whose thunder is its knell; he, as I guess,
Had gazed on Nature's naked loveliness,
Actaeon-like, and now he fled astray
With feeble steps o'er the world's wilderness,
And his own thoughts, along that rugged way,
Pursued, like raging hounds, their father and their prey.

A pardlike Spirit beautiful and swift—
A Love in desolation masked—a Power
Girt round with weaknesses:—it can scarce uplift
The weight of the superincumbent hour;
It is a dying lamp, a falling shower,

[3] *Byron, who attacked the venomous critics as Apollo attacked the Python.*
[4] *Byron.* [5] *Ireland.* [6] *Thomas Moore.*
[7] *Shelley himself, mixing self-pity with pity for Keats.*

A breaking billow—even whilst we speak
Is it not broken? On the withering flower
The killing sun smiles brightly; on a cheek
The life can burn in blood, even while the heart may break.

His head was bound with pansies overblown,
And faded violets, white, and pied, and blue;
And a light spear topped with a cypress cone,
Round whose rude shaft dark ivy-tresses grew
Yet dripping with the forest's noonday dew,
Vibrated, as the ever-beating heart
Shook the weak hand that grasped it; of that crew
He came the last, neglected and apart;
A herd-abandoned deer, struck by the hunter's dart.

All stood aloof, and at his partial moan
Smiled through their tears; well knew that gentle band
Who in another's fate now wept his own;
As, in the accents of an unknown land,
He sung new sorrow; sad Urania scanned
The Stranger's mien, and murmured, "Who art thou?"
He answered not, but with a sudden hand
Made bare his branded and ensanguined brow,
Which was like Cain's or Christ's—Oh! that it should be so!

What softer voice is hushed over the dead?
Athwart what brow is that dark mantle thrown?
What form leans sadly o'er the white deathbed,
In mockery of monumental stone,
The heavy heart heaving without a moan?
If it be He,[8] who, gentlest of the wise,
Taught, soothed, loved, honored the departed one,
Let me not vex with inharmonious sighs
The silence of that heart's accepted sacrifice.

Our Adonais has drunk poison—oh!
What deaf and viperous murderer could crown
Life's early cup with such a draught of woe?
The nameless worm would now itself disown.
It felt, yet could escape, the magic tone
Whose prelude held all envy, hate, and wrong,
But what was howling in one breast alone,
Silent with expectation of the song,
Whose master's hand is cold, whose silver lyre unstrung.

[8] *Leigh Hunt, close friend of Keats.*

Live thou, whose infamy is not thy fame!
Live! fear no heavier chastisement from me,
Thou noteless blot on a remembered name!
But be thyself, and know thyself to be!
And ever at thy season be thou free
To spill the venom when thy fangs o'erflow.
Remorse and self-contempt shall cling to thee;
Hot shame shall burn upon thy secret brow,
And like a beaten hound tremble thou shalt—as now.

Nor let us weep that our delight is fled
Far from these carrion kites that scream below;
He wakes or sleeps with the enduring dead;
Thou canst not soar where he is sitting now.—
Dust to the dust! but the pure spirit shall flow
Back to the burning fountain whence it came,
A portion of the Eternal, which must glow
Through time and change, unquenchably the same,
Whilst thy cold embers choke the sordid hearth of shame.

Peace, peace! he is not dead, he doth not sleep—
He hath awakened from the dream of life—
'Tis we who, lost in stormy visions, keep
With phantoms an unprofitable strife,
And in mad trance strike with our spirit's knife
Invulnerable nothings.—*We* decay
Like corpses in a charnel; fear and grief
Convulse us and consume us day by day,
And cold hopes swarm like worms within our living clay.

He has outsoared the shadow of our night;
Envy and calumny and hate and pain,
And that unrest which men miscall delight,
Can touch him not and torture not again;
From the contagion of the world's slow stain
He is secure, and now can never mourn
A heart grown cold, a head grown gray in vain;
Nor, when the spirit's self has ceased to burn,
With sparkless ashes load an unlamented urn.

He lives, he wakes—'tis Death is dead, not he;
Mourn not for Adonais.—Thou young Dawn,
Turn all thy dew to splendor, for from thee
The spirit thou lamentest is not gone;

Ye caverns and ye forests, cease to moan!
Cease, ye faint flowers and fountains, and thou Air,
Which like a mourning veil thy scarf hadst thrown
O'er the abandoned Earth, now leave it bare
Even to the joyous stars which smile on its despair!

He is made one with Nature; there is heard
His voice in all her music, from the moan
Of thunder, to the song of night's sweet bird;
He is a presence to be felt and known
In darkness and in light, from herb and stone,
Spreading itself where'er that Power may move
Which has withdrawn his being to its own;
Which wields the world with never-wearied love,
Sustains it from beneath, and kindles it above.

He is a portion of the loveliness
Which once he made more lovely; he doth bear
His part, while the one Spirit's plastic stress
Sweeps through the dull, dense world, compelling there
All new successions to the forms they wear;
Torturing th' unwilling dross that checks its flight
To its own likeness, as each mass may bear;
And bursting in its beauty and its might
From trees and beasts and men into the Heaven's light.

The splendors of the firmament of time
May be eclipsed, but are extinguished not;
Like stars to their appointed height they climb
And death is a low mist which cannot blot
The brightness it may veil. When lofty thought
Lifts a young heart above its mortal lair,
And love and life contend in it for what
Shall be its earthly doom, the dead live there
And move like winds of light on dark and stormy air.

The inheritors of unfulfilled renown
Rose from their thrones, built beyond mortal thought,
Far in the Unapparent. Chatterton
Rose pale; his solemn agony had not
Yet faded from him. Sidney, as he fought
And as he fell and as he lived and loved,
Sublimely mild, a Spirit without spot,
Arose. And Lucan, by his death approved—
Oblivion, as they rose, shrank like a thing reproved.

And many more, whose names on earth are dark
But whose transmitted effluence cannot die
So long as fire outlives the parent spark,
Rose, robed in dazzling immortality.
"Thou art become as one of us," they cry,
"It was for thee yon kingless sphere has long
Swung blind in unascended majesty,
Silent alone amid an Heaven of Song.
Assume thy winged throne, thou Vesper of our throng!"

Who mourns for Adonais? oh, come forth,
Fond wretch! and know thyself and him aright.
Clasp with thy panting soul the pendulous Earth;
As from a center, dart thy spirit's light
Beyond all worlds, until its spacious might
Satiate the void circumference. Then shrink
Even to a point within our day and night;
And keep thy heart light, lest it make thee sink,
When hope has kindled hope, and lured thee to the brink.

Or go to Rome, which is the sepulchre,
Oh, not of him, but of our joy; 'tis naught
That ages, empires, and religions there
Lie buried in the ravage they have wrought;
For such as he can lend—they borrow not
Glory from those who made the world their prey;
And he is gathered to the kings of thought
Who waged contention with their time's decay,
And of the past are all that cannot pass away.

Go thou to Rome—at once the Paradise,
The grave, the city, and the wilderness;
And where its wrecks like shattered mountains rise,
And flowering weeds and fragrant copses dress
The bones of Desolation's nakedness,
Pass, till the Spirit of the spot shall lead
Thy footsteps to a slope of green access
Where, like an infant's smile, over the dead
A light of laughing flowers along the grass is spread.

And gray walls molder round, on which dull Time
Feeds, like slow fire upon a hoary brand;
And one keen pyramid with wedge sublime,
Pavilioning the dust of him who planned

This refuge for his memory, doth stand
Like flame transformed to marble; and beneath,
A field is spread, on which a newer band
Have pitched in Heaven's smile their camp of death,
Welcoming him we lose with scarce extinguished breath.

Here pause. These graves are all too young as yet
To have outgrown the sorrow which consigned
Its charge to each; and if the seal is set,
Here, on one fountain of a mourning mind,
Break it not thou! too surely shalt thou find
Thine own well full, if thou returnest home,
Of tears and gall. From the world's bitter wind
Seek shelter in the shadow of the tomb.
What Adonais is, why fear we to become?

The One [9] remains, the many change and pass;
Heaven's light forever shines, earth's shadows fly;
Life, like a dome of many-colored glass,
Stains the white radiance of Eternity,
Until Death tramples it to fragments.—Die,
If thou wouldst be with that which thou dost seek!
Follow where all is fled!—Rome's azure sky,
Flowers, ruins, statues, music, words, are weak
The glory they transfuse with fitting truth to speak.

Why linger, why turn back, why shrink, my Heart?
Thy hopes are gone before; from all things here
They have departed; thou shouldst now depart!
A light is past from the revolving year,
And man, and woman; and what still is dear
Attracts to crush, repels to make thee wither.
The soft sky smiles—the low wind whispers near;
'Tis Adonais calls! oh, hasten thither,
No more let Life divide what Death can join together.

That Light whose smile kindles the universe,
That Beauty in which all things work and move,
That Benediction which the eclipsing Curse
Of birth can quench not, that sustaining Love
Which, through the web of being blindly wove
By man and beast and earth and air and sea,

[9] *Ultimate Reality, "the white radiance of Eternity," unseen until Death shatters the colored dome of life.*

Burns bright or dim, as each are mirrors of
The fire for which all thirst, now beams on me,
Consuming the last clouds of cold mortality.

The breath whose might I have invoked in song
Descends on me; my spirit's bark is driven,
Far from the shore, far from the trembling throng
Whose sails were never to the tempest given;
The massy earth and spherèd skies are riven!
I am borne darkly, fearfully, afar;
Whilst burning through the inmost veil of Heaven,
The soul of Adonais, like a star,
Beacons from the abode where the Eternal are.

The first collected edition of Shelley's poems was not published until 1839, seventeen years after his death, and the collection was prefaced by Mrs. Shelley. Many readers were surprised by the penetration of the foreword. They should not have been, for Mary Wollstonecraft Shelley was the author of some seven or eight volumes, including the celebrated macabre FRANKENSTEIN, which she had written at the age of twenty-one. Two of Mrs. Shelley's sentences have never been bettered: "No poet was ever warmed by a more genuine and unforced inspiration. His extreme sensibility gave the intensity of passion to his intellectual pursuits and rendered his mind keenly alive to every perception of outward objects, as well as to his internal sensations."

Shelley's failures are those of excess. He erred on the side of brilliance, of overenergetic compulsion. He was not always able to give body to his abstractions or to idealize reality. But the best of his work has not been surpassed by any lyric poet, with the possible exception of Keats. It is not in a single poem that Shelley's full greatness may be felt, but, as the poet W. J. Turner wrote, "in the impression made by his work as a whole—an impression of one of the most exalted and sublime spirits the world has ever seen."

Ozymandias

I met a traveler from an antique land,
Who said: Two vast and trunkless legs of stone
Stand in the desert. Near them, on the sand,
Half sunk, a shattered visage lies, whose frown,

And wrinkled lip, and sneer of cold command,
Tell that its sculptor well those passions read,
Which yet survive, stamped on these lifeless things,
The hand that mocked them, and the heart that fed:
And on the pedestal these words appear:
"My name is Ozymandias, King of Kings:
Look on my works, ye Mighty, and despair!"
Nothing beside remains. Round the decay
Of that colossal wreck, boundless and bare
The lone and level sands stretch far away.

The Cloud

I bring fresh showers for the thirsting flowers,
    From the seas and the streams;
I bear light shade for the leaves when laid
    In their noonday dreams.
From my wings are shaken the dews that waken
    The sweet buds every one,
When rocked to rest on their mother's breast,
    As she dances about the sun.
I wield the flail of the lashing hail,
    And whiten the green plains under,
And then again I dissolve it in rain,
    And laugh as I pass in thunder.

I sift the snow on the mountains below,
    And their great pines groan aghast;
And all the night 'tis my pillow white,
    While I sleep in the arms of the blast.
Sublime on the towers of my skiey bowers,
    Lightning, my pilot, sits;
In a cavern under is fettered the thunder,
    It struggles and howls at fits;

Over earth and ocean, with gentle motion,
    This pilot is guiding me,
Lured by the love of the genii that move
    In the depths of the purple sea;
Over the rills, and the crags, and the hills,
    Over the lakes and the plains,

Wherever he dream, under mountain or stream,
    The Spirit he loves remains;
And I all the while bask in Heaven's blue smile,
    Whilst he is dissolving in rains.

The sanguine Sunrise, with his meteor eyes,
    And his burning plumes outspread,
Leaps on the back of my sailing rack,
    When the morning star shines dead;
As on the jag of a mountain crag,
    Which an earthquake rocks and swings,
An eagle alit one moment may sit
    In the light of its golden wings.
And when Sunset may breathe, from the lit sea beneath,
    Its ardors of rest and of love,
And the crimson pall of eve may fall
    From the depth of Heaven above,
With wings folded I rest, on mine aery nest,
    As still as a brooding dove.

That orbèd maiden with white fire laden,
    Whom mortals call the Moon,
Glides glimmering o'er my fleece-like floor,
    By the midnight breezes strewn;
And wherever the beat of her unseen feet,
    Which only the angels hear,
May have broken the woof of my tent's thin roof,
    The stars peep behind her and peer;
And I laugh to see them whirl and flee,
    Like a swarm of golden bees,
When I widen the rent in my wind-built tent,
    Till the calm rivers, lakes, and seas,
Like strips of the sky fallen through me on high,
    Are each paved with the moon and these.

I bind the Sun's throne with a burning zone,
    And the Moon's with a girdle of pearl;
The volcanoes are dim, and the stars reel and swim
    When the whirlwinds my banner unfurl.
From cape to cape, with a bridge-like shape,
    Over a torrent sea,
Sunbeam-proof, I hang like a roof,—
    The mountains its columns be.
The triumphal arch through which I march
    With hurricane, fire, and snow,

When the Powers of the air are chained to my chair,
    Is the million-colored bow;
The sphere-fire above its soft colors wove,
    While the moist Earth was laughing below.

I am the daughter of Earth and Water,
    And the nursling of the Sky;
I pass through the pores of the ocean and shores;
    I change, but I cannot die.
For after the rain when with never a stain
    The pavilion of Heaven is bare,
And the winds and sunbeams with their convex gleams
    Build up the blue dome of air,
I silently laugh at my own cenotaph,
    And out of the caverns of rain,
Like a child from the womb, like a ghost from the tomb,
    I arise and unbuild it again.

A Lament

O world! O life! O time!
On whose last steps I climb,
    Trembling at that where I had stood before;
When will return the glory of your prime?
        No more—Oh, never more!

Out of the day and night
A joy has taken flight;
    Fresh spring, and summer, and winter hoar,
Move my faint heart with grief, but with delight
        No more—Oh, never more!

A Dirge

Rough wind, that moanest loud
    Grief too sad for song;
Wild wind, when sullen cloud
    Knells all the night long;
Sad storm, whose tears are vain,
Bare woods, whose branches strain,
Deep caves and dreary main,—
    Wail, for the world's wrong!

Music

Silver key of the fountain of tears,
  Where the spirit drinks till the brain is wild;
Softest grave of a thousand fears,
  Where their mother, Care, like a drowsy child,
    Is laid asleep in flowers.

JOHN KEATS

[1795–1821]

READING some of the titles of Keats's poems—ENDYMION, HYPERION, SONNET TO HOMER, HYMN TO APOLLO, ON SEEING THE ELGIN MARBLES, ODE ON A GRECIAN URN—the ignorant reader might conclude that the poet was the product of a special environment, a cloistered spirit, perhaps the son of an aristocrat or a professor of Greek. But Keats was not reared in an ivory tower. His father took care of the horses and cleaned the stalls in his grandfather's livery stable.

Born in London in 1795—the day is variously given as October 29 and October 31—John Keats was the oldest son of Thomas Keats and Frances Jennings, daughter of the livery-stable proprietor. When Keats was ten years old his father was killed by a fall from a horse; his mother remarried within a year, but was soon separated from her new husband and returned to her mother's house in Edmonton. During his boyhood, Keats alternated between his grandmother's home in the country and the school at Enfield, a suburb of London, for the widow could not afford to send him to Harrow. Although he was finely built, he was not frail. Instead of the delicate legendary poet, Keats was anything but effeminate; he overcompensated for inner insecurity by an outer pugnacity. At school he was well known as a fighter. Cowden Clarke, son of the headmaster at Enfield, remembered his "terrier courage" and wrote that Keats's passion often grew ungovernable: "His brother George, being considerably taller and stronger, used frequently to hold him down by main force."

His mother died of tuberculosis when he was fifteen, and a guardian was appointed for John and his brother—a relationship described with sensitive irony in E. M. Forster's short story MR. AND MRS. ABBEY'S DIFFICULTIES. At sixteen Keats was apprenticed to a surgeon of Edmonton; at nineteen he ran away to London and studied sporadically at hospitals in the metropolis. Before Keats left Edmonton, Cowden Clarke had given him a copy of Spenser's THE FAERIE QUEENE; when Clarke came up to London, the young men found Homer in Chapman's spirited translation. They spent a whole autumn night in excited discovery, reading the rich passages aloud. At ten o'clock the following morning Clarke, who had had little sleep, received a communication from Keats, who had not slept at all. It was the poem ON FIRST LOOKING INTO CHAPMAN'S HOMER, one of the world's most famous sonnets.

On First Looking into Chapman's Homer

Much have I travell'd in the realms of gold,
  And many goodly states and kingdoms seen,
  Round many western islands have I been
Which bards in fealty to Apollo hold.
Oft of one wide expanse had I been told
  That deep-brow'd Homer ruled as his demesne:
  Yet did I never breathe its pure serene
Till I heard Chapman speak out loud and bold.

Then felt I like some watcher of the skies
  When a new planet swims into his ken;
Or like stout Cortez when with eagle eyes
  He stared at the Pacific—and all his men
Look'd at each other with a wild surmise—
  Silent, upon a peak in Darien.

Keats's adventurous mind may have been wandering when, in the magnificent picture of the explorer staring at the Pacific, he wrote "Cortez" instead of "Balboa," but his sensitivity to words was never keener. Two manuscripts of this poem exist; the first, in the Amy Lowell collection, is a remarkable contrast to the second. In the first draft Homer was not "deep-brow'd" but "low-brow'd." The seventh line was originally "Yet could I never judge what men could mean," but Keats's fine ear made him alter the awkward syllables to the highly suggestible and unforgettable "Yet never did I breathe its pure serene." That "pure serene" is the essence of Keats distilled in a phrase.

Although Keats was duly licensed, he never practiced medicine. Unhappy events crowded fast upon him; he withdrew from the contemporary world of difficult experience to live in a world of antique dreams. "Glory and loveliness have passed away," he wrote to Leigh Hunt in the dedication of his first volume. A year later, in a Preface to ENDYMION, he emphasized the sentiment: "I hope I have not in too late a day touched the beautiful mythology of Greece and dulled its brightness." He took to haunting the British Museum, and in particular the rooms which contained the Greek vases, marbles, and ruined portions of the Parthenon. "Poetry must surprise by a fine excess," Keats had declared; and in the British Museum there was a superfluity of beauty to delight the most romantic and sensation-loving spirit. ODE ON A GRECIAN URN unites with "fine excess" the two aspects of reality: beauty and truth—the beauty of the sensual world and the truth of the imagination.

Ode on a Grecian Urn

Thou still unravish'd bride of quietness,
  Thou foster-child of silence and slow time,
Sylvan historian. who canst thus express
  A flowery tale more sweetly than our rhyme:
What leaf-fring'd legend haunts about thy shape
  Of deities or mortals, or of both,
    In Tempe or the dales of Arcady?
  What men or gods are these? What maidens loth?
What mad pursuit? What struggle to escape?
    What pipes and timbrels? What wild ecstasy?

Heard melodies are sweet, but those unheard
  Are sweeter; therefore, ye soft pipes, play on;
Not to the sensual ear, but, more endear'd,
  Pipe to the spirit ditties of no tone:
Fair youth, beneath the trees, thou canst not leave
  Thy song, nor ever can those trees be bare;
    Bold Lover, never, never canst thou kiss,
Though winning near the goal—yet, do not grieve;
  She cannot fade, though thou hast not thy bliss,
    For ever wilt thou love, and she be fair!

Ah, happy, happy boughs! that cannot shed
  Your leaves, nor ever bid the Spring adieu;
And, happy melodist, unwearièd,
  For ever piping songs for ever new;
More happy love! more happy, happy love!
  For ever warm and still to be enjoy'd,
    For ever panting, and for ever young;
All breathing human passion far above,
  That leaves a heart high-sorrowful and cloy'd,
    A burning forehead, and a parching tongue.

Who are these coming to the sacrifice?
  To what green altar, O mysterious priest,
Lead'st thou that heifer lowing at the skies,
  And all her silken flanks with garlands drest?
What little town by river or sea shore,
  Or mountain-built with peaceful citadel,
    Is emptied of this folk, this pious morn?
And, little town, thy streets for evermore
  Will silent be; and not a soul to tell
    Why thou art desolate, can e'er return.

O Attic shape! Fair attitude! with brede
  Of marble men and maidens overwrought,
With forest branches and the trodden weed;
  Thou, silent form, dost tease us out of thought
As doth eternity. Cold Pastoral!
  When old age shall this generation waste,
    Thou shalt remain, in midst of other woe
Than ours, a friend to man, to whom thou say'st,
  "Beauty is truth, truth beauty—that is all
    Ye know on earth, and all ye need to know."

The ODE ON A GRECIAN URN was a direct result of Keats's preoccupation with Greek myths and the plastic embodiments of it which he found in the British Museum. It seems improbable that the ode was a description of any particular urn. It is far more likely that Keats was reconstructing the design from the Parthenon, recalling it through the eye of imagination. The "mad pursuit" and "wild ecstasy" are no longer part of a sculptured ritual; the "marble men and maidens" take on warm flesh and leaping blood.

It is a cultural oddity that the passion for Greek legend, which affected Byron and Shelley no less than Keats, was not given its first great impetus by a poet but by a political envoy. Had it not been for Lord Elgin's spoliation of the Parthenon, the famous frieze and pediment of Phidias would have remained in Athens. With the acquisition of the marble pieces, the British Museum became an ally of Greece, and the poets turned to an older romanticism than their immediate predecessors; without quite repudiating Scott and Coleridge they deserted medievalism for Hellenism. Keats acknowledged his debt to Lord Elgin without uncertainty; the twenty-one-year-old poet—already "a sick eagle looking at the sky"—paid his tribute in a sonnet of praise.

On Seeing the Elgin Marbles

My spirit is too weak—mortality
  Weighs heavily on me like unwilling sleep,
  And each imagined pinnacle and steep
Of godlike hardship tells me I must die
Like a sick eagle looking at the sky.
  Yet 'tis a gentle luxury to weep
  That I have not the cloudy winds to keep,
Fresh for the opening of the morning's eye.
Such dim-conceived glories of the brain,
  Bring round the heart an indescribable feud;
So do these wonders a most dizzy pain,
  That mingles Grecian grandeur with the rude
Wasting of old Time—with a billowy main—
  A sun—a shadow of a magnitude.

At twenty-one Keats met his first "sponsor," the poet Leigh Hunt, who was generous in his recognition of younger and better poets. For the first time Keats moved in a wholly literary atmosphere; through Hunt he met Shelley, Coleridge, and Wordsworth. With none of these except Hunt did the acquaintance ripen into real friendship; Shelley esteemed Keats, but objected that he wrote on principles which Shelley opposed, and Wordsworth dampened the young poet's fervor by referring to his HYMN TO PAN as "a pretty piece of paganism." Encouraged by Hunt, Keats published his first volume, POEMS, before he was twenty-one. It was followed in a year by ENDYMION.

Keats had gone to the countryside in the hope of curing a throat trouble which was to develop into the consumption that caused his death three years later. When he returned to London, he found himself viciously attacked by the two leading critical reviews, BLACKWOOD'S MAGAZINE and THE QUARTERLY REVIEW. The articles were not merely critical onslaughts but personal assaults. The reviewers commented harshly on the friendship of Hunt, who had made many enemies, spoke sneeringly of Keats's humble beginnings, and treated the young poet as a vicious example of the "Cockney school." Keats was deeply hurt as well as discouraged by the reviews; he even considered abandoning literature. Several of his friends believed that the brutality of the attacks hastened his end. Byron wrote:

"Who killed John Keats?"
"I," said the *Quarterly*,
So savage and tartarly;
" 'Twas one of my feats."

But, although depressed by the offending criticisms, Keats was not killed by them. He had other and more personal troubles. The family was breaking up. His brother George had left for America. His brother Tom, whom he had nursed for months, died of tuberculosis. By this time it was obvious to Keats that he himself had inherited the fatal family weakness. To make the situation still more tragic, he fell hopelessly in love with the charming but lightly flirtatious Fanny Brawne.

Keats's passion for Fanny Brawne, complicated by the increasing malignancy of his disease and the uncertainty of his future, was a headlong desperation. Unable to possess her, he became abnormally possessive. He tormented himself and her with frantic talks, letters, and poems. In the sonnet beginning "I cry your mercy—pity," Keats revealed his uncontrollable and jealous love. The poem is not a smoothly molded work of art, but an agonized self-expression. It stammers with the lover's anguish, stumbles on in a wild demand, pauses breathlessly to tantalize the unfortunate dreamer with the "sweet minor zest of love, your kiss," with the beloved's hands and her "warm, white, lucent, million-pleasured breast," and rushes on to its fevered conclusion.

To Fanny

I cry your mercy—pity—love!—aye, love!
  Merciful love that tantalizes not,
One-thoughted, never-wandering, guileless love,
  Unmasked, and being seen—without a blot!
O! let me have thee whole,—all—all—be mine!
  That shape, that fairness, that sweet minor zest
Of love, your kiss,—those hands, those eyes divine,
  That warm, white, lucent, million-pleasured breast,—
Yourself—your soul—in pity give me all,
  Withhold no atom's atom or I die,
Or living on perhaps, your wretched thrall,
  Forget, in the mist of idle misery,
Life's purposes,—the palate of my mind
Losing its gust, and my ambition blind!

It was in the unhappiest period of Keats's life that he wrote the poems by which he is most remembered. In one year, 1819, he created most of the great odes, THE EVE OF ST. AGNES, and the beautifully archaic LA BELLE DAME SANS MERCI. LA BELLE DAME SANS MERCI is a splendid example of Keats's "remaking" power. Written more than three centuries after the ballad of TRUE THOMAS (see page 146), Keats's poem is also about a mortal seduced by an immortal. But in the modern ballad the poet becomes a knight and the Queen of Elfland is a "faery's child." Here also the woman is an enchantress, and magic and doom—the doom of love—establish a kinship between the despairing poet of the nineteenth century and the unknown balladist of the sixteenth.

La Belle Dame Sans Merci

Ah, what can ail thee, wretched wight,
  Alone and palely loitering?
The sedge is withered from the lake,
  And no birds sing.

Ah, what can ail thee, wretched wight,
  So haggard and so woe-begone?
The squirrel's granary is full,
  And the harvest's done.

I see a lily on thy brow
  With anguish moist and fever dew,
And on thy cheek a fading rose
  Fast withereth too.

I met a lady in the meads,
  Full beautiful, a faery's child:
Her hair was long, her foot was light,
  And her eyes were wild.

I set her on my pacing steed,
  And nothing else saw all day long;
For sideways would she lean, and sing
  A faery's song.

I made a garland for her head,
  And bracelets too, and fragrant zone;
She looked at me as she did love,
  And made sweet moan.

She found me roots of relish sweet,
  And honey wild, and manna dew,
And sure in language strange she said,
  "I love thee true!"

She took me to her elfin grot,
  And there she gazed and sighed deep,
And there I shut her wild, sad eyes—
  So kissed to sleep.

And there we slumbered on the moss,
  And there I dreamed, ah! woe betide,
The latest dream I ever dreamed
  On the cold hill side.

I saw pale kings, and princes too,
  Pale warriors, death-pale were they all;
Who cried—"La belle Dame sans merci
  Hath thee in thrall!"

I saw their starved lips in the gloam,
  With horrid warning gaped wide,
And I awoke and found me here,
  On the cold hill side.

And this is why I sojourn here,
  Alone and palely loitering,
Though the sedge is withered from the lake,
  And no birds sing.

In 1820 Keats knew that his illness was becoming progressively worse. He tried the English seashore, again to no avail. Fanny Brawne nursed him, but her nearness aggravated his pain. In July his last and best volume was issued, but the cordiality with which it was received could not restore him to health. In September Keats sailed for Italy, and composed his last poem, the sonnet beginning "Bright star, would I were stedfast as thou art," while he was passing down the Channel. Significantly enough, this most moving of Keats's love poems was written in a volume of Shakespeare's, facing A LOVER'S COMPLAINT.

Bright Star, Would I Were Stedfast

Bright star, would I were stedfast as thou art—
Not in lone splendor hung aloft the night,
And watching, with eternal lids apart,
Like nature's patient sleepless Eremite,[1]
The moving waters at their priestlike task
Of pure ablution round earth's human shores,
Or gazing on the new soft fallen mask
Of snow upon the mountains and the moors:
No—yet still stedfast, still unchangeable,
Pillowed upon my fair love's ripening breast
To feel for ever its soft fall and swell,
Awake for ever in a sweet unrest;
Still, still to hear her tender-taken breath,
And so live ever—or else swoon to death.

Keats reached Rome in November. Within a month he had a final relapse. He died February 23, 1821, and was buried in the Protestant Cemetery in Rome. His first published poem had appeared when he was twenty-two; he was dead at twenty-six.

Keats's short life was a flash of painful ecstasy, and the intensity of his nature is everywhere in his poetry. The verse is vivid and definite, lavish with a feeling of textures, with minute felicities of touch and taste, "filling every sense with spiritual sweets." The

[1] *Hermit.*

early poems are almost too profuse, too lush in sensuousness, too decoratively detailed. But the later work is both more brilliant and more controlled. The perceptions are delicately exact, the pictures are translucent. No poet has more subtly communicated complex and luxuriant sensations.

THE EVE OF ST. AGNES is opulent in storytelling and in suggestion, a tale which is also a painting, an old-world tapestry, and an allegory of young love triumphing over a world of hate. The kaleidoscope of sensations begins dramatically with the first verse. St. Agnes' Eve—January 20—is proverbially the coldest of the year, and the effect of cold is emphasized not only by the "bitter chill" of the first line, but by the owl hunched miserably in his feathers, the hare limping and trembling through the frozen grass, the silently huddled flock, the numb fingers of the Beadsman (literally, a praying man), and the breath visibly suspended in the freezing air. The wintry atmosphere is heightened by the hot proclamation of "silver, snarling trumpets"; fragrant quiet succeeds the boisterous revelry, and the lovers vanish in "an elfin-storm from faery land."

In this poem three devices reveal Keats's debt to antiquity. He repeats and elaborates the legend that girls are permitted a vision of their future husbands on St. Agnes' Eve; the lover awakes his beloved with "an ancient ditty, long since mute" entitled LA BELLE DAME SANS MERCI; and the poem itself is written in the stately nine-line stanza invented by Spenser in the sixteenth century.

The Eve of St. Agnes

St. Agnes' Eve—Ah, bitter chill it was!
The owl, for all his feathers, was a-cold;
The hare limped trembling through the frozen grass,
And silent was the flock in woolly fold:
Numb were the Beadsman's fingers while he told
His rosary, and while his frosted breath,
Like pious incense from a censer old,
Seemed taking flight for heaven, without a death,
Past the sweet Virgin's picture, while his prayer he saith.

His prayer he saith, this patient, holy man;
Then takes his lamp, and riseth from his knees,
And back returneth, meager, barefoot, wan,
Along the chapel aisle by slow degrees:

The sculptured dead, on each side, seem to freeze,
Imprisoned in black, purgatorial rails:
Knights, ladies, praying in dumb orat'ries,
He passeth by, and his weak spirit fails
To think how they may ache in icy hoods and mails.

Northward he turneth through a little door,
And scarce three steps, ere Music's golden tongue
Flattered to tears this aged man and poor;
But no—already had his death-bell rung:
The joys of all his life were said and sung;
His was harsh penance on St. Agnes' Eve:
Another way he went, and soon among
Rough ashes sat he for his soul's reprieve,
And all night kept awake, for sinners' sake to grieve.

That ancient Beadsman heard the prelude soft;
And so it chanced, for many a door was wide,
From hurry to and fro. Soon, up aloft,
The silver, snarling trumpets 'gan to chide:
The level chambers, ready with their pride,
Were glowing to receive a thousand guests.
The carved angels, ever eager-eyed,
Stared, where upon their heads the cornice rests,
With hair blown back, and wings put crosswise on their breasts.

At length burst in the argent revelry,
With plume, tiara, and all rich array,
Numerous as shadows haunting faerily
The brain new-stuffed, in youth, with triumphs gay
Of old romance. These let us wish away,
And turn, sole-thoughted, to one Lady there,
Whose heart had brooded, all that wintry day,
On love, and winged St. Agnes' saintly care,
As she had heard old dames full many times declare.

They told her how, upon St. Agnes' Eve,
Young virgins might have visions of delight,
And soft adorings from their loves receive
Upon the honeyed middle of the night,
If ceremonies due they did aright;
As, supperless to bed they must retire,
And couch supine their beauties, lily white;
Nor look behind, nor sideways, but require
Of Heaven with upward eyes for all that they desire.

Full of this whim was thoughtful Madeline:
The music, yearning like a God in pain,
She scarcely heard: her maiden eyes divine,
Fixed on the floor, saw many a sweeping train
Pass by—she heeded not at all: in vain
Came many a tiptoe, amorous cavalier,
And back retired; not cooled by high disdain,
But she saw not: her heart was otherwhere;
She sighed for Agnes' dreams, the sweetest of the year.

She danced along with vague, regardless eyes,
Anxious her lips, her breathing quick and short:
The hallowed hour was near at hand: she sighs
Amid the timbrels, and the thronged resort
Of whisperers in anger or in sport;
'Mid looks of love, defiance, hate, and scorn,
Hoodwinked with faery fancy; all amort,
Save to St. Agnes and her lambs unshorn,
And all the bliss to be before tomorrow morn.

So, purposing each moment to retire,
She lingered still. Meantime, across the moors,
Had come young Porphyro, with heart on fire
For Madeline. Beside the portal doors,
Buttressed from moonlight, stands he, and implores
All saints to give him sight of Madeline,
But for one moment in the tedious hours,
That he might gaze and worship all unseen;
Perchance speak, kneel, touch, kiss—in sooth such things have been.

He ventures in: let no buzzed whisper tell,
All eyes be muffled, or a hundred swords
Will storm his heart, Love's feverous citadel:
For him, those chambers held barbarian hordes,
Hyena foemen, and hot-blooded lords,
Whose very dogs would execrations howl
Against his lineage; not one breast affords
Him any mercy in that mansion foul,
Save one old beldame, weak in body and in soul.

Ah, happy chance! the aged creature came,
Shuffling along with ivory-headed wand,
To where he stood, hid from the torch's flame,
Behind a broad hall pillar, far beyond

The sound of merriment and chorus bland.
He startled her: but soon she knew his face,
And grasped his fingers in her palsied hand,
Saying, "Mercy, Porphyro! hie thee from this place;
They are all here tonight, the whole bloody-thirsty race!

"Get hence! get hence! there's dwarfish Hildebrand:
He had a fever late, and in the fit
He cursed thee and thine, both house and land:
Then there's that old Lord Maurice, not a whit
More tame for his gray hairs–Alas me! flit!
Flit like a ghost away."—"Ah, Gossip dear,
We're safe enough; here in this arm-chair sit,
And tell me how–" "Good saints! not here, not here!
Follow me, child, or else these stones will be thy bier."

He followed through a lowly arched way,
Brushing the cobwebs with his lofty plume;
And as she muttered "Well-a–well-a-day!"
He found him in a little moonlight room,
Pale, latticed, chill, and silent as a tomb.
"Now tell me where is Madeline," said he,
"O tell me, Angela, by the holy loom
Which none but secret sisterhood may see,
When they St. Agnes' wool are weaving piously."

"St. Agnes! Ah! it is St. Agnes' Eve–
Yet men will murder upon holy days.
Thou must hold water in a witch's sieve,
And be liege-lord of all the Elves and Fays
To venture so: it fills me with amaze
To see thee, Porphyro!–St. Agnes' Eve!
God's help! my lady fair the conjurer plays
This very night: good angels her deceive!
But let me laugh awhile,–I've mickle time to grieve."

Feebly she laugheth in the languid moon,
While Porphyro upon her face doth look,
Like puzzled urchin on an aged crone
Who keepeth closed a wondrous riddle-book,
As spectacled she sits in chimney nook.
But soon his eyes grew brilliant, when she told
His lady's purpose; and he scarce could brook
Tears, at the thought of those enchantments cold,
And Madeline asleep in lap of legends old.

Sudden a thought came like a full-blown rose,
Flushing his brow, and in his pained heart
Made purple riot: then doth he propose
A stratagem, that makes the beldame start:
"A cruel man and impious thou art!
Sweet lady, let her pray, and sleep and dream
Alone with her good angels, far apart
From wicked men like thee. Go, go! I deem
Thou canst not surely be the same that thou didst seem."

"I will not harm her, by all saints I swear!"
Quoth Porphyro: "O may I ne'er find grace
When my weak voice shall whisper its last prayer,
If one of her soft ringlets I displace,
Or look with ruffian passion in her face.
Good Angela, believe me, by these tears;
Or I will, even in a moment's space,
Awake, with horrid shout, my foemen's ears,
And beard them, though they be more fanged than wolves and bears."

"Ah! why wilt thou affright a feeble soul?
A poor, weak, palsy-stricken, churchyard thing,
Whose passing-bell may ere the midnight toll;
Whose prayers for thee, each morn and evening,
Were never missed." Thus plaining, doth she bring
A gentler speech from burning Porphyro;
So woeful, and of such deep sorrowing,
That Angela gives promise she will do
Whatever he shall wish, betide her weal or woe.

Which was, to lead him, in close secrecy,
Even to Madeline's chamber, and there hide
Him in a closet, of such privacy
That he might see her beauty unespied,
And win perhaps that night a peerless bride,
While legioned fairies paced the coverlet,
And pale enchantment held her sleepy-eyed.
Never on such a night have lovers met,
Since Merlin paid his Demon all the monstrous debt.

"It shall be as thou wishest," said the Dame:
"All cates and dainties shall be stored there
Quickly on this feast-night: by the tambour frame
Her own lute thou wilt see: no time to spare,

For I am slow and feeble, and scarce dare
On such a catering trust my dizzy head.
Wait here, my child, with patience: kneel in prayer
The while. Ah! thou must needs the lady wed,
Or may I never leave my grave among the dead."

So saying she hobbled off with busy fear.
The lover's endless minutes slowly passed;
The dame returned, and whispered in his ear
To follow her; with aged eyes aghast
From fright of dim espial. Safe at last
Through many a dusky gallery, they gain
The maiden's chamber, silken, hushed and chaste;
Where Porphyro took covert, pleased amain.
His poor guide hurried back with agues in her brain.

Her faltering hand upon the balustrade,
Old Angela was feeling for the stair,
When Madeline, St. Agnes' charmed maid,
Rose, like a missioned spirit, unaware:
With silver taper's light, and pious care,
She turned, and down the aged gossip led
To a safe level matting. Now prepare,
Young Porphyro, for gazing on that bed;
She comes, she comes again, like ring-dove frayed and fled.

Out went the taper as she hurried in;
Its little smoke, in pallid moonshine, died:
She closed the door, she panted, all akin
To spirits of the air, and visions wide:
No uttered syllable, or, woe betide!
But to her heart, her heart was voluble,
Paining with eloquence her balmy side;
As though a tongueless nightingale should swell
Her throat in vain, and die, heart-stifled, in her dell.

A casement high and triple-arched there was,
All garlanded with carven imageries,
Of fruits, and flowers, and bunches of knot-grass,
And diamonded with panes of quaint device,
Innumerable of stains and splendid dyes,
As are the tiger-moth's deep-damasked wings;
And in the midst, 'mong thousand heraldries,
And twilight saints, and dim emblazonings,
A shielded scutcheon blushed with blood of queens and kings.

Full on this casement shone the wintry moon,
And threw warm gules on Madeline's fair breast,
As down she knelt for Heaven's grace and boon;
Rose-bloom fell on her hands, together prest,
And on her silver cross soft amethyst,
And on her hair a glory, like a saint:
She seemed a splendid angel, newly drest,
Save wings, for heaven:—Porphyro grew faint:
She knelt, so pure a thing, so free from mortal taint.

Anon his heart revives: her vespers done,
Of all its wreathed pearls her hair she frees;
Unclasps her warmed jewels one by one;
Loosens her fragrant bodice; by degrees
Her rich attire creeps rustling to her knees:
Half-hidden, like a mermaid in sea-weed,
Pensive awhile she dreams awake, and sees,
In fancy, fair St. Agnes in her bed,
But dares not look behind, or all the charm is fled.

Soon, trembling in her soft and chilly nest,
In sort of wakeful swoon, perplexed she lay,
Until the poppied warmth of sleep oppressed
Her soothed limbs, and soul fatigued away;
Flown, like a thought, until the morrow-day;
Blissfully havened both from joy and pain;
Clasped like a missal where swart Paynims pray;
Blinded alike from sunshine and from rain,
As though a rose should shut, and be a bud again.

Stolen to this paradise, and so entranced,
Porphyro gazed upon her empty dress,
And listened to her breathing, if it chanced
To wake into a slumberous tenderness;
Which when he heard, that minute did he bless,
And breathed himself: then from the closet crept,
Noiseless as fear in a wide wilderness,
And over the hushed carpet, silent, stept,
And 'tween the curtains peeped, where, lo!—how fast she slept.

Then by the bed-side, where the faded moon
Made a dim, silver twilight, soft he set
A table, and, half anguished, threw thereon
A cloth of woven crimson, gold, and jet:—

O for some drowsy Morphean amulet!
The boisterous, midnight, festive clarion,
The kettle-drum, and far-heard clarinet,
Affray his ears, though but in dying tone:—
The hall-door shuts again, and all the noise is gone.

And still she slept an azure-lidded sleep,
In blanched linen, smooth, and lavendered,
While he from forth the closet brought a heap
Of candied apple, quince, and plum, and gourd;
With jellies soother than the creamy curd,
And lucent syrops, tinct with cinnamon;
Manna and dates, in argosy transferred
From Fez; and spiced dainties, every one,
From silken Samarcand to cedared Lebanon.

These delicates he heaped with glowing hand
On golden dishes and in baskets bright
Of wreathed silver: sumptuous they stand
In the retired quiet of the night,
Filling the chilly room with perfume light.—
"And now, my love, my seraph fair, awake!
Thou art my heaven, and I thine eremite:
Open thine eyes, for meek St. Agnes' sake,
Or I shall drowse beside thee, so my soul doth ache."

Thus whispering, his warm, unnerved arm
Sank in her pillow. Shaded was her dream
By the dusk curtains:—'twas a midnight charm
Impossible to melt as iced stream:
The lustrous salvers in the moonlight gleam;
Broad golden fringe upon the carpet lies:
It seemed he never, never could redeem
From such a stedfast spell his lady's eyes;
So mused awhile, entoiled in woofed phantasies.

Awakening up, he took her hollow lute,—
Tumultuous,—and, in chords that tenderest be,
He played an ancient ditty, long since mute,
In Provence called, "La belle dame sans mercy":
Close to her ear touching the melody;—
Wherewith disturbed, she uttered a soft moan:
He ceased—she panted quick—and suddenly
Her blue affrayed eyes wide open shone:
Upon his knees he sank, pale as smooth-sculptured stone.

Her eyes were open, but she still beheld,
Now wide awake, the vision of her sleep:
There was a painful change, that nigh expelled
The blisses of her dream so pure and deep
At which fair Madeline began to weep,
And moan forth witless words with many a sigh,
While still her gaze on Porphyro would keep;
Who knelt, with joined hands and piteous eye,
Fearing to move or speak, she looked so dreamingly.

"Ah, Porphyro!" said she, "but even now
Thy voice was at sweet tremble in mine ear,
Made tuneable with every sweetest vow;
And those sad eyes were spiritual and clear:
How changed thou art! how pallid, chill, and drear!
Give me that voice again, my Porphyro,
Those looks immortal, those complainings dear!
Oh, leave me not in this eternal woe,
For if thou diest, my Love, I know not where to go."

Beyond a mortal man impassioned far
At these voluptuous accents, he arose,
Ethereal, flushed, and like a throbbing star
Seen 'mid the sapphire heaven's deep repose;
Into her dream he melted, as the rose
Blendeth its odor with the violet,—
Solution sweet: meantime the frost-wind blows
Like Love's alarum, pattering the sharp sleet
Against the window-panes; St. Agnes' moon hath set.

'Tis dark: quick pattereth the flaw-blown sleet.
"This is no dream, my bride, my Madeline!"
'Tis dark: the iced gusts still rave and beat:
"No dream, alas! alas! and woe is mine!
Porphyro will leave me here to fade and pine.
Cruel! what traitor could thee hither bring?
I curse not, for my heart is lost in thine,
Though thou forsakest a deceived thing;—
A dove forlorn and lost with sick unpruned wing."

"My Madeline! sweet dreamer! lovely bride!
Say, may I be for aye thy vassal blest?
Thy beauty's shield, heart-shaped and vermeil-dyed?
Ah, silver shrine, here will I take my rest

After so many hours of toil and quest,
A famished pilgrim,—saved by miracle.
Though I have found, I will not rob thy nest,
Saving of thy sweet self; if thou think'st well
To trust, fair Madeline, to no rude infidel.

"Hark! 'tis an elfin-storm from faery land,
Of haggard seeming, but a boon indeed:
Arise—arise! the morning is at hand;—
The bloated wassailers will never heed;—
Let us away, my love, with happy speed;
There are no ears to hear, or eyes to see,—
Drowned all in Rhenish and the sleepy mead:
Awake! arise! my love, and fearless be,
For o'er the southern moors I have a home for thee."

She hurried at his words, beset with fears,
For there were sleeping dragons all around,
At glaring watch, perhaps, with ready spears—
Down the wide stairs a darkling way they found;
In all the house was heard no human sound.
A chain-drooped lamp was flickering by each door;
The arras, rich with horseman, hawk, and hound,
Fluttered in the besieging wind's uproar;
And the long carpets rose along the gusty floor.

They glide, like phantoms, into the wide hall;
Like phantoms, to the iron porch they glide,
Where lay the Porter, in uneasy sprawl,
With a huge empty flagon by his side:
The wakeful bloodhound rose, and shook his hide,
But his sagacious eye an inmate owns:
By one, and one, the bolts full easy slide:—
The chains lie silent on the footworn stones;
The key turns, and the door upon its hinges groans.

And they are gone: aye, ages long ago
These lovers fled away into the storm.
That night the Baron dreamt of many a woe,
And all his warrior-guests with shade and form
Of witch, and demon, and large coffin-worm,
Were long be-nightmared. Angela the old
Died palsy-twitched, with meager face deform;
The Beadsman, after thousand aves told,
For aye unsought-for slept among his ashes cold.

Sensory richness fills all the great odes of Keats. ODE TO AUTUMN, seemingly a picture and little more, exudes a "mellow fruitfulness" and the drowsy "fume of poppies" while small gnats mourn "in a wailful choir . . . and gathering swallows twitter in the skies." The ODE ON MELANCHOLY, one of the shortest as well as one of the most poignant of the odes, achieves solemnity and a sense of heaviness by the weighted movement of the lines. The ODE TO A NIGHTINGALE, the most quoted as well as the most carefully elaborated, is magic throughout. Charles Armitage Brown, with whom Keats stayed in 1819, gave this account of the poem's genesis: "In the spring a nightingale had built her nest near my house. Keats felt a tranquil and continual joy in her song; one morning he took his chair from the breakfast table to the grass plot under a plum tree, where he sat for two or three hours. When he came into the house, I perceived he had some scraps of paper in his hand, and these he was quietly thrusting behind the books. On inquiry, I found those scraps, four or five in number; the writing was not well legible, and it was difficult to arrange the stanzas. With his assistance I succeeded, and this was his ODE TO A NIGHTINGALE."

Ode to a Nightingale

My heart aches, and a drowsy numbness pains
  My sense, as though of hemlock I had drunk,
Or emptied some dull opiate to the drains
  One minute past, and Lethe-wards had sunk:
'Tis not through envy of thy happy lot,
  But being too happy in thy happiness,—
    That thou, light-winged Dryad of the trees,
        In some melodious plot
  Of beechen green, and shadows numberless,
    Singest of summer in full-throated ease.

O for a draught of vintage, that hath been
  Cooled a long age in the deep-delved earth,
Tasting of Flora and the country green,
  Dance, and Provençal song, and sun-burnt mirth!
O for a beaker full of the warm South,
  Full of the true, the blushful Hippocrene,
    With beaded bubbles winking at the brim,
        And purple-stained mouth;
That I might drink, and leave the world unseen,
  And with thee fade away into the forest dim:

Fade far away, dissolve, and quite forget
  What thou among the leaves hast never known,
The weariness, the fever, and the fret
  Here, where men sit and hear each other groan;
Where palsy shakes a few, sad, last gray hairs,
  Where youth grows pale, and spectre-thin, and dies;
    Where but to think is to be full of sorrow
        And leaden-eyed despairs;
Where beauty cannot keep her lustrous eyes,
  Or new love pine at them beyond tomorrow.

Away! away! for I will fly to thee,
  Not charioted by Bacchus and his pards,
But on the viewless wings of Poesy,
  Though the dull brain perplexes and retards:
Already with thee! tender is the night,
  And haply the Queen-Moon is on her throne,
    Clustered around by all her starry fays;
        But here there is no light,
  Save what from heaven is with the breezes blown
    Through verdurous glooms and winding mossy ways.

I cannot see what flowers are at my feet,
  Nor what soft incense hangs upon the boughs,
But, in embalmed darkness, guess each sweet
  Wherewith the seasonable month endows
The grass, the thicket, and the fruit-tree wild;
  White hawthorn, and the pastoral eglantine;
    Fast-fading violets covered up in leaves;
        And mid-May's eldest child,
  The coming musk-rose, full of dewy wine,
    The murmurous haunt of flies on summer eves.

Darkling I listen; and for many a time
  I have been half in love with easeful Death,
Called him soft names in many a mused rhyme,
  To take into the air my quiet breath;
Now more than ever seems it rich to die,
  To cease upon the midnight with no pain,
    While thou art pouring forth thy soul abroad
        In such an ecstasy!
  Still wouldst thou sing, and I have ears in vain—
    To thy high requiem become a sod

Thou wast not born for death, immortal Bird!
No hungry generations tread thee down;
The voice I hear this passing night was heard
In ancient days by emperor and clown:
Perhaps the self-same song that found a path
Through the sad heart of Ruth, when, sick for home,
She stood in tears amid the alien corn;
The same that oft-times hath
Charmed magic casements, opening on the foam
Of perilous seas, in faery lands forlorn.

Forlorn! the very word is like a bell
To toll me back from thee to my sole self!
Adieu! the fancy cannot cheat so well
As she is famed to do, deceiving elf.
Adieu! adieu! thy plaintive anthem fades
Past the near meadows, over the still stream,
Up the hill-side; and now 'tis buried deep
In the next valley-glades:
Was it a vision, or a waking dream?
Fled is that music:—do I wake or sleep?

Ode to Autumn

Season of mists and mellow fruitfulness,
Close bosom-friend of the maturing sun;
Conspiring with him how to load and bless
With fruit the vines that round the thatch-eaves run;
To bend with apples the mossed cottage-trees,
And fill all fruit with ripeness to the core;
To swell the gourd, and plump the hazel shells
With a sweet kernel; to set budding more,
And still more, later flowers for the bees,
Until they think warm days will never cease,
For Summer has o'er-brimmed their clammy cells.

Who hath not seen thee oft amid thy store?
Sometimes whoever seeks abroad may find
Thee sitting careless on a granary floor,
Thy hair soft-lifted by the winnowing wind;
Or on a half-reaped furrow sound asleep,
Drowsed with the fume of poppies, while thy hook
Spares the next swath and all its twined flowers;

And sometimes like a gleaner thou dost keep
  Steady thy laden head across a brook;
  Or by a cider-press, with patient look,
    Thou watchest the last oozings, hours by hours.

Where are the songs of Spring? Ay, where are they?
  Think not of them, thou hast thy music too,—
While barred clouds bloom the soft-dying day,
  And touch the stubble-plains with rosy hue;
Then in a wailful choir, the small gnats mourn
  Among the river sallows, borne aloft
    Or sinking as the light wind lives or dies;
And full-grown lambs loud bleat from hilly bourn;
  Hedge-crickets sing; and now with treble soft
  The redbreast whistles from a garden-croft,
    And gathering swallows twitter in the skies.

Ode on Melancholy

No, no! go not to Lethe, neither twist
  Wolf's-bane, tight-rooted, for its poisonous wine;
Nor suffer thy pale forehead to be kissed
  By nightshade, ruby grape of Proserpine;
Make not your rosary of yew-berries,
  Nor let the beetle nor the death-moth be
    Your mournful Psyche, nor the downy owl
A partner in your sorrow's mysteries;
  For shade to shade will come too drowsily,
    And drown the wakeful anguish of the soul.

But when the melancholy fit shall fall
  Sudden from heaven like a weeping cloud,
That fosters the droop-headed flowers all,
  And hides the green hill in an April shroud;
Then glut thy sorrow on a morning rose,
  Or on the rainbow of the salt sand-wave,
    Or on the wealth of globed peonies;
Or if thy mistress some rich anger shows,
  Emprison her soft hand, and let her rave,
    And feed deep, deep upon her peerless eyes.

She dwells with Beauty—Beauty that must die;
  And Joy, whose hand is ever at his lips

Bidding adieu; and aching Pleasure nigh,
Turning to poison while the bee-mouth sips:
Ay, in the very temple of delight
Veiled Melancholy has her sovran shrine,
Though seen of none save him whose strenuous tongue
Can burst Joy's grape against his palate fine:
His soul shall taste the sadness of her might,
And be among her cloudy trophies hung.

One of Keats's most charming small poems was an impromptu performance, the result of a challenge. One December day while Hunt and Keats were seated in front of the hearth, listening to the crickets, "the cheerful little grasshoppers of the fireside," Hunt proposed that they should both write competing sonnets ON THE GRASSHOPPER AND CRICKET. Cowden Clarke, friend of Keats's youth, timed them, and Keats won. Hunt wrote a pretty little tribute to the "sweet and tiny cousins" of the field and hearth, but Keats, who modestly preferred Hunt's treatment to his own, achieved one of his almost perfect effects. The calm finality of the first line is not diminished by Keats's characteristic contrast of hot sun and cool shade. The return of the grasshopper at the end is a particularly happy touch. "This end," wrote Amy Lowell in her comprehensive biography, "is not only beautiful as regards the technical pattern, it is so in regard to the mental pattern as well."

On the Grasshopper and Cricket

The poetry of earth is never dead:
When all the birds are faint with the hot sun,
And hide in cooling trees, a voice will run
From hedge to hedge about the new-mown mead;
That is the grasshopper's—he takes the lead
In summer luxury,—he has never done
With his delights, for when tired out with fun
He rests at ease beneath some pleasant weed.
The poetry of earth is ceasing never:
On a lone winter evening, when the frost
Has wrought a silence, from the stove there shrills
The cricket's song, in warmth increasing ever,
And seems to one, in drowsiness half-lost,
The grasshopper's among some grassy hills

"I am certain of nothing," Keats wrote in one of those letters which eloquently complement his poetry, "but the holiness of the heart's affections and the truth of imagination. . . . What the imagination seizes as beauty must be truth, whether it existed before or not. The imagination may be compared to Adam's dream—he awoke and found it true." The principle of beauty, the concluding "motto" of the ODE ON A GRECIAN URN, was Keats's highest truth, a truth not inconsistent with his cry, "O for a life of sensations rather than of thoughts!"

Like Milton, to whom Keats progressively turned, Keats lived in "poetical luxury." Recent commentators have exalted Keats even beyond Milton. Commenting on his power of "concentrating all the far-reaching resources of language on one point," the late poet laureate, Robert Bridges, wrote: "This is only found in the greatest poets, and is rare even in them. It is no doubt for the possession of this power that Keats has often been likened to Shakespeare, and very justly, for Shakespeare is of all poets the greatest master of it."

A Thing of Beauty

A thing of beauty is a joy for ever:
Its loveliness increases; it will never
Pass into nothingness; but still will keep
A bower quiet for us, and a sleep
Full of sweet dreams, and health, and quiet breathing.
Therefore, on every morrow, are we wreathing
A flowery band to bind us to the earth,
Spite of despondence, of the inhuman dearth
Of noble natures, of the gloomy days,
Of all the unhealthy and o'er-darkened ways
Made for our searching: yes, in spite of all,
Some shape of beauty moves away the pall
From our dark spirits. Such the sun, the moon,
Trees old and young, sprouting a shady boon
For simple sheep; and such are daffodils
With the green world they live in; and clear rills
That for themselves a cooling covert make
'Gainst the hot season; the mid-forest brake,
Rich with a sprinkling of fair musk-rose blooms:
And such too is the grandeur of the dooms

We have imagined for the mighty dead;
All lovely tales that we have heard or read:
An endless fountain of immortal drink,
Pouring unto us from the heaven's brink.
from ENDYMION

To One Who Has Been Long in City Pent

To one who has been long in city pent,
'Tis very sweet to look into the fair
And open face of heaven,—to breathe a prayer
Full in the smile of the blue firmament.
Who is more happy, when, with heart's content,
Fatigued he sinks into some pleasant lair
Of wavy grass, and reads a debonair
And gentle tale of love and languishment?
Returning home at evening, with an ear
Catching the notes of Philomel,—an eye
Watching the sailing cloudlet's bright career,
He mourns that day so soon has glided by,
E'en like the passage of an angel's tear
That falls through the clear ether silently.

On the Sea

It keeps eternal whisperings around
Desolate shores, and with its mighty swell
Gluts twice ten thousand caverns, till the spell
Of Hecate leaves them their old shadowy sound.
Often 'tis in such gentle temper found,
That scarcely will the very smallest shell
Be moved for days from where it sometime fell,
When last the winds of heaven were unbound.
Oh ye! who have your eye-balls vexed and tired,
Feast them upon the wideness of the Sea;
Oh ye! whose ears are dinned with uproar rude,
Or fed too much with cloying melody,—
Sit ye near some old cavern's mouth, and brood
Until ye start, as if the sea-nymphs quired!

Keats never completed his most ambitious work, HYPERION, an epic of the overthrow of the elder gods, but the first lines of that massive fragment are among his greatest accomplishments. "The whole sentiment of gigantic despair," wrote H. Buxton Forman, "reflected around the fallen god of the Titan dynasty, and permeating the landscape, is resumed in the most perfect manner in the incident of the motionless fallen leaf, a line almost as intense and full of the essence of poetry as any line in our language."

Saturn

Deep in the shady sadness of a vale
Far sunken from the healthy breath of morn,
Far from the fiery noon, and eve's one star,
Sat gray-haired Saturn, quiet as a stone,
Still as the silence round about his lair;
Forest on forest hung about his head
Like cloud on cloud. No stir of air was there,
Not so much life as on a summer's day
Robs not one light seed from the feathered grass,
But where the dead leaf fell, there did it rest.
A stream went voiceless by, still deadened more
By reason of his fallen divinity
Spreading a shade: the Naiad 'mid her reeds
Pressed her cold finger closer to her lips.

Along the margin-sand large foot-marks went,
No further than to where his feet had strayed,
And slept there since. Upon the sodden ground
His old right hand lay nerveless, listless, dead,
Unsceptred; and his realmless eyes were closed;
While his bowed head seemed listening to the Earth,
His ancient mother, for some comfort yet.

from HYPERION

When I Have Fears That I May Cease to Be

When I have fears that I may cease to be
  Before my pen has gleaned my teeming brain,
Before high-piled books, in charactery,
  Hold like rich garners the full ripened grain;
When I behold, upon the night's starred face,
  Huge cloudy symbols of a high romance,

And think that I may never live to trace
  Their shadows, with the magic hand of chance;
And when I feel, fair creature of an hour,
  That I shall never look upon thee more,
Never have relish in the faery power
  Of unreflecting love;—then on the shore
Of the wide world I stand alone, and think
Till love and fame to nothingness do sink.

The poetry of Keats may be limited because of its very concentration, its rapt attention to detail and absorption in beauty. But never has poetry been enclosed in an atmosphere of purer enchantment.

XIII

Faith, Doubt, and Democracy

WILLIAM CULLEN BRYANT

[1794–1878]

THANATOPSIS, the first important American poem, was written by a boy of seventeen and, when first published, was considered a hoax. Bryant's father found the manuscript in the family desk, copied it, and sent it to the NORTH AMERICAN REVIEW. Richard Henry Dana, author of TWO YEARS BEFORE THE MAST, told the editor he had been imposed upon. "No one, on this side of the Atlantic," said Dana, "is capable of writing such verses."

Born in a log house at Cummington, Massachusetts, November 3, 1794, William Cullen Bryant was descended from *Mayflower* Pilgrims. He was a frail but scarcely pampered child. His father, a country doctor, attempted to reduce his son's abnormally large head by soaking it every morning in a spring of cold water, and the boy was put to work raising timber frames, helping at the mill, and cutting the twigs for the whipping birch which was "as much a part of the necessary furniture as the crane that hung in the fireplace."

Although the boy was kept busy doing countless chores, he was precociously studious. Two months after learning the Greek alphabet, he read the entire New Testament. In 1808 he printed his first book of verse, THE EMBARGO: OR SKETCHES OF THE TIMES, which bore the subtitle "A Satire by a Youth of Thirteen," and which called upon President Thomas Jefferson "to resign because he was incapable of managing the Government." Entering Williams College at sixteen, he left in his sophomore year because of lack of means to continue.

One evening when Bryant was about twenty-two he was going along the road, worried about his prospects. It was December, an overcast twilight. Suddenly the clouds broke, the heavens glowed "with the last steps of day," and a lone bird flew up and vanished into the sunset. The dissolving clouds, the solitary bird, and Bryant's own meditation fused in TO A WATERFOWL, a poem which, frankly didactic, transcends sermonizing.

To a Waterfowl

Whither, 'midst falling dew,
While glow the heavens with the last steps of day,
Far, through their rosy depths, dost thou pursue
Thy solitary way!

Vainly the fowler's eye
Might mark thy distant flight to do thee wrong,
As, darkly painted on the crimson sky,
Thy figure floats along.

Seek'st thou the plashy brink
Of weedy lake, or marge of river wide,
Or where the rocking billows rise and sink
On the chafed ocean side?

There is a power whose care
Teaches thy way along that pathless coast,—
The desert and illimitable air,—
Lone wandering, but not lost.

All day thy wings have fanned,
At that far height, the cold, thin atmosphere,
Yet stoop not, weary, to the welcome land,
Though the dark night is near.

And soon that toil shall end;
Soon shalt thou find a summer home, and rest,
And scream among thy fellows; reeds shall bend,
Soon, o'er thy sheltered nest.

Thou'rt gone, the abyss of heaven
Hath swallowed up thy form; yet, on my heart
Deeply hath sunk the lesson thou hast given,
And shall not soon depart.

He who, from zone to zone,
Guides through the boundless sky thy certain flight,
In the long way that I must tread alone,
Will lead my steps aright.

A few months later Bryant studied law, practiced at Great Barrington, Massachusetts, married at twenty-six, and at thirty became one of the editors of the NEW YORK EVENING POST. After two years he was made editor in chief, and held that position for fifty years. He was acclaimed "the first citizen of the Republic," and divided his days between poetry and journalism. In his eighty-fourth year he stood uncovered in the blazing sun while he delivered an address at the dedication of a statue to Mazzini in Central Park, New York. Ascending a flight of stairs a little later, he was overcome by dizziness and fell, suffering a concussion of the brain. He died June 12, 1878.

It has been said that in youth Bryant wrote for old men and in his old age for children. Death is the traditional preoccupation of adolescence, and THANATOPSIS is perhaps the most famous projection of that concern. The poem triumphs over its pompous beginning, and with the line "Yet not to thine eternal resting-place" rises from expansive rhetoric to clear eloquence.

Thanatopsis

To him who in the love of nature holds
Communion with her visible forms, she speaks
A various language; for his gayer hours
She has a voice of gladness, and a smile
And eloquence of beauty; and she glides
Into his darker musings, with a mild
And healing sympathy that steals away
Their sharpness ere he is aware. When thoughts
Of the last bitter hour come like a blight
Over thy spirit, and sad images
Of the stern agony, and shroud, and pall,
And breathless darkness, and the narrow house,

Make thee to shudder, and grow sick at heart;—
Go forth, under the open sky, and list
To Nature's teachings, while from all around—
Earth and her waters, and the depths of air—
Comes a still voice. Yet a few days, and thee
The all-beholding sun shall see no more
In all his course; nor yet in the cold ground,
Where thy pale form was laid, with many tears,
Nor in the embrace of ocean, shall exist
Thy image. Earth, that nourished thee, shall claim
Thy growth, to be resolved to earth again,
And, lost each human trace, surrendering up
Thine individual being, shalt thou go
To mix forever with the elements,
To be a brother to the insensible rock
And to the sluggish clod, which the rude swain
Turns with his share, and treads upon. The oak
Shall send his roots abroad, and pierce thy mold.

Yet not to thine eternal resting-place
Shalt thou retire alone, nor couldst thou wish
Couch more magnificent. Thou shalt lie down
With patriarchs of the infant world—with kings,
The powerful of the earth—the wise, the good,
Fair forms, and hoary seers of ages past,
All in one mighty sepulchre. The hills
Rock-ribbed and ancient as the sun,—the vales
Stretching in pensive quietness between;
The venerable woods—rivers that move
In majesty, and the complaining brooks
That make the meadows green; and, poured round all,
Old Ocean's gray and melancholy waste,—
Are but the solemn decorations all
Of the great tomb of man. The golden sun,
The planets, all the infinite host of heaven,
Are shining on the sad abodes of death
Through the still lapse of ages. All that tread
The globe are but a handful to the tribes
That slumber in its bosom.—Take the wings
Of morning, pierce the Barcan wilderness,
Or lose thyself in the continuous woods
Where rolls the Oregon, and hears no sound,
Save his own dashings—yet the dead are there:
And millions in those solitudes, since first

The flight of years began, have laid them down
In their last sleep—the dead reign there alone.

So shalt thou rest—and what if thou withdraw
In silence from the living, and no friend
Take note of thy departure? All that breathe
Will share thy destiny. The gay will laugh
When thou art gone, the solemn brood of care
Plod on, and each one as before will chase
His favorite phantom; yet all these shall leave
Their mirth and their employments, and shall come
And make their bed with thee. As the long train
Of ages glides away, the sons of men—
The youth in life's fresh spring, and he who goes
In the full strength of years, matron and maid,
The speechless babe, and the gray-headed man—
Shall one by one be gathered to thy side,
By those, who in their turn shall follow them.

So live, that when thy summons comes to join
The innumerable caravan, which moves
To that mysterious realm, where each shall take
His chamber in the silent halls of death,
Thou go not, like the quarry-slave at night,
Scourged to his dungeon, but, sustained and soothed
By an unfaltering trust, approach thy grave
Like one who wraps the drapery of his couch
About him, and lies down to pleasant dreams.

Bryant's world is neither an exciting nor a romantic one, but it is a world to which the reader may come, after heat and turbulence, for reassuring quiet. It is not enchanted ground, but it is a true haven.

JOHN GREENLEAF WHITTIER

[1807–1892]

THE most militant of the New England poets, John Greenleaf Whittier, was born December 17, 1807, at Haverhill, Massachu setts. Unlike his famous contemporaries, Whittier had a background of little education and practically no money. The first eighteen years of his life were spent on a farm, and it was not until he had turned nineteen that he was able to attend Haverhill Academy for two terms. He paid for the tuition with his own savings, chiefly from shoemaking, and, according to his first biographer, "calculated every item of expense so closely that he knew before the beginning of the term he would have twenty-five cents to spare at its close."

At eighteen Whittier had seen his first poem printed in a local newspaper, the Newburyport FREE PRESS. The editor was William Lloyd Garrison, and under Garrison's influence Whittier was stirred to a fever of abolitionism. Born a Quaker, Whittier became a crusader, the poet and politician of the antislavery cause. He served in the legislature, and was assailed as a fanatic. He edited a newspaper, and saw his office burned down by a pro-slavery mob. After his fortieth year, he lived in Amesbury, with his sister, in Wordsworthian seclusion. He died at the patriarchal age of eighty-five, September 7, 1892.

A more vehement spirit than his noted compatriots, Whittier was a less skillful craftsman. His homely ballads, however, have never lost their appeal. Such a poem as BARBARA FRIETCHIE continues to be relished partly because of the straightforwardness of the simple couplets, partly because it seems to belong to the folk stuff of a nation. Even if, as historians have insisted, the event is fictitious, it is the sort of gallant incident that should have happened.

Barbara Frietchie

Up from the meadows rich with corn,
Clear in the cool September morn,

The clustered spires of Frederick stand
Green-walled by the hills of Maryland.

Round about them orchards sweep,
Apple and peach tree fruited deep,

Fair as a garden of the Lord,
To the eyes of the famished rebel horde,

On that pleasant morn of the early fall
When Lee marched over the mountain wall—

Over the mountains, winding down,
Horse and foot into Frederick town.

Forty flags with their silver stars,
Forty flags with their crimson bars,

Flapped in the morning wind; the sun
Of noon looked down, and saw not one.

Up rose old Barbara Frietchie then,
Bowed with her fourscore years and ten;

Bravest of all in Frederick town,
She took up the flag the men hauled down;

In her attic-window the staff she set,
To show that one heart was loyal yet.

Up the street came the rebel tread,
Stonewall Jackson riding ahead.

Under his slouch hat left and right
He glanced: the old flag met his sight.

"Halt!"—the dust-brown ranks stood fast;
"Fire!"—out blazed the rifle-blast.

It shivered the window, pane and sash;
It rent the banner with seam and gash.

Quick, as it fell, from the broken staff
Dame Barbara snatched the silken scarf;

She leaned far out on the window-sill,
And shook it forth with a royal will.

"Shoot, if you must, this old gray head,
But spare your country's flag," she said.

A shade of sadness, a blush of shame,
Over the face of the leader came;

The nobler nature within him stirred
To life at that woman's deed and word:

"Who touches a hair of yon gray head
Dies like a dog! March on!" he said.

All day long through Frederick street
Sounded the tread of marching feet;

All day long that free flag tost
Over the heads of the rebel host.

Ever its torn folds rose and fell
On the loyal winds that loved it well;

And through the hill-gaps sunset light
Shone over it with a warm good-night.

Barbara Frietchie's work is o'er,
And the rebel rides on his raids no more.

Honor to her! and let a tear
Fall, for her sake, on Stonewall's bier.

Over Barbara Frietchie's grave,
Flag of freedom and union wave!

Peace and order and beauty draw
Round thy symbol of light and law;

And ever the stars above look down
On thy stars below in Frederick town.

The bucolic elements in his verse have led many readers to think of Whittier as a ruder Wordsworth, a Massachusetts Burns without the Scottish plowman's gift of song. But Whittier's country verse exhales native air. It is American colonial life which is lovingly recorded in SNOW-BOUND, Whittier's highest poetic achievement. Rich in characterization, graphic in interior details, it is an almost perfect genre poem, a small epic in homespun.

Winter Day

The sun that brief December day
Rose cheerless over hills of gray,
And, darkly circled, gave at noon
A sadder light than waning moon.

Slow tracing down the thickening sky
Its mute and ominous prophecy,
A portent seeming less than threat,
It sank from sight before it set.
A chill no coat, however stout,
Of homespun stuff could quite shut out,
A hard, dull bitterness of cold,
That checked, mid-vein, the circling race
Of life-blood in the sharpened face
The coming of the snow-storm told.
The wind blew east; we heard the roar
Of Ocean on his wintry shore,
And felt the strong pulse throbbing there
Beat with low rhythm our inland air.
Meanwhile we did our nightly chores,
Brought in the wood from out of doors,
Littered the stalls, and from the mows
Raked down the herd's-grass for the cows:
Heard the horse whinnying for his corn;
And, sharply clashing horn on horn,
Impatient down the stanchion rows
The cattle shake their walnut bows;
While, peering from his early perch
Upon the scaffold's pole of birch,
The cock his crested helmet bent
And down his querulous challenge sent.

from SNOW-BOUND

Winter Night

As night drew on, and, from the crest
Of wooded knolls that ridged the west,
The sun, a snow-blown traveller, sank
From sight beneath the smothering bank,
We piled, with care, our nightly stack
Of wood against the chimney-back,—
The oaken log, green, huge, and thick,
And on its top the stout back-stick;
The knotty forestick laid apart,
And filled between with curious art
The ragged brush; then, hovering near,
We watched the first red blaze appear,
Heard the sharp crackle, caught the gleam

On whitewashed wall and sagging beam,
Until the old, rude-furnished room
Burst, flower-like, into rosy bloom;
While radiant with a mimic flame
Outside the sparkling drift became,
And through the bare-boughed lilac-tree
Our own warm hearth seemed blazing free.
The crane and pendent trammels showed,
The Turks' heads on the andirons glowed;
While childish fancy, prompt to tell
The meaning of the miracle,
Whispered the old rhyme: "*Under the tree,*
When fire outdoors burns merrily,
There the witches are making tea."

The moon above the eastern wood
Shone at its full; the hill-range stood
Transfigured in the silver flood,
Its blown snows flashing cold and keen,
Dead white, save where some sharp ravine
Took shadow, or the sombre green
Of hemlocks turned to pitchy black
Against the whiteness at their back.
For such a world and such a night
Most fitting that unwarming light,
Which only seemed where'er it fell
To make the coldness visible.

from SNOW-BOUND

RALPH WALDO EMERSON

[1803–1882]

BORN May 25, 1803, in Boston, Massachusetts, of ministerial stock, Ralph Waldo Emerson was destined for the ministry. After graduating from Harvard College and Harvard Divinity School, he was ordained in his twenty-sixth year. Three years later he left the pulpit, unable to believe in the ritual.

At twenty-nine one part of Emerson's life had ended. He had married Ellen Tucker, and was in a fair way of becoming influential not only as a chaplain but as an educator. Three years after his marriage, his wife—like Emerson's father and two of his brothers—died of tuberculosis. Emerson journeyed abroad, met Coleridge, formed a warm friendship with Carlyle, recovered his health, and returned to America, where he became a resident of Concord, Massachusetts. He remarried, turned to the lecture platform, and published his first volume, NATURE, a milestone in American letters. "Nature," Emerson contended, "is the incarnation of thought. The world is the mind precipitated." Poems and essays followed with ever-growing strength and conviction. Emerson spoke up for intellectual as well as religious independence; he held that humanity had lost self-rule and self-reliance, that man was dominated by things rather than by thought. As a result of Emerson's attack on the conventions, clergymen assailed his "heresies" and Harvard closed its lecture rooms to him. Thirty years later he received an honorary degree from Harvard and was chosen one of its overseers. At sixty-seven he gave a course in philosophy at Cambridge.

His house had burned down in his seventieth year, and Emerson had been weakened by exposure and disheartened by the loss of his books and furniture. Friends sent him abroad and admirers rebuilt the house to the last detail. Emerson returned as "The Sage of Concord" to spend his days in increasing solitude. But he was still energetic; at seventy-seven he loved to swim naked in Walden Pond. His memory faded. Nevertheless, when he had trouble remembering people and even words, he recalled characteristics. Once, wishing for his umbrella, he said, "I can't tell its name, but I can tell its history. Strangers take it away." At the burial of Longfellow he declared, "That gentleman was a sweet and beautiful soul—but I have forgotten his name." The end was a gradual diminishing, and Emerson died at Concord, April 27, 1882.

Emerson's love of Concord reveals itself in one of his most characteristic although one of his least-quoted poems, TWO RIVERS. The Indian name "Musketaquit" is explained in Thoreau's A WEEK ON THE CONCORD AND MERRIMACK RIVERS:

> The Musketaquit, or Grass-ground River, though probably as old as the Nile or Euphrates, did not begin to have a place in civilized history until the fame of its grassy meadows and its fish attracted settlers out of England in 1635, when it received the other but kindred name of Concord from the first plantation on its banks, which appears to have been commenced in a spirit of peace and harmony. It will be Grass-ground River as long as grass grows

and water runs here; it will be Concord River only while men lead peaceable lives on its banks.

Two Rivers

Thy summer voice, Musketaquit,
Repeats the music of the rain;
But sweeter rivers pulsing flit
Through thee, as thou through Concord Plain.

Thou in thy narrow banks are pent:
The stream I love unbounded goes
Through flood and sea and firmament;
Through light, through life, it forward flows.

I see the inundation sweet,
I hear the spending of the stream
Through years, through men, through Nature fleet,
Through love and thought, through power and dream.

Musketaquit, a goblin strong,
Of shard and flint makes jewels gay;
They lose their grief who hear his song,
And where he winds is the day of day.

So forth and brighter fares my stream—
Who drink it shall not thirst again;
No darkness stains its equal gleam,
And ages drop in it like rain.

The suavity of Emerson's verse is deceptive. The surface is so limpid, so easily persuasive, that it appears conventional. But the ideas embodied in the poems are energetic and radical ideas; they are, like Emerson himself, not only truth-loving but truth-living. They celebrate the democratic man, but they do not idealize him; they recognize evil as well as good; they regard doubt not as a fixed denial but as "a cry for faith rising from the dust of dead creeds." Even love, which demands every sacrifice, must be free of moral impositions; for "when half-gods go, the gods arrive."

Give All to Love

Give all to love;
Obey thy heart;
Friends, kindred, days,
Estate, good-fame,
Plans, credit, and the Muse—
Nothing refuse.

'Tis a brave master;
Let it have scope:
Follow it utterly,
Hope beyond hope:
High and more high
It dives into noon,
With wing unspent,
Untold intent;
But it is a god,
Knows its own path,
And the outlets of the sky.

It was not for the mean;
It requireth courage stout,
Souls above doubt,
Valor unbending;
Such 'twill reward—
They shall return
More than they were,
And ever ascending.

Leave all for love;
Yet, hear me, yet,
One word more thy heart behoved,
One pulse more of firm endeavor—
Keep thee today,
Tomorrow, forever,
Free as an Arab
Of thy beloved.

Cling with life to the maid;
But when the surprise,
First vague shadow of surmise
Flits across her bosom young

Of a joy apart from thee,
Free be she, fancy-free;
Nor thou detain her vesture's hem,
Nor the palest rose she flung
From her summer diadem.

Though thou loved her as thyself,
As a self of purer clay,
Though her parting dims the day,
Stealing grace from all alive;
Heartily know,
When half-gods go,
The gods arrive.

In a long poem, MERLIN, Emerson tells the poet—and, by inference, the reader—that he must

. . . . . mount to Paradise
By the stairway of surprise.

Surprise is the element which characterizes Emerson's best poetry, the pithy suggestiveness which influenced his Amherst disciple, Emily Dickinson. His meaning has often been questioned. The pantheistic BRAHMA has been parodied and misunderstood, although the title should make it plain that the speaker is not meant to be Emerson but the god of nature. In this poem, accident and design, life and death, are harmonized in the all-resolving paradox of existence.

Brahma

If the red slayer think he slays,
  Or if the slain think he is slain,
They know not well the subtle ways
  I keep, and pass, and turn again.

Far or forgot to me is near;
  Shadow and sunlight are the same;
The vanished gods to me appear;
  And one to me are shame and fame.

They reckon ill who leave me out;
  When me they fly, I am the wings;
I am the doubter and the doubt,
  And I the hymn the Brahmin sings.

The strong gods pine for my abode,
  And pine in vain the sacred Seven;
But thou, meek lover of the good!
  Find me, and turn thy back on heaven.

Emerson's range and integrity overcome his occasional lack of melody and structural carelessness. His scope includes the passion of the CONCORD HYMN, the pictorial delicacy of THE SNOWSTORM, and the Thoreaulike sententiousness of THE RHODORA and FORBEARANCE. The value of Emerson's poetry, however, is not in what it teaches but what it confirms. A hint here, a phrase there, a gnomic suggestion taking us breathlessly—we seize him by intuition or not at all.

Concord Hymn

By the rude bridge that arched the flood,
  Their flag to April's breeze unfurled,
Here once the embattled farmers stood,
  And fired the shot heard round the world.

The foe long since in silence slept;
  Alike the conqueror silent sleeps;
And Time the ruined bridge has swept
  Down the dark stream that seaward creeps.

On this green bank, by this soft stream,
  We set to-day a votive stone;
That memory may their deed redeem,
  When, like our sires, our sons are gone.

Spirit, that made those heroes dare
  To die, and leave their children free,
Bid Time and Nature gently spare
  The shaft we raise to them and thee.

The Snowstorm

Announced by all the trumpets of the sky,
Arrives the snow, and, driving o'er the fields,
Seems nowhere to alight: the whited air
Hides hills and woods, the river, and the heaven,
And veils the farmhouse at the garden's end.
The sled and traveler stopped, the courier's feet
Delayed, all friends shut out, the housemates sit
Around the radiant fireplace, inclosed
In a tumultuous privacy of storm.

Come, see the north wind's masonry.
Out of an unseen quarry evermore
Furnished with tile, the fierce artificer
Curves his white bastions with projected roof
Round every windward stake, or tree, or door.
Speeding, the myriad-handed, his wild work
So fanciful, so savage, naught cares he
For number or proportion. Mockingly
On coop or kennel he hangs Parian wreaths;
A swan-like form invests the hidden thorn;
Fills up the farmer's lane from wall to wall,
Maugre the farmer's sighs; and at the gate
A tapering turret overtops the work.
And when his hours are numbered, and the world
Is all his own, retiring, as he were not,
Leaves, when the sun appears, astonished Art
To mimic in slow structures, stone by stone,
Built in an age, the mad wind's night-work,
The frolic architecture of the snow.

Days

Daughters of Time, the hypocritic Days,
Muffled and dumb like barefoot dervishes,
And marching single in an endless file,
Bring diadems and fagots in their hands.
To each they offer gifts after his will,
Bread, kingdoms, stars, and sky that holds them all.

I, in my pleached garden, watched the pomp,
Forgot my morning wishes, hastily
Took a few herbs and apples, and the Day
Turned and departed silent. I, too late,
Under her solemn fillet saw the scorn.

The Rhodora

ON BEING ASKED, WHENCE IS THE FLOWER?

In May, when sea-winds pierced our solitudes,
I found the fresh Rhodora in the woods,
Spreading its leafless blooms in a damp nook,
To please the desert and the sluggish brook.
The purple petals, fallen in the pool,
Made the black water with their beauty gay;
Here might the red-bird come his plumes to cool,
And court the flower that cheapens his array.
Rhodora! if the sages ask thee why
This charm is wasted on the earth and sky,
Tell them, dear, that if eyes were made for seeing,
Then Beauty is its own excuse for being:
Why thou wert there, O rival of the rose!
I never thought to ask, I never knew:
But, in my simple ignorance, suppose
The self-same Power that brought me there brought you.

Forbearance

Hast thou named all the birds without a gun?
Loved the wood-rose, and left it on its stalk?
At rich men's tables eaten bread and pulse?
Unarmed, faced danger with a heart of trust?
And loved so well a high behavior,
In man or maid, that thou from speech refrained,
Nobility more nobly to repay?—
O, be my friend, and teach me to be thine!

THOMAS LOVELL BEDDOES

[1803–1849]

THOMAS LOVELL BEDDOES was a lost anachronism, a bizarre Elizabethan dramatist who happened to live in the nineteenth century. Beddoes' father was a famous physician and quasi scientist; his mother was a sister of Maria Edgeworth, the novelist. At seventeen Beddoes entered Pembroke College, Oxford, immersed himself in the works of the lesser Elizabethan and Jacobean playwrights, and at nineteen published the violent but fragmentary THE BRIDE'S TRAGEDY. A fantastic and still more uneven drama, DEATH'S JEST-BOOK, was begun in Beddoes' twenty-second year, completed in his twenty-sixth, and continually revised until his death. "I am convinced that the man who is to awaken the drama must be a bold, trampling fellow," Beddoes wrote to a friend, "no creeper into wormholes!" But Beddoes was unable to live up to his audacious program. If he was, as he was sometimes called, "the last of the Elizabethans," he was not influenced by the greatest of these; "he imbibed," wrote Saintsbury, "rather from the night-shade of Webster and Tourneur than from the vine of Shakespeare."

Beddoes himself might have been a character in the most macabre of his plays. He lived in Europe practically all his life, practiced medicine in Zurich, and lived with a baker whom he resolved to turn into a great actor. He hired a theater for one night so that the baker could play the part of Hotspur; and when the two friends separated after a quarrel, Beddoes tried to kill himself. At forty-three he visited England and called upon his relatives, gravely riding upon a donkey. He tried to set fire to Drury Lane Theater with a five-pound note as a protest against the English stage. Returning to the Continent, he died in Basel, January 26, 1849; it was suspected, though never proved, that he committed suicide by taking poison.

If Beddoes' dramas are spasmodic, his poems are not. The songs interpolated in the plays are exquisite and almost perfect. Whether the mood is sensuous, as in lines beginning "If there were dreams to sell," insinuatingly chill, as in THE PHANTOM WOOER with its "little snakes of silver throat," or grimly jocular, as in THE CARRION CROW, the music is as persuasive as it is precise. If the lyrics are

Gothic, preoccupied with death and decay, they are authentic in their fitful genius. If they are fragmentary, they are fragments of gold.

Dream-Pedlary

If there were dreams to sell,
  What would you buy?
Some cost a passing bell;
  Some a light sigh,
That shakes from Life's fresh crown
Only a rose-leaf down.
If there were dreams to sell,
Merry and sad to tell,
And the crier rung the bell,
  What would you buy?

A cottage lone and still,
  With bowers nigh,
Shadowy, my woes to still,
  Until I die.
Such pearl from Life's fresh crown
Fain would I shake me down.
Were dreams to have at will,
This would best heal my ill,
  This would I buy.

If there are ghosts to raise,
  What shall I call,
Out of hell's murky haze,
  Heaven's blue pall?
Raise my loved long-lost boy
To lead me to his joy.
  There are no ghosts to raise;
  Out of death lead no ways;
    Vain is the call.

Know'st thou not ghosts to sue?
  No love thou hast.
Else lie, as I will do,
  And breathe thy last.
So out of Life's fresh crown
Fall like a rose-leaf down.
  Thus are the ghosts to woo;
  Thus are all dreams made true,
    Ever to last!

Stanzas

The mighty thought of an old world
Fans, like a dragon's wing unfurled,
The surface of my yearnings deep;
And solemn shadows then awake,
Like the fish-lizard in the lake,
Troubling a planet's morning sleep.

My waking is a Titan's dream,
Where a strange sun, long set, doth beam
Through Montezuma's cypress bough:
Through the fern wilderness forlorn
Glisten the giant hart's great horn
And serpents vast with helmèd brow.

The measureless from caverns rise
With steps of earthquake, thunderous cries,
And graze upon the lofty wood;
The palmy grove, through which doth gleam
Such antediluvian ocean's stream,
Haunts shadowy my domestic mood.

from THE IVORY GATE

Song

How many times do I love thee, dear?
  Tell me how many thoughts there be
    In the atmosphere
    Of a new-fall'n year,
Whose white and sable hours appear
  The latest flake of Eternity:
So many times do I love thee, dear.

How many times do I love again?
  Tell me how many beads there are
    In a silver chain
    Of evening rain,
Unravelled from the tumbling main,
  And threading the eye of a yellow star:
So many times do I love again.

from TORRISMOND

The Phantom Wooer

A ghost, that loved a lady fair,
Ever in the starry air
Of midnight at her pillow stood;
And, with a sweetness skies above
The luring words of human love,
Her soul the phantom wooed.
Sweet and sweet is their poisoned note,
The little snakes of silver throat,
In mossy skulls that nest and lie,
Ever singing 'die, oh! die.'

Young soul put off your flesh, and come
With me into the quiet tomb,
Our bed is lovely, dark, and sweet;
The earth will swing us, as she goes,
Beneath our coverlid of snows,
And the warm leaden sheet.
Dear and dear is their poisoned note,
The little snakes of silver throat,
In mossy skulls that nest and lie,
Ever singing 'die, oh! die.'

The Carrion Crow

Old Adam, the carrion crow,
The old crow of Cairo;
He sat in the shower, and let it flow
Under his tail and over his crest;
And through every feather
Leaked the wet weather;
And the bough swung under his nest;
For his beak it was heavy with marrow.
Is that the wind dying? O no;
It's only two devils, that blow
Through a murderer's bones, to and fro,
In the ghosts' moonshine.

Ho! Eve, my grey carrion wife,
When we have supped on kings' marrow,

Where shall we drink and make merry our life?
  Our nest it is queen Cleopatra's skull,
    'Tis cloven and cracked,
    And battered and hacked,
  But with tears of blue eyes it is full:
  Let us drink them, my raven of Cairo.
    Is that the wind dying? O no;
    It's only two devils, that blow
    Through a murderer's bones, to and fro,
      In the ghosts' moonshine.

from DEATH'S JEST-BOOK

ELIZABETH BARRETT BROWNING

[1806–1861]

WHEN Robert Browning stormed into her life, Elizabeth Barrett was a thirty-nine-year-old invalid. Daughter of a jealously dominating father, Elizabeth was born near Durham, March 6, 1806. At twelve she wrote THE BATTLE OF MARATHON, an "epic" of four books, which her father caused to be printed. At fifteen she injured her spine, and confinement in the London house on Wimpole Street ("Newgate prison turned inside out") affected her lungs. The grief caused by the death of a beloved brother by drowning and her father's refusal to allow any of his children to marry made her a recluse. Approaching her forties, she seemed destined for a life of gloom and uneventfulness.

Two events suddenly dispelled the gloom. On May 20, 1845, after a protracted correspondence, Elizabeth Barrett granted Robert Browning's request for a visit. On September 12, 1846, she escaped the possessive vigilance of her father and was secretly married to the poet, who was six years her junior. The couple left immediately for Italy, partly because of the mild climate, partly because of the cost of living; and in Italy they remained until her death.

"I love your verses with all my heart, dear Miss Barrett," Robert Browning began his first letter to the poet, who was, at that time, far more famous than he. Then after a page or two of critical compliments, he added impetuously, "And I love you too." That love was increasingly returned. It was rewarded by countless tributes, pre-eminently by the SONNETS FROM THE PORTUGUESE. The poems had been written by stealth, with no thought of publication; even the title was a slight effort at concealment. But it was obvious that these sonnets were not translations, and the title was an intimate acknowledgment of her husband's playful way of calling her "my little Portuguese" because of her olive skin.

Sonnets from the Portuguese

3

Unlike are we, unlike, O princely Heart!
Unlike our uses and our destinies.
Our ministering two angels look surprise
On one another, as they strike athwart
Their wings in passing. Thou, bethink thee, art
A guest for queens to social pageantries,
With gages from a hundred brighter eyes
Than tears even can make mine, to play thy part
Of chief musician. What hast *thou* to do
With looking from the lattice-lights at me,
A poor, tired, wandering singer, singing through
The dark, and leaning up a cypress-tree?
The chrism is on thine head—on mine, the dew—
And Death must dig the level where these agree.

6

Go from me. Yet I feel that I shall stand
Henceforward in thy shadow. Nevermore
Alone upon the threshold of my door
Of individual life, I shall command
The uses of my soul, nor lift my hand
Serenely in the sunshine as before,
Without the sense of that which I forbore—
Thy touch upon the palm. The widest land
Doom takes to part us, leaves thy heart in mine
With pulses that beat double. What I do
And what I dream include thee, as the wine
Must taste of its own grapes. And when I sue
God for myself, He hears that name of thine,
And sees within my eyes the tears of two.

14

If thou must love me, let it be for naught
Except for love's sake only. Do not say,
"I love her for her smile—her look—her way
Of speaking gently—for a trick of thought
That falls in well with mine, and certes brought
A sense of pleasant ease on such a day"—
For these things in themselves, Belovèd, may
Be changed, or change for thee—and love, so wrought,
May be unwrought so. Neither love me for
Thine own dear pity's wiping my cheeks dry—
A creature might forget to weep, who bore
Thy comfort long, and lose thy love thereby!
But love me for love's sake, that evermore
Thou may'st love on, through love's eternity.

22

When our two souls stand up erect and strong,
Face to face, silent, drawing nigh and nigher,
Until the lengthening wings break into fire
At either curvèd point,—what bitter wrong
Can the earth do to us, that we should not long
Be here contented? Think. In mounting higher,
The angels would press on us and aspire
To drop some golden orb of perfect song
Into our deep, dear silence. Let us stay
Rather on earth, Belovèd,—where the unfit,
Contrarious moods of men recoil away
And isolate pure spirits, and permit
A place to stand and love in for a day,
With darkness and the death-hour rounding it.

43

How do I love thee? Let me count the ways.
I love thee to the depth and breadth and height
My soul can reach, when feeling out of sight
For the ends of Being and ideal Grace.
I love thee to the level of every day's
Most quiet need, by sun and candle-light.
I love thee freely, as men strive for right;

I love thee purely, as they turn from praise.
I love thee with the passion put to use
In my old griefs, and with my childhood's faith.
I love thee with a love I seemed to lose
With my lost saints—I love thee with the breath,
Smiles, tears, of all my life!—and, if God choose,
I shall but love thee better after death.

Mrs. Browning's eminence has declined during the last half century. Her sonnets were once considered "the finest in any language since Shakespeare's"; but a few years ago the late Virginia Woolf cruelly declared that "the only place in the mansion of literature" to which Mrs. Browning could be assigned "is downstairs in the servants' quarters in company with Mrs. Hemans, Eliza Cook, Jean Ingelow . . ." It is true that Mrs. Browning's poetry is too diffuse, too unreservedly "emotional." As G. K. Chesterton recently wrote, "She cannot leave anything alone, she cannot write a line, without a conceit. She gives the reader the impression that she never declined a fancy." Nevertheless, her sincere femininity more than compensates for any sentimentality; the sonnet beginning "How do I love thee" is one of the most eloquent love poems in the language. Her best work, especially where the strict form of the sonnet compels concentration, is her gentlest. If it sometimes fails in control, it never lacks fervor.

Grief

I tell you hopeless grief is passionless,
That only men incredulous of despair,
Half-taught in anguish, through the midnight air
Beat upward to God's throne in loud access
Of shrieking and reproach. Full desertness
In souls, as countries, lieth silent-bare
Under the blanching, vertical eye-glare
Of the absolute heavens. Deep-hearted man, express
Grief for thy dead in silence like to death—
Most like a monumental statue set
In everlasting watch and moveless woe
Till itself crumble to the dust beneath.
Touch it; the marble eyelids are not wet;
If it could weep, it could arise and go.

After he heard that his favorite daughter had dared to defy his authority by a runaway marriage, Mr. Barrett forbade his children ever to mention Elizabeth's name, and melodramatically foretold an early end of the romance. His prophecy was not fulfilled. Mrs. Browning recovered her health sufficiently to bear a son in her forty-fourth year, to enjoy the company of many visitors, and live an idyllic life with her poet-husband in Florence for fifteen years after her escape from Wimpole Street. She died in Browning's arms June 30, 1861.

HENRY WADSWORTH LONGFELLOW

[1807–1882]

OVERPRAISED in his time, underrated in our own, Longfellow seems to be remembered for his worst. He has been misrepresented in textbooks as a prosy preacher in verse; schoolchildren have been forced to memorize his most sententious platitudes. The poet has suffered from unhappy repetitions of:

> Life is real! Life is earnest!
> And the grave is not its goal;
> "Dust thou art, to dust returnest"
> Was not spoken of the soul.

and the moral but meaningless:

> "Oh stay," the maiden said, "and rest
> Thy weary head upon this breast."
> A tear stood in his bright blue eye,
> But still he answered with a sigh,
> "Excelsior!"

But Longfellow was not only a writer of maxims and wall mottoes. He was a true scholar, a devoted teacher—he held his first class at Bowdoin at six in the morning—and, as a poet, something of a pioneer. Born February 27, 1807, in Portland, Maine, of an old New England family, Longfellow was descended from Priscilla and

John Alden. He entered Bowdoin College at fifteen, traveled abroad at twenty, and, after two years of absorption, returned to bring the romantic tradition to America. He became an expert linguist—Dutch was the only language that resisted him—and steeped himself in German literature. His lyrics are an embodiment of his favorite mood, *Gemütlichkeit,* twilight lengthening into evening, "the children's hour," the genial lamp, the undisturbing book. His study of the Finnish national epic, the KALEVALA, was reflected in an attempt to create an American Indian epic, HIAWATHA. One of the first American poets to employ American themes, Longfellow stressed the charms of legendry rather than the problems of contemporary affairs. His POEMS OF SLAVERY were thin and nostalgic instead of forceful; tales of the past inspired (and prettified) EVANGELINE and THE COURTSHIP OF MILES STANDISH. American history prompted one of his most vigorous ballads, PAUL REVERE'S RIDE, a poem that has never lost its power as a story told in swinging rhyme.

Paul Revere's Ride

Listen, my children, and you shall hear
Of the midnight ride of Paul Revere,
On the eighteenth of April, in Seventy-five;
Hardly a man is now alive
Who remembers that famous day and year.

He said to his friend, "If the British march
By land or sea from the town tonight,
Hang a lantern aloft in the belfry arch
Of the North Church tower as a signal light—
One, if by land, and two, if by sea;
And I on the opposite shore will be,
Ready to ride and spread the alarm
Through every Middlesex village and farm,
For the country folk to be up and to arm."

Then he said, "Good night!" and with muffled oar
Silently rowed to the Charlestown shore,
Just as the moon rose over the bay,
Where swinging wide at her moorings lay
The Somerset, British man-of-war;

A phantom ship, with each mast and spar
Across the moon like a prison bar,
And a huge black hulk, that was magnified
By its own reflection in the tide.

Meanwhile, his friend, through alley and street,
Wanders and watches with eager ears,
Till in the silence around him he hears
The muster of men at the barrack door,
The sound of arms, and the tramp of feet,
And the measured tread of the grenadiers,
Marching down to their boats on the shore.

Then he climbed the tower of the Old North Church
By the wooden stairs, with stealthy tread,
To the belfry-chamber overhead,
And startled the pigeons from their perch
On the somber rafters, that round him made
Masses and moving shapes of shade—
By the trembling ladder, steep and tall,
To the highest window in the wall,
Where he paused to listen and look down
A moment on the roofs of the town,
And the moonlight flowing over all.

Beneath, in the churchyard, lay the dead,
In their night-encampment on the hill,
Wrapped in silence so deep and still
That he could hear, like a sentinel's tread,
The watchful night-wind, as it went
Creeping along from tent to tent,
And seeming to whisper, "All is well!"
A moment only he feels the spell
Of the place and the hour, and the secret dread
Of the lonely belfry and the dead;
For suddenly all his thoughts are bent
On a shadowy something far away,
Where the river widens to meet the bay—
A line of black that bends and floats
On the rising tide, like a bridge of boats.

Meanwhile, impatient to mount and ride,
Booted and spurred, with a heavy stride
On the opposite shore walked Paul Revere.

Now he patted his horse's side,
Now gazed at the landscape far and near,
Then, impetuous, stamped the earth,
And turned and tightened his saddle-girth;
But mostly he watched with eager search
The belfry-tower of the Old North Church,
As it rose above the graves on the hill,
Lonely and spectral and somber and still.
And lo! as he looks, on the belfry's height
A glimmer, and then a gleam of light!
He springs to the saddle, the bridle he turns,
But lingers and gazes, till full on his sight
A second lamp in the belfry burns!

A hurry of hoofs in a village street,
A shape in the moonlight, a bulk in the dark,
And beneath, from the pebbles, in passing, a spark
Struck out by a steed flying fearless and fleet;
That was all! And yet, through the gloom and the light,
The fate of a nation was riding that night;
And the spark struck out by that steed in his flight,
Kindled the land into flame with its heat.

He has left the village and mounted the steep,
And beneath him, tranquil and broad and deep,
Is the Mystic, meeting the ocean tides;
And under the alders that skirt its edge,
Now soft on the sand, now loud on the ledge,
Is heard the tramp of his steed as he rides.

It was twelve by the village clock
When he crossed the bridge into Medford town.
He heard the crowing of the cock,
And the barking of the farmer's dog,
And felt the damp of the river fog,
That rises after the sun goes down.

It was one by the village clock,
When he galloped into Lexington.
He saw the gilded weathercock
Swim in the moonlight as he passed,
And the meeting-house windows, blank and bare,
Gaze at him with a spectral glare,
As if they already stood aghast
At the bloody work they would look upon.

It was two by the village clock,
When he came to the bridge in Concord town.
He heard the bleating of the flock,
And the twitter of birds among the trees,
And felt the breath of the morning breeze
Blowing over the meadows brown.
And one was safe and asleep in his bed
Who at the bridge would be first to fall,
Who that day would be lying dead,
Pierced by a British musket-ball.

You know the rest. In the books you have read,
How the British Regulars fired and fled—
How the farmers gave them ball for ball,
From behind each fence and farmyard wall,
Chasing the redcoats down the lane,
Then crossing the fields to emerge again
Under the trees at the turn of the road,
And only pausing to fire and load.
So through the night rode Paul Revere;
And so through the night went his cry of alarm
To every Middlesex village and farm—
A cry of defiance, and not of fear,
A voice in the darkness, a knock at the door,
And a word that shall echo forevermore!
For, borne on the night-wind of the Past,
Through all our history, to the last,
In the hour of darkness and peril and need,
The people will waken and listen to hear
The hurrying hoofbeats of that steed,
And the midnight message of Paul Revere.

At twenty-four Longfellow married Mary Potter, daughter of a Portland judge. A dozen years after her death in childbed, the poet took a second wife, the lovely Frances Elizabeth Appleton. One afternoon, thirty years later, Mrs. Longfellow was sealing up some envelopes, and the burning wax fell on her flimsy dress, which immediately caught fire. Although Longfellow extinguished the blaze, she was so badly burned that she died the next morning. Longfellow never recovered from the shock. He continued to write and travel, but "the household poet" was no longer at home in the world. He died March 24, 1882, and his death was mourned in Europe as well as America. England set up his marble bust in the Poets' Corner of Westminster Abbey.

While it is true that Longfellow's facility too often betrays him into fatuousness, and his didacticism, as Friedrich Schoenemann says, "turns the poet of the people into a poet for the pedagogues," his serenity is apparent even in his literary poems. Greater poets have penned tributes to Chaucer and Milton; none have written more quietly and sympathetically of "the poet of the dawn" and the "mighty undulations" of England's "sightless bard."

Chaucer

An old man in a lodge within a park;
  The chamber walls depicted all around
  With portraitures of huntsman, hawk, and hound,
  And the hurt deer. He listeneth to the lark,
Whose song comes with the sunshine through the dark
  Of painted glass in leaden lattice bound;
  He listeneth and he laugheth at the sound,
  Then writeth in a book like any clerk.
He is the poet of the dawn, who wrote
  The Canterbury Tales, and his old age
  Made beautiful with song; and as I read
I hear the crowing cock, I hear the note
  Of lark and linnet, and from every page
  Rise odors of ploughed field or flowery mead.

Milton

I pace the sounding sea-beach and behold
  How the voluminous billows roll and run,
  Upheaving and subsiding, while the sun
  Shines through their sheeted emerald far unrolled
And the ninth wave, slow gathering fold by fold
  All its loose-flowing garments into one,
  Plunges upon the shore, and floods the dun
  Pale reach of sands, and changes them to gold.
So in majestic cadence rise and fall
  The mighty undulations of thy song,
  O sightless bard, England's Mæonides!
And ever and anon, high over all
  Uplifted, a ninth wave superb and strong,
  Floods all the soul with its melodious seas.

Although Longfellow has been justly criticized for putting into ambling verse everything he heard, read, and remembered, the best of his poetry is not bookish. If he relies too often on mere naturalness and the quiet *Abendstimmung,* his lines are tender and transparent.

The Day Is Done

The day is done, and the darkness
  Falls from the wings of Night,
As a feather is wafted downward
  From an eagle in his flight.

I see the lights of the village
  Gleam through the rain and the mist,
And a feeling of sadness comes o'er me
  That my soul cannot resist:

A feeling of sadness and longing,
  That is not akin to pain,
And resembles sorrow only
  As the mist resembles the rain.

Come, read to me some poem,
  Some simple and heartfelt lay,
That shall soothe this restless feeling,
  And banish the thoughts of day.

Not from the grand old masters,
  Not from the bards sublime,
Whose distant footsteps echo
  Through the corridors of Time.

For, like strains of martial music,
  Their mighty thoughts suggest
Life's endless toil and endeavor;
  And tonight I long for rest.

Read from some humbler poet,
  Whose songs gushed from his heart,
As showers from the clouds of summer,
  Or tears from the eyelids start:

Who, through long days of labor,
  And nights devoid of ease,
Still heard in his soul the music
  Of wonderful melodies.

Such songs have power to quiet
  The restless pulse of care,
And come like the benediction
  That follows after prayer.

Then read from the treasured volume
  The poem of thy choice,
And lend to the rhyme of the poet
  The beauty of thy voice.

And the night shall be filled with music,
  And the cares, that infest the day,
Shall fold their tents, like the Arabs,
  And as silently steal away.

Nature

As a fond mother, when the day is o'er,
  Leads by the hand her little child to bed,
  Half willing, half reluctant to be led,
  And leave his broken playthings on the floor,
Still gazing at them through the open door,
  Nor wholly reassured and comforted
  By promises of others in their stead,
  Which, though more splendid, may not please him more;
So Nature deals with us, and takes away
  Our playthings one by one, and by the hand
  Leads us to rest so gently, that we go
Scarce knowing if we wish to go or stay,
  Being too full of sleep to understand
  How far the unknown transcends the what we know.

Hymn to the Night

I heard the trailing garments of the Night
  Sweep through her marble halls!
I saw her sable skirts all fringed with light
  From the celestial walls.

I felt her presence, by its spell of might,
  Stoop o'er me from above;
The calm, majestic presence of the Night,
  As of the one I love.

I heard the sounds of sorrow and delight,
  The manifold, soft chimes,
That fill the haunted chambers of the Night,
  Like some old poet's rhymes.

From the cool cisterns of the midnight air
  My spirit drank repose;
The fountain of perpetual peace flows there—
  From those deep cisterns flows.

O holy Night! from thee I learn to bear
  What man has borne before.
Thou layest thy finger on the lips of Care,
  And they complain no more.

Peace! Peace! Orestes-like I breathe this prayer!
  Descend with broad-winged flight,
The welcome, the thrice-prayed for, the most fair,
  The best-beloved Night!

EDGAR ALLAN POE

[1809–1849]

THE stormy, star-crossed life of Edgar Allan Poe was prefigured in his youth. His parents were actors, and he was born, January 19, 1809, in Boston, Massachusetts, during one of their spasmodic peregrinations. Less than a year after his birth, his father disappeared. Two years later his mother died, and the child Edgar was adopted by John Allan, a prosperous merchant of Richmond, Virginia, who gave him a home as well as his middle name.

Young Poe entered boyhood with every advantage. His foster father sent him to an exclusive school in England and to the University of Virginia, but, by the time he was seventeen, Poe already exhibited the combination of weakness and recklessness which was to plague him the rest of his life. He drank and ran into debt, and was obliged to leave the university before he was eighteen. The period was one of painful confusion. Poe had become engaged to a pretty girl of fifteen; returning to Richmond in disgrace, he learned that his Sarah Elmira was about to be married. He quarreled with his foster father, and ran away from home. He enlisted in the army, and published his first volume, TAMERLANE AND OTHER POEMS, five months after his eighteenth birthday. It is significant that the book was published anonymously "By a Bostonian" and that the motto chosen for the title page was a couplet from Cowper:

> Young heads are giddy, and young hearts are warm,
> And make mistakes for manhood to reform.

As a first step toward "reform" Poe returned South, patched up the quarrel with his foster father, and visited his aunt, Mrs. Maria Clemm, her seven-year-old daughter Virginia, and his brother William Henry, who was dying of drink and consumption. Mr. Allan made it possible for Poe to enter West Point in his twenty-second year. Six months later Poe was dismissed for disobeying orders.

Repudiated by his foster father, Poe was now homeless and penniless. Resolved to earn his living by hack-work, he came to New York and worked as a proofreader. From this time on the outcast fought a losing struggle with poverty, illness, and alcohol. He drove himself to creation; he wrote desperately in every medium and on every subject—short stories, essays, poems, analyses of handwriting, a plagiarized book on conchology. At twenty-four he achieved momentary success when his story MS. FOUND IN A BOTTLE won a prize; the award was fifty dollars. At twenty-six the "weary, wayworn wanderer" married his cousin Virginia, then thirteen years old and tubercular. Poe's next ten years were a succession of brief triumphs and long defeats. He was irregularly engaged as editor and regularly discharged. He disappeared for days and was brought home delirious; he could no longer exist without stimulants. For every friend he made he lost two. He fluttered for a while in literary dovecotes among the "female poets" of the day, a bedraggled raven among the twitterers. The situation became hopeless. In a frantic effort to live on the little money that he had borrowed and Mrs. Clemm had begged, Poe moved the battered family to Fordham, then a little village thirteen miles out of New York. Here Poe was in such need that he could not afford stamps to mail his manuscripts or wood to heat the stove. His old army coat served as a blanket, and Virginia was warmed by a tortoise-shell cat that slept on her bosom. At Fordham Virginia died, and Poe collapsed completely.

Poe was now thirty-eight, obviously neurotic and almost insanely depressed. He turned to various women for platonic friendship and mothering. At thirty-nine he became practically engaged to the widowed Sarah Helen Whitman, who was forty-five; at the same time he wrote passionate letters to Mrs. Richmond ("Annie"), a Massachusetts married woman. He attempted suicide, and was saved because his stomach could not tolerate the overdose. Pursued by hallucinations, Poe disappeared in Baltimore. On October 3, 1849, he was found in a tavern, "his face haggard and unwashed, his hair unkempt, and his whole physique repulsive." On October 7, 1849, he died in a Baltimore hospital.

Although criticism has raged about Poe's character and the final importance of his poetry, his original and intense genius cannot be questioned. The quality of his gift as well as the tragedy of his life is indicated in the words of Sir Francis Bacon which are on the Poe Memorial Gate at West Point: "There is no exquisite beauty without some strangeness in the proportion."

Strangeness is the chief characteristic of Poe's multiform work. It is manifest in the lyric TO HELEN which stems from his youth and which fulfills Poe's attempt to create "pure poetry"—"no mere appreciation of the beauty before us, but a wild effort to reach the beauty above."

TO HELEN was Poe's tribute to Mrs. Jane Stanard, mother of one of his boyhood friends, and sixteen years older than Poe. She died when the poet was fifteen, and he haunted her grave with morbid persistence. So great was Poe's fixation that when he proposed to another woman twenty years later, he compared her to "the friend of my boyhood, the tenderest of this world's most womanly souls, and an angel to my forlorn and darkened nature."

To Helen

Helen, thy beauty is to me
  Like those Nicéan barks of yore,
That gently, o'er a perfumed sea,
  The weary, way-worn wanderer bore
  To his own native shore.

On desperate seas long wont to roam,
  Thy hyacinth hair, thy classic face,
Thy Naiad airs have brought me home
  To the glory that was Greece,
  And the grandeur that was Rome.

Lo! in yon brilliant window-niche
  How statue-like I see thee stand,
The agate lamp within thy hand!
  Ah, Psyche, from the regions which
  Are Holy-Land!

Toward the end of his career Poe's conduct became so erratic that he seemed to leave reality. Too distracted to make decisions, he evaded action; unable to choose between security and emotional fantasy, he hoped, somehow, to achieve both. He could give up neither the wealthy widow, Mrs. Whitman, nor the fluttering Annie Richmond, who appears as the unhappy heroine of FOR ANNIE and the backward-longing ANNABEL LEE. As was inevitable, he lost both.

Annabel Lee

It was many and many a year ago,
  In a kingdom by the sea,
That a maiden there lived whom you may know
  By the name of Annabel Lee;–
And this maiden she lived with no other thought
  Than to love and be loved by me.

She was a child and I was a child,
  In this kingdom by the sea,
But we loved with a love that was more than love–
  I and my Annabel Lee–
With a love that the winged seraphs of Heaven
  Coveted her and me.

And this was the reason that, long ago,
  In this kingdom by the sea,
A wind blew out of a cloud, by night
  Chilling my Annabel Lee;
So that her highborn kinsmen came
  And bore her away from me,
To shut her up in a sepulchre
  In this kingdom by the sea.

The angels, not half so happy in Heaven,
  Went envying her and me:
Yes! that was the reason (as all men know,
  In this kingdom by the sea)
That the wind came out of the cloud, chilling
  And killing my Annabel Lee.

But our love it was stronger by far than the love
  Of those who were older than we—
  Of many far wiser than we—
And neither the angels in Heaven above
  Nor the demons down under the sea,
Can ever dissever my soul from the soul
  Of the beautiful Annabel Lee:—

For the moon never beams without bringing me dreams
  Of the beautiful Annabel Lee;
And the stars never rise but I see the bright eyes
  Of the beautiful Annabel Lee;
And so, all the night-tide, I lie down by the side
Of my darling, my darling, my life and my bride,
  In her sepulchre there by the sea—
  In her tomb by the sounding sea.

This indefiniteness affected Poe's work. Recognizing it, he made it part of his program. "A poem, in my opinion," wrote Poe, "is opposed to a work of science by having, for its immediate object, an indefinite instead of a definite pleasure—being a poem only so far as this object is attained." Although Poe's definition is so restricted that it is false, he lived up to it. There are few recognizable emotions and no "messages" in his lines; Poe scarcely ever united penetrating experience with persuasive words. Words were his strength and weakness; words fascinated and betrayed him. With few exceptions, Poe's most often quoted poems are his worst. THE RAVEN is a declamation piece in which the serious idea is made ridiculous by cheap theatricalism, hypnotic rhythm, and a comic rhyme scheme. THE BELLS is a childish piling up of sounds, a wearisome echolalia; as George Barker recently wrote, it "is not a poem, it is a game." Emerson spoke of Poe as the "jingle man," and there is some basis for the characterization. But the best of his poems move with the magic of unreality, with the impossible but inescapable logic of a dream.

To One in Paradise

Thou wast all that to me, love,
  For which my soul did pine—
A green isle in the sea, love,
  A fountain and a shrine,
All wreathed with fairy fruits and flowers,
  And all the flowers were mine.

Ah, dream too bright to last!
  Ah, starry Hope! that didst arise
But to be overcast!
  A voice from out the Future cries,
"On! on!"—but o'er the Past
  (Dim gulf!) my spirit hovering lies
Mute, motionless, aghast!

For, alas! alas! with me
  The light of Life is o'er!
No more—no more—no more—
  (Such language holds the solemn sea
To the sands upon the shore)
  Shall bloom the thunder-blasted tree,
Or the stricken eagle soar!

And all my days are trances,
  And all my nightly dreams
Are where thy gray eye glances,
  And where thy footstep gleams—
In what ethereal dances,
  By what eternal streams.

A Dream Within a Dream

Take this kiss upon thy brow!
And, in parting from you now,
Thus much let me avow—
You are not wrong, to deem
That my days have been a dream;
Yet if Hope has flown away
In a night, or in a day,

In a vision, or in none,
Is it therefore the less *gone?*
All that we see or seem
Is but a dream within a dream.

I stand amid the roar
Of a surf-tormented shore,
And I hold within my hand
Grains of the golden sand—
How few! yet how they creep
Through my fingers to the deep,
While I weep—while I weep!
O God! can I not grasp
Them with a tighter clasp?
O God! can I not save
One from the pitiless wave?
Is *all* that we see or seem
But a dream within a dream?

The Sleeper

At midnight, in the month of June,
I stand beneath the mystic moon.
An opiate vapor, dewy, dim,
Exhales from out her golden rim,
And, softly dropping, drop by drop,
Upon the quiet mountain-top,
Steals drowsily and musically
Into the universal valley.
The rosemary nods upon the grave;
The lily lolls upon the wave;
Wrapping the fog about its breast,
The ruin molders into rest;
Looking like Lethe, see! the lake
A conscious slumber seems to take,
And would not, for the world, awake.
All beauty sleeps!—and lo! where lies
Irene, with her destinies!

O lady bright! can it be right,
This window open to the night?
The wanton airs, from the tree-top,
Laughingly through the lattice drop;

The bodiless airs, a wizard rout,
Flit through thy chamber in and out,
And wave the curtain canopy
So fitfully, so fearfully,
Above the closed and fringéd lid
'Neath which thy slumbering soul lies hid,
That, o'er the floor, and down the wall,
Like ghosts the shadows rise and fall.
O lady dear, hast thou no fear?
Why and what art thou dreaming here?
Sure thou art come o'er far-off seas,
A wonder to these garden trees!
Strange is thy pallor: strange thy dress:
Strange, above all, thy length of tress,
And all this solemn silentness!

The lady sleeps. Oh, may her sleep,
Which is enduring, so be deep!
Heaven have her in its sacred keep!
This chamber changed for one more holy,
This bed for one more melancholy,
I pray to God that she may lie
Forever with unopened eye,
While the pale sheeted ghosts go by.

My love, she sleeps. Oh, may her sleep,
As it is lasting, so be deep!
Soft may the worms about her creep!
Far in the forest, dim and old,
For her may some tall vault unfold:
Some vault that oft hath flung its black
And winged panels fluttering back,
Triumphant, o'er the crested palls
Of her grand family funerals;
Some sepulchre, remote, alone,
Against whose portal she hath thrown,
In childhood, many an idle stone:
Some tomb from out whose sounding door
She ne'er shall force an echo more,
Thrilling to think, poor child of sin,
It was the dead who groaned within!

The Haunted Palace

In the greenest of our valleys
  By good angels tenanted,
Once a fair and stately palace—
  Radiant palace—reared its head.
In the monarch Thought's dominion—
  It stood there!
Never seraph spread a pinion
  Over fabric half so fair!

Banners yellow, glorious, golden,
  On its roof did float and flow,
(This—all this—was in the olden
  Time long ago),
And every gentle air that dallied,
  In that sweet day,
Along the ramparts plumed and pallid,
  A winged odor went away.

Wanderers in that happy valley,
  Through two luminous windows, saw
Spirits moving musically,
  To a lute's well-tuned law,
Round about a throne where, sitting,
  (Porphyrogene!) [1]
In state his glory well befitting,
  The ruler of the realm was seen.

And all with pearl and ruby glowing
  Was the fair palace door,
Through which came flowing, flowing, flowing.
  And sparkling evermore,
A troop of Echoes, whose sweet duty
  Was but to sing,
In voices of surpassing beauty,
  The wit and wisdom of their king.

But evil things, in robes of sorrow,
  Assailed the monarch's high estate.
(Ah, let us mourn!—for never morrow
  Shall dawn upon him, desolate!)

[1] *Of royal blood.*

And round about his home the glory
  That blushed and bloomed,
Is but a dim-remembered story
  Of the old time entombed.

And travellers, now, within that valley,
  Through the red-litten windows see
Vast forms, that move fantastically
  To a discordant melody,
While, like a ghastly rapid river,
  Through the pale door
A hideous throng rush out forever
  And laugh—but smile no more.
from THE FALL OF THE HOUSE OF USHER

The future may rate Poe as a poet and author of bizarre tales less highly than as the inventor of the short story whose descendants in fiction are such masters of deduction as Conan Doyle and such experts in pseudo science as Jules Verne and H. G. Wells. It is possible that Poe's lurid history may continue to overshadow his work; it becomes progressively harder to believe in his misty mid-region of dank tarns, dim lakes, and scoriac rivers—especially since his life was so much more terrible than his museum of Gothic horrors. But there can be no doubt about the persistence of his aim, a pure passion of dedication, and the spell of his strange and melancholy music. Poe himself said it in ROMANCE:

That little time with lyre and rhyme
To while away—forbidden things!
My heart would feel to be a crime
Unless it trembled with the strings.

Too often Poe wallows in ornate banalities, in a gaudy tastelessness. But there are, as in the powerful THE CITY IN THE SEA, the moments of ascending beauty, unearthly radiance. Poe's world is the "ultimate, dim Thule," a realm forsaken and ghost-ridden. But if the landscape is dark, it is enchanted; and, though the outlines are wavering, they are drawn to the last shadowy inlet.

The City in the Sea

Lo! Death has reared himself a throne
In a strange city lying alone
Far down within the dim West,
Where the good and the bad and the worst and the best
Have gone to their eternal rest.
There shrines and palaces and towers
(Time-eaten towers that tremble not!)
Resemble nothing that is ours.
Around, by lifting winds forgot,
Resignedly beneath the sky
The melancholy waters lie.

No rays from the holy heaven come down
On the long night-time of that town;
But light from out the lurid sea
Streams up the turrets silently—
Gleams up the pinnacles far and free—
Up domes—up spires—up kingly halls—
Up fanes—up Babylon-like walls—
Up shadowy long-forgotten bowers
Of sculptured ivy and stone flowers—
Up many and many a marvelous shrine
Whose wreathed friezes intertwine
The viol, the violet, and the vine.

Resignedly beneath the sky
The melancholy waters lie.
So blend the turrets and shadows there
That all seem pendulous in air,
While from a proud tower in the town
Death looks gigantically down.

There open fanes and gaping graves
Yawn level with the luminous waves;
But not the riches there that lie
In each idol's diamond eye—
Not the gaily-jeweled dead
Tempt the waters from their bed;
For no ripples curl, alas!
Along that wilderness of glass—

No swellings tell that winds may be
Upon some far-off happier sea—
No heavings hint that winds have been
On seas less hideously serene.

But lo, a stir is in the air!
The wave—there is a movement there!
As if the towers had thrust aside,
In slightly sinking, the dull tide—
As if their tops had feebly given
A void within the filmy Heaven.
The waves have now a redder glow—
The hours are breathing faint and low—
And when, amid no earthly moans,
Down, down that town shall settle hence,
Hell, rising from a thousand thrones,
Shall do it reverence.

ALFRED TENNYSON

[1809–1892]

UNLIKE most poets, Alfred Tennyson was reared in comfort and died in the peerage. The fourth of twelve children, he was born August 6, 1809, at Somersby, in Lincolnshire, and the placid scenery of his childhood is continually reflected in his work. Precocious as a child, he composed blank verse at the age of eight, wrote hundreds of lines in imitation of Pope at the age of ten, and at twelve made an analysis of Milton's SAMSON AGONISTES. At eighteen, a few months before he entered Trinity College, Cambridge, he collaborated with his brother Charles on his first published volume, POEMS BY TWO BROTHERS.

At Cambridge Tennyson became the center of an admiring group which included Arthur Henry Hallam, who was to be memorialized by the poet, and Edward FitzGerald, who achieved his own immortality. At twenty-one, while still an undergraduate, Tennyson published his POEMS, CHIEFLY LYRICAL. Two years later he presented a larger collection, POEMS, and received his first rude public affront.

The same critic who had attacked Keats in THE QUARTERLY REVIEW castigated the young Tennyson for his voluptuousness, his ornate images, his few metrical innovations and errors in taste. He belittled Tennyson's fecundity and scorned the "self-assured prodigy" as "another star in that galaxy of poetry of which the lamented Keats was the harbinger." The sneer is the more astonishing since this early volume contained some of Tennyson's most accomplished poems, such as THE LADY OF SHALOTT, THE LOTOS EATERS, THE MILLER'S DAUGHTER, and MARIANA.

Mariana

"Mariana in the moated grange."—MEASURE FOR MEASURE

With blackest moss the flower-plots
  Were thickly crusted, one and all:
The rusted nails fell from the knots
  That held the peach to the garden-wall.
The broken sheds look'd sad and strange:
  Unlifted was the clinking latch;
  Weeded and worn the ancient thatch
Upon the lonely moated grange.
    She only said, "My life is dreary,
      He cometh not," she said;
    She said, "I am aweary, aweary,
      I would that I were dead!"

Her tears fell with the dews at even;
  Her tears fell ere the dews were dried;
She could not look on the sweet heaven,
  Either at morn or eventide.
After the flitting of the bats,
  When thickest dark did trance the sky,
  She drew her casement-curtain by,
And glanced athwart the glooming flats.
    She only said, "The night is dreary,
      He cometh not," she said;
    She said, "I am aweary, aweary,
      I would that I were dead!"

Upon the middle of the night,
  Waking she heard the night-fowl crow:

The cock sung out an hour ere light:
  From the dark fen the oxen's low
Came to her: without hope of change,
  In sleep she seem'd to walk forlorn,
  Till cold winds woke the gray-eyed morn
About the lonely moated grange.
    She only said, "The day is dreary,
      He cometh not," she said;
    She said, "I am aweary, aweary,
      I would that I were dead!"

About a stone-cast from the wall
  A sluice with blacken'd waters slept,
And o'er it many, round and small,
  The cluster'd marish-mosses crept.
Hard by a poplar shook alway,
  All silver-green with gnarlèd bark:
  For leagues no other tree did mark
The level waste, the rounding gray.
    She only said, "My life is dreary,
      He cometh not," she said;
    She said, "I am aweary, aweary,
      I would that I were dead!"

And ever when the moon was low,
  And the shrill winds were up and away,
In the white curtain, to and fro,
  She saw the gusty shadow sway.
But when the moon was very low,
  And wild winds bound within their cell,
  The shadow of the poplar fell
Upon her bed, across her brow.
    She only said, "The night is dreary,
      He cometh not," she said;
    She said, "I am aweary, aweary,
      I would that I were dead!"

All day within the dreamy house,
  The doors upon their hinges creak'd;
The blue fly sung in the pane; the mouse
  Behind the mouldering wainscot shriek'd,
Or from the crevice peer'd about.
  Old faces glimmer'd thro' the doors,
  Old footsteps trod the upper floors,

Old voices called her from without.
  She only said, "The day is dreary,
    He cometh not," she said;
  She said, "I am aweary, aweary,
    I would that I were dead!"

The Miller's Daughter

It is the miller's daughter,
  And she is grown so dear, so dear,
That I would be the jewel
  That trembles at her ear:
For hid in ringlets day and night,
I'd touch her neck so warm and white.

And I would be the girdle
  About her dainty, dainty waist,
And her heart would beat against me,
  In sorrow and in rest:
And I should know if it beat right,
I'd clasp it round so close and tight.

And I would be the necklace,
  And all day long to fall and rise
Upon her balmy bosom,
  With her laughter or her sighs:
And I would lie so light, so light,
I scarce should be unclasped at night.

The bond between Tennyson and Hallam was unusually close. It grew firmer when, upon graduation, the two friends volunteered for a few months in the Spanish insurgent army, and was cemented when Hallam became betrothed to Tennyson's sister. It was tragically broken when, three years later, Hallam burst a blood vessel and died before he was twenty-three. Tennyson was so affected that he withdrew from ordinary activities; even his health was impaired. His long IN MEMORIAM A. H. H. is not only a record of his grief but a revelation of Tennyson's philosophy, the conflict of faith and doubt and final affirmation.

FROM

In Memoriam A. H. H.

PROEM

Strong Son of God, immortal Love,
  Whom we, that have not seen thy face,
  By faith, and faith alone, embrace,
Believing where we cannot prove;

Thine are these orbs of light and shade;
  Thou madest Life in man and brute;
  Thou madest Death; and lo, thy foot
Is on the skull which thou hast made.

Thou wilt not leave us in the dust;
  Thou madest man, he knows not why,
  He thinks he was not made to die;
And thou hast made him: thou art just.

Thou seemest human and divine,
  The highest, holiest manhood, thou.
  Our wills are ours, we know not how;
Our wills are ours, to make them thine.

Our little systems have their day;
  They have their day and cease to be;
  They are but broken lights of thee,
And thou, O Lord, art more than they.

We have but faith: we cannot know,
  For knowledge is of things we see;
  And yet we trust it comes from thee,
A beam in darkness: let it grow.

Let knowledge grow from more to more,
  But more of reverence in us dwell;
  That mind and soul, according well,
May make one music as before,

But vaster. We are fools and slight;
  We mock thee when we do not fear:
  But help thy foolish ones to bear;
Help thy vain worlds to bear thy light.

Forgive what seemed my sin in me;
  What seemed my worth since I began;
  For merit lives from man to man,
And not from man, O Lord, to thee.

Forgive my grief for one removed,
  Thy creature, whom I found so fair.
  I trust he lives in thee, and there
I find him worthier to be loved.

Forgive these wild and wandering cries,
  Confusions of a wasted youth;
  Forgive them where they fail in truth,
And in thy wisdom make me wise.

CALM IS THE MORN

Calm is the morn without a sound,
  Calm as to suit a calmer grief,
  And only through the faded leaf
The chestnut pattering to the ground:

Calm and deep peace on this high wold,
  And on these dews that drench the furze,
  And all the silvery gossamers
That twinkle into green and gold:

Calm and still light on yon great plain
  That sweeps with all its autumn bowers,
  And crowded farms and lessening towers,
To mingle with the bounding main:

Calm and deep peace in this wide air,
  These leaves that redden to the fall;
  And in my heart, if calm at all,
If any calm, a calm despair:

Calm on the seas, and silver sleep,
  And waves that sway themselves in rest,
  And dead calm in that noble breast
Which heaves but with the heaving deep.

OH YET WE TRUST

Oh yet we trust that somehow good
  Will be the final goal of ill,
  To pangs of nature, sins of will,
Defects of doubt, and taints of blood;

That nothing walks with aimless feet;
  That not one life shall be destroyed,
  Or cast as rubbish to the void,
When God hath made the pile complete;

That not a worm is cloven in vain;
  That not a moth with vain desire
  Is shriveled in a fruitless fire,
Or but subserves another's gain.

Behold, we know not anything;
  I can but trust that good shall fall
  At last—far off—at last, to all,
And every winter change to spring.

So runs my dream: but what am I?
  An infant crying in the night:
  An infant crying for the light:
And with no language but a cry.

RING OUT, WILD BELLS

Ring out, wild bells, to the wild sky,
  The flying cloud, the frosty light:
  The year is dying in the night;
Ring out, wild bells, and let him die.

Ring out the old, ring in the new,
  Ring, happy bells, across the snow:
  The year is going, let him go;
Ring out the false, ring in the true.

Ring out the grief that saps the mind,
  For those that here we see no more;
  Ring out the feud of rich and poor,
Ring in redress to all mankind.

Ring out a slowly dying cause,
  And ancient forms of party strife;
  Ring in the nobler modes of life,
With sweeter manners, purer laws.

Ring out the want, the care, the sin,
  The faithless coldness of the times;
  Ring out, ring out my mournful rhymes,
But ring the fuller minstrel in.

Ring out false pride in place and blood,
  The civic slander and the spite;
  Ring in the love of truth and right,
Ring in the common love of good.

Ring out old shapes of foul disease;
  Ring out the narrowing lust of gold;
  Ring out the thousand wars of old,
Ring in the thousand years of peace.

Ring in the valiant man and free,
  The larger heart, the kindlier hand;
  Ring out the darkness of the land,
Ring in the Christ that is to be.

After Hallam's death Tennyson underwent a long and unhappy period of apathy. He shunned society and turned his back upon those in power. He visited the Lake District but was reluctant to intrude upon Wordsworth, who had expressed a desire to meet the young poet. He sold the estate he had inherited, invested the proceeds in a "Patent Decorative Carving Company," and lost all his money. It was ten years before he could be induced to issue another volume.

Suddenly, with the publication of the two-volume edition of his POEMS in 1842, Tennyson became famous. He was acclaimed everywhere. Wordsworth hailed him as "decidedly the first of our living poets," and Sir Robert Peel bestowed upon him a pension of two hundred pounds a year. In 1850, at the age of forty-one, Tennyson was happily married to Emily Sellwood, to whom he had been engaged during fourteen years of poverty—"the peace of God came into my life when I wedded her"—and Queen Victoria appointed him poet laureate. Two years later his first child was born and was christened Hallam.

Fortitude had come back into Tennyson's life. In ULYSSES he firmly expressed the quality of courage. Here is the heroism which has "enjoyed greatly, suffered greatly," the determination to venture "beyond the utmost bound of human thought." It is true that the Victorian poet could not resist moralizing. But his was a moralizing age, and Tennyson lifted the strain to a triumphant persistence:

To strive, to seek, to find, and not to yield.

Ulysses

It little profits that an idle king,
By this still hearth, among these barren crags,
Matched with an aged wife, I mete and dole
Unequal laws unto a savage race,
That hoard, and sleep, and feed, and know not me.
I cannot rest from travel: I will drink
Life to the lees: all times I have enjoyed
Greatly, have suffered greatly, both with those
That loved me, and alone; on shore, and when
Through scudding drifts the rainy Hyades
Vext the dim sea. I am become a name;
For always roaming with a hungry heart
Much have I seen and known: cities of men
And manners, climates, councils, governments,
Myself not least, but honored of them all,—
And drunk delight of battle with my peers,
Far on the ringing plains of windy Troy.
I am a part of all that I have met;
Yet all experience is an arch wherethrough
Gleams that untraveled world, whose margin fades
For ever and for ever when I move.
How dull it is to pause, to make an end,
To rust unburnished, not to shine in use!
As though to breathe were life. Life piled on life
Were all too little, and of one to me
Little remains: but every hour is saved
From that eternal silence, something more,
A bringer of new things; and vile it were
For some three suns to store and hoard myself,
And this gray spirit yearning in desire
To follow knowledge, like a sinking star,
Beyond the utmost bound of human thought.

This is my son, mine own Telemachus,
To whom I leave the scepter and the isle—
Well-loved of me, discerning to fulfill
This labor, by slow prudence to make mild
A rugged people, and through soft degrees
Subdue them to the useful and the good.
Most blameless is he, centered in the sphere
Of common duties, decent not to fail
In offices of tenderness, and pay
Meet adoration to my household gods,
When I am gone. He works his work, I mine.
There lies the port: the vessel puffs her sail:
There gloom the dark broad seas. My mariners,
Souls that have toiled, and wrought, and thought with me—
That ever with a frolic welcome took
The thunder and the sunshine, and opposed
Free hearts, free foreheads—you and I are old;
Old age hath yet his honor and his toil;
Death closes all: but something ere the end,
Some work of noble note, may yet be done,
Not unbecoming men that strove with Gods.
The lights begin to twinkle from the rocks:
The long day wanes: the slow moon climbs: the deep
Moans round with many voices. Come, my friends,
'Tis not too late to seek a newer world.
Push off, and sitting well in order smite
The sounding furrows; for my purpose holds
To sail beyond the sunset, and the baths
Of all the western stars, until I die.
It may be that the gulfs will wash us down:
It may be we shall touch the Happy Isles,
And see the great Achilles, whom we knew.
Though much is taken, much abides; and though
We are not now that strength which in old days
Moved earth and heaven, that which we are, we are,—
One equal temper of heroic hearts,
Made weak by time and fate, but strong in will
To strive, to seek, to find, and not to yield.

From his forties until the end of his life, Tennyson's position as England's most popular poet was unchallenged. He wrote plays and poems with increasing energy; one of his dramas, BECKET, was successfully produced by Sir Henry Irving. He was often invited to read before Queen Victoria, and it was said that Her Majesty turned to Tennyson for her poetry as instinctively as she turned to Disraeli for her politics. This was natural enough, for Tennyson, as G. K. Chesterton tartly observed, "held a great many of the same views as Queen Victoria, though he was gifted with a more fortunate literary style."

In his early seventies Tennyson became intimately associated with Gladstone, then Prime Minister, and the two men made a voyage together to Norway and Denmark. Gladstone offered Tennyson a peerage and, after some hesitation, the poet accepted the honor. He was seventy-five years old. Nine years later, while reading Shakespeare's CYMBELINE, he died, October 6, 1892.

Tennyson has suffered from his adulators as well as from his detractors, and it has never been determined whether he merely reflected or helped to establish the smug optimism and sentimentality of his day. Many critics have pictured him as a cross between the people's traditional minstrel and the conventional maiden aunt. He has been attacked for primness; for his transformation of Malory's MORTE D'ARTHUR, that savage pageant of the Middle Ages, into the IDYLLS OF THE KING, that Victorian Sunday-school picnic; for celebrating small ideas rather than great causes. But if Tennyson lacks passion, he does not lack picturesqueness. His craftsmanship redeems his too-perfect niceties; in his hands the devices of poetry become supple and self-concealing. The variety of his music has seldom been surpassed. THE PRINCESS is a veritable anthology of lyrics.

Songs from The Princess

SWEET AND LOW

Sweet and low, sweet and low,
  Wind of the western sea,
Low, low, breathe and blow,
  Wind of the western sea!
Over the rolling waters go,
Come from the dying moon, and blow,
  Blow him again to me;
While my little one, while my pretty one, sleeps.

Sleep and rest, sleep and rest,
  Father will come to thee soon;

Rest, rest, on mother's breast,
  Father will come to thee soon;
Father will come to his babe in the nest,
Silver sails all out of the west
  Under the silver moon:
Sleep, my little one, sleep, my pretty one, sleep.

THE SPLENDOR FALLS

The splendor falls on castle walls
  And snowy summits old in story:
The long light shakes across the lakes,
  And the wild cataract leaps in glory.
Blow, bugle, blow, set the wild echoes flying,
Blow, bugle; answer, echoes, dying, dying, dying.

O hark, O hear! how thin and clear,
  And thinner, clearer, farther going!
O sweet and far from cliff and scar
  The horns of Elfland faintly blowing!
Blow, let us hear the purple glens replying:
Blow, bugle; answer, echoes, dying, dying, dying.

O love, they die in yon rich sky,
  They faint on hill or field or river:
Our echoes roll from soul to soul,
  And grow for ever and for ever.
Blow, bugle, blow, set the wild echoes flying,
And answer, echoes, answer, dying, dying, dying.

TEARS, IDLE TEARS

Tears, idle tears, I know not what they mean,
Tears from the depth of some divine despair
Rise in the heart, and gather to the eyes,
In looking on the happy autumn-fields,
And thinking of the days that are no more.

Fresh as the first beam glittering on a sail,
That brings our friends up from the underworld,
Sad as the last which reddens over one
That sinks with all we love below the verge;
So sad, so fresh, the days that are no more.

Ah, sad and strange as in dark summer dawns
The earliest pipe of half-awakened birds
To dying ears, when unto dying eyes
The casement slowly grows a glimmering square;
So sad, so strange, the days that are no more.

Dear as remembered kisses after death,
And sweet as those by hopeless fancy feigned
On lips that are for others; deep as love,
Deep as first love, and wild with all regret;
O Death in Life, the days that are no more!

THY VOICE IS HEARD

Thy voice is heard through rolling drums
That beat to battle where he stands;
Thy face across his fancy comes,
And gives the battle to his hands.
A moment, while the trumpets blow,
He sees his brood about thy knee;
The next, like fire he meets the foe,
And strikes him dead for thine and thee.

HOME THEY BROUGHT HER WARRIOR

Home they brought her warrior dead:
She nor swooned, nor uttered cry:
All her maidens, watching, said,
"She must weep or she will die."

Then they praised him, soft and low,
Called him worthy to be loved,
Truest friend and noblest foe;
Yet she neither spoke nor moved.

Stole a maiden from her place,
Lightly to the warrior stept,
Took the face-cloth from the face;
Yet she neither moved nor wept.

Rose a nurse of ninety years,
Set his child upon her knee—
Like summer tempest came her tears—
"Sweet my child, I live for thee."

ASK ME NO MORE

Ask me no more. The moon may draw the sea;
The cloud may stoop from heaven and take the shape,
With fold to fold, of mountain or of cape;
But O too fond, when have I answered thee?
Ask me no more.

Ask me no more. What answer should I give?
I love not hollow cheek or faded eye;
Yet, O my friend, I will not have thee die!
Ask me no more, lest I should bid thee live;
Ask me no more.

Ask me no more. Thy fate and mine are sealed;
I strove against the stream and all in vain;
Let the great river take me to the main.
No more, dear love, for at a touch I yield;
Ask me no more.

NOW SLEEPS THE CRIMSON PETAL

Now sleeps the crimson petal, now the white;
Nor waves the cypress in the palace walk;
Nor winks the gold fin in the porphyry font.
The firefly wakens. Waken thou with me.

Now droops the milk-white peacock like a ghost,
And like a ghost she glimmers on to me.

Now lies the Earth all Danaë to the stars,
And all thy heart lies open unto me.

Now slides the silent meteor on, and leaves
A shining furrow, as thy thoughts in me.

Now folds the lily all her sweetness up,
And slips into the bosom of the lake;
So fold thyself, my dearest, thou, and slip
Into my bosom and be lost in me.

An Idyl

Come down, O maid, from yonder mountain height.
What pleasure lives in height (the shepherd sang)
In height and cold, the splendor of the hills?
But cease to move so near the heavens, and cease
To glide a sunbeam by the blasted pine,
To sit a star upon the sparkling spire;
And come, for Love is of the valley, come,
For Love is of the valley, come thou down
And find him; by the happy threshold, he,
Or hand in hand with Plenty in the maize,
Or red with spirted purple of the vats,
Or foxlike in the vine; nor cares to walk
With Death and Morning on the silver horns,
Nor wilt thou snare him in the white ravine,
Nor find him dropt upon the firths of ice
That huddling slant in furrow-cloven falls
To roll the torrent out of dusky doors.
But follow; let the torrent dance thee down
To find him in the valley; let the wild
Lean-headed eagles yelp alone, and leave
The monstrous ledges there to slope, and spill
Their thousand wreaths of dangling water-smoke
That like a broken purpose waste in air.
So waste not thou, but come; for all the vales
Await thee; azure pillars of the hearth
Arise to thee; the children call, and I
Thy shepherd pipe, and sweet is every sound,
Sweeter thy voice, but every sound is sweet;
Myriads of rivulets hurrying thro' the lawn,
The moan of doves in immemorial elms,
And murmuring of innumerable bees.

from THE PRINCESS

Although Tennyson did not assume the prophetic mantle of a Nostradamus, some of his poems embody prophecies much less veiled than the cryptic French astrologer's. In LOCKSLEY HALL, which contains the most famous of Tennyson's predictions, the hero prefigured the future long before the days of the airplane, and saw:

. . . the heavens fill with commerce, argosies of magic sails,
Pilots of the purple twilight, dropping down with costly bales;

Heard the heavens fill with shouting, and there rained a ghastly dew
From the nations' airy navies grappling in the central blue;

Far along the world-wide whisper of the southwind rushing warm,
With the standards of the peoples plunging through the thunder-
storm.

Tennyson, envisioning the materialism of an age "staled by frequence, shrunk by usage," looked beyond international conflicts. He predicted that humanity would rise above its material and competitive successes to a universal brotherhood.

Till the war-drum throbbed no longer, and the battle-
flags were furled
In the Parliament of man, the Federation of the world.

It is, however, not in prophecy but in lucidity and music that Tennyson excels, in what Edmund Gosse terms "his broad undulating sweetness." It is eminently a power of clear condensation which distinguishes Tennyson's lyrics, which concentrates the spirit of the long IN MEMORIAM in the four brief stanzas of BREAK, BREAK, BREAK and in the valedictory CROSSING THE BAR, which Tennyson requested to be placed at the end of his poems.

Break, Break, Break

Break, break, break,
On thy cold gray stones, O Sea!
And I would that my tongue could utter
The thoughts that arise in me.

O well for the fisherman's boy,
That he shouts with his sister at play!
O well for the sailor lad,
That he sings in his boat on the bay!

And the stately ships go on
To their haven under the hill;
But O for the touch of a vanished hand,
And the sound of a voice that is still!

Break, break, break,
  At the foot of thy crags, O Sea!
But the tender grace of a day that is dead
  Will never come back to me.

The Eagle

He clasps the crag with crooked hands:
Close to the sun in lonely lands,
Ringed with the azure world, he stands.

The wrinkled sea beneath him crawls;
He watches from his mountain walls,
And like a thunderbolt he falls.

Flower in the Crannied Wall

Flower in the crannied wall,
I pluck you out of the crannies,
I hold you here, root and all, in my hand,
Little flower—but *if* I could understand
What you are, root and all, and all in all,
I should know what God and man is.

In Love, If Love Be Love

In Love, if Love be Love, if Love be ours,
Faith and unfaith can ne'er be equal powers:
Unfaith in aught is want of faith in all.

It is the little rift within the lute,
That by and by will make the music mute,
And ever widening slowly silence all.

The little rift within the lover's lute
Or little pitted speck in garnered fruit,
That rotting inward slowly moulders all.

It is not worth the keeping: let it go:
But shall it? answer, darling, answer, no.
And trust me not at all or all in all.

from IDYLLS OF THE KING

Crossing the Bar

Sunset and evening star,
  And one clear call for me!
And may there be no moaning of the bar,
  When I put out to sea,

But such a tide as moving seems asleep,
  Too full for sound and foam,
When that which drew from out the boundless deep
  Turns again home.

Twilight and evening bell,
  And after that the dark!
And may there be no sadness of farewell,
  When I embark;

For though from out our bourne of Time and Place
  The flood may bear me far,
I hope to see my Pilot face to face
  When I have crossed the bar.

EDWARD FITZGERALD

[1809–1883]

THE name of Edward FitzGerald is so bound up with the name of Omar Khayyám that (to English readers, at least) the biography of one inevitably involves the other. To establish the odd relationship, we must go back almost eight centuries to a village in northeast Persia.

The manufacture of carpets, for which the district of Khorasan is still noted, was practiced by old Ibráhim, who specialized in tough woven cloth for tents. So, when his son was born at Naishapur in Khorasan, the child was named Ghiáthuddin Abulfath Omar bin Ibráhim al-Khayyámi, which signified nothing more portentous than that Omar was the true son of al-Khayyámi, or the Tentmaker. The boy seems to have followed his father's trade. But during youth he frequented the haunts of the dialecticians, the wandering Sufis, whom he enjoyed and distrusted, and the scientists, whom he feared and worshiped. Soon he was dabbling with, and attempting to fuse, mysticism and mathematics. He became known as Persia's outstanding astronomer. He wrote an authoritative text on algebra; he revised the old astronomical tables; he persuaded the Sultan Malik-Shah to reform the calendar.

When he was not consulting the stars and balancing equations, Omar permitted himself the luxury of poetry. His chief indulgence was the celebration of two intoxicants: verse and the vine. Before he died in 1123 he had composed some five hundred epigrams in quatrains, or *rubais,* peculiar in rhyme and pungent in tone. The stanzas were, for the most part, independent; they embodied a tight and self-contained idea. But they were connected, if not unified, by a careless philosophy: a light, free-thinking hedonism, a frank appeal to enjoy the pleasures of life without too much reflection.

The astronomer died; the tables were again revised; and for six centuries Omar's work was unknown to the Western world. It remained for a secluded English country gentleman to establish the Persian poet-mathematician among the glories of literature. Edward FitzGerald was born at Bredfield House on March 31, 1809, into a well-to-do family. Educated at Trinity College, Cambridge, where he became a friend of Thackeray, FitzGerald did the leisurely studying and traveling expected of him, cultivated music and botany, and, even as a young man, was relieved when he was permitted to retire to the Suffolk countryside. There he settled himself snugly, devoted his days to his friends and his flowers, and led a pleasantly unproductive life until his late forties.

In his fiftieth year, FitzGerald printed a little paper-bound pamphlet of translations which he called THE RUBÁIYÁT OF OMAR KHAYYÁM. The pamphlet was published anonymously; it attracted little attention. A year later, in 1860, the poets Swinburne and Rossetti discovered the poem; but, legend to the contrary, the work did not thereupon leap into immediate popularity. Eight years passed before a second edition was called for.

Suddenly the poem became a favorite. The mocking quatrains of the eleventh-century Persian were used as a challenge by the nineteenth-century undergraduates, repeated by rebellious lovers, and flung out as a credo by restless men and women. There had already been an undercurrent of protest against the rigidity and moral earnestness of the period. The RUBÁIYÁT served as a small but concentrated expression of the revolt against Victorian conventions, the prevailing smugness, the acquiescent prudery. Religion had been defied by science; noble ideals had come into conflict with practical necessity; smoke-belching machinery was threatening to dispel the once pervasive "sweetness and light." The "message" of FitzGerald's RUBÁIYÁT was something of a slogan and something of an escape. It turned away from commercial imperialism toward an idealized paganism. Half defiantly, half desperately, the younger men and women made FitzGerald-Omar a vogue. Perhaps the most-quoted quatrain of the century was the alluring:

> A Book of Verses underneath the Bough
> A Jug of Wine, a Loaf of Bread—and Thou
>   Beside me singing in the Wilderness—
> Oh, Wilderness were Paradise enow!

Here was a panacea, half tonic, half opiate. It was not so much a compromise of values as a combination of desirables: an avoidance of ordinary existence and a participation in a richer, if somewhat unreal, life. This was the opposite of Mrs. Grundy's middle-class taboos; this was a very denial of negations. "Wine, Woman, and Song" were affirmed and glorified in a mounting paean to pleasure. A Persian Ecclesiastes, through the medium of a staid English squire, assured a perplexed generation that all was vanity; that the glories of this world are better than Paradise to come; that it is wise to take the cash and let the credit go; that life is a meaningless game played by helpless pieces; that worldly ambitions turn into ashes; that in the end—an end which comes all too quickly—wine is a more trustworthy friend and a better comforter than all the philosophers.

Thrust into undesired notice by THE RUBÁIYÁT, FitzGerald attempted for a while to live up to his reputation. He published translations of the AGAMEMNON and the two OEDIPUS tragedies of Sophocles; he wrote a biography of Bernard Barton, his father-in-law and friend of Charles Lamb; he made a compilation of the homely verse of George Crabbe. But he was not designed to be an Eminent Victorian. He was, even among retired gentlemen, unusually reticent ("an idle fellow, one whose friendships were more like loves"), and his wit was kept for private communications. It was not until the letters of "Old Fitz" were published that FitzGerald's personal charm was revealed. He sank back into semiobscurity as though it were a comfortable couch, and died, almost a quarter of a century after the publication of his masterpiece, on June 14, 1883. His end was characteristically calm. He slipped from life painlessly, almost imperceptibly.

Appreciation of Omar-FitzGerald continued to grow. Tennyson wrote a reminiscent poem lauding the "golden Eastern lay" of "that large infidel, your Omar." It is said that when Thomas Hardy was dying in his eighty-eighth year, he asked to have his favorite stanza read to him. It was the verse which runs:

> O Thou, who Man of baser Earth didst make,
> And ev'n with Paradise devise the Snake:
>   For all the Sin wherewith the Face of Man
> Is blackened—Man's forgiveness give—and take!

No longer dependent upon the vagaries of a period or the tricks of fashion, THE RUBÁIYÁT has outlived cults and commentaries. It has had its influences and imitators. Its spirit is reflected in Housman's A SHROPSHIRE LAD (see page 1023) in which fortitude and fatalism are pitted against each other and finally reconciled. Omar might well have applauded the Shropshire lad's cynical conclusion that

> . . . malt does more than Milton can
> To justify God's way to man—

But the philosophy scarcely matters. The cynicism may be persistent; the mood may be (as FitzGerald himself said) "a desperate sort of thing, at the bottom of all thinking men's minds." But the tune is so gay that even the pessimism seems blithe. The quick but melodic turns of the poem "tease us out of thought." We may argue about the meaning, but we are indisputably held by the music.

FitzGerald's first version of THE RUBÁIYÁT contained only seventy-five quatrains; subsequently he enlarged the work and changed the order of the stanzas. It is generally considered that the best arrangement is the fourth edition, which is the one reprinted here.

The Rubáiyát of Omar Khayyám

Wake! for the Sun, who scattered into flight
The Stars before him from the Field of Night,
  Drives Night along with them from Heav'n, and strikes
The Sultán's Turret with a Shaft of Light.

Before the phantom of False morning died,
Methought a Voice within the Tavern cried,
"When all the Temple is prepared within,
Why nods the drowsy Worshipper outside?"

And, as the cock crew, those who stood before
The Tavern shouted—"Open then the Door!
You know how little while we have to stay,
And, once departed, may return no more."

Now the New Year reviving old Desires,
The thoughtful Soul to Solitude retires,
Where the White Hand of Moses on the Bough
Puts out, and Jesus from the Ground suspires.

Iram indeed is gone with all his Rose,
And Jamshyd's Sev'n-ring'd Cup where no one knows;
But still a Ruby kindles in the Vine,
And many a Garden by the Water blows.

And David's lips are lockt; but in divine
High-piping Pehleví, with "Wine! Wine! Wine!
Red Wine!"—the Nightingale cries to the Rose
That sallow cheek of hers to incarnadine.

Come, fill the Cup, and in the fire of Spring
Your Winter-garment of Repentance fling:
The Bird of Time has but a little way
To flutter—and the Bird is on the Wing.

Whether at Naishápúr or Babylon,
Whether the Cup with sweet or bitter run,
The Wine of Life keeps oozing drop by drop,
The Leaves of Life keep falling one by one.

Each morn a thousand Roses brings, you say;
Yes, but where leaves the Rose of Yesterday?
And this first Summer month that brings the Rose
Shall take Jamshyd and Kaikobád away.

Well, let it take them! What have we to do
With Kaikobád the Great, or Kaikhosrú?
Let Zál and Rustum bluster as they will,
Or Hátim call to Supper—heed not you.

With me along the strip of Herbage strown
That just divides the desert from the sown,
  Where name of Slave and Sultán is forgot—
And Peace to Mahmúd on his golden Throne!

A Book of Verses underneath the Bough,
A Jug of Wine, a Loaf of Bread—and Thou
  Beside me singing in the Wilderness—
Oh, Wilderness were Paradise enow!

Some for the Glories of This World; and some
Sigh for the Prophet's Paradise to come;
  Ah, take the Cash, and let the Credit go,
Nor heed the rumble of a distant Drum!

Look to the blowing Rose about us—"Lo,
Laughing," she says, "into the world I blow,
  At once the silken tassel of my Purse
Tear, and its Treasure on the Garden throw."

And those who husbanded the Golden grain,
And those who flung it to the winds like Rain,
  Alike to no such aureate Earth are turned
As, buried once, Men want dug up again.

The Worldly Hope men set their Hearts upon
Turns Ashes—or it prospers; and anon,
  Like Snow upon the Desert's dusty Face,
Lighting a little hour or two—is gone.

Think, in this battered Caravanserai
Whose Portals are alternate Night and Day,
  How Sultán after Sultán with his Pomp
Abode his destined Hour, and went his way.

They say the Lion and the Lizard keep
The Courts where Jamshyd gloried and drank deep:
  And Bahrám, the great Hunter—the Wild Ass
Stamps o'er his Head, but cannot break his Sleep.

I sometimes think that never blows so red
The Rose as where some buried Cæsar bled;
  That every Hyacinth the Garden wears
Dropt in her Lap from some once lovely Head.

And this reviving Herb whose tender Green
Fledges the River-Lip on which we lean—
  Ah, lean upon it lightly! for who knows
From what once lovely Lip it springs unseen!

Ah, my Belovéd, fill the Cup that clears
To-day of past Regret and future Fears:
  To-morrow!—Why, To-morrow I may be
Myself with Yesterday's Sev'n thousand Years.

For some we loved, the loveliest and the best
That from his Vintage rolling Time hath prest,
  Have drunk their Cup a Round or two before,
And one by one crept silently to rest.

And we, that now make merry in the Room
They left, and Summer dresses in new bloom,
  Ourselves must we beneath the Couch of Earth
Descend—ourselves to make a Couch—for whom?

Ah, make the most of what we yet may spend,
Before we too into the Dust descend;
  Dust into Dust, and under Dust, to lie,
Sans Wine, sans Song, sans Singer, and—sans End!

Alike for those who for To-day prepare,
And those that after some To-morrow stare,
  A Muezzín from the Tower of Darkness cries,
"Fools, your Reward is neither Here nor There."

Why, all the Saints and Sages who discussed
Of the Two Worlds so wisely—they are thrust
  Like foolish Prophets forth; their Words to Scorn
Are scattered, and their Mouths are stopt with Dust.

Myself when young did eagerly frequent
Doctor and Saint, and heard great argument
  About it and about: but evermore
Came out by the same Door where in I went.

With them the seed of Wisdom did I sow,
And with mine own hand wrought to make it grow;
  And this was all the Harvest that I reaped—
"I came like Water, and like Wind I go."

Into this Universe, and *Why* not knowing
Nor *Whence,* like Water willy-nilly flowing;
  And out of it, as Wind along the Waste,
I know not *Whither,* willy-nilly blowing.

What, without asking, hither hurried *Whence?*
And, without asking, *Whither* hurried hence!
  Oh, many a Cup of this forbidden Wine
Must drown the memory of that insolence!

Up from Earth's Centre through the Seventh Gate
I rose, and on the Throne of Saturn sate,
  And many a Knot unravelled by the Road;
But not the Master-knot of Human Fate.

There was the Door to which I found no Key;
There was the Veil through which I might not see:
  Some little talk awhile of Me and Thee
There was—and then no more of Thee and Me.

Earth could not answer; nor the Seas that mourn
In flowing Purple, of their Lord forlorn;
  Nor rolling Heaven, with all his Signs revealed
And hidden by the sleeve of Night and Morn.

Then of the Thee in Me who works behind
The Veil, I lifted up my hands to find
  A Lamp amid the Darkness; and I heard,
As from Without—"The Me within Thee blind!"

Then to the Lip of this poor earthen Urn
I leaned, the Secret of my Life to learn:
  And Lip to Lip it murmured—"While you live,
Drink!—for, once dead, you never shall return."

I think the Vessel, that with fugitive
Articulation answered, once did live,
  And drink; and Ah! the passive Lip I kissed,
How many Kisses might it take—and give!

For I remember stopping by the way
To watch a Potter thumping his wet Clay;
  And with its all-obliterated Tongue
It murmured—"Gently, Brother, gently, pray!"

And has not such a Story from of Old
Down Man's successive generations rolled
  Of such a clod of saturated Earth
Cast by the Maker into Human mould?

And not a drop that from our Cups we throw
For Earth to drink of, but may steal below
  To quench the fire of Anguish in some Eye
There hidden—far beneath, and long ago.

As then the Tulip for her morning sup,
Of Heav'nly Vintage from the soil looks up,
  Do you devoutly do the like, till Heav'n
To Earth invert you—like an empty Cup.

Perplext no more with Human or Divine,
To-morrow's tangle to the winds resign,
  And lose your fingers in the tresses of
The Cypress-slender Minister of Wine.

And if the Wine you drink, the Lip you press,
End in what All begins and ends in—Yes;
  Think then you are To-day what Yesterday
You were—To-morrow you shall not be less.

So when the Angel of the darker Drink
At last shall find you by the river-brink,
  And offering his Cup, invite your Soul
Forth to your Lips to quaff—you shall not shrink.

Why, if the Soul can fling the Dust aside,
And naked on the Air of Heaven ride,
  Were't not a Shame—were't not a Shame for him
n this clay carcase crippled to abide?

'Tis but a Tent where takes his one day's rest
A Sultán to the realm of Death addrest;
  The Sultán rises, and the dark Ferrásh
Strikes, and prepares it for another Guest.

And fear not lest Existence closing your
Account, and mine, should know the like no more;
  The Eternal Sákí[1] from that Bowl has poured
Millions of Bubbles like us, and will pour.

[1] *The cupbearer.*

When You and I behind the Veil are past,
Oh, but the long, long while the World shall last,
  Which of our Coming and Departure heeds
As the Sea's self should heed a pebble-cast.

A Moment's Halt—a momentary taste
Of Being from the Well amid the Waste—
  And Lo!—the phantom Caravan has reached
The Nothing it set out from—Oh, make haste!

Would you that spangle of Existence spend
About The Secret—quick about it, Friend!
  A Hair perhaps divides the False and True—
And upon what, prithee, may life depend?

A Hair perhaps divides the False and True—
Yes; and a single Alif were the clue—
  Could you but find it—to the Treasure-house,
And peradventure to The Master too;

Whose secret Presence, through Creation's veins
Running Quicksilver-like, eludes your pains;
  Taking all shapes from Máh to Máhi; and
They change and perish all—but He remains;

A moment guessed—then back behind the Fold
Immerst of Darkness round the Drama rolled
  Which, for the Pastime of Eternity,
He doth himself contrive, enact, behold.

But if in vain, down on the stubborn floor
Of Earth, and up to Heav'n's unopening Door,
  You gaze To-day, while You are You—how then
To-morrow, when You shall be You no more?

Waste not your Hour, nor in the vain pursuit
Of This and That endeavor and dispute;
  Better be jocund with the fruitful Grape
Than sadden after none, or bitter, Fruit.

You know, my Friends, with what a brave Carouse
I made a Second Marriage in my house;
  Divorced old barren Reason from my Bed,
And took the Daughter of the Vine to Spouse.

For "Is" and "Is-not" though with Rule and Line
And "Up-and-down" by Logic I define,
  Of all that one should care to fathom, I
Was never deep in anything but—Wine.

Ah, but my Computations, People say,
Reduced the Year to better reckoning?—Nay,
  'Twas only striking from the Calendar
Unborn To-morrow, and dead Yesterday.

And lately, by the Tavern Door agape,
Came shining through the Dusk an Angel Shape
  Bearing a Vessel on his Shoulder; and
He bid me taste of it; and 'twas—the Grape!

The Grape that can with Logic Absolute
The Two and Seventy jarring Sects confute:
  The sovereign Alchemist that in a trice
Life's leaden metal into Gold transmute:

The mighty Mahmúd, Allah-breathing Lord,
That all the misbelieving and black Horde
  Of fears and Sorrows that infest the Soul
Scatters before him with his whirlwind Sword.

Why, be this Juice the growth of God, who dare
Blaspheme the twisted tendril as a Snare?
  A Blessing, we should use it, should we not?
And if a Curse—why, then, Who set it there?

I must abjure the Balm of Life, I must,
Scared by some After-reckoning ta'en on trust,
  Or lured with Hope of some Diviner Drink,
To fill the Cup—when crumbled into Dust!

O threats of Hell and Hopes of Paradise!
One thing at least is certain—*This* Life flies;
  One thing is certain and the rest is Lies;
The Flower that once has blown for ever dies.

Strange, is it not? that of the myriads who
Before us passed the door of Darkness through,
  Not one returns to tell us of the Road,
Which to discover we must travel too.

The Revelations of Devout and Learned
Who rose before us, and as Prophets burned,
  Are all but Stories, which, awoke from Sleep
They told their comrades, and to Sleep returned.

I sent my soul through the Invisible,
Some letter of that After-life to spell:
  And by and by my Soul returned to me,
And answered "I Myself am Heav'n and Hell:"

Heav'n but the Vision of fulfilled Desire,
And Hell the Shadow from a Soul on fire
  Cast on the Darkness into which Ourselves,
So late emerged from, shall so soon expire.

We are no other than a moving row
Of Magic Shadow-shapes that come and go
  Round with the Sun-illumined Lantern held
In Midnight by the Master of the Show;

But helpless Pieces of the Game He plays
Upon this Chequer-board of Nights and Days;
  Hither and thither moves, and checks, and slays,
And one by one back in the Closet lays.

The Ball no question makes of Ayes and Noes,
But Here or There as strikes the Player goes;
  And He that tossed you down into the Field,
He knows about it all—HE knows—HE knows!

The Moving Finger writes; and, having writ,
Moves on: nor all your Piety nor Wit
  Shall lure it back to cancel half a Line,
Nor all your Tears wash out a Word of it.

And that inverted Bowl they call the Sky,
Whereunder crawling cooped we live and die,
  Lift not your hands to *It* for help—for It
As impotently moves as you or I.

With Earth's first Clay They did the Last Man knead,
And there of the Last Harvest sowed the Seed:
  And the first Morning of Creation wrote
What the Last Dawn of Reckoning shall read.

Yesterday *This* Day's Madness did prepare;
To-morrow's Silence, Triumph, or Despair:
  Drink! for you know not whence you came, nor why:
Drink! for you know not why you go, nor where.

What! from his helpless Creature be repaid
Pure Gold for what he lent him dross-allayed–
  Sue for a Debt we never did contract,
And cannot answer–Oh, the sorry trade!

O Thou, who didst with Pitfall and with Gin
Beset the Road I was to wander in,
  Thou wilt not with Predestined Evil round
Enmesh, and then impute my Fall to Sin!

O Thou, who Man of baser Earth didst make,
And ev'n with Paradise devise the Snake:
  For all the Sin wherewith the Face of Man
Is blackened–Man's forgiveness give–and take!

As under cover of departing Day
Slunk hunger-stricken Ramazán away,
  Once more within the Potter's house alone
I stood, surrounded by the Shapes of Clay.

Shapes of all Sorts and Sizes, great and small,
That stood along the floor and by the wall;
  And some loquacious Vessels were; and some
Listen'd perhaps, but never talked at all.

Said one among them–"Surely not in vain
My substance of the common Earth was ta'en
  And to this Figure moulded, to be broke,
Or trampled back to shapeless Earth again."

Then said a Second–"Ne'er a peevish Boy
Would break the Bowl from which he drank in joy;
  And He that with his hand the Vessel made
Will surely not in after Wrath destroy."

After a momentary silence spake
Some Vessel of a more ungainly Make;
  "They sneer at me for leaning all awry:
What! did the Hand then of the Potter shake?"

Whereat some one of the loquacious Lot—
I think a Súfi pipkin—waxing hot—
"All this of Pot and Potter—Tell me then,
Who is the Potter, pray, and who the Pot?"

"Why," said another, "Some there are who tell
Of one who threatens he will toss to Hell
The luckless Pots he marred in making—Pish!
He's a Good Fellow, and 'twill all be well."

"Well," murmured one, "Let whoso make or buy,
My Clay with long Oblivion is gone dry:
But fill me with the old familiar Juice,
Methinks I might recover by and by."

So while the Vessels one by one were speaking,
The little Moon looked in that all were seeking:
And then they jogged each other, "Brother! Brother!
Now for the Porter's shoulder-knot a-creaking!"

Ah, with the Grape my fading Life provide,
And wash the Body whence the Life has died,
And lay me, shrouded in the living Leaf,
By some not unfrequented Garden-side.

That ev'n my buried Ashes such a snare
Of Vintage shall fling up into the Air
As not a True-believer passing by
But shall be overtaken unaware.

Indeed the Idols I have loved so long
Have done my credit in this World much wrong:
Have drowned my Glory in a shallow Cup,
And sold my Reputation for a Song.

Indeed, indeed, Repentance oft before
I swore—but was I sober when I swore?
And then and then came Spring, and Rose-in-hand
My thread-bare Penitence apieces tore.

And much as Wine has played the Infidel,
And robbed me of my Robe of Honor—Well,
I wonder often what the Vintners buy
One half so precious as the stuff they sell.

Yet Ah, that Spring should vanish with the Rose!
That Youth's sweet-scented manuscript should close!
  The Nightingale that in the branches sang,
Ah whence, and whither flown again, who knows!

Would but the desert of the Fountain yield
One glimpse—if dimly, yet indeed, revealed,
  To which the fainting Traveller might spring,
As springs the trampled herbage of the field!

Would but some wingéd Angel ere too late
Arrest the yet unfolded Roll of Fate,
  And make the stern Recorder otherwise
Enregister, or quite obliterate!

Ah Love! could you and I with Him conspire
To grasp this sorry Scheme of Things entire,
  Would not we shatter it to bits—and then
Remould it nearer to the Heart's Desire!

Yon rising Moon that looks for us again—
How oft hereafter will she wax and wane;
  How oft hereafter rising look for us
Through this same Garden—and for *one* in vain!

And when like her, O Sákí, you shall pass
Among the Guests Star-scattered on the Grass,
  And in your joyous errand reach the spot
Where I made One—turn down an empty Glass!

EDWARD LEAR

[1812–1888]

EDWARD LEAR never wanted to be known as a great humorist; he hoped—and tried hard—to be a great painter. Born in London, May 12, 1812, of Danish ancestry, he was the youngest of twelve children. Brought up by his sister, who was twenty-one years older than he, Edward suffered from asthma and epilepsy from the age of seven onward. Nevertheless, he lived through seventy-six restless years, and his malady seems to have interfered little with either his work or his play.

At twenty, already a gifted ornithologist, Lear published a set of drawings of the more uncommon parrots, a work which brought favorable comparisons with Audubon. The thirteenth Earl of Derby engaged him to paint his whole menagerie, and the water-colorist became a permanent favorite with the Derby family—it was for the fifteenth Earl of Derby that he designed his BOOK OF NONSENSE. After his success as a delineator of birds, he determined to become a landscape painter. For ten years he lived and studied abroad. But, although he was the most indefatigable of artisans, a draftsman whose accuracy was such that experts could recognize the geology of the country from Lear's sketches, he never became a successful artist.

Seeking new backgrounds for new stimuli, Lear visited Greece, explored unfrequented Calabria, penetrated the wilds of Albania, traveled to Constantinople, wintered on the Nile, and finally built himself a villa at San Remo, on the Italian Riviera, where he died January 30, 1888. He left countless canvases, water colors, and notebooks; one of his friends inherited over ten thousand of his designs.

It was in his thirty-fourth year that Lear interrupted his serious pursuits (including drawing lessons to Queen Victoria) to write his comic limericks, for which he provided the weird illustrations, and the fantastic poems which have become classics of their kind. Established for years in the nursery, such poems as THE YONGHY-BONGHY-BO and THE OWL AND THE PUSSY-CAT have been strangely revalued. In our own time T. S. Eliot has commended the purity of Lear's lyrical gift, and Robert Graves has found unsuspected emotional depths in THE DONG WITH A LUMINOUS NOSE, which seems to Mr. Graves "as tragic as the Greek legend of Cadmus seeking his lost Europa." Mr. Graves also believes that the song which Edward Lear lightly called CALICO PIE presents grief in terms of childish invention; to him it is "as poignant as the idea of Hamlet played by Burbage, the actor, as a comic part," and the little birds suggest "the familiar emblem of unrealized love." But one does not have to believe that Lear wore "the pantomime mask over a tear-stained face" to relish the delight of his laughing syllables.

Calico Pie

Calico pie,
The little birds fly
Down to the calico tree:
Their wings were blue,
And they sang "Tilly-loo!"
Till away they flew;
And they never came back to me.
They never came back,
They never came back,
They never came back to me!

Calico ban,
The little Mice ran
To be ready in time for tea;
Flippity flup,
They drank it all up,
And danced in the cup:
But they never came back to me;
They never came back,
They never came back,
They never came back to me.

Calico drum,
The Grasshoppers come,
The Butterfly, Beetle, and Bee,
Over the ground,
Around and round,
With a hop and a bound;
But they never came back to me:
They never came back,
They never came back,
They never came back to me.

Once in a while Lear exchanged sheer drollery for parody. INCIDENTS IN THE LIFE OF MY UNCLE ARLY is a burlesque of Wordsworth's sentimental RESOLUTION AND INDEPENDENCE, also known as THE LEECH-GATHERER. But it is the sheer pleasure in whimsical and unmeaning sound which draws the reader. THE OWL AND THE PUSSY-CAT and a half-dozen other wild whimsicalities have secured for Lear the affection of the world. He is eternal childhood's madcap laureate.

Incidents in the Life of My Uncle Arly

O my agéd Uncle Arly!
Sitting on a heap of Barley
    Through the silent hours of night—
Close beside a leafy thicket:—
On his nose there was a Cricket,
In his hat a Railway-Ticket;—
    (But his shoes were far too tight.)

Long ago, in youth, he squandered
All his goods away, and wandered
    To the Tiniskoop-hills afar.
There on golden sunsets blazing,
Every evening found him gazing—
Singing—"Orb! you're quite amazing!
    How I wonder what you are!"

Like the ancient Medes and Persians,
Always by his own exertions
    He subsisted on those hills;
Whiles—by teaching children spelling;
Or at times by merely yelling,
Or at intervals by selling
    "Propter's Nicodemus Pills."

Later, in his morning rambles
He perceived the moving brambles
    Something square and white disclose;
'Twas a First-class Railway-Ticket;
But, on stooping down to pick it
Off the ground, a pea-green Cricket
    Settled on my uncle's Nose.

Never—never more—oh! never
Did that Cricket leave him ever,
    Dawn or evening, day or night;
Clinging as a constant treasure,
Chirping with a cheerious measure.
Wholly to my uncle's pleasure;—
    (Though his shoes were far too tight.)

So for three-and-forty winters,
Till his shoes were worn to splinters,
    All those hills he wandered o'er—
Sometimes silent, sometimes yelling—
Till he came to Borley-Melling,
Near his old ancestral dwelling;—
    (But his shoes were far too tight.)

On a little heap of Barley
Died my agéd Uncle Arly,
    And they buried him one night—
Close beside the leafy thicket;
There—his hat and Railway-Ticket;
There—his ever-faithful Cricket;—
    (But his shoes were far too tight.)

The Owl and the Pussy-cat

The Owl and the Pussy-cat went to sea
  In a beautiful pea-green boat:
They took some honey, and plenty of money
  Wrapped up in a five-pound note.
The Owl looked up to the stars above,
  And sang to a small guitar,
"O lovely Pussy, O Pussy, my love,
  What a beautiful Pussy you are,
        You are,
        You are!
  What a beautiful Pussy you are!"

Pussy said to the Owl, "You elegant fowl,
  How charmingly sweet you sing!
Oh! let us be married; too long we have tarried:
  But what shall we do for a ring?"
They sailed away, for a year and a day,
  To the land where the bong-tree grows;
And there in a wood a Piggy-wig stood,
  With a ring at the end of his nose,
        His nose,
        His nose,
  With a ring at the end of his nose.

"Dear Pig, are you willing to sell for one shilling
  Your ring?" Said the Piggy, "I will."
So they took it away, and were married next day
  By the turkey who lives on the hill.
They dined on mince and slices of quince,
  Which they ate with a runcible spoon;
And hand in hand, on the edge of the sand,
  They danced by the light of the moon,
    The moon,
    The moon,
  They danced by the light of the moon.

ROBERT BROWNING

[1812–1889]

BROWNING and Tennyson spanned the nineteenth century—a longevity in startling contrast to the brief careers of Keats and Shelley. Both poets reflected the changing standards of their times: the economic struggles sharpened by the contradictory claims of science and religion, the grudging compromises and gradual reforms. Tennyson indicated the Victorian values from priggishness to liberalism; Browning emphasized the shift from abstract morality to psychological speculation.

Robert Browning, the most erudite of modern poets, never attended a university. Born May 7, 1812, in Camberwell, a suburb of London, Browning was educated in the cradle. His mother was the daughter of a German shipowner who had married a Scottish woman in Dundee. His father, a well-to-do official in the Bank of England, was unusually cultured: a good draftsman, a competent versifier, and a lover of the classics. He is pictured, in one of Browning's poems, as illustrating the siege of Troy by piling up chairs and tables for the beleaguered city; placing the boy on top of the pile in the role of Priam; calling the family cat Helen because she had so often been enticed from home; and pointing to the pony as Achilles sulking in the stable. His father's library of seven thousand volumes was supplemented by a few tutors, and Browning's literary career was determined in boyhood. At twelve he completed a collection of verses, INCONDITA, which he later destroyed. He discovered

Shelley during adolescence, and at twenty-one published his first volume, PAULINE; it is Shelleyan in idea and manner, the only work of Browning which is frankly imitative.

In his early twenties, Browning learned the delights of travel. He journeyed to Russia and the hill towns of Tuscany; he fell in love with Venice. "Italy," he declared, "was my university." He wrote a drama, PARACELSUS, in which the Renaissance physician seeks to save mankind; and Macready, the most influential actor-manager of the day, urged Browning to write or adapt a play for him. Browning took as his next subject the great Earl of Strafford, whose devotion to Charles I was his undoing, and Macready produced the play at Covent Garden in 1837. STRAFFORD was an instantaneous failure. Macready blamed the play; Browning blamed the actors. The poet swore he would never again be tempted to write for the theater, but in less than two years he was at work on new plays.

In his twenty-eighth year Browning published a long narrative poem so compressed in phrase and large in thought that it was dismissed as a piece of willful obscurity. The poem, SORDELLO, became the butt of literary London. Douglas Jerrold, who tried to read the book while recovering from a severe illness, thought he had lost his mind, and was reassured only when his wife confessed her own failure to understand it. Tennyson said that of SORDELLO's 5800 lines there were just two which he could comprehend. They were the first line of the poem:

> Who will may hear Sordello's story told

and the last line:

> Who would has heard Sordello's story told

and both were lies.

Although few could read SORDELLO with pleasure—few, indeed, read it at all—Browning's essential gift of characterization was apparent, if not yet acknowledged. Browning said it took him twenty-five years to recover from the work on the poem and its reception.

The poems which followed were more comprehensible and far more forcible. THE LOST LEADER was written upon Wordsworth's acceptance of the laureateship. Wordsworth was then seventy-three; and Browning, at thirty-one, recoiled from what he considered a reward for political defection and "a regular face-about of his party." Still influenced by Shelley, the young Browning could not forgive the old poet's "apostasy," his abandonment of liberalism.

The Lost Leader

Just for a handful of silver he left us,
  Just for a riband to stick in his coat—
Found the one gift of which fortune bereft us,
  Lost all the others she lets us devote;
They, with the gold to give, doled him out silver,
  So much was theirs who so little allowed:
How all our copper had gone for his service!
  Rags—were they purple, his heart had been proud!
We that had loved him so, followed him, honored him,
  Lived in his mild and magnificent eye,
Learned his great language, caught his clear accents,
  Made him our pattern to live and to die!
Shakespeare was of us, Milton was for us,
  Burns, Shelley, were with us,—they watch from their graves!
He alone breaks from the van and the freemen,
  He alone sinks to the rear and the slaves!

We shall march prospering,—not thro' his presence;
  Songs may inspirit us,—not from his lyre;
Deeds will be done,—while he boasts his quiescence,
  Still bidding crouch whom the rest bade aspire:
Blot out his name, then, record one lost soul more,
  One task more declined, one more footpath untrod,
One more triumph for devils and sorrow for angels,
  One wrong more to man, one more insult to God!
Life's night begins: let him never come back to us!
  There would be doubt, hesitation and pain,
Forced praise on our part—the glimmer of twilight,
  Never glad confident morning again!
Best fight on well, for we taught him,—strike gallantly,
  Menace our heart ere we master his own;
Then let him receive the new knowledge and wait us,
  Pardoned in Heaven, the first by the throne!

It is unlikely that Wordsworth saw THE LOST LEADER or, seeing it, realized that he had been attacked. Browning later regretted the youthful assault. In a mood that was partly disillusioned, partl self-exonerating, Browning wrote a companion piece, THE PATRIOT, a poem which grew out of Browning's sympathy with the revolution. Here a "world-loser and world-forsaker" pits his courage against the fickleness of the crowd, and the pathos of his defeat is heightened by the ironic tone of the poem.

The Patriot

It was roses, roses, all the way,
  With myrtle mixed in my path like mad:
The house-roofs seemed to heave and sway,
  The church-spires flamed, such flags they had,
A year ago on this very day!

The air broke into a mist with bells,
  The old walls rocked with the crowd and cries.
Had I said, "Good folk, mere noise repels—
  But give me your sun from yonder skies!"
They had answered, "And afterward, what else?"

Alack, it was I who leaped at the sun
  To give it my loving friends to keep!
Nought man could do, have I left undone:
  And you see my harvest, what I reap
This very day, now a year is run.

There's nobody on the house-tops now—
  Just a palsied few at the windows set;
For the best of the sight is, all allow,
  At the Shambles' Gate—or, better yet,
By the very scaffold's foot, I trow.

I go in the rain, and, more than needs,
  A rope cuts both my wrists behind;
And I think, by the feel, my forehead bleeds,
  For they fling, whoever has a mind,
Stones at me for my year's misdeeds.

Thus I entered, and thus I go!
  In triumphs, people have dropped down dead.
"Paid by the World,—what dost thou owe
  Me?" God might question: now instead,
'Tis God shall repay. I am safer so.

Browning's life was almost wholly given to his writing; its milestones are his books. His career was uneventful except for one romance, and that romance, as much a part of literature as anything Browning ever wrote, began in his thirty-third year. Elizabeth Barrett, a poet six years his senior and far more popular than he, had praised Browning in one of her poems. Although she was a confirmed invalid, guarded by a father who was a jealous and oppressive God—the very opposite of Browning's sympathetic father—Browning practically forced his way into the gloomy house, courted her passionately, and eloped with her to his rejuvenating Italy. Wordsworth expressed the hope that the two poets might understand each other.

For fifteen years the Brownings enjoyed a rich life in Italy. Theirs was a busy idyl. Mrs. Browning's health improved, and she gave birth to a son; the once hopeless recluse entertained visitors from England and America. Husband and wife grew deeply interested in Italian politics and art, and the new spirit stimulated a warmer poetry than either had previously written.

Song

The year's at the spring
And day's at the morn;
Morning's at seven;
The hill-side's dew-pearled;
The lark's on the wing;
The snail's on the thorn:
God's in his heaven—
All's right with the world!

from PIPPA PASSES

Song

The moth's kiss, first!
Kiss me as if you made believe
You were not sure, this eve,
How my face, your flower, had pursed
Its petals up; so, here and there
You brush it, till I grow aware
Who wants me, and wide open burst.

The bee's kiss, now!
Kiss me as if you entered gay
My heart at some noonday,
A bud that dares not disallow
The claim, so all is rendered up,
And passively its shattered cup
Over your head to sleep I bow.

from IN A GONDOLA

Two in the Campagna

I wonder do you feel today
  As I have felt since, hand in hand,
We sat down on the grass, to stray
  In spirit better through the land,
This morn of Rome and May?

For me, I touched a thought, I know,
  Has tantalized me many times,
(Like turns of thread the spiders throw
  Mocking across our path) for rhymes
To catch at and let go.

Help me to hold it! First it left
  The yellowing fennel, run to seed
There, branching from the brickwork's cleft,
  Some old tomb's ruin; yonder weed
Took up the floating weft,

Where one small orange cup amassed
  Five beetles—blind and green they grope
Among the honey-meal; and last,
  Everywhere on the grassy slope
I traced it. Hold it fast!

The champaign with its endless fleece
  Of feathery grasses everywhere!
Silence and passion, joy and peace,
  An everlasting wash of air—
Rome's ghost since her decease.

Such life here, through such length of hours
  Such miracles performed in play,

Such primal naked forms of flowers,
  Such letting Nature have her way
While Heaven looks from its towers!

How say you? Let us, O my dove,
  Let us be unashamed of soul,
As earth lies bare to heaven above!
  How is it under our control
To love or not to love?

I would that you were all to me,
  You that are just so much, no more,
Nor yours, nor mine, nor slave nor free!
  Where does the fault lie? What the core
O' the wound, since wound must be?

I would I could adopt your will,
  See with your eyes, and set my heart
Beating by yours, and drink my fill
  At your soul's springs—your part, my part
In life, for good and ill.

No. I yearn upward—touch you close,
  Then stand away. I kiss your cheek,
Catch your soul's warmth,—I pluck the rose
  And love it more than tongue can speak—
Then the good minute goes.

Already how am I so far
  Out of that minute? Must I go
Still like the thistle-ball, no bar,
  Onward, whenever light winds blow,
Fixed by no friendly star?

Just when I seemed about to learn!
  Where is the thread now? Off again!
The old trick! Only I discern
  Infinite passion and the pain
Of finite hearts that yearn.

Home-Thoughts, from Abroad

Oh, to be in England
Now that April's there,
And whoever wakes in England
Sees, some morning, unaware,
That the lowest boughs and the brush-wood sheaf
Round the elm-tree bole are in tiny leaf,
While the chaffinch sings on the orchard bough
In England—now!

And after April, when May follows,
And the whitethroat builds, and all the swallows!
Hark, where my blossomed pear-tree in the hedge
Leans to the field and scatters on the clover
Blossoms and dewdrops—at the bent-spray's edge—
That's the wise thrush; he sings each song twice over,
Lest you should think he never could recapture
The first fine careless rapture!
And though the fields look rough with hoary dew,
All will be gay when noontide wakes anew
The buttercups, the little children's dower,
—Far brighter than this gaudy melon-flower!

Evelyn Hope

Beautiful Evelyn Hope is dead!
  Sit and watch by her side an hour.
That is her book-shelf, this her bed;
  She plucked that piece of geranium-flower,
Beginning to die, too, in the glass.
  Little has yet been changed, I think—
The shutters are shut, no light may pass
  Save two long rays through the hinge's chink.

Sixteen years old when she died!
  Perhaps she had scarcely heard my name;
It was not her time to love: beside,
  Her life had many a hope and aim,
Duties enough and little cares,
  And now was quiet, now astir—
Till God's hand beckoned unawares,
  And the sweet white brow is all of her.

Is it too late then, Evelyn Hope?
  What, your soul was pure and true,
The good stars met in your horoscope,
  Made you of spirit, fire and dew—
And, just because I was thrice as old,
  And our paths in the world diverged so wide
Each was nought to each, must I be told?
  We were fellow mortals, naught beside?

No, indeed! for God above
  Is great to grant, as mighty to make,
And creates the love to reward the love,—
  I claim you still, for my own love's sake!
Delayed it may be for more lives yet,
  Through worlds I shall traverse, not a few;
Much is to learn, much to forget
  Ere the time be come for taking you.

But the time will come,—at last it will,
  When, Evelyn Hope, what meant (I shall say)
In the lower earth, in the years long still,
  That body and soul so pure and gay?
Why your hair was amber, I shall divine,
  And your mouth of your own geranium's red—
And what you would do with me, in fine,
  In the new life come in the old one's stead.

I have lived (I shall say) so much since then,
  Given up myself so many times,
Gained me the gains of various men,
  Ransacked the ages, spoiled the climes;
Yet one thing, one, in my soul's full scope.
  Either I missed or itself missed me—
And I want and find you, Evelyn Hope!
  What is the issue? let us see!

I loved you, Evelyn, all the while!
  My heart seemed full as it could hold;
There was place and to spare for the frank young smile
  And the red young mouth and the hair's young gold.
So, hush—I will give you this leaf to keep—
  See, I shut it inside the sweet cold hand.
There, that is our secret: go to sleep!
  You will wake, and remember, and understand.

Life in a Love

Escape me?
Never—
Beloved!
While I am I, and you are you,
So long as the world contains us both,
Me the loving and you the loth,
While the one eludes, must the other pursue.
My life is a fault at last, I fear:
It seems too much like a fate, indeed
Though I do my best I shall scarce succeed.
But what if I fail of my purpose here?
It is but to keep the nerves at strain,
To dry one's eyes and laugh at a fall,
And baffled, get up and begin again,—
So the chase takes up one's life, that's all.
While, look but once from your farthest bound
At me so deep in the dust and dark,
No sooner the old hope drops to ground
Than a new one, straight to the self-same mark,
I shape me—
Ever
Removed!

Meeting at Night

The grey sea and the long black land;
And the yellow half-moon large and low;
And the startled little waves that leap
In fiery ringlets from their sleep,
As I gain the cove with pushing prow,
And quench its speed i' the slushy sand.

Then a mile of warm sea-scented beach;
Three fields to cross till a farm appears;
A tap at the pane, the quick sharp scratch
And blue spurt of a lighted match,
And a voice less loud, through its joys and fears,
Than the two hearts beating each to each!

With MEN AND WOMEN, published in his forty-fourth year, Browning reached the peak of his career. No poet of the period—indeed, no poet of any time, with the exception of Shakespeare—had so successfully embodied in poetry the complex variations of the human spirit. Browning turned ideas into persons. He gave philosophy substance and made thought take on the form of personal experience. A dramatic poet, he was not a dramatist. It was not in his plays but in his tersely packed poems that his dramatic power is manifest. Never since Shakespeare has there been such a pageant of extraordinary figures. The range is indicated even in a few of Browning's most familiar pieces. Here, in MY LAST DUCHESS, is the brutal and egocentric duke, about to marry the daughter of a count, discussing the marriage settlement with the count's legate; and here, unseen, is his victim, the late duchess. Here, in SOLILOQUY OF THE SPANISH CLOISTER, is the narrow-minded, ritual-loving friar with his sustaining hatred of the ascetic Brother Lawrence, and his plans to ruin the gentle monk. Here, in INCIDENT OF THE FRENCH CAMP, a poem founded upon an actual event, is heroic action without ostentation. And here, in A WOMAN'S LAST WORD, is an uncanny capture of the feminine tone, an amazing assumption of character in which the delicate adjustments of marriage are revealed by the wife.

My Last Duchess

SCENE: FERRARA

That's my last Duchess painted on the wall,
Looking as if she were alive. I call
That piece a wonder, now: Frà Pandolf's hands
Worked busily a day, and there she stands.
Will't please you sit and look at her? I said
"Frà Pandolf" by design, for never read
Strangers like you that pictured countenance,
The depth and passion of its earnest glance,
But to myself they turned (since none puts by
The curtain I have drawn for you, but I)
And seemed as they would ask me, if they durst,
How such a glance came there; so, not the first
Are you to turn and ask thus. Sir, 'twas not
Her husband's presence only, called that spot
Of joy into the Duchess' cheek: perhaps

Frà Pandolf chanced to say, "Her mantle laps
Over my Lady's wrist too much," or "Paint
Must never hope to reproduce the faint
Half-flush that dies along her throat"; such stuff
Was courtesy, she thought, and cause enough
For calling up that spot of joy. She had
A heart—how shall I say?—too soon made glad,
Too easily impressed; she liked whate'er
She looked on, and her looks went everywhere.
Sir, 'twas all one! My favor at her breast,
The dropping of the daylight in the West,
The bough of cherries some officious fool
Broke in the orchard for her, the white mule
She rode with round the terrace—all and each
Would draw from her alike the approving speech,
Or blush, at least. She thanked men,—good; but thanked
Somehow—I know not how—as if she ranked
My gift of a nine-hundred-years'-old name
With anybody's gift. Who'd stoop to blame
This sort of trifling? Even had you skill
In speech—(which I have not)—to make your will
Quite clear to such an one, and say, "Just this
Or that in you disgusts me; here you miss,
Or there exceed the mark"—and if she let
Herself be lessoned so, nor plainly set
Her wits to yours, forsooth, and made excuse,
—E'en then would be some stooping, and I choose
Never to stoop. Oh, sir, she smiled, no doubt,
Whene'er I passed her; but who passed without
Much the same smile? This grew; I gave commands;
Then all smiles stopped together. There she stands
As if alive. Will't please you rise? We'll meet
The company below, then. I repeat,
The Count your master's known munificence
Is ample warrant that no just pretence
Of mine for dowry will be disallowed;
Though his fair daughter's self, as I avowed
At starting, is my object. Nay, we'll go
Together down, sir! Notice Neptune, though,
Taming a sea-horse, thought a rarity,
Which Claus of Innsbruck cast in bronze for me!

Soliloquy of the Spanish Cloister

Gr-r-r—there go, my heart's abhorrence!
  Water your damned flower-pots, do!
If hate killed men, Brother Lawrence,
  God's blood, would not mine kill you!
What? your myrtle-bush wants trimming?
  Oh, that rose has prior claims—
Needs its leaden vase filled brimming?
  Hell dry you up with its flames!

At the meal we sit together;
  Salve tibi! I must hear
Wise talk of the kind of weather,
  Sort of season, time of year:
Not a plenteous cork-crop: scarcely
  Dare we hope oak-galls, I doubt:
What's the Latin name for "parsley"?
  What's the Greek name for Swine's Snout?

Whew! We'll have our platter burnished,
  Laid with care on our own shelf!
With a fire-new spoon we're furnished,
  And a goblet for ourself,
Rinsed like something sacrificial
  Ere 'tis fit to touch our chaps—
Marked with L. for our initial!
  (He-he! There his lily snaps!)

Saint, forsooth! While brown Dolores
  Squats outside the Convent bank
With Sanchicha, telling stories,
  Steeping tresses in the tank,
Blue-black, lustrous, thick like horsehairs,
  —Can't I see his dead eye glow,
Bright as 'twere a Barbary corsair's?
  (That is, if he'd let it show!)

When he finishes refection,
  Knife and fork he never lays
Cross-wise, to my recollection,
  As do I, in Jesu's praise.

I, the Trinity illustrate,
  Drinking watered orange-pulp—
In three sips the Arian frustrate;
  While he drains his at one gulp!

Oh, those melons! If he's able
  We're to have a feast; so nice!
One goes to the Abbot's table,
  All of us get each a slice.
How go on your flowers? None double?
  Not one fruit-sort can you spy?
Strange!—And I, too, at such trouble,
  Keep them close-nipped on the sly!

There's a great text in Galatians,
  Once you trip on it, entails
Twenty-nine distinct damnations,
  One sure, if another fails;
If I trip him just a-dying,
  Sure of heaven as sure can be,
Spin him round and send him flying
  Off to hell, a Manichee?

Or, my scrofulous French novel
  On grey paper with blunt type!
Simply glance at it, you grovel
  Hand and foot in Belial's gripe;
If I double down its pages
  At the woeful sixteenth print,
When he gathers his greengages,
  Ope a sieve and slip it in't?

Or, there's Satan!—One might venture
  Pledge one's soul to him, yet leave
Such a flaw in the indenture
  As he'd miss, till, past retrieve,
Blasted lay that rose-acacia
  We're so proud of. *Hy, Zy, Hine* . . .
'St! There's Vespers! *Plena gratiâ*
  Ave, Virgo! Gr-r-r—you swine!

Incident of the French Camp

You know we French stormed Ratisbon:
  A mile or so away,
On a little mound, Napoleon
  Stood on our storming-day;
With neck out-thrust, you fancy how,
  Legs wide, arms locked behind,
As if to balance the prone brow,
  Oppressive with its mind.

Just as perhaps he mused, "My plans
  That soar, to earth may fall,
Let once my army-leader Lannes
  Waver at yonder wall,"—
Out 'twixt the battery-smokes there flew
  A rider, bound on bound
Full galloping; nor bridle drew
  Until he reached the mound.

Then off there flung in smiling joy,
  And held himself erect
By just his horse's mane, a boy;
  You hardly could suspect
(So tight he kept his lips compressed,
  Scarce any blood came through),
You looked twice ere you saw his breast
  Was all but shot in two.

"Well," cried he, "Emperor, by God's grace
  We've got you Ratisbon!
The Marshal's in the market-place,
  And you'll be there anon
To see your flag-bird flap his vans
  Where I, to heart's desire,
Perched him!" The chief's eye flashed; his plans
  Soared up again like fire.

The chief's eye flashed, but presently
  Softened itself, as sheathes
A film the mother eagle's eye
  When her bruised eaglet breathes:

"You're wounded!" "Nay," his soldier's pride
  Touched to the quick, he said,
"I'm killed, sire!" And, his chief beside,
  Smiling, the boy fell dead.

A Woman's Last Word

Let's contend no more, Love,
  Strive nor weep;
All be as before, Love,
  —Only sleep!

What so wild as words are?
  I and thou
In debate, as birds are,
  Hawk on bough!

See the creature stalking
  While we speak!
Hush and hide the talking,
  Cheek on cheek!

What so false as truth is,
  False to thee?
Where the serpent's tooth is
  Shun the tree—

Where the apple reddens
  Never pry—
Lest we lose our Edens,
  Eve and I.

Be a god and hold me
  With a charm!
Be a man and fold me
  With thine arm!

Teach me, only teach, Love!
  As I ought
I will speak thy speech, Love,
  Think thy thought—

Meet, if thou require it,
  Both demands,
Laying flesh and spirit
  In thy hands.

That shall be tomorrow
  Not tonight:
I must bury sorrow
  Out of sight:

—Must a little weep, Love,
  (Foolish me!)
And so fall asleep, Love,
  Loved by thee.

To his MEN AND WOMEN Browning added a significant poem dedicated to his wife. It was entitled ONE WORD MORE and it began:

There they are, my fifty men and women
Naming me the fifty poems finished!
Take them, Love, the book and me together:
Where the heart lies, let the brain lie also.

Six years after its publication Mrs. Browning died, and Browning left Florence for England. He never returned to the city which had been the center of their common life. Fame, long delayed, came to him in his fifties with DRAMATIS PERSONAE and THE RING AND THE BOOK, a long narrative poem based on a Roman murder trial, in which the story is presented from a dozen points of view with the exactness of a court record.

The last twenty years of Browning's life brought increasing honors. He wrote constantly and with an ever-growing variety of subject and style. ASOLANDO, a volume prepared at Ásolo, was published on the very day of Browning's death, December 12, 1889, at Venice. He was buried in Westminster Abbey the last day of the year.

The Epilogue to ASOLANDO may well stand as Browning's epitaph. Speaking of it shortly before his death, Browning commented, "It almost looks like bragging to say this, and as if I ought to cancel it. But it's the simple truth; and as it's true, I shall let it stand." Walter Savage Landor, whom the Brownings had befriended during his most trying days, confirmed the poet's estimate. Landor wrote:

. . . Since Chaucer was alive and hale,
No man hath walked along our roads with step
So active, so inquiring eye, or tongue
So varied in discourse.

Epilogue

to ASOLANDO

At the midnight in the silence of the sleep-time,
  When you set your fancies free,
Will they pass to where—by death, fools think, imprisoned—
Low he lies who once so loved you, whom you loved so,
      —Pity me?

Oh to love so, be so loved, yet so mistaken!
  What had I on earth to do
With the slothful, with the mawkish, the unmanly?
Like the aimless, helpless, hopeless, did I drivel
      —Being—who?

One who never turned his back but marched breast forward,
  Never doubted clouds would break,
Never dreamed, though right were worsted, wrong would triumph,
Held we fall to rise, are baffled to fight better,
      Sleep to wake.

No, at noonday in the bustle of man's work-time
  Greet the unseen with a cheer!
Bid him forward, breast and back as either should be,
"Strive and thrive!" cry "Speed,—fight on, fare ever
      There as here!"

Much has been made of Browning's morality and his obscurity. The obscurity, when it occurs, happens because Browning sometimes uses a subtle and elliptical mode of speech. It does not arise, as some have charged, from a desire to impress the reader with the author's erudition. It is not vanity but modesty that takes the intelligence of the reader for granted and assumes (perhaps unwarrantably) a background of many associations.

Browning's moralizing, once quoted like Scripture by Browning Societies, is obvious enough; but it is less religious than ethical. His was a philosophy of imperfection. As the poet wrote in ABT VOGLER:

The evil is null, is nought, is silence implying sound. . .
On the earth the broken arcs; in the heaven, the perfect round.

It was the striving toward perfection rather than the attainment that mattered most; the onward-going rather than the goal itself. Browning's determined cheerfulness wells up like a dependable geyser. It is the spring of the robust if overlong RABBI BEN EZRA:

Grow old along with me!
The best is yet to be,
The last of life, for which the first was made:
Our times are in his hand
Who saith: "A whole I planned,
Youth shows but half; trust God, see all, nor be afraid."

Accompanying Browning's hopefulness is a devotion to the ideal of service. This high regard echoes Herbert's THE ELIXIR (see page 418), especially the lines:

A servant with this clause
Makes drudgery divine;
Who sweeps a room, as for thy laws,
Makes that and the action fine.

The sentiment finds its fulfillment in an inconspicuous but significant lyric from PIPPA PASSES:

Service

All service ranks the same with God.
If now, as formerly He trod
Paradise, His presence fills
Our earth, each only as God wills
Can work—God's puppets, best and worst,
Are we; there is no last nor first.

Say not "a small event!" Why "small?"
Costs it more pain than this, ye call
A "great event," should come to pass,
Than that? Untwine me from the mass
Of deeds which make up life, one deed
Power shall fall short in, or exceed!

from PIPPA PASSES

Browning's other preoccupation was with human aspirations, with the upward struggle of the human soul, with the very failures that test the nobility of man.

> Ah, but a man's reach should exceed his grasp,
> Or what's a heaven for?

Heartiness is perhaps overstressed, and optimism is too unrelievedly buoyant in Browning. It is not easy to "welcome each rebuff that turns earth's smoothness rough," nor, in a bitter age, to concede that "the best is yet to be." But it is impossible to deny the value of Browning's affirmation, the blind faith in perfectibility, even in imperfection. It is the high courage rising from such a poem as PROSPICE ("Look Forward") that endears the yea-saying singer to those who love a poet who is "ever a fighter."

Prospice

Fear death?—to feel the fog in my throat,
    The mist in my face,
When the snows begin, and the blasts denote
    I am nearing the place,
The power of the night, the press of the storm,
    The post of the foe;
Where he stands, the Arch Fear in a visible form,
    Yet the strong man must go:
For the journey is done and the summit attained,
    And the barriers fall,
Though a battle's to fight ere the guerdon be gained,
    The reward of it all.
I was ever a fighter, so—one fight more,
    The best and the last!
I would hate that death bandaged my eyes, and forbore,
    And bade me creep past.
No! let me taste the whole of it, fare like my peers
    The heroes of old,
Bear the brunt, in a minute pay glad life's arrears
    Of pain, darkness and cold.
For sudden the worse turns the best to the brave,
    The black minute's at end,
And the elements' rage, the fiend-voices that rave,
    Shall dwindle, shall blend,

Shall change, shall become first a peace out of pain,
    Then a light, then thy breast,
O thou soul of my soul! I shall clasp thee again,
    And with God be the rest!

Today Browning is honored less as a teacher and more as a pioneer in a difficult art, the art of psychological portraiture in verse. His soliloquies and narratives hold us with their dramatic tension rather than with their philosophy. He spoke often of the ultimate goal, but it was the urgency, the human adventure, the "one fight more, the best and the last," with which he was most deeply concerned.

After

Take the cloak from his face, and at first
  Let the corpse do its worst.

How he lies in his rights of a man!
  Death has done all death can.
And, absorbed in the new life he leads,
  He recks not, he heeds
Nor his wrong nor my vengeance—both strike
  On his senses alike,
And are lost in the solemn and strange
  Surprise of the change.

Ha, what avails death to erase
  His offence, my disgrace?
I would we were boys as of old
  In the field, by the fold—
His outrage, God's patience, man's scorn
  Were so easily borne!

I stand here now, he lies in his place—
  Cover the face.

Porphyria's Lover

The rain set early in tonight,
  The sullen wind was soon awake,
It tore the elm-tops down for spite,
  And did its worst to vex the lake:
  I listened with heart fit to break.

When glided in Porphyria; straight
  She shut the cold out and the storm,
And kneeled and made the cheerless grate
  Blaze up, and all the cottage warm;
  Which done, she rose, and from her form
Withdrew the dripping cloak and shawl,
  And laid her soiled gloves by, untied
Her hat and let the damp hair fall,
  And, last, she sat down by my side
  And called me. When no voice replied,
She put my arm about her waist,
  And made her smooth white shoulder bare
And all her yellow hair displaced,
  And, stooping, made my cheek lie there,
  And spread, o'er all, her yellow hair,
Murmuring how she loved me—she
  Too weak, for all her heart's endeavor,
To set its struggling passion free
  From pride, and vainer ties dissever,
  And give herself to me for ever.
But passion sometimes would prevail,
  Nor could tonight's gay feast restrain
A sudden thought of one so pale
  For love of her, and all in vain:
  So, she was come through wind and rain.
Be sure I looked up at her eyes
  Happy and proud; at last I knew
Porphyria worshiped me; surprise
  Made my heart swell, and still it grew
  While I debated what to do.
That moment she was mine, mine, fair,
  Perfectly pure and good: I found
A thing to do, and all her hair
  In one long yellow string I wound
  Three times her little throat around,
And strangled her. No pain felt she;
  I am quite sure she felt no pain.
As a shut bud that holds a bee,
  I warily oped her lids: again
  Laughed the blue eyes without a stain.
And I untightened next the tress
  About her neck; her cheek once more
Blushed bright beneath my burning kiss:
  I propped her head up as before,
  Only, this time my shoulder bore

Her head, which droops upon it still:
  The smiling rosy little head,
So glad it has its utmost will,
  That all it scorned at once is fled,
  And I, its love, am gained instead!
Porphyria's love: she guessed not how
  Her darling one wish would be heard.
And thus we sit together now,
  And all night long we have not stirred,
  And yet God has not said a word!

Song

Nay, but you, who do not love her,
  Is she not pure gold, my mistress?
Holds earth aught—speak truth—above her?
  Aught like this tress, see, and this tress,
And this last fairest tress of all,
So fair, see, ere I let it fall?

Because, you spend your lives in praising;
  To praise, you search the wide world over;
Then, why not witness, calmly gazing,
  If earth holds aught—speak truth—above her?
Above this tress, and this I touch
But cannot praise, I love so much!

My Star

All that I know
  Of a certain star
Is, it can throw
  (Like the angled spar)
Now a dart of red,
  Now a dart of blue;
Till my friends have said
  They would fain see, too,
My star that dartles the red and the blue!
Then it stops like a bird; like a flower, hangs furled:
  They must solace themselves with the Saturn above it.
What matter to me if their star is a world?
  Mine has opened its soul to me; therefore I love it.

Browning's rugged individuality is mirrored in the unprecedented range of his work. If it is sometimes too energetic, it is always exciting; if it is overloaded, it expresses the complete man. Browning was never satisfied with easy victories. He had determined, as G. K. Chesterton wrote, "to leave no spot of the cosmos unadorned by his poetry," and he almost succeeded.

EMILY BRONTË

[1818–1848]

IT IS hard to separate the Brontës; they were not only a closely knit family but a group of collaborators. So great a literature of biography and speculation has grown up about them that the individuals have been obscured by the tradition.

The father of the family was Patrick Prunty, an Irishman, who changed his name to Brontë when he came to England, accepted a curacy, and married Maria, daughter of Thomas Branwell, a Penzance merchant. Nine years after the marriage Mrs. Brontë died, leaving six children, two of whom died before they reached the age of twelve. The others were gifted to an extraordinary degree. The one son, Branwell, was educated to be a genius, but his precocity vanished in youth; he failed at everything he attempted, and drank himself to death at thirty-one. The surviving sisters were equally at home in prose and verse. Anne, the mildest of the three, died at twenty-nine, author of two novels, AGNES GREY and THE TENANT OF WILDFELL HALL. Charlotte, author of THE PROFESSOR, VILLETTE, and JANE EYRE, was the only one of the sisters to marry, but her wedded life lasted less than twelve months; she died as a consequence of childbirth in her fortieth year. Emily, the most self-revealing as well as the most stoic of the sisters, surpassed them—as she surpassed all women in literature—in creative intensity. Sent to the school at Roe Head, the institution unforgettably described by Charlotte in JANE EYRE, she suffered from bad food, brutal discipline, and continual homesickness. "Every morning when she awoke," Charlotte wrote in her diary concerning Emily's failure to remain in school, "the vision of home and the moors rushed on her and darkened and saddened the day that lay before her." Emily ventured into the world only at rare intervals. She taught briefly at a seminary for girls and, with Charlotte, attended a girls' school in Brussels. But she longed for the bleak moors of Haworth:

> Where the grey fox in ferny glens are feeding,
> Where the wild wind blows on the mountain side.

A tendency toward tuberculosis marked the entire Brontë family. Standing at her brother's grave in a sharp wind, Emily took cold. She was in great pain and sank rapidly. "Stronger than a man," Charlotte wrote, "simpler than a child, her nature stood alone. I have seen nothing like it; but, indeed, I have never seen her parallel in anything." Emily knew she was dying, but she insisted on getting out of bed and dressing herself before she permitted a doctor to attend her. Stoical to the end, she died at thirty, December 19, 1848.

Last Lines

No coward soul is mine,
No trembler in the world's storm-troubled sphere:
I see Heaven's glories shine,
And faith shines equal, arming me from fear.

O God within my breast,
Almighty, ever-present Deity!
Life—that in me hast rest,
As I, undying Life, have power in thee!

Vain are the thousand creeds
That move men's hearts, unalterably vain;
Worthless as withered weeds,
Or idlest froth amid the boundless main,

To waken doubt in one
Holding so fast by thine infinity;
So surely anchored on
The steadfast rock of immortality.

With wide-embracing love
Thy spirit animates eternal years,
Pervades and broods above,
Changes, sustains, dissolves, creates, and rears.

Though earth and moon were gone,
And suns and universes ceased to be,
And Thou wert left alone,
Every existence would exist in Thee.

There is not room for Death,
Nor atom that his might could render void:
Thou—Thou art Being and Breath,
And what Thou art may never be destroyed.

Only one volume of poems was published during the Brontës lifetime, and that was carefully disguised. The three girls assumed names that were "positively masculine," using the initials of their first names in choosing pseudonyms. Since no publisher would assume the commercial risk, the girls at their own expense brought out POEMS BY CURRER, ELLIS, AND ACTON BELL. Exactly two copies were sold; most of the edition was used to line trunks.

Until recently it was impossible to determine how much of Emily Brontë's poetry was concealed autobiography and how much was unconcealed fantasy. The mystery was cleared up in 1941 by Fanny Elizabeth Ratchford's THE BRONTËS' WEB OF CHILDHOOD. More clearly than any of her predecessors in research, and at odds with most, Miss Ratchford showed that it was futile to base a biography on a subjective interpretation of Emily Brontë's poems. In a remarkable piece of scholarly detective work Miss Ratchford revealed that as children the Brontës escaped from the unhappy Haworth parsonage into a world of shining make-believe. But they did not merely dream of an imaginary country; they created one, called it Gondal, made maps of this fancied island in the Pacific, composed countless poems and legends of its past, and designed a complete if miniature epic. The poems, continued into maturity, were not written, according to Miss Ratchford, "as progressive plot incidents, but were merely the poetic expression of scenes, dramas, and emotions long familiar to her [Emily's] inner vision, carried over, no doubt, from her prose creations." Many students have sought to find Emily's "lover" in the intense and seemingly personal REMEMBRANCE. But the poem is part of the Gondalian cycle, and is uttered by the grieving Rosina of Alcona upon the death of Julius Brenzaida, two leading characters in the Gondal saga.

Remembrance

Cold in the earth, and the deep snow piled above thee!
Far, far removed, cold in the dreary grave!
Have I forgot, my only Love, to love thee,
Severed at last by Time's all-wearing wave?

Now, when alone, do my thoughts no longer hover
Over the mountains, on Angora's shore,
Resting their wings where heath and fern-leaves cover
That noble heart for ever, ever more?

Cold in the earth, and fifteen wild Decembers
From those brown hills, have melted into spring:
Faithful, indeed, is the spirit that remembers
After such years of change and suffering!

Sweet Love of youth, forgive, if I forget thee,
While the world's tide is bearing me along;
Sterner desires and darker hopes beset me,
Hopes which obscure, but cannot do thee wrong.

No other sun has lightened up my heaven,
No other star has ever shone for me;
All my life's bliss from thy dear life was given,
All my life's bliss is in the grave with thee.

But, when the days of golden dreams had perished,
And even Despair was powerless to destroy;
Then did I learn how existence could be cherished,
Strengthened, and fed without the aid of joy.

Then did I check the tears of useless passion,
Weaned my young soul from yearning after thine;
Sternly denied its burning wish to hasten
Down to that tomb already more than mine.

And, even yet, I dare not let it languish,
Dare not indulge in memory's rapturous pain;
Once drinking deep of that divinest anguish,
How could I seek the empty world again?

So many of Emily Brontë's poems had been carelessly copied and incorrectly printed that no authoritative edition was in existence until 1941, when C. W. Hatfield masterfully edited THE COMPLETE POEMS OF EMILY JANE BRONTË from the scattered manuscripts. New treasures were unearthed and long-cherished poems were given their original luster. In a little-known and strongly subjective poem, which Miss Ratchford calls "the noblest apology for genius in the language," Emily Brontë acknowledged her dependence on the "phantom thing" which was her slave yet ruled her imagination. If she steadfastly shunned "the paths that others run" and "cast the world away," it was not Reason but the God of Visions who spoke for her.

God of Visions

Oh, thy bright eyes must answer now,
When Reason, with a scornful brow,
Is mocking at my overthrow;
Oh, thy sweet tongue must plead for me
And tell why I have chosen thee!

Stern Reason is to judgment come,
Arrayed in all her forms of gloom:
Wilt thou, my advocate, be dumb?
No, radiant angel, speak and say
Why I did cast the world away.

Why I have persevered to shun
The common paths that others run;
And on a strange road journeyed on,
Heedless alike of wealth and power—
Of glory's wreath and pleasure's flower.

These, once, indeed, seemed Beings divine;
And they, perchance, heard vows of mine,
And saw my offerings on their shrine;
But careless gifts are seldom prized,
And mine were worthily despised.

So, with a ready heart, I swore
To seek their altar-stone no more;

And gave my spirit to adore
Thee, ever-present, phantom thing—
My slave, my comrade, and my king.

A slave, because I rule thee still;
Incline thee to my changeful will,
And make thy influence good or ill:
A comrade, for by day and night
Thou art my intimate delight—

My darling pain that wounds and sears,
And wrings a blessing out from tears
By deadening me to real cares;
And yet, a king, though prudence well
Have taught thy subject to rebel.

And am I wrong to worship where
Faith cannot doubt, nor hope despair,
Since my own soul can grant my prayer?
Speak, God of visions, plead for me,
And tell why I have chosen thee!

"My sister Emily loved the moors," Charlotte Brontë wrote. "Flowers brighter than the rose bloomed in the blackest of the heath for her; out of a sullen hollow in a livid hillside her mind could make an Eden. She found in the bleak solitude many and dear delights, and the best loved was—liberty." This wildness, this love of bleakness and freedom, strengthens the poems and makes WUTHERING HEIGHTS the greatest novel ever achieved by a woman. With singular melancholy and concentered passion Emily Brontë created a dream world, and made it more real than reality.

Fall, Leaves, Fall

Fall, leaves, fall; die, flowers, away;
Lengthen night and shorten day;
Every leaf speaks bliss to me
Fluttering from the autumn tree.

I shall smile when wreaths of snow
Blossom where the rose should grow;
I shall sing when night's decay
Ushers in a drearier day.

The Old Stoic

Riches I hold in light esteem,
And love I laugh to scorn;
And lust of fame was but a dream
That vanished with the morn:

And if I pray, the only prayer
That moves my lips for me
Is, "Leave the heart that now I bear,
And give me liberty!"

Yes, as my swift days near their goal,
'Tis all that I implore–
Through life and death a chainless soul,
With courage to endure.

ARTHUR HUGH CLOUGH

[1819–1861]

BORN on the first day of 1819, son of a prosperous cotton merchant in Liverpool, Arthur Hugh Clough was taken to Charleston, South Carolina, at the age of four. He remained there during his childhood and returned to England to enter Rugby, where he became a favorite of the noted headmaster, Dr. Thomas Arnold. In his early thirties, encouraged by Emerson, he came to the United States to lecture and teach. It was an unsuccessful venture, although Clough considered America "beyond all question the happiest country going."

Back in England, Clough was appointed secretary to a Commission of Report on military education, and his official duties took him abroad. At forty-one his health, never robust, failed; a year later he succumbed to malarial fever. Upon his death Matthew Arnold (see page 921), son of Dr. Thomas Arnold, wrote a commemorating poem, THYRSIS, which some critics have ranked among the great English elegies.

Clough's life was greater in promise than in performance. It is thought that his religious doubts cost him a career. It is certain that intellectual unrest disturbs most of his poetry, and even his "austere love of truth" does not lift his verse above dogged honesty. F. T. Palgrave, the famous Victorian anthologist, said that Clough "lived rather than wrote his poems." But there is one poem which contains Clough's whole spiritual conviction and which has a timeless power. Its long echoes continue to be heard in plays and poems. In April, 1941, it was quoted with great effect by Winston Churchill, Prime Minister of England, as a culmination of one of his most stirring speeches.

Say Not the Struggle Naught Availeth

Say not the struggle naught availeth,
The labor and the wounds are vain,
The enemy faints not, nor faileth,
And as things have been they remain.

If hopes were dupes, fears may be liars;
It may be, in yon smoke conceal'd,
Your comrades chase e'en now the fliers,
And, but for you, possess the field.

For while the tired waves, vainly breaking,
Seem here no painful inch to gain,
Far back, through creeks and inlets making,
Comes silent, flooding in, the main.

And not by eastern windows only,
When daylight comes, comes in the light;
In front the sun climbs slow, how slowly.
But westward, look, the land is bright!

XIV

Challenge to Tradition

WALT WHITMAN

[1819–1892]

"LITERATURE, strictly considered, has never recognized the people, and whatever may be said, does not today. It seems as if, so far, there were some natural repugnance between a literary and professional life, and the rude rank spirit of the democracies. . . . I know nothing more rare, even in this country, than a fit scientific estimate and reverent application of the People—of their measureless wealth of latent worth and capacity, their vast artistic contrasts of lights and shades." Thus, in DEMOCRATIC VISTAS, wrote Walt Whitman, in whom the people, with their conflicting expressions of faith, doubt, and democracy, found a confident voice.

He was born Walter Whitman, May 31, 1819, at West Hills, near Huntington, Long Island, of a family of workers. His mother's people were Dutch Quakers, and his maternal grandfather had been a horse breeder. His paternal ancestors had been farmers, but his father turned carpenter and moved his family to Brooklyn, New York. Here the country child became a town boy. He roamed about the docks, explored the alleys, loved the sharp wood smell of his father's shop and the exciting noises of the streets. There were no uneventful days. One Fourth of July, when a library cornerstone was being laid, he was singled out and embraced by Lafayette.

At eleven the young Whitman went to work as an errand boy. At twelve he learned to set type, and at fourteen he was in the composing room of THE LONG ISLAND STAR. For the next twenty years he earned a living as a printer-journalist, reporter, and intermittent teacher. He wrote short and sentimental pieces, innocuous verses, and undistinguished editorials for forgotten newspapers. In his twenty-third year he published FRANKLIN EVANS, OR THE INEBRIATE, a temperance tract disguised as a novel, and which he admitted, with some embarrassment, was written for seventy-five dollars "cash down." In his thirtieth year Whitman left New York to become a special writer on the staff of the New Orleans CRESCENT.

Much has been made of Whitman's sojourn in New Orleans. Certain biographers, worried by passages in his poems which suggest homosexuality, have been quick to supply an orthodox clandestine and unhappy romance. They have furnished various inamoratas to explain not only Whitman's failure to marry, but also his avoidance of women; one of his most recent biographers convinced herself that Whitman's secret love was a young octoroon. Later in life, in order to offset suspicions of sexual abnormality, Whitman boasted that he was the father of six illegitimate children. At another time he implied that he had signed a contract with his father-in-law never to see his wife or children again. Yet Whitman had specifically said he was never married. No child ever came forth to claim him as a father. Although his executors examined everything with microscopic care, no "incriminating" letters were ever unearthed. Until documentary evidence is forthcoming, it is impossible to believe in Whitman's illicit affairs; the New Orleans mistress disappears, and the six children are nothing more than a patriarchal wish-fulfillment.

At thirty-one Walter Whitman, the itinerant journalist, vanished, and the Walt Whitman of tradition emerged. He ceased to write polite sketches and began to fashion a rough and capacious poetry. He exchanged his well-tailored suit for the clothes of a workman and consorted with ferrymen, bus drivers, and other "powerful, uneducated persons." It is related that once when a driver, with whom Walt had often ridden, was sick, Whitman drove the omnibus down Broadway for him and sent the proceeds to his family.

At thirty-one Whitman discovered the American language. Later he planned something between a lecture and a book to be called AN AMERICAN PRIMER, but even now he was in love with muscular sounds, place names, tavern words, words with native brawn. "A perfect user of words uses things," he wrote. "They exude in power and beauty from him—miracles from his hands, miracles from his mouth . . . Monongahela—it rolls with venison richness upon the palate. Mississippi—the word winds with chutes; it rolls a stream three thousand miles long." He continued prophetically, "The appetite of the people of These States is for unhemmed latitude, coarseness, directness, live epithets, expletives, words of opprobrium, resistance."

Prophet and poet spoke together in LEAVES OF GRASS, first published in Whitman's thirty-seventh year. Here were force and flexibility. Here the poet dispensed with "delicate lady-words" and "gloved gentleman-words" in a fierce and limber speech, an idiom like nothing else ever framed. In a quasi-autobiographical set of poems, Whitman identified word and flesh: "Who touches this book touches a man." But LEAVES OF GRASS was not only devoted to a man; its theme was mankind. It dedicated itself to brave, cowardly, chaste, lewd, spiritual and sweating humanity. Whittier literally threw the book into the flames; but Emerson wrote to Whitman, "I give you joy for your free and brave thought. . . . I find the courage of treatment which so delights us, and which large perception only can inspire. I greet you at the beginning of a great career."

Emerson's prediction was not to be fulfilled in Whitman's own time. The "great career" was wholly posthumous; LEAVES OF GRASS was so neglected that Whitman had to write his own inflated reviews in the hope of provoking a controversy. As late as 1900, Barrett Wendell, in his LITERARY HISTORY OF AMERICA, spoke of Whitman's "eccentric insolence of phrase and temper" and concluded that "he was an exotic member of that sterile brotherhood which eagerly greeted him abroad." The critics were revolted not only by Whitman's use of the vernacular, but by his egotism. They failed to realize that Whitman's "I" was a symbol representing the common man and that, when he seemed to celebrate himself, he was celebrating all men.

FROM

Song of Myself

1

I celebrate myself, and sing myself,
And what I assume you shall assume,
For every atom belonging to me as good belongs to you.

I loafe and invite my soul,
I lean and loafe at my ease observing a spear of summer grass.

My tongue, every atom of my blood, form'd from this soil, this air,
Born here of parents born here from parents the same, and their
    parents the same,
I, now thirty-seven years old in perfect health begin,
Hoping to cease not till death.
Creeds and schools in abeyance,
Retiring back a while sufficed at what they are, but never forgotten,
I harbor for good or bad, I permit to speak at every hazard,
Nature without check with original energy.

2

Houses and rooms are full of perfumcs, the shelves are crowded
    with perfumes,
I breathe the fragrance myself and know it and like it,
The distillation would intoxicate me also, but I shall not let it.

The atmosphere is not a perfume, it has no taste of the distillation,
    it is odorless,
It is for my mouth forever, I am in love with it,
I will go to the bank by the wood and become undisguised and
    naked,
I am mad for it to be in contact with me.

The smoke of my own breath,
Echoes, ripples, buzz'd whispers, love-root, silk-thread, crotch and
    vine,
My respiration and inspiration, the beating of my heart, the passing
    of blood and air through my lungs,
The sniff of green leaves and dry leaves, and of the shore and dark-
    color'd sea-rocks, and of hay in the barn,
The sound of the belch'd words of my voice loos'd to the eddies of
    the wind,
A few light kisses, a few embraces, a reaching around of arms,
The play of shine and shade on the trees as the supple boughs wag,
The delight alone or in the rush of the streets, or along the fields
    and hill-sides,
The feeling of health, the full-noon trill, the song of me rising
    from bed and meeting the sun.

Have you reckon'd a thousand acres much? have you reckon'd the
earth much?
Have you practic'd so long to learn to read?
Have you felt so proud to get at the meaning of poems?

Stop this day and night with me and you shall possess the origin of
all poems,
You shall possess the good of the earth and sun, (there are millions
of suns left,)
You shall no longer take things at second or third hand, nor look
through the eyes of the dead, nor feed on the specters in books,
You shall not look through my eyes either, nor take things from me,
You shall listen to all sides and filter them from your self.

6

A child said, *What is the grass?* fetching it to me with full hands;
How could I answer the child? I do not know what it is any more
than he.

I guess it must be the flag of my disposition, out of hopeful green
stuff woven.
Or I guess it is the handkerchief of the Lord,
A scented gift and remembrancer designedly dropt,
Bearing the owner's name someway in the corner, that we may see
and remark, and say *Whose?*

Or I guess the grass is itself a child, the produced babe of the vegeta-
tion.
Or I guess it is a uniform hieroglyphic,
And it means, Sprouting alike in broad zones and narrow zones,
Growing among black folks as among white,
Kanuck, Tuckahoe, Congressman, Cuff, I give them the same, I re-
ceive them the same.

And now it seems to me the beautiful uncut hair of graves,

Tenderly will I use you curling grass,
It may be you transpire from the breasts of young men,
It may be if I had known them I would have loved them,
It may be you are from old people, or from offspring taken soon out
of their mothers' laps,
And here you are the mothers' laps.

This grass is very dark to be from the white heads of old mothers,
Darker than the colorless beards of old men,
Dark to come from under the faint red roofs of mouths.
O I perceive after all so many uttering tongues,
And I perceive they do not come from the roofs of mouths for nothing.
I wish I could translate the hints about the dead young men and women,
And the hints about old men and mothers, and the offspring taken soon out of their laps.

What do you think has become of the young and old men?
And what do you think has become of the women and children?

They are alive and well somewhere,
The smallest sprout shows there is really no death,
And if ever there was it led forward life, and does not wait at the end to arrest it,
And ceas'd the moment life appear'd.

All goes onward and outward, nothing collapses,
And to die is different from what anyone supposed, and luckier.

8

The little one sleeps in its cradle,
I lift the gauze and look a long time, and silently brush away flies with my hand.

The youngster and the red-faced girl turn aside up the bushy hill,
I peeringly view them from the top.

The suicide sprawls on the bloody floor of the bedroom,
I witness the corpse with its dabbled hair, I note where the pistol has fallen.

The blab of the pave, tires of carts, sluff of boot-soles, talk of the promenaders,
The heavy omnibus, the driver with his interrogating thumb, the clank of the shod horses on the granite floor,
The snow-sleighs, clinking, shouted jokes, pelts of snow-balls,
The hurrahs for popular favorites, the fury of rous'd mobs,
The flap of the curtain'd litter, a sick man inside borne to the hospital,

The meeting of enemies, the sudden oath, the blows and fall,
The excited crowd, the policeman with his star quickly working his passage to the center of the crowd,
The impassive stones that receive and return so many echoes,
What groans of over-fed or half-starv'd who fall sunstruck or in fits
What exclamations of women taken suddenly who hurry home and give birth to babes,
What living and buried speech is always vibrating here, what howls restrain'd by decorum,
Arrests of criminals, slights, adulterous offers made, acceptances, rejections with convex lips,
I mind them or the show or resonance of them—I come and I depart.

18

With music strong I come, with my cornets and my drums,
I play not marches for accepted victors only, I play marches for conquer'd and slain persons.

Have you heard that it was good to gain the day?
I also say it is good to fall, battles are lost in the same spirit in which they are won.

I beat and pound for the dead,
I blow through my embouchures my loudest and gayest for them.

Vivas to those who have fail'd!
And to those whose war-vessels sank in the sea!
And to those themselves who sank in the sea!
And to all generals that lost engagements, and all overcome heroes!
And the numberless unknown heroes equal to the greatest heroes known!

20

Who goes there? hankering, gross, mystical, nude;
How is it I extract strength from the beef I eat?

What is a man anyhow? what am I? what are you?

All I mark as my own you shall offset it with your own,
Else it were time lost listening to me.

I do not snivel that snivel the world over,
That months are vacuums and the ground but wallow and filth.

Whimpering and truckling fold with powders for invalids, conformity goes to the fourth-remov'd,
I wear my hat as I please indoors or out.

Why should I pray? why should I venerate and be ceremonious?

Having pried through the strata, analyzed to a hair, counsel'd with doctors and calculated close,
I find no sweeter fat than sticks to my own bones.

In all people I see myself, none more and not one a barleycorn less,
And the good or bad I say of myself I say of them.
I know I am solid and sound,
To me the converging objects of the universe perpetually flow,
All are written to me, and I must get what the writing means.

I know I am deathless,
I know this orbit of mine cannot be swept by a carpenter's compass,
I know I shall not pass like a child's carlacue cut with a burnt stick at night.

I know I am august,
I do not trouble my spirit to vindicate itself or be understood,
I see that the elementary laws never apologize,
(I reckon I behave no prouder than the level I plant my house by, after all.)

I exist as I am, that is enough,
If no other in the world be aware I sit content,
And if each and all be aware I sit content.

One world is aware and by far the largest to me, and that is myself,
And whether I come to my own today or in ten thousand or ten million years,
I can cheerfully take it now, or with equal cheerfulness I can wait.

My foothold is tenon'd and mortis'd in granite,
I laugh at what you call dissolution,
And I know the amplitude of time.

21

I am the poet of the Body and I am the poet of the Soul,
The pleasures of heaven are with me and the pains of hell are with me,
The first I graft and increase upon myself, the latter I translate into a new tongue.

I am the poet of the woman the same as the man,
And I say it is as great to be a woman as to be a man,
And I say there is nothing greater than the mother of men.

I chant the chant of dilation or pride,
We have had ducking and deprecating about enough,
I show that size is only development.

Have you outstript the rest? are you the President?
It is a trifle, they will more than arrive there every one, and still pass on.

I am he that walks with the tender and growing night,
I call to the earth and sea half-held by the night.

Press close bare-bosom'd night—press close magnetic nourishing night!
Night of south winds—night of the large few stars!
Still nodding night—mad naked summer night.

Smile O voluptuous cool-breath'd earth!
Earth of the slumbering and liquid trees!
Earth of departed sunset—earth of the mountains misty-topt!
Earth of the vitreous pour of the full moon just tinged with blue!
Earth of shine and dark mottling the tide of the river!
Earth of the limpid gray of clouds brighter and clearer for my sake!
Far-swooping elbow'd earth—rich apple-blossom'd earth!
Smile, for your lover comes.

Prodigal, you have given me love—therefore I to you give love!
O unspeakable passionate love.

31

I believe a leaf of grass is no less than the journeywork of the stars,
And the pismire is equally perfect, and a grain of sand, and the egg of the wren,

And the tree-toad is a chef-d'œuvre for the highest,
And the running blackberry would adorn the parlors of heaven,
And the narrowest hinge in my hand puts to scorn all machinery,
And the cow crunching with depress'd head surpasses any statue,
And a mouse is miracle enough to stagger sextillions of infidels.

I find I incorporate gneiss, coal, long-threaded moss, fruits, grains
esculent roots,
And am stucco'd with quadrupeds and birds all over,
And have distanced what is behind me for good reasons,
But call any thing back again when I desire it.

In vain the speeding or shyness,
In vain the plutonic rocks send their old heat against my approach,
In vain the mastodon retreats beneath its own powder'd bones,
In vain objects stand leagues off and assume manifold shapes,
In vain the ocean settling in hollows and the great monsters lying
low,
In vain the buzzard houses herself with the sky,
In vain the snake slides through the creepers and logs,
In vain the elk takes to the inner passes of the woods,
In vain the razor-bill'd auk sails far north to Labrador,
I follow quickly, I ascend to the nest in the fissure of the cliff.

32

I think I could turn and live with animals, they are so placid and
self-contain'd,
I stand and look at them long and long.

They do not sweat and whine about their condition,
They do not lie awake in the dark and weep for their sins,
They do not make me sick discussing their duty to God,
Not one is dissatisfied, not one is demented with the mania of own-
ing things,
Not one kneels to another, nor to his kind that lived thousands of
years ago,
Not one is respectable or unhappy over the whole earth.

So they show their relations to me and I accept them,
They bring me tokens of myself, they evince them plainly in their
possession.

I wonder where they get those tokens,
Did I pass that way huge times ago and negligently drop them?
Myself moving forward then and now and forever,
Gathering and showing more always and with velocity,
Infinite and omnigenous, and the like of these among them,
Not too exclusive toward the reachers of my remembrancers,
Picking out here one that I love, and now go with him on brotherly
terms.

A gigantic beauty of a stallion, fresh and responsive to my caresses,
Head high in the forehead, wide between the ears,
Limbs glossy and supple, tail dusting the ground,
Eyes full of sparkling wickedness, ears finely cut, flexibly moving.
His nostrils dilate as my heels embrace him,
His well-built limbs tremble with pleasure as we race around and
return.

I but use you a minute, then I resign you, stallion,
Why do I need your paces when I myself out-gallop them?
Even as I stand or sit passing faster than you.

35

Would you hear of an old-time sea-fight?
Would you learn who won by the light of the moon and stars?
List to the yarn, as my grandmother's father the sailor told it to me.

Our foe was no skulk in his ship I tell you, (said he,)
His was the surly English pluck, and there is no tougher or truer,
and never was, and never will be;
Along the lower'd eve he came horribly raking us.

We closed with him, the yards entangled, the cannon touch'd,
My captain lash'd fast with his own hands.

We had receiv'd some eighteen pound shots under the water,
On our lower-gun-deck two large pieces had burst at the first fire,
killing all around and blowing up overhead.

Fighting at sun-down, fighting at dark,
Ten o'clock at night, the full moon well up, our leaks on the gain,
and five feet of water reported,
The master-at-arms loosing the prisoners confined in the afterhold
to give them a chance for themselves.

The transit to and from the magazine is now stopt by the sentinels,
They see so many strange faces they do not know whom to trust.

Our frigate takes fire,
The other asks if we demand quarter?
If our colors are struck and the fighting done?

Now I laugh content, for I hear the voice of my little captain,
We have not struck, he composedly cries, *we have just begun our part of the fighting.*

Only three guns are in use,
One is directed by the captain himself against the enemy's main-mast,
Two well-serv'd with grape and canister silence his musketry and clear his decks.
The tops alone second the fire of this little battery, especially the main-top,
They hold out bravely during the whole of the action.

Not a moment's cease.
The leaks gain fast on the pumps, the fire eats toward the powder-magazine.

One of the pumps has been shot away, it is generally thought we are sinking.

Serene stands the little captain,
He is not hurried, his voice is neither high nor low,
His eyes give more light to us than our battle-lanterns.

Toward twelve there in the beams of the moon they surrender to us.

40

Flaunt of the sunshine I need not your bask—lie over!
You light surfaces only, I force surfaces and depths also.

Earth! you seem to look for something at my hands,
Say, old top-knot, what do you want?

Behold, I do not give lectures or a little charity,
When I give I give myself.

You there, impotent, loose in the knees,
Open your scarf'd chops till I blow grit within you,
Spread your palms and lift the flaps of your pockets,
I am not to be denied, I compel, I have stores plenty and to spare,
And any thing I have I bestow.

I do not ask who you are, that is not important to me,
You can do nothing and be nothing but what I will infold you.

To cotton-field drudge or cleaner of privies I lean,
On his right cheek I put the family kiss,
And in my soul I swear I never will deny him.

To anyone dying, thither I speed and twist the knob of the door,
Turn the bed-clothes toward the foot of the bed,
Let the physician and the priest go home.

I seize the descending man and raise him with resistless will,
O despairer, here is my neck,
By God, you shall not go down! hang your whole weight upon me.

48

I have said that the soul is not more than the body,
And I have said that the body is not more than the soul,
And nothing, not God, is greater to one than one's self is,
And whoever walks a furlong without sympathy walks to his own
funeral drest in his shroud,
And I or you pocketless of a dime may purchase the pick of the
earth,
And to glance with an eye or show a bean in its pod confounds the
learning of all times,
And there is no trade or employment but the young man following
it may become a hero,
And there is no object so soft but it makes a hub for the wheel'd
universe,
And I say to any man or woman, Let your soul stand cool and com-
posed before a million universes.

And I say to mankind, Be not curious about God,
For I who am curious about each am not curious about God,
(No array of terms can say how much I am at peace about God and
about death.)

I hear and behold God in every object, yet understand God not in
the least,
Nor do I understand who there can be more wonderful than myself.

Why should I wish to see God better than this day?
I see something of God each hour of the twenty-four, and each moment then,
In the faces of men and women I see God, and in my own face in
the glass,
I find letters from God dropt in the street, and every one is sign'd
by God's name,
And I leave them where they are, for I know that wheresoe'er I go,
Others will punctually come for ever and ever.

52

The spotted hawk swoops by and accuses me, he complains of my
gab and my loitering.

I too am not a bit tamed, I too am untranslatable,
I sound my barbaric yawp over the roofs of the world.

The last scud of day holds back for me,
It flings my likeness after the rest and true as any on the shadow'd
wilds,
It coaxes me to the vapor and the dusk.

I depart as air, I shake my white locks at the runaway sun,
I effuse my flesh in eddies, and drift it in lacy jags.

I bequeath myself to the dirt to grow from the grass I love,
If you want me again look for me under your boot-soles.

You will hardly know who I am or what I mean,
But I shall be good health to you nevertheless,
And filter and fiber your blood.

Failing to fetch me at first keep encouraged,
Missing me one place search another,
I stop somewhere waiting for you.

Nothing was mean, nothing was rejected. A leaf of grass was a miracle as great as the galaxy; the running roadside blackberry was "fit to adorn the parlors of heaven." In a dream of a new world

Whitman precipitated the American spirit. He implored the Muse to migrate from Greece, to turn away from the past:

Cross out please those immensely overpaid accounts,
That matter of Troy and Achilles' wrath, and Aeneas', Odysseus' wanderings,
Placard "Removed" and "To Let" on the rocks of your snowy Parnassus . . .

And the Muse responded. She made herself at home among "the divine average"; she was not dismayed by the thud of machinery, "not a bit by drainpipe and artificial fertilizers." The "glory of the commonplace" touched new and democratic vistas.

I Hear America Singing

I hear America singing, the varied carols I hear,
Those of mechanics, each one singing his as it should be blithe and strong,
The carpenter singing his as he measures his plank or beam,
The mason singing his as he makes ready for work, or leaves off work,
The boatman singing what belongs to him in his boat, the deckhand singing on the steamboat deck,
The shoemaker singing as he sits on his bench, the hatter singing as he stands,
The wood-cutter's song, the plowboy's on his way in the morning, or at noon intermission or at sundown,
The delicious singing of the mother, or of the young wife at work, or of the girl sewing or washing,
Each singing what belongs to him or her and to none else,
The day what belongs to the day—at night the party of young fellows, robust, friendly,
Singing with open mouths their strong melodious songs.

For You, O Democracy

Come, I will make the continent indissoluble,
I will make the most splendid race the sun ever shone upon,
I will make divine magnetic lands,
With the love of comrades,
With the life-long love of comrades.

I will plant companionship thick as trees along all the rivers of America, and along the shores of the great lakes, and all over the prairies,
I will make inseparable cities with their arms about each other's necks,
By the love of comrades,
By the manly love of comrades.

For you these from me, O Democracy, to serve you, ma femme!
For you, for you I am trilling these songs.

Whitman's challenge to tradition did not go unpunished. It affected his private life as well as his public career. After serving as a wound dresser during the Civil War, he was given a minor clerkship in the Department of the Interior. His chief, who had been a Methodist preacher, discovered evidences of "immorality" in CHILDREN OF ADAM, and Whitman was summarily dismissed. William Douglas O'Connor, an abolitionist author, wrote a pamphlet in defense of Whitman and coined the phrase "the Good Gray Poet." Whitman's phrase about Abraham Lincoln is less well-known, but it is equally apt: "a Hoosier Michael Angelo."

Lincoln was assassinated while Whitman was still in the Department of the Interior. In the fourth edition of LEAVES OF GRASS, a volume which was steadily growing in size and strength, Whitman included a series of DRUM TAPS which reflected the Civil War and its consequences. Among the war poems were four MEMORIES OF PRESIDENT LINCOLN. One in rhyme soon became popular; another, WHEN LILACS LAST IN THE DOORYARD BLOOM'D, had to wait almost half a century before it was recognized as one of the greatest poems, and certainly the greatest elegy, ever written in America.

O Captain! My Captain!

O Captain! my Captain! our fearful trip is done,
The ship has weathered every rack, the prize we sought is won.
The port is near, the bells I hear, the people all exulting,
While follow eyes the steady keel, the vessel grim and daring;
But O heart! heart! heart!
O the bleeding drops of red.
Where on the deck my Captain lies,
Fallen cold and dead.

O Captain! my Captain! rise up and hear the bells;
Rise up—for you the flag is flung—for you the bugle trills,
For you bouquets and ribboned wreaths—for you the shores a-crowd-
    ing,
For you they call, the swaying mass, their eager faces turning;
        Here Captain! dear father!
          This arm beneath your head!
            It is some dream that on the deck,
              You've fallen cold and dead.

My Captain does not answer, his lips are pale and still,
My father does not feel my arm, he has no pulse nor will,
The ship is anchored safe and sound, its voyage closed and done,
From fearful trip the victor ship comes in with object won;
        Exult, O shores, and ring, O bells!
          But I with mournful tread,
            Walk the deck my Captain lies,
              Fallen cold and dead.

When Lilacs Last in the Dooryard Bloom'd

1

When lilacs last in the dooryard bloom'd,
And the great star early droop'd in the western sky in the night,
I mourn'd, and yet shall mourn with ever-returning spring.

Ever-returning spring, trinity sure to me you bring,
Lilac blooming perennial and drooping star in the west,
And thought of him I love.

2

O powerful western fallen star!
O shades of night—O moody, tearful night!
O great star disappear'd—O the black murk that hides the star!
O cruel hands that hold me powerless—O helpless soul of me!
O harsh surrounding cloud that will not free my soul.

3

In the dooryard fronting an old farm-house near the whitewash'd
    palings,
Stands the lilac-bush tall-growing with heart-shaped leaves of rich
    green,

With many a pointed blossom rising delicate, with the perfume
strong I love,
With every leaf a miracle—and from this bush in the dooryard,
With delicate-color'd blossoms and heart-shaped leaves of rich green,
A sprig with its flower I break.

4

In the swamp in secluded recesses,
A shy and hidden bird is warbling a song.

Solitary the thrush,
The hermit withdrawn to himself, avoiding the settlements,
Sings by himself a song.

Song of the bleeding throat,
Death's outlet song of life, (for well dear brother I know,
If thou wast not granted to sing thou would'st surely die.)

5

Over the breast of the spring, the land, amid cities,
Amid lanes and through old woods, where lately the violets peep'd
from the ground, spotting the gray débris,
Amid the grass in the fields each side of the lanes, passing the end-
less grass,
Passing the yellow-spear'd wheat, every grain from its shroud in the
dark-brown fields uprisen,
Passing the apple-tree blows of white and pink in the orchards,
Carrying a corpse to where it shall rest in the grave,
Night and day journeys a coffin.

6

Coffin that passes through lanes and streets,
Through day and night with the great cloud darkening the land,
With the pomp of the inloop'd flags with the cities draped in black,
With the show of the States themselves as of crape-veil'd women
standing,
With processions long and winding and the flambeaus of the night,
With the countless torches lit, with the silent sea of faces and the
unbared heads,

With the waiting depot, the arriving coffin, and the somber faces,
With dirges through the night, with the thousand voices rising
strong and solemn,
With all the mournful voices of the dirges pour'd around the coffin,
The dim-lit churches and the shuddering organs—where amid these
you journey,
With the tolling tolling bells' perpetual clang,
Here, coffin that slowly passes,
I give you my sprig of lilac.

7

(Nor for you, for one alone,
Blossoms and branches green to coffins all I bring,
For fresh as the morning, thus would I chant a song for you O sane
and sacred death.

All over bouquets of roses,
O death, I cover you over with roses and early lilies,
But mostly and now the lilac that blooms the first,
Copious I break, I break the sprigs from the bushes,
With loaded arms I come, pouring for you,
For you and the coffins all of you O death.)

8

O western orb sailing the heaven,
Now I know what you must have meant as a month since I walk'd,
As I walk'd in silence the transparent shadowy night,
As I saw you had something to tell as you bent to me night after
night,
As you droop'd from the sky low down as if to my side, (while the
other stars all look'd on,)
As we wander'd together the solemn night, (for something I know
not what kept me from sleep,)
As the night advanced, and I saw on the rim of the west how full
you were of woe,
As I stood on the rising ground in the breeze in the cool transparent
night,
As I watch'd where you pass'd and was lost in the netherward black
of the night,
As my soul in its trouble dissatisfied sank, as where you sad orb.
Concluded, dropt in the night, and was gone.

9

Sing on there in the swamp,
O singer bashful and tender, I hear your notes, I hear your call,
I hear, I come presently, I understand you,
But a moment I linger, for the lustrous star has detain'd me,
The star my departing comrade holds and detains me.

10

O how shall I warble myself for the dead one there I loved?
And how shall I deck my song for the large sweet soul that has gone?
And what shall my perfume be for the grave of him I love?

Sea-winds blown from east and west,
Blown from the Eastern sea and blown from the Western sea, till there on the prairies meeting,
These and with these and the breath of my chant,
I'll perfume the grave of him I love.

11

O what shall I hang on the chamber walls?
And what shall the pictures be that I hang on the walls,
To adorn the burial-house of him I love?
Pictures of growing spring and farms and homes,
With the Fourth-month eve at sundown, and the gray smoke lucid and bright,
With floods of the yellow gold of the gorgeous, indolent, sinking sun, burning, expanding the air,
With the fresh sweet herbage under foot, and the pale green leaves of the trees prolific,
In the distance the flowing glaze, the breast of the river, with a wind-dapple here and there,
With ranging hills on the banks, with many a line against the sky, and shadows,
And the city at hand, with dwellings so dense, and stacks of chimneys,
And all the scenes of life and the workshops, and the workmen homeward returning.

12

Lo, body and soul—this land,
My own Manhattan with spires, and the sparkling and hurrying tides, and the ships,
The varied and ample land, the South and the North in the light, Ohio's shores and flashing Missouri,
And ever the far-spreading prairies cover'd with grass and corn.

Lo, the most excellent sun so calm and haughty,
The violet and purple morn with just-felt breezes,
The gentle soft-born measureless light,
The miracle spreading bathing all, the fulfill'd noon,
The coming eve delicious, the welcome night and the stars,
Over my cities shining all, enveloping man and land.

13

Sing on, sing on you gray-brown bird,
Sing from the swamps, the recesses, pour your chant from the bushes,
Limitless out of the dusk, out of the cedars and pines.
Sing on dearest brother, warble your reedy song,
Loud human song, with voice of uttermost woe.

O liquid and free and tender!
O wild and loose to my soul—O wondrous singer!
You only I hear—yet the star holds me, (but will soon depart,)
Yet the lilac with mastering odor holds me.

14

Now while I sat in the day and look'd forth,
In the close of the day with its light and the fields of spring, and the farmers preparing their crops,
In the large unconscious scenery of my land with its lakes and forests,
In the heavenly aerial beauty, (after the perturb'd winds and the storms,)
Under the arching heavens of the afternoon swift passing, and the voices of children and women,
The many-moving sea-tides, and I saw the ships how they sail'd,

And the summer approaching with richness, and the fields all busy
with labor,
And the infinite separate houses, how they all went on, each with
its meals and minutia of daily usages,
And the streets how their throbbings throbb'd, and the cities pent
—lo, then and there,
Falling upon them all and among them all, enveloping me with
the rest,
Appear'd the cloud, appear'd the long black trail,
And I knew death, its thought, and the sacred knowledge of death.

Then with the knowledge of death as walking one side of me,
And the thought of death close-walking the other side of me,
And I in the middle as with companions, and as holding the hands
of companions,
I fled forth to the hiding receiving night that talks not,
Down to the shores of the water, the path by the swamp in the
dimness,
To the solemn shadowy cedars and ghostly pines so still.

And the singer so shy to the rest receiv'd me,
The gray-brown bird I know receiv'd us comrades three,
And he sang the carol of death, and a verse for him I love.

From deep secluded recesses,
From the fragrant cedars and the ghostly pines so still,
Came the carol of the bird.

And the charm of the carol rapt me
As I held as if by their hands my comrades in the night,
And the voice of my spirit tallied the song of the bird.

Come lovely and soothing death,
Undulate round the world, serenely arriving, arriving,
In the day, in the night, to all, to each,
Sooner or later delicate death.

Prais'd be the fathomless universe,
For life and joy, and for objects and knowledge curious,
And for love, sweet love—but praise! praise! praise!
For the sure-enwinding arms of cool-enfolding death.

Dark mother always gliding near with soft feet,
Have none chanted for thee a chant of fullest welcome?

Then I chant it for thee, I glorify thee above all,
I bring thee a song that when thou must indeed come, come unfalteringly.

Approach strong deliveress,
When it is so, when thou hast taken them I joyously sing the dead,
Lost in the loving floating ocean of thee,
Laved in the flood of thy bliss O death.

From me to thee glad serenades,
Dances for thee I propose saluting thee, adornments and feastings for thee,
And the sights of the open landscape and the high-spread sky are fitting,
And life and the fields, and the huge and thoughtful night.

The night in silence under many a star,
The ocean shore and the husky whispering wave whose voice I know,
And the soul turning to thee O vast and well-veil'd death,
And the body gratefully nestling close to thee.

Over the tree-tops I float thee a song,
Over the rising and sinking waves, over the myriad fields and the prairies wide,
Over the dense-pack'd cities all and the teeming wharves and ways,
I float this carol with joy, with joy to thee O death.

15

To the tally of my soul,
Loud and strong kept up the gray-brown bird,
With pure deliberate notes spreading filling the night.

Loud in the pines and cedars dim,
Clear in the freshness moist and the swamp-perfume,
And I with my comrades there in the night.

While my sight that was bound in my eyes unclosed,
As to long panoramas of visions.

And I saw askant the armies,
I saw as in noiseless dreams hundreds of battle-flags,
Borne through the smoke of the battles and pierc'd with missiles I saw them,
And carried hither and yon through the smoke, and torn and bloody,

And at last but a few shreds left on the staffs, (and all in silence,)
And the staffs all splinter'd and broken.

I saw battle-corpses, myriads of them,
And the white skeletons of young men, I saw them,
I saw the débris and débris of all the slain soldiers of the war,
But I saw they were not as was thought,
They themselves were fully at rest, they suffer'd not,
The living remain'd and suffer'd, the mother suffer'd,
And the wife and the child and the musing comrade suffer'd,
And the armies that remain'd suffer'd.

16

Passing the visions, passing the night,
Passing, unloosing the hold of my comrades' hands,
Passing the song of the hermit bird and the tallying song of my soul,
Victorious song, death's outlet song, yet varying ever-altering song,
As low and wailing, yet clear the notes, rising and falling, flooding
the night,
Sadly sinking and fainting, as warning and warning, and yet again
bursting with joy,
Covering the earth and filling the spread of the heaven,
As that powerful psalm in the night I heard from recesses,
Passing, I leave thee lilac with heart-shaped leaves,
I leave thee there in the dooryard, blooming, returning with spring.

I cease from my song for thee,
From my gaze on thee in the west, fronting the west, communing
with thee,
O comrade lustrous with silver face in the night.

Yet each to keep and all, retrievements out of the night,
The song, the wondrous chant of the gray-brown bird,
And the tallying chant, the echo arous'd in my soul,
With the lustrous and drooping star with the countenance full of
woe,
With the holders holding my hand nearing the call of the bird,
Comrades mine and I in the midst, and their memory ever to keep,
for the dead I loved so well,
For the sweetest, wisest soul of all my days and lands—and this for
his dear sake,
Lilac and star and bird twined with the chant of my soul,
There in the fragrant pines and the cedars dusk and dim.

In his fifty-fourth year Whitman was struck by paralysis. Three months later his mother died, and he seems never to have recovered from the effect of her death. Years later he wrote that he was "still enveloped in thoughts of my dear mother, the most perfect and magnetic character, the rarest combination of practical, moral, and spiritual of all and any I have ever known—and by me O so much the most deeply loved."

Whitman spent the last years of his life in Camden, New Jersey, where his mother had died. Confined by paralysis and poverty-stricken, he was helped by a few friends. In 1891 he prepared the final "deathbed edition" of LEAVES OF GRASS, which had grown from thirty-two poems to approximately three hundred, and pictured himself "much like some hard-cased dilapidated grim ancient shell-fish or time-banged conch—no legs, utterly nonlocomotive—cast up high and dry on the shore sands." He died at Camden, in his seventy-third year, March 26, 1892.

The Last Invocation

At the last, tenderly,
From the walls of the powerful fortress'd house,
From the clasp of the knitted locks, from the keep of the well-closed
doors,
Let me be wafted.

Let me glide noiselessly forth;
With the key of softness unlock the locks—with a whisper,
Set ope the doors O soul.

Tenderly—be not impatient,
(Strong is your hold O mortal flesh.
Strong is your hold O love.)

Poets to Come

Poets to come! orators, singers, musicians to come!
Not to-day is to justify me and answer what I am for,
But you, a new brood, native, athletic, continental, greater than
before known,

Arouse! for you must justify me.
I myself but write one or two indicative words for the future,
I but advance a moment only to wheel and hurry back in the darkness.

I am a man who, sauntering along without fully stopping, turns a casual look upon you and then averts his face,
Leaving it to you to prove and define it,
Expecting the main things from you.

When I Heard the Learn'd Astronomer

When I heard the learn'd astronomer,
When the proofs, the figures, were ranged in columns before me,
When I was shown the charts and diagrams, to add, divide, and measure them,
When I sitting heard the astronomer where he lectured with much applause in the lecture-room,
How soon unaccountable I became tired and sick,
Till rising and gliding out I wander'd off by myself,
In the mystical moist night-air, and from time to time,
Look'd up in perfect silence at the stars.

The Commonplace

The commonplace I sing;
How cheap is health! how cheap nobility!
Abstinence, no falsehood, no gluttony, lust;
The open air I sing, freedom, toleration,
(Take here the mainest lesson—less from books—less from the schools,)
The common day and night—the common earth and waters,
Your farm—your work, trade, occupation,
The democratic wisdom underneath, like solid ground for all.

A Noiseless Patient Spider

A noiseless patient spider,
I mark'd where on a little promontory it stood isolated,
Mark'd how to explore the vacant vast surrounding,
It launch'd forth filament, filament, filament, out of itself.
Ever unreeling them, ever tirelessly speeding them.

And you O my soul where you stand,
Surrounded, detached, in measureless oceans of space,
Ceaselessly musing, venturing, throwing, seeking the spheres to
connect them.
Till the bridge you will need be form'd, till the ductile anchor hold,
Till the gossamer thread you fling catch somewhere, O my soul.

Reconciliation

Word over all, beautiful as the sky,
Beautiful that war and all its deeds of carnage must in time be
utterly lost,
That the hands of the sisters Death and Night incessantly softly
wash again, and ever again, this soil'd world;
For my enemy is dead, a man divine as myself is dead,
I look where he lies white-faced and still in the coffin—I draw near,
Bend down and touch lightly with my lips the white face in the
coffin.

Darest Thou Now, O Soul

Darest thou now, O soul,
Walk out with me toward the unknown region,
Where neither ground is for the feet nor any path to follow?

No map there, nor guide,
Nor voice sounding, nor touch of human hand,
Nor face with blooming flesh, nor lips, nor eyes, are in that land.

I know it not, O soul,
Nor dost thou; all is a blank before us;
All waits undreamed of in that region, that inaccessible land.

Till when the ties loosen,
All but the ties eternal, Time and Space,
Nor darkness, gravitation, sense, nor any bounds bounding us.

Then we burst forth, we float,
In Time and Space, O soul, prepared for them,
Equal, equipped at last (O joy! O fruit of all!) them to fulfill, O soul.

"What I assume you shall assume," wrote Whitman in an all-embracing exaltation of the democratic character. "In all people I see myself." Buoyed up by tremendous expectations and unrestrained by the gathering threats to his idealism, Whitman was guilty of overinclusiveness. He tried to force the reader to a comprehension of a vast world by a catalogue of its details. To overemphasis he added overconfidence. Kenneth Allott, in (of all places!) a biography of Jules Verne, speaks of "Whitman's exuberant Rousseau-Rotarian voice," and there is justice as well as wit in the incongruous epigram. Whitman's unflagging optimism and high hopes were dashed by events he could not foresee. In THE BEGINNINGS OF CRITICAL REALISM IN AMERICA, V. L. Parrington remarks that Whitman was "a great figure, the greatest assuredly in our literature—yet perhaps only a great child."

Whitman was "a great child" in the sense that he was both a realist and a mystic. A single, separate person, he sang of all existence, of "Life immense in passion, pulse, and power." A visionary, he beheld a future greater than all the past, a land of "inseparable cities" teeming with "the lifelong love of comrades." Prophet for a possible millennium, he was also an indomitable pioneer; exploring new roads, he was swept by tidal rhythms. Biographer of democracy, he contained a continent.

HERMAN MELVILLE

[1819–1891]

LIKE Whitman, Herman Melville fought a losing battle with fate. A pioneer in American giantism, writing novels that were extended poems in prose, scorned by the critics and neglected by the public, he died in obscurity.

Melville's beginnings were auspicious enough. He was born in New York City, August 1, 1819, in a well-to-do family. When Melville was twelve, his father died, leaving a wife with eight children to be taken care of by her relatives near Albany, New York. Orphaned and half educated, young Melville attempted to teach school. Failing as a teacher, he became a clerk. A failure again, he ran away to sea and shipped as a common sailor. After a disillusioning experience abroad, he returned to America and hoped to settle in the little town of Lansingburgh, New York. But the sea was in his veins; at twenty-one he began pursuing the great whale which, to him, was not only an adventure and an education, but a symbol. He wrote: "If, at my death my executors (or more properly, my creditors) find any precious manuscripts in my desk, then I prospectively ascribe all the honor and glory to whaling; for a whale-ship was my Yale and Harvard." Twice Melville jumped ship, lived among South Sea cannibals, and made a dusky Eden in Tahiti. The need of medical attention to an infected leg forced him to return reluctantly to what he termed "snivelization."

At twenty-six Melville entered the literary world with TYPEE, and on the promise of its reception he married the daughter of Judge Shaw, a Boston Brahmin. TYPEE was an adventure story in which the criticism of contemporary society was present but submerged; it was his one popular success. The volumes which followed questioned current standards; for fifteen years Melville dared to create works which challenged values and assailed the political-moral structure of his day. It took years to produce his masterpiece, MOBY-DICK, and Melville emerged from the work with energy drained and health impaired. Few readers recognized the overpowering force of the book, a book which has since been recognized as a prose epic and a poetic allegory; "one of the first great mythologies to be created in the modern world," wrote Lewis Mumford, "created out of the stuff of that world, its science, its exploration, its terrestrial daring." Most of the critics appraised MOBY-DICK as a fair yarn ruined by the author's perverse symbolism. One of them termed Melville's style "mad as a March hare; gibbering, screaming, like an incurable Bedlamite, reckless of keeper or strait jacket." It is true that the narration sprawls and that the pattern is sometimes twisted. But a prodigious current runs through the book; it impels Ahab's Shakespearean soliloquies as well as the lyrical digressions. The power of the sea is in MOBY-DICK as the power of the earth is in LEAVES OF GRASS.

The Whale

The ribs and terrors in the whale,
  Arched over me a dismal gloom,
While all God's sun-lit waves rolled by,
  And left me deepening down to doom.

I saw the opening maw of hell,
  With endless pains and sorrows there;
Which none but they that feel can tell—
  Oh, I was plunging to despair.

In black distress, I called my God,
  When I could scarce believe Him mine,
He bowed His ear to my complaints—
  No more the whale did me confine.

With speed He flew to my relief,
  As on a radiant dolphin borne;
Awful, yet bright, as lightning shone
  The face of my Deliverer God.

My song for ever shall record
  That terrible, that joyful hour;
I give the glory to my God,
  His all the mercy and the power.

from MOBY-DICK

Melville's last forty years were unhappy spasms of creation and ill-health. He had ceased to be a popular novelist. At fifty he turned to poetry; his last book was a collection of verse. "All Fame is patronage," Melville once wrote. "Let me be infamous." He died September 28, 1891, a foundered ship, sinking (in Raymond Weaver's phrase) "without a ripple of renown."

MOBY-DICK is not an isolated peak. Melville's verses, and particularly his BATTLE PIECES, are eminences illumined by lightning strokes. Much of the poetry has been lost, much of it is out of print. But the living flame burns in the fragments. The young sailor, buried for years, comes to life; the adventurer who had withdrawn from the world, refusing to share its slavery, re-enters it with a dream of freedom.

The Martyr

Indicative of the passion of the people on the 15th of April, 1865, after the assassination of Lincoln

Good Friday was the day
  Of the prodigy and crime,
When they killed him in his pity,
  When they killed him in his prime

Of clemency and calm—
    When with yearning he was filled
    To redeem the evil-willed,
And, though conqueror, be kind;
  But they killed him in his kindness,
  In their madness and their blindness,
And they killed him from behind.

  There is sobbing of the strong,
    And a pall upon the land;
  But the People in their weeping
    Bare the iron hand;
  Beware the People weeping
    When they bare the iron hand.

He lieth in his blood—
  The father in his face;
They have killed him, the Forgiver—
  The Avenger takes his place,
The Avenger wisely stern,
    Who in righteousness shall do
    What the heavens call him to,
And the parricides remand;
  For they killed him in his kindness,
  In their madness and their blindness,
And his blood is on their hand.

  There is sobbing of the strong,
    And a pall upon the land;
  But the People in their weeping
    Bare the iron hand;
  Beware the People weeping
    When they bare the iron hand.

The March into Virginia

JULY, 1861

Did all the lets and bars appear
  To every just or larger end,
Whence should come the trust and cheer?
  Youth must its ignorant impulse lend—
Age finds place in the rear.
  All wars are boyish, and are fought by boys,

The champions and enthusiasts of the state:
  Turbid ardors and vain joys
    Not barrenly abate—
  Stimulants to the power mature,
    Preparatives of fate.

Who here forecasteth the event?
What heart but spurns at precedent
And warnings of the wise,
Contemned foreclosures of surprise?
The banners play, the bugles call,
The air is blue and prodigal.
  No berrying party, pleasure-wooed,
No picnic party in the May,
Ever went less loth than they
  Into that leafy neighborhood.
In Bacchic glee they file toward Fate,
Moloch's uninitiate;
Expectancy, and glad surmise
Of battle's unknown mysteries.
All they feel is this: 'tis glory,
A rapture sharp, though transitory,
Yet lasting in belaureled story.
So they gaily go to fight,
Chatting left and laughing right.

But some who this blithe mood present,
  As on in lightsome files they fare,
Shall die experienced ere three days are spent—
  Perish, enlightened by the volleyed glare;
Or shame survive, and like to adamant,
  The throe of Second Manassas share.

In strength and amplitude Melville has only two equals in America: Emerson and Whitman, both of whom, being children of light, are alien to his dark grandeur. Against their positive yea-saying, Melville pits his challenging No. He is their disturbing opponent, and he measures up to them.

MATTHEW ARNOLD

[1822–1888]

MATTHEW ARNOLD was destined to be a poet who preached wistfully to the world. His blend of skepticism and faith expressed the spirit of two generations, and, until recently, his prim canons of poetry dominated English criticism.

Son of Thomas Arnold, the famous headmaster of Rugby, Matthew Arnold was born near Staines, December 24, 1822. At eighteen his first publication, ALARIC AT ROME, won a prize at Rugby; at twenty-one, his poem CROMWELL won the important Newdigate Prize at Oxford. For four years after graduation he earned a small living as private secretary, but marriage at the age of twenty-nine compelled him to seek an increased income. He accepted an appointment as inspector of schools, a position which was more conducive to criticism than creation and which he held for thirty-five years. Toward the end of his life he came to the United States to lecture. He died of heart failure at Liverpool in his sixty-sixth year.

It has been said that Arnold's much-anthologized verse is respected but no longer loved, that his social criticism is infrequently read, and that he is quoted only for a few phrases, such as "sweetness and light" and his definition of poetry as "a criticism of life." His poetic activity lasted less than ten years, yet Arnold did not underestimate his verse. "My poems," he wrote, "represent, on the whole, the main movement of mind of the last quarter of a century, and thus they will probably have their day as people become conscious of what that movement of mind is, and interested in the literary productions which reflect it. It might fairly be urged that I have less poetical sentiment than Tennyson, and less intellectual vigor and abundance than Browning; yet, because I have perhaps more of a fusion of the two than either of them, I am likely enough to have my turn, as they have had theirs."

Whether or not Arnold's estimate of his own poetry was accurate, his verse unquestionably justifies his definition. It is distinctly "a criticism of life." It is ethical, earnest, and melancholy in tone. What was once considered to be its great virtue now seems to be its chief defect: its purposeful "high seriousness" is muted by the low emotional pitch. But poetry is not all song; and here, for the most part, instead of singing, it searches.

Dover Beach

The sea is calm tonight,
The tide is full, the moon lies fair
Upon the straits;—on the French coast the light
Gleams and is gone; the cliffs of England stand,
Glimmering and vast, out in the tranquil bay.
Come to the window, sweet is the night-air!

Only, from the long line of spray
Where the sea meets the moon-blanched land,
Listen! you hear the grating roar
Of pebbles which the waves draw back, and fling,
At their return, up the high strand,
Begin, and cease, and then again begin,
With tremulous cadence slow, and bring
The eternal note of sadness in.

Sophocles long ago
Heard it on the Aegean, and it brought
Into his mind the turbid ebb and flow
Of human misery; we
Find also in the sound a thought,
Hearing it by this distant northern sea.

The Sea of Faith
Was once, too, at the full, and round earth's shore
Lay like the folds of a bright girdle furled.
But now I only hear
Its melancholy, long, withdrawing roar,
Retreating, to the breath
Of the night-wind, down the vast edges drear
And naked shingles of the world.

Ah, love, let us be true
To one another! for the world, which seems
To lie before us like a land of dreams,
So various, so beautiful, so new,
Hath really neither joy, nor love, nor light.

Nor certitude, nor peace, nor help for pain;
And we are here as on a darkling plain
Swept with confused alarms of struggle and flight,
Where ignorant armies clash by night.

Quiet Work

One lesson, Nature, let me learn of thee,
One lesson which in every wind is blown,
One lesson of two duties kept at one
Though the loud world proclaim their enmity—
Of toil unsevered from tranquillity,
Of labor, that in lasting fruit outgrows
Far noisier schemes, accomplished in repose,
Too great for haste, too high for rivalry!

Yes, while on earth a thousand discords ring,
Man's fitful uproar mingling with his toil,
Still do thy sleepless ministers move on,
Their glorious tasks in silence perfecting;
Still working, blaming still our vain turmoil,
Laborers that shall not fail, when man is gone.

Shakespeare

Others abide our question. Thou art free.
We ask and ask. Thou smilest, and art still,
Out-topping knowledge. For the loftiest hill,
Who to the stars uncrowns his majesty,
Planting his steadfast footsteps in the sea,
Making the heaven of heavens his dwelling-place,
Spares but the cloudy border of his base
To the foiled searching of mortality;
And thou, who didst the stars and sunbeams know,
Self-schooled, self-scanned, self-honored, self-secure,
Didst tread on earth unguessed at.—Better so!
All pains the immortal spirit must endure,
All weakness which impairs, all griefs which bow,
Find their sole speech in that victorious brow.

Requiescat

Strew on her roses, roses,
And never a spray of yew:
In quiet she reposes;
Ah, would that I did too!

Her mirth the world required;
She bathed it in smiles of glee.
But her heart was tired, tired,
And now they let her be.

Her life was turning, turning,
In mazes of heat and sound.
But for peace her soul was yearning,
And now peace laps her round.

Her cabined, ample spirit,
It fluttered and failed for breath;
Tonight it doth inherit
The vasty hall of death.

The Last Word

Creep into thy narrow bed,
Creep, and let no more be said!
Vain thy onset! all stands fast.
Thou thyself must break at last.

Let the long contention cease!
Geese are swans, and swans are geese.
Let them have it how they will!
Thou art tired; best be still.

They out-talked thee, hissed thee, tore thee?
Better men fared thus before thee;
Fired their ringing shot and passed,
Hotly charged—and sank at last.

Charge once more, then, and be dumb!
Let the victors, when they come,
When the forts of folly fall,
Find thy body by the wall!

COVENTRY PATMORE

[1823–1896]

BORN July 23, 1823, in Epping Forest, Coventry Kersey Dighton Patmore was almost crippled by his name. His father was an ambitious if commonplace author, and the Patmores expected great things of their offspring. It was planned that Coventry should become a painter; he joined the Pre-Raphaelite group and contributed to its organ THE GERM. His gift as an artist being negligible, he turned to literature, and Thackeray hailed him as a coming genius. Unfortunately, POEMS, published in Patmore's twenty-first year, was thin and mawkish, and, although Dante Gabriel Rossetti befriended the book, the critics condemned it. At twenty-four, Patmore became an assistant librarian in the British Museum, married happily, and devoted most of his life to a celebration of domesticity.

THE ANGEL IN THE HOUSE, a collection of some one hundred and fifty poems in praise of married love, is characterized by its sentimental title. Yet Ruskin spoke of the verses as "sparkling humilities," and if they are not passionate, they are gently persuasive.

A Farewell

With all my will, but much against my heart,
We two now part.
My Very Dear,
Our solace is, the sad road lies so clear.
It needs no art,
With faint, averted feet
And many a tear,
In our opposéd paths to persevere.
Go thou to East, I West.
We will not say
There's any hope, it is so far away.
But, O my Best,
When the one darling of our widowhead,
The nursling Grief,
Is dead.

And no dews blur our eyes
To see the peach-bloom come in evening skies,
Perchance we may,
Where now this night is day,
And even through faith of still averted feet,
Making full circle of our banishment,
Amazéd meet;
The bitter journey to the bourne so sweet
Seasoning the termless feast of our content
With tears of recognition never dry.

After fifteen years of uneventful felicity, Mrs. Patmore died. Three years later Patmore married a recent convert to Catholicism and became a Catholic himself. His second wife was a woman of means, and Patmore was able to give up his post in the British Museum and purchase a large place in Ashdown Forest. He was so proud of his status as country squire that he wrote and published HOW I MANAGED MY ESTATE. His second wife died in 1880, and, within a year, Patmore married again. He died in his seventy-fourth year, November 26, 1896.

After his death Alice Meynell wrote, "Essentially he had but one subject: human love as a mystery; and but one character: an impassioned spirituality." Today Patmore's verse seems more intimate than impassioned. There is no doubt about its warmth, its true simplicity. As Patmore himself wrote in one of the shortest but one of his most profound poems:

For want of me the world's course will not fail;
When all its work is done the lie shall rot.
The truth is great, and shall prevail,
When none cares whether it prevail or not.

The Toys

My little son, who looked from thoughtful eyes
And moved and spoke in quiet grown-up wise,
Having my law the seventh time disobeyed,
I struck him, and dismissed
With hard words and unkissed,
—His mother, who was patient, being dead.
Then, fearing lest his grief should hinder sleep,
I visited his bed,

But found him slumbering deep,
With darkened eyelids, and their lashes yet
From his late sobbing wet.
And I, with moan,
Kissing away his tears, left others of my own;
For, on a table drawn beside his head,
He had put, within his reach,
A box of counters and a red-veined stone,
A piece of glass abraded by the beach,
And six or seven shells,
A bottle with bluebells,
And two French copper coins, ranged there with careful art,
To comfort his sad heart.
So when that night I prayed
To God, I wept, and said:
"Ah, when at last we lie with trancéd breath,
Not vexing Thee in death,
And Thou rememberest of what toys
We made our joys,
How weakly understood
Thy great commanded good,
Then, fatherly not less
Than I whom Thou hast molded from the clay,
Thou'lt leave Thy wrath, and say,
'I will be sorry for their childishness.' "

The Married Lover

Why, having won her, do I woo?
  Because her spirit's vestal grace
Provokes me always to pursue,
  But, spirit-like, eludes embrace. . . .

Because, although in act and word
  As lowly as a wife can be,
Her manners, when they call me lord,
  Remind me 'tis by courtesy.

Because her gay and lofty brows,
  When all is won which hope can ask,
Reflect a light of hopeless snows
  That bright in virgin ether bask;

Because, tho' free of the outer court
I am, this Temple keeps its shrine
Sacred to Heaven; because, in short,
She's not and never can be mine.

Truth

Here, in this little bay,
Full of tumultous life and great repose,
Where, twice a day,
The purposeless, glad ocean comes and goes,
Under high cliffs, and far from the huge town,
I sit me down.
For want of me the world's course will not fail;
When all its work is done, the lie shall rot.
The truth is great, and shall prevail,
When none cares whether it prevail or not.

GEORGE MEREDITH

[1828–1909]

ONE of the few novelists whose poetry excelled their prose, George Meredith was born in Portsmouth, in Hampshire, February 12, 1828. His father was a tailor and outfitter at the naval station, but the family affairs deteriorated after the death of Meredith's mother. The boy's education was fitful; he was taught privately at home and at a Moravian school in Germany. At sixteen he began to study law and entered a London solicitor's office. Having neither inclination nor talent for the legal profession, he attempted journalism, for which he was scarcely better fitted. At twenty-one he married the daughter of the novelist Thomas Love Peacock, a widow eight years older than he. The marriage was not a success. Meredith himself recognized it as a blunder, and his wife deserted him and their young son some years later. When his wife died, Meredith remarried at thirty-six, and his second wife was his devoted companion until her death in 1885. The discordant ending of Meredith's first marriage ("the union of this ever-diverse pair) is reflected in the sequence of semisonnets—actually, poems of four united quatrains—which Meredith ironically entitled MODERN LOVE.

FROM

Modern Love

Thus piteously Love closed what he begat:
The union of this ever-diverse pair!
These two were rapid falcons in a snare,
Condemned to do the flitting of the bat.
Lovers beneath the singing sky of May,
They wandered once, clear as the dew on flowers,
But they fed not on the advancing hours:
Their hearts held cravings for the buried day.
Then each applied to each that fatal knife,
Deep questioning, which probes to endless dole.
Ah, what a dusty answer gets the soul
When hot for certainties in this our life!
In tragic hints here see what evermore
Moves dark as yonder midnight ocean's force,
Thundering like ramping hosts of warrior horse,
To throw that faint thin line upon the shore!

Meanwhile, Meredith had acted as war correspondent in Italy (a period reflected in several of his novels) and had become editorial adviser. Thomas Hardy, the other Victorian who became equally famous as poet and novelist, was one of Meredith's discoveries. Although he wrote continually and energetically—one edition of his works ran to thirty-nine volumes—Meredith's vogue did not begin until forty years after the publication of his first books. In his seventy-seventh year he received the Order of Merit, rarely bestowed upon men of letters. He died at eighty-one, May 18, 1909.

Meredith's prose style has been a stumbling block for many. It is mannered and involved, devoted to pretentious characters and preposterous conversations. His novels have a way of elaborating and dissecting the smallest nuance of meaning; praised for their subtlety, many of them seem to be nothing more than tremendous trifles.

Meredith's poems, liberated from tortuous narration, are free of his prose mannerisms. They are thoughtful and vigorous, and some times (as in LUCIFER IN STARLIGHT) richly imaginative. Tennyson declared that he could never get the music of LOVE IN THE VALLEY out of his mind.

Lucifer in Starlight

On a starred night Prince Lucifer uprose.
Tired of his dark dominion swung the fiend
Above the rolling ball in cloud part screened,
Where sinners hugged their spectre of repose.
Poor prey to his hot fit of pride were those.
And now upon his western wing he leaned,
Now his huge bulk o'er Afric's sands careened,
Now the black planet shadowed Arctic snows.
Soaring through wider zones that pricked his scars
With memory of the old revolt from Awe,
He reached a middle height, and at the stars,
Which are the brain of heaven, he looked, and sank.
Around the ancient track marched, rank on rank,
The army of unalterable law.

FROM

Love in the Valley

Under yonder beech-tree single on the greensward,
  Couched with her arms behind her golden head,
Knees and tresses folded to slip and ripple idly,
  Lies my young love sleeping in the shade.
Had I the heart to slide an arm beneath her,
  Press her parting lips as her waist I gather slow,
Waking in amazement she could not but embrace me:
  Then would she hold me and never let me go?

Shy as the squirrel and wayward as the swallow,
  Swift as the swallow along the river's light
Circleting the surface to meet his mirrored winglets,
  Fleeter she seems in her stay than in her flight.
Shy as the squirrel that leaps among the pine-tops,
  Wayward as the swallow overhead at set of sun,
She whom I love is hard to catch and conquer;
  Hard. but O the glory of the winning were she won!

When her mother tends her before the laughing mirror,
  Tying up her laces, looping up her hair,
Often she thinks, were this wild thing wedded,
  More love should I have, and much less care.
When her mother tends her before the lighted mirror,
  Loosening her laces, combing down her curls,
Often she thinks, were this wild thing wedded,
  I should miss but one for many boys and girls.

Heartless she is as the shadow in the meadows
  Flying to the hills on a blue and breezy noon.
No, she is athirst and drinking up her wonder:
  Earth to her is young as the slip of the new moon.
Deals she an unkindness, 'tis but her rapid measure,
  Even as in a dance; and her smile can heal no less:
Like the swinging May-cloud that pelts the flowers with hailstones
  Off a sunny border, she was made to bruise and bless.

Lovely are the curves of the white owl sweeping
  Wavy in the dusk lit by one large star.
Lone on the fir-branch, his rattle-note unvaried,
  Brooding o'er the gloom, spins the brown eve-jar.
Darker grows the valley, more and more forgetting:
  So were it with me if forgetting could be willed.
Tell the grassy hollow that holds the bubbling well-spring,
  Tell it to forget the source that keeps it filled.

Stepping down the hill with her fair companions,
  Arm in arm, all against the raying West,
Boldly she sings, to the merry tune she marches,
  Brave in her shape, and sweeter unpossessed.
Sweeter, for she is what my heart first awaking
  Whispered the world was; morning light is she.
Love that so desires would fain keep her changeless;
  Fain would fling the net, and fain have her free.

DANTE GABRIEL ROSSETTI

[1828–1882]

THE alien Rossettis were a queer family to have made so deep an impression on English art and literature. The father was an Italian poet, a political refugee who became a professor at King's College; the mother was half Italian. There were four children born within a year of each other. The oldest, Maria Francesca Rossetti, became a nun. The elder son, Dante Gabriel Rossetti, soon established himself as a painter, poet, and head of a furiously controversial group. The second son, William Michael, was an art critic and man of letters, editor of THE GERM. Christina Georgina Rossetti, youngest of the children, became a devout and purely lyrical poet.

Born in London, May 12, 1828, Dante Gabriel Rossetti grew up in the "strange society of Italian exiles and English eccentrics which his father had gathered about him." He wrote and illustrated his own poems even as a child. At twenty, ambitious to design great allegories, he became a pupil of the artist Ford Madox Brown; Brown made him draw pickle jars. But Rossetti was impatient for public notice. A few months later, he gathered about him a group of students and organized the Pre-Raphaelite Brotherhood as a revolt from current academic standards and a protest against an accelerated industrialism. The name, intimating that the art of painting had declined with Raphael, began as a slogan and became a trade-mark.

Rossetti's paintings set the standard for the group. They were realistic in detail yet vaguely symbolic in effect, full of odd "off" colors and a sexless sensuality. The matching poetry was equally sultry and languid. The Brotherhood was violently attacked, even by Charles Dickens, as "ugly," "impertinent," "sacrilegious." But Rossetti was undisturbed; he was seeking not only "perfect fidelity" but the perfect model. He found the latter in Elizabeth Siddall. She was seventeen, a milliner's assistant, tall, with gray-green eyes and hair "like dazzling copper," delicately built and slightly tubercular. She became Rossetti's mistress and the Brotherhood's favorite model. It was presumed that Rossetti and Elizabeth Siddall were engaged, but Rossetti waited ten years before he married her. Her health became steadily worse and her husband more difficult. She took laudanum in ever-increasing quantities. Two years after the marriage Rossetti came home and found his wife dying of an overdose of the drug. It was never known whether her death was accidental or suicidal. Overcome with grief, and possibly remorse, Rossetti put all his love poems in the casket. Nine years later, in order to bring out a collection of his poems, the coffin was dug up and the manuscript exhumed.

FROM
The House of Life

LOVE-SIGHT

When do I see thee most, beloved one?
When in the light the spirits of mine eyes
Before thy face, their altar, solemnize
The worship of that Love through thee made known?
Or when, in the dusk hours (we two alone),
Close-kissed and eloquent of still replies
Thy twilight-hidden glimmering visage lies,
And my soul only sees thy soul its own?

O love, my love! if I no more should see
Thyself, nor on the earth the shadow of thee,
Nor image of thine eyes in any spring,—
How then should sound upon Life's darkening slope
The ground-whirl of the perished leaves of Hope,
The wind of Death's imperishable wing?

SILENT NOON

Your hands lie open in the long fresh grass,
The finger-points look through like rosy blooms;
Your eyes smile peace. The pasture gleams and glooms
'Neath billowing skies that scatter and amass.
All round our nest, far as the eye can pass,
Are golden kingcup-fields with silver edge
Where the cow-parsley skirts the hawthorn-hedge.
'Tis visible silence, still as the hour-glass.

Deep in the sun-searched growths the dragon-fly
Hangs like a blue thread loosened from the sky:—
So this winged hour is dropt to us from above.
Oh! clasp we to our hearts, for deathless dower,
This close-companioned inarticulate hour
When twofold silence was the song of love.

BODY'S BEAUTY

Of Adam's first wife, Lilith, it is told
(The witch he loved before the gift of Eve,)
That, ere the snake's, her sweet tongue could deceive,
And her enchanted hair was the first gold.
And still she sits, young while the earth is old,
And, subtly of herself contemplative,
Draws men to watch the bright net she can weave,
Till heart and body and life are in its hold.

The rose and poppy are her flowers; for where
Is he not found, O Lilith, whom shed scent
And soft-shed kisses and soft sleep shall snare?
Lo! as that youth's eyes burned at thine, so went
Thy spell through him, and left his straight neck bent,
And round his heart one strangling golden hair.

Sudden Light

I have been here before,
  But when or how I cannot tell:
I know the grass beyond the door,
  The sweet keen smell,
The sighing sound, the lights around the shore.

You have been mine before,—
  How long ago I may not know:
But just when at that swallow's soar
  Your neck turned so,
Some veil did fall,—I knew it all of yore.

Has this been thus before?
  And shall not thus time's eddying flight
Still with our lives our loves restore
  In death's despite,
And day and night yield one delight once more?

After his wife's death Rossetti continued to work in many mediums. Besides mingling the arts of writing and painting, he made designs for stained glass and murals. His reputation mounted, his income rose to three thousand pounds a year, but he grew more and more depressed. Gloomy and suspicious, he drew near the edge of insanity; he lived on fantasy and narcotics. Shunning people, he cultivated the society of beasts. Deluding himself that his wife's spirit was reincarnated in some animal, his home became a menagerie. At various times he housed woodchucks, owls, an Irish deerhound, a raven (in homage of Poe), an Australian opossum that slept in a centerpiece on the table, a white peacock that died under a sofa, a zebu, and (without humorous intent) a laughing jackass. A raccoon lived in a bureau drawer, and an armadillo gnawed its way out through a neighbor's kitchen. A prey to insomnia, Rossetti found a new drug, chloral, which made him still more melancholy and accelerated his end. He died April 9, 1882, while his best book, BALLADS AND SONNETS, was being printed.

Rossetti is not only a poet's poet, but a painter's poet. His verse is composed as though for a canvas—rich, and sometimes stiff, with color. Instead of being "fleshly," as was once charged, it is disembodied, unearthly, and hypnotic. Its supernatural overtones recall Poe, and Rossetti was not unaware of the influence. THE BLESSED DAMOZEL, Rossetti's most famous poem, was written as a complement to THE RAVEN. "I saw at once," Rossetti said, "that Poe had done the utmost it was possible to do with the grief of the lover on earth; I determined to reverse the conditions, and give utterance to the yearning of the loved one in heaven." Rossetti thereupon created not only a more mystical poem than his model, but a far more beautiful one.

The Blessed Damozel

The blessed damozel leaned out
  From the gold bar of Heaven;
Her eyes were deeper than the depth
  Of waters stilled at even;
She had three lilies in her hand,
  And the stars in her hair were seven.

Her robe, ungirt from clasp to hem,
  No wrought flowers did adorn,

But a white rose of Mary's gift,
  For service meetly worn;
Her hair that lay along her back
  Was yellow like ripe corn.

Herseemed she scarce had been a day
  One of God's choristers;
The wonder was not yet quite gone
  From that still look of hers;
Albeit, to them she left, her day
  Had counted as ten years.

(To one, it is ten years of years.
  . . . Yet now, and in this place,
Surely she leaned o'er me—her hair
  Fell all about my face. . . .
Nothing: the autumn fall of leaves.
  The whole year sets apace.)

It was the rampart of God's house
  That she was standing on;
By God built over the sheer depth
  The which is Space begun;
So high, that looking downward thence
  She scarce could see the sun.

It lies in Heaven, across the flood
  Of ether, as a bridge.
Beneath the tides of day and night
  With flame and darkness ridge
The void, as low as where this earth
  Spins like a fretful midge.

Around her, lovers, newly met
  'Mid deathless love's acclaims,
Spoke evermore among themselves
  Their heart-remembered names;
And the souls mounting up to God
  Went by her like thin flames.

And still she bowed herself and stooped
  Out of the circling charm;
Until her bosom must have made
  The bar she leaned on warm,
And the lilies lay as if asleep
  Along her bended arm.

From the fixed place of Heaven she saw
  Time like a pulse shake fierce
Through all the worlds. Her gaze still strove
  Within the gulf to pierce
Its path; and now she spoke as when
  The stars sang in their spheres.

The sun was gone now; the curled moon
  Was like a little feather
Fluttering far down the gulf; and now
  She spoke through the still weather.
Her voice was like the voice the stars
  Had when they sang together.

(Ah sweet! Even now, in that bird's song,
  Strove not her accents there,
Fain to be hearkened? When those bells
  Possessed the mid-day air,
Strove not her steps to reach my side
  Down all the echoing stair?)

"I wish that he were come to me,
  For he will come," she said.
"Have I not prayed in Heaven?—on earth,
  Lord, Lord, has he not prayed?
Are not two prayers a perfect strength?
  And shall I feel afraid?

"When round his head the aureole clings,
  And he is clothed in white,
I'll take his hand and go with him
  To the deep wells of light;
As unto a stream we will step down,
  And bathe there in God's sight.

"We two will stand beside that shrine,
  Occult, withheld, untrod,
Whose lamps are stirred continually
  With prayer sent up to God;
And see our old prayers, granted, melt
  Each like a little cloud.

"We two will lie i' the shadow of
  That living mystic tree
Within whose secret growth the Dove
  Is sometimes felt to be.

While every leaf that His plumes touch
  Saith His Name audibly.

"And I myself will teach to him,
  I myself, lying so,
The songs I sing here; which his voice
  Shall pause in, hushed and slow,
And find some knowledge at each pause,
  Or some new thing to know."

(Alas! We two, we two, thou say'st!
  Yea, one wast thou with me
That once of old. But shall God lift
  To endless unity
The soul whose likeness with thy soul
  Was but its love for thee?)

"We two," she said, "will seek the groves
  Where the lady Mary is,
With her five handmaidens, whose names
  Are five sweet symphonies,
Cecily, Gertrude, Magdalen,
  Margaret and Rosalys.

"Circlewise sit they, with bound locks
  And foreheads garlanded;
Into the fine cloth white like flame
  Weaving the golden thread,
To fashion the birth-robes for them
  Who are just born, being dead.

"He shall fear, haply, and be dumb:
  Then will I lay my cheek
To his, and tell about our love,
  Not once abashed or weak:
And the dear Mother will approve
  My pride, and let me speak.

"Herself shall bring us, hand in hand,
  To Him round whom all souls
Kneel, the clear-ranged unnumbered heads
  Bowed with their aureoles:
And angels meeting us shall sing
  To their citherns and citoles.

"There will I ask of Christ the Lord
  Thus much for him and me:—
Only to live as once on earth
  With Love, only to be,
As then awhile, for ever now
  Together, I and he."

She gazed and listened and then said,
  Less sad of speech than mild:—
"All this is when he comes." She ceased.
  The light thrilled towards her, filled
With angels in strong level flight.
  Her eyes prayed, and she smiled.

(I saw her smile.) But soon their path
  Was vague in distant spheres:
And then she cast her arms along
  The golden barriers,
And laid her face between her hands,
  And wept. (I heard her tears.)

CHRISTINA ROSSETTI

[1830–1894]

Christina Georgina, youngest of the Rossettis, was born December 5, 1830, in London. Although her mother was half English, her father was wholly Italian, a famous scholar in exile, and the Rossetti household was crowded with literary refugees, "good-natured Neapolitans, keen Tuscans, and emphatic Romans." The melodic Italian speech must have inspired Christina Rossetti's musical verse, for at twelve she was writing English lyrics of singular fluency. Unpretentious and devoted, neither she nor her work was happy. Differing from her Bohemian brother, Dante Gabriel, and more like her older sister, who became a nun, she found the world evil. She repudiated pleasure: "I cannot possibly use the word 'happy' without meaning something beyond this present life."

Uphill, one of her most famous poems, expresses her prevailing attitude with dignity and pathos. The lines owe their appeal, as Viola Mevnell wrote, "to the simplicity which could reduce the whole struggle of man to that single day's faring along a road, with an inn and its open door at the end."

Uphill

Does the road wind uphill all the way?
  Yes, to the very end.
Will the day's journey take the whole long day?
  From morn to night, my friend.

But is there for the night a resting-place?
  A roof for when the slow dark hours begin.
May not the darkness hide it from my face?
  You cannot miss that inn.

Shall I meet other wayfarers at night?
  Those who have gone before.
Then must I knock, or call when just in sight?
  They will not keep you standing at that door.

Shall I find comfort, travel-sore and weak?
  Of labor you shall find the sum.
Will there be beds for me and all who seek?
  Yea, beds for all who come.

Twice she refused to marry because of religious scruples. Baptized in the Church of England, she dismissed James Collinson, a minor Pre-Raphaelite, because he was a Catholic convert. Later, in love with Charles Cayley, a scholar of her own faith, she feared marriage with one who did not seem to be "religious enough." Spiritually committed to the Heavenly Bridegroom, she could not surrender to any earthly lover. Confident neither of self nor of salvation, she became a recluse; for fifteen years she rarely spent a night away from her mother.

Suffering from a chronic weakness of heart most of her life, Christina Rossetti never ceased ministering to the poor. In her early sixties she was operated on for cancer, but the inevitable end was only postponed. She died, literally in the act of prayer, December 29, 1894.

Christina Rossetti's spirit persists in her poetry. The verse, limited in range, is exquisite in phrase, flexible in music. Slight in form, transparent in texture, it defies analysis. One of the most reticent spirits, she was also one of the few women whose lyrics and sonnets will survive.

A Birthday

My heart is like a singing bird
  Whose nest is in a watered shoot;
My heart is like an apple-tree
  Whose boughs are bent with thick-set fruit;
My heart is like a rainbow shell
  That paddles in a halcyon sea;
My heart is gladder than all these
  Because my love is come to me.

Raise me a dais of silk and down;
  Hang it with vair and purple dyes;
Carve it in doves and pomegranates,
  And peacocks with a hundred eyes;
Work it in gold and silver grapes,
  In leaves and silver fleur-de-lys;
Because the birthday of my life
  Is come, my love is come to me.

When I Am Dead, My Dearest

When I am dead, my dearest,
Sing no sad songs for me;
Plant thou no roses at my head,
Nor shady cypress-tree:
Be the green grass above me
With showers and dewdrops wet;
And if thou wilt, remember,
And if thou wilt, forget.

I shall not see the shadows,
I shall not feel the rain;
I shall not hear the nightingale
Sing on, as if in pain:
And dreaming through the twilight
That doth not rise nor set,
Haply I may remember,
And haply may forget.

Aloof

The irresponsive silence of the land,
The irresponsive sounding of the sea,
Speak both one message of one sense to me:—
"Aloof, aloof, we stand aloof; so stand
Thou too aloof bound with the flawless band
Of inner solitude; we bind not thee.
But who from thy self-chain shall set thee free?
What heart shall touch thy heart? what hand thy hand?"

And I am sometimes proud and sometimes meek,
And sometimes I remember days of old
When fellowship seemed not so far to seek
And all the world and I seemed much less cold,
And at the rainbow's foot lay surely gold,
And hope felt strong and life itself not weak.

Remember

Remember me when I am gone away,
Gone far away into the silent land;
When you can no more hold me by the hand,
Nor I half turn to go, yet turning stay.
Remember me when no more, day by day,
You tell me of our future that you planned;
Only remember me; you understand
It will be late to counsel then or pray.

Yet if you should forget me for a while
And afterwards remember, do not grieve;
For if the darkness and corruption leave
A vestige of the thoughts that once I had,
Better by far you should forget and smile
Than that you should remember and be sad.

Rest

O Earth, lie heavily upon her eyes;
Seal her sweet eyes weary of watching, Earth;
Lie close around her: leave no room for mirth
With its harsh laughter, nor for sound of sighs.

She hath no questions, she hath no replies,
Hushed in and curtained with a blessèd dearth
Of all that irked her from the hour of birth;
With stillness that is almost Paradise.

Darkness more clear than noonday holdeth her,
Silence more musical than any song;
Even her very heart has ceased to stir.
Until the morning of Eternity
Her rest shall not begin nor end, but be;
And when she wakes she will not think it long.

SLEEPING AT LAST is as characteristic as it is appropriately named. The poem, Christina Rossetti's last, was written shortly before her death.

Sleeping at Last

Sleeping at last, the struggle and horror past,
Sleeping at last, the trouble and tumult over,
Cold and white, out of sight of friend and of lover,
Sleeping at last.

No more a tired heart downcast or overcast,
No more pangs that wring or shifting fears that hover,
Sleeping at last in a dreamless sleep locked fast.

Fast asleep. Singing birds in their leafy cover
Cannot wake her, nor shake her the gusty blast.
Under the purple thyme and the purple clover
Sleeping at last.

EMILY DICKINSON

[1830–1886]

THE two greatest women poets of the century were strangely paired. Born in the same year, the English Christina Rossetti and the American Emily Dickinson matched each other and were each other's integral opposite. Their outer lives were strikingly similar: both women were abnormally reticent; both loved deeply but remained unmarried; both secluded themselves from the world. But the mingling of frustration and resignation was wholly different in their expressions. Christina Rossetti wrote as a devout Anglican who abased herself before God; Emily Dickinson disclosed herself as a protesting Puritan who challenged the Deity. Christina Rossetti's tone is melancholy, a sadness that affects the soul but never probes the intellect; Emily Dickinson's note is sharp and impertinent, yet searchingly introspective. In technique the differences are even more marked. The Englishwoman's verse is formal, traditional in pattern and phrase. The American woman's poetry is experimental, reckless in rhyme and audacious in idiom.

Emily Dickinson's biography is brief and almost bare of events. She was born December 10, 1830, in Amherst, Massachusetts, and at Amherst she lived, except for a few excursions, all her fifty-six years. At seventeen she entered South Hadley Female Seminary a few miles from town, disliked it at once, and, a determined rebel, returned home. At twenty-three she spent a few weeks in Washington with her father, whom she adored, and visited in Philadelphia. After her return to Amherst, she became a recluse. She rarely crossed her threshold; even in the house, visitors saw her only as a figure vanishing down a corridor. Little was known of her except that she was an indefatigable letter writer but made others address her envelopes, that she always wore white but refused to be fitted for her clothes, and that her gifts of cookies and garden flowers were usually accompanied by a few cryptic lines of verse. She became the village oddity, and died of Bright's disease, May 15, 1886, in the house in which she was born.

Three biographers published mutually contradictory accounts of the event which made Emily Dickinson a hermit. Two of the stories were sensational; only one, guardedly related by her niece, Martha Dickinson Bianchi, was plausible. Further research by George F. Whicher made it plain that, in Philadelphia, Emily Dickinson fell in love with the Reverend Charles Wadsworth, who was married, and only three or four meetings took place. "So we must keep apart," she wrote at the end of one of her secret poems:

With just the door ajar
That oceans are,
And prayer,
And that pale sustenance,
Despair.

There was no love affair in the ordinary sense, but the poet felt herself dedicated to the man's spirit, if not to the man. It is possible that the pastor was unconscious of the profound emotion he had awakened; it is also possible that the poet was dramatizing her abnegation and grief. But the love poems are there, greater than the experience, poignant, transfigured, among the finest poems ever written by a woman.

The Soul Selects

The soul selects her own society,
Then shuts the door;
On her divine majority
Obtrude no more.

Unmoved, she notes the chariots pausing
At her low gate;
Unmoved, an emperor is kneeling
Upon her mat.

I've known her from an ample nation
Choose one;
Then close the valves of her attention
Like stone.

My Life Closed Twice

My life closed twice before its close;
It yet remains to see
If Immortality unveil
A third event to me,

So huge, so hopeless to conceive,
As these that twice befell.
Parting is all we know of heaven,
And all we need of hell.

Of All the Souls That Stand Create

Of all the souls that stand create
I have elected one.
When sense from spirit files away,
And subterfuge is done;

When that which is and that which was
Apart, intrinsic, stand,
And this brief tragedy of flesh
Is shifted like a sand;

When figures show their royal front
And mists are carved away—
Behold the atom I preferred
To all the lists of clay!

Although love was a preoccupation, it was not Emily Dickinson's single, or even dominating, theme. Alone and disdainful of notice, she ranged the universe. During her life only four of her poems appeared in print, and these were published "by stealth," without her knowledge. After her death more than one thousand poems were unearthed, most of them hidden in boxes and bureau drawers; many are still unpublished. Six volumes appeared posthumously, the first in 1890, the most recent as late as 1935. Originally her editors divided the poems, none of which bore a title, into four categories: Life, Love, Nature, Time and Eternity. In each of the groups the paradoxical poet is supreme, a mystic and a madcap. She announces whimsically:

To make a prairie it takes a clover and one bee—
And revery.
The revery alone will do
If bees are few.

Her profundities are always achieved with nimble delicacy. Lightnings "skip like mice" and intuitions flash from her pages casually, almost inconsequentially.

The Mountains Grow Unnoticed

The mountains grow unnoticed,
Their purple figures rise
Without attempt, exhaustion,
Assistance or applause.

In their eternal faces
The sun with broad delight
Looks long—and last—and golden,
For fellowship at night.

Nowhere in poetry is there a style more precise and unpredictable. Exact observation heightened by accurate fancy reveals the hummingbird as "a resonance of emerald," the wind "tapping like a tired man," a dog's "belated" feet like "intermittent plush," a gentlewoman's "dimity convictions," frost as "the blond assassin," Indian summer repeating "the old, old sophistries of June." Everywhere there is an appropriateness which is both discriminating and startling.

I Never Saw a Moor

I never saw a moor,
I never saw the sea;
Yet know I how the heather looks,
And what a wave must be.

I never spoke with God,
Nor visited in Heaven;
Yet certain am I of the spot
As if the chart were given.

Apparently With No Surprise

Apparently with no surprise
To any happy flower,
The frost beheads it at its play
In accidental power.

The blond assassin passes on;
The sun proceeds unmoved
To measure off another day
For an approving God.

The Heart Asks Pleasure First

The heart asks pleasure first;
And then, excuse from pain;
And then, those little anodynes
That deaden suffering;

And then, to go to sleep;
And then, if it should be
The will of its Inquisitor,
The liberty to die.

There Is No Frigate Like a Book

There is no frigate like a book
  To take us lands away,
Nor any courser like a page
  Of prancing poetry.

This traverse may the poorest take
  Without oppress of toll;
How frugal is the chariot
  That bears a human soul!

Although her experiences were few, Emily Dickinson ventured further than most of her contemporaries in the uncharted territory of the mind. She dared the darkness with a light but confident foot, an explorer whose compass was divination.

LEWIS CARROLL

[1832–1898]

THE two greatest English masters of nonsense were also masters in arts and sciences which were anything but nonsensical. The maddest verbal music in the language was perfected by Edward Lear, a topographical landscape painter. His successor in inspired nonsense was Lewis Carroll, a university lecturer, a noted mathematician, and a deacon in holy orders.

Lewis Carroll was born Charles Lutwidge Dodgson in Cheshire, January 27, 1832. He entered Christ Church College at nineteen, became a deacon at twenty-nine, and lectured on mathematics at Oxford for twenty-six years. He published many treatises under such alluring titles as THE FORMULAE OF PLANE TRIGONOMETRY and A SYLLABUS of ALGEBRAICAL GEOMETRY. It is said that when Queen Victoria discovered that Dodgson was the author of ALICE'S ADVENTURES IN WONDERLAND, she made it known that more of the author's work would be acceptable to the royal eye. Dodgson thereupon presented the Queen with AN ELEMENTARY TREATISE ON DETERMINANTS.

Fond of children, and particularly attached to young Alice Liddell, Dodgson, using the pseudonym of "Lewis Carroll," wrote a series of books which are appreciated far more by sophisticated maturity than by the children to whom they were addressed. This is understandable, for Lewis Carroll's nonsense is not only logical but symbolical. THROUGH THE LOOKING-GLASS is an elaborately disguised game of chess, and the whimsical rhymes which appear through Carroll's volumes for uncritical youngsters are, for the most part, critical parodies of the didactic poems of the period. THE CROCODILE, from ALICE'S ADVENTURES IN WONDERLAND, is a burlesque of Isaac Watts's moral stanzas AGAINST IDLENESS AND MISCHIEF beginning:

> How doth the little busy bee
>   Improve each shining hour,
> And gather honey all the day
>   From every opening flower!

The Crocodile

How doth the little crocodile
  Improve his shining tail,
And pour the waters of the Nile
  On every shining scale!

How cheerfully he seems to grin,
  How neatly spreads his claws,
And welcomes little fishes in
  With gently smiling jaws!

Carroll's lines beginning "Twinkle, twinkle, little bat" is a joke on Jane Taylor, author of ORIGINAL POEMS FOR INFANT MINDS. The captivating FATHER WILLIAM, a seemingly irresponsible set of rhymes, is actually a satire. It is a brilliant if cruel caricature of Robert Southey's THE OLD MAN'S COMFORTS, AND HOW HE GAINED THEM, which begins:

"You are old, Father William," the young man cried,
  "The few locks which are left you are gray;
You are hale, Father William, a hearty old man,
  Now tell me the reason, I pray."

"In the days of my youth," Father William replied,
  "I remembered that youth would fly fast,
And abused not my health, and my vigor at first,
  That I never might need them at last."

Carroll's "hearty old man" is anything but the sanctimonious babbler of Southey's poem. His logic is even more startling than his vigor.

Father William

"You are old, Father William," the young man said,
  "And your hair has become very white;
And yet you incessantly stand on your head—
  Do you think, at your age, it is right?"

"In my youth," Father William replied to his son,
"I feared it might injure the brain;
But, now that I'm perfectly sure I have none,
Why, I do it again and again."

"You are old," said the youth, "as I mentioned before,
And have grown most uncommonly fat;
Yet you turned a back-somersault in at the door—
Pray, what is the reason of that?"

"In my youth," said the sage, as he shook his gray locks,
"I kept all my limbs very supple
By the use of this ointment—one shilling the box—
Allow me to sell you a couple?"

"You are old," said the youth, "and your jaws are too weak
For anything tougher than suet;
Yet you finished the goose, with the bones and the beak—
Pray, how did you manage to do it?"

"In my youth," said his father, "I took to the law,
And argued each case with my wife;
And the muscular strength which it gave to my jaw
Has lasted the rest of my life."

"You are old," said the youth, "one would hardly suppose
That your eye was as steady as ever;
Yet you balanced an eel on the end of your nose—
What made you so awfully clever?"

"I have answered three questions, and that is enough,"
Said his father. "Don't give yourself airs!
Do you think I can listen all day to such stuff?
Be off, or I'll kick you down-stairs!"

Even JABBERWOCKY, from THROUGH THE LOOKING-GLASS, is logical in its puzzling language. Carroll furnished a glossary of the invented words, paraphrasing the proverb about pence and pounds: "Take care of the sounds and the sense will take care of itself." Some of the words have ceased to be nonsense—"chortle" and "burble" for example—and have become part of our vocabulary. Carroll declared that many of the adjectives were "portmanteau words"—two meanings packed into one word, such as *slithy: lithe* and *slimy,* and *frumious,* a combination of *fuming* and *furious.*

Jabberwocky

'Twas brillig, and the slithy toves
  Did gyre and gimble in the wabe:
All mimsy were the borogoves,
  And the mome raths outgrabe.

"Beware the Jabberwock, my son!
  The jaws that bite, the claws that catch!
Beware the Jubjub bird, and shun
  The frumious Bandersnatch!"

He took his vorpal sword in hand;
  Long time the manxome foe he sought–
So rested he by the Tumtum tree,
  And stood awhile in thought.

And, as in uffish thought he stood,
  The Jabberwock, with eyes of flame,
Came whiffling through the tulgey wood,
  And burbled as it came!

One, two! One, two! And through and through
  The vorpal blade went snicker-snack!
He left it dead, and with its head
  He went galumphing back.

"And hast thou slain the Jabberwock?
  Come to my arms, my beamish boy!
O frabjous day! Callooh, Callay!"
  He chortled in his joy.

'Twas brillig, and the slithy toves
  Did gyre and gimble in the wabe:
All mimsy were the borogoves,
  And the mome raths outgrabe.

Dodgson always kept himself apart from Carroll. To the last he refused to be identified with his pseudonym. Nevertheless, he continued to invent a kind of nonsense which was mathematically precise, to design ingenious games, problems, and memory systems, as though, wrote Eleanor Farjeon, "most of the affairs of life could be conducted delightfully through a series of games and tricks." He died at Guildford, January 14, 1898.

W. S. GILBERT

[1836–1911]

THE names of Gilbert and Sullivan suggest a union as close as the Siamese Twins or, since they were separable, an attachment no less traditional than Beaumont and Fletcher. Yet the two friends had divergent aims, quarreled about careers, and parted over a triviality.

William Schwenck Gilbert, the librettist of the partnership, was born November 18, 1836, in London. He was educated at King's College, became a militia officer, a clerk in the Privy Council office, and a practicing lawyer. In his twenty-fifth year he began writing for the magazine FUN, making his own drawings. His combination of verses and drawings, later christened THE BAB BALLADS, reminded some critics of Edward Lear, but Gilbert owed nothing to any model. "For THE BAB BALLADS," Deems Taylor wrote recently, "Gilbert invented a new race of people, creatures who were not so much caricatures of existing humans as a strange, autochthonous goblin species that was like nothing on land or sea. . . . In insane reasonableness THE BAB BALLADS are surpassed only by the two ALICE books." One of the best, and possibly the most famous of THE BAB BALLADS, was rejected by PUNCH on the ground that it was "too cannibalistic for its readers' tastes." It was THE YARN OF THE "NANCY BELL."

The Yarn of the "Nancy Bell"

'T was on the shores that round our coast
  From Deal to Ramsgate span,
That I found alone on a piece of stone
  An elderly naval man.

His hair was weedy, his beard was long,
  And weedy and long was he,
And I heard this wight on the shore recite,
  In a singular minor key:

"Oh, I am a cook and the captain bold,
  And the mate of the *Nancy* brig,
And a bo'sun tight, and a midshipmite,
  And the crew of the captain's gig."

And he shook his fists and he tore his hair,
  Till I really felt afraid,
For I couldn't help thinking the man had been drinking,
  And so I simply said:

"Oh, elderly man, it's little I know
  Of the duties of men of the sea,
And I'll eat my hand if I understand
  How you can possibly be

"At once a cook, and a captain bold,
  And the mate of the *Nancy* brig,
And a bo'sun tight, and midshipmite,
  And the crew of the captain's gig."

Then he gave a hitch to his trousers, which
  Is a trick all seamen larn,
And having got rid of a thumping quid,
  He spun this painful yarn:

" 'T was in the good ship *Nancy Bell*
  That we sailed to the Indian Sea,
And there on a reef we come to grief,
  Which has often occurred to me.

"And pretty nigh all the crew was drowned
  (There was seventy-seven o' soul),
And only ten of the *Nancy's* men
  Said 'Here!' to the muster-roll.

"There was me and the cook and the captain bold,
  And the mate of the *Nancy* brig,
And the bo'sun tight, and a midshipmite,
  And the crew of the captain's gig.

"For a month we'd neither wittles nor drink,
  Till a-hungry we did feel,
So we drawed a lot, and accordin' shot
  The captain for our meal.

"The next lot fell to the *Nancy's* mate,
  And a delicate dish he made;
Then our appetite with the midshipmite
  We seven survivors stayed.

"And then we murdered the bo'sun tight,
  And he much resembled pig;
Then we wittled free, did the cook and me,
  On the crew of the captain's gig.

"Then only the cook and me was left,
  And the delicate question, 'Which
Of us two goes to the kettle?' arose,
  And we argued it out as sich.

"For I loved that cook as a brother, I did,
  And the cook he worshipped me;
But we'd both be blowed if we'd either be stowed
  In the other chap's hold, you see.

" 'I'll be eat if you dines off me,' says Tom.
  'Yes, that,' says I, 'you'll be,—
I'm boiled if I die, my friend,' quoth I.
  And 'Exactly so,' quoth he.

"Says he, 'Dear James, to murder me
  Were a foolish thing to do,
For don't you see that you can't cook *me*,
  While I can—and will—cook *you!*'

"So he boils the water, and takes the salt
  And the pepper in portions true
(Which he never forgot), and some chopped shalot,
  And some sage and parsley too.

" 'Come here,' says he, with a proper pride,
  Which his smiling features tell,
' 'T will soothing be if I let you see
  How extremely nice you'll smell.'

"And he stirred it round and round and round,
  And he sniffed at the foaming froth;
When I ups with his heels, and smothers his squeals
  In the scum of the boiling broth.

"And I eat that cook in a week or less,
  And—as I eating be
The last of his chops, why, I almost drops,
  For a vessel in sight I see.

. . . . . .

"And I never larf, and I never smile,
  And I never lark nor play,
But sit and croak, and a single joke
  I have—which is to say:

"Oh, I am a cook and a captain bold,
  And the mate of the *Nancy* brig,
And a bo'sun tight, and midshipmite,
  And the crew of the captain's gig!"

In his thirty-first year, Gilbert turned to the stage and wrote pantomimes, melodramas, burlesques, and sentimental pieces. Ten years later he met the ideal partner, Arthur Sullivan, and the two men collaborated on the most brilliant series of light operas ever composed. Many of the plots were taken from THE BAB BALLADS, enlarged, and pointed at the foibles of the day. The Gilbert and Sullivan operas were hilariously received and enjoyed no less because of their social criticism. PINAFORE is still a sardonic commentary on political officeholders. PATIENCE ridicules the pretentions of every aesthetic "school." IOLANTHE mocks blue blood in general and stuffy, somnolent peers in particular.

The House of Lords

When Britain *really* ruled the waves
  (In good Queen Bess's time)
The House of Peers made no pretence
To intellectual eminence
  Or scholarship sublime;
Yet Britain won her proudest bays
In good Queen Bess's glorious days.

When Wellington thrashed Bonaparte,
  As every child can tell,
The House of Peers throughout the war
Did nothing in particular

And did it very well;
Yet Britain set the world ablaze
In good King George's glorious days.

And while the House of Peers withholds
Its legislative hand,
And noble statesmen do not itch
To interfere with matters which
They do not understand,
As bright will shine Great Britain's rays
As in King George's glorious days.

from IOLANTHE

A Policeman's Lot

When a felon's not engaged in his employment,
Or maturing his felonious little plans,
His capacity for innocent enjoyment
Is just as great as any honest man's.
Our feelings we with difficulty smother
When constabulary duty's to be done;
Ah, take one consideration with another,
A policeman's lot is not a happy one.

When the enterprising burglar's not a-burgling,
When the cut-throat isn't occupied in crime,
He loves to hear the little brook a-gurgling,
And listen to the merry village chime.
When the coster's finished jumping on his mother,
He loves to lie a-basking in the sun;
Ah, take one consideration with another,
A policeman's lot is not a happy one.

from THE PIRATES OF PENZANCE

Unusually dexterous in technique, Gilbert's light verse has been the delight and despair of a hundred imitators. His rhymes are as astounding as they are fresh; his meters are tricky but exact; the ideas nonchalantly mingle absurdity and satire. A librettist by profession, Gilbert was a writer of true lyrics by instinct.

To the Terrestrial Globe

BY A MISERABLE WRETCH

Roll on, thou ball, roll on!
Through pathless realms of Space
        Roll on!
What though I'm in a sorry case?
What though I cannot meet my bills?
What though I suffer toothache's ills?
What though I swallow countless pills?
    Never *you* mind!
        Roll on!

Roll on, thou ball, roll on!
Through seas of inky air
        Roll on!
It's true I've got no shirts to wear;
It's true my butcher's bill is due;
It's true my prospects all look blue—
But don't let that unsettle you!
    Never *you* mind!
        Roll on!
                [*It rolls on.*]

In 1911 Gilbert was entertaining two young ladies near his home. They went swimming; one of the young women found herself out of her depth and cried for help. Although Gilbert was over seventy-four, he plunged in and attempted to rescue her. The exertion was too much for him. He died of heart failure May 29, 1911.

ALGERNON CHARLES SWINBURNE

[1837–1909]

ALGERNON CHARLES SWINBURNE has been more variously described than any other poet of his century. Edmund Gosse pictured him, with his thin body, waving red hair, and birdlike head, as a brilliant but ridiculous flamingo. T. Earle Welby likened him to a pagan apparition at a Victorian tea party, "leaping onto the sleek lawn to stamp its goat foot in challenge, to deride with its screech of laughter the admirable decorum of the conversation."

The personality who, according to Edgell Rickword, "shattered the virginal reticence of Victoria's serenest years with a book of poems," was born in London April 5, 1837. His forebears were distinguished aristocrats. His father was an admiral, descendant of an old Northumbrian family; his grandfather was Sir John Edward Swinburne; his mother was the daughter of the third Earl of Ashburnham. Spoiled and precocious, Swinburne attended Eton and Oxford without being graduated from either. He fell in love with medievalism and its interpretation by the Pre-Raphaelites. In his early twenties he attempted to outdo the excesses of the young Bohemians, and was successful, although at great cost to his physique and character. His unusually frail hands and delicate features gave him an elfin look, which was belied by his appetite for alcohol. He was, however, not a robust drinker, and soon passed into a state of unconsciousness. It is said that Rossetti always pinned his address to his coat collar so that Swinburne would be sure of being delivered to his own home.

At twenty-three Swinburne published his first volume, two poetic dramas dedicated to Rossetti. The blank verse was fluent, and the interspersed lyrics were graceful, but the critics were not impressed. Five years later there appeared his ATALANTA IN CALYDON, and the critics squandered their superlatives. In ATALANTA IN CALYDON Swinburne attempted to "reproduce for English readers the likeness of a Greek tragedy with something of its true poetic life and charm." But the exuberance was anything but Greek, and the mounting syllables carried a sumptuous and orchestral music new to English ears. The spirit was rebellious, a defiance of the creeds by which men live, but it was the melodiousness which made the young men of the period shout the choruses to each other. The pure extravagance, the happy (if too insistent) alliteration—the "lisp of leaves and ripple of rain," the "leaf to flower and flower to fruit"—and the unflagging verve created an effect of magic to which we are not yet immune.

When the Hounds of Spring

When the hounds of spring are on winter's traces,
  The mother of months in meadow or plain
Fills the shadows and windy places
  With lisp of leaves and ripple of rain;
And the brown bright nightingale amorous
Is half assuaged for Itylus,
For the Thracian ships and the foreign faces,
  The tongueless vigil, and all the pain.

Come with bows bent and with emptying of quivers,
  Maiden most perfect, lady of light,
With a noise of winds and many rivers,
  With a clamor of waters, and with might;
Bind on thy sandals, O thou most fleet,
Over the splendor and speed of thy feet;
For the faint east quickens, the wan west shivers,
  Round the feet of the day and the feet of the night.

Where shall we find her, how shall we sing to her,
  Fold our hands round her knees, and cling?
O that man's heart were as fire and could spring to her,
  Fire, or the strength of the streams that spring!
For the stars and the winds are unto her
As raiment, as songs of the harp-player;
For the risen stars and the fallen cling to her,
  And the southwest-wind and the west-wind sing.

For winter's rains and ruins are over,
  And all the season of snows and sins;
The days dividing lover and lover,
  The light that loses, the night that wins;
And time remembered is grief forgotten,
And frosts are slain and flowers begotten,
And in green underwood and cover
  Blossom by blossom the spring begins.

The full streams feed on flower of rushes,
  Ripe grasses trammel a traveling foot,
The faint fresh flame of the young year flushes
  From leaf to flower and flower to fruit;

And fruit and leaf are as gold and fire,
And the oat is heard above the lyre,
And the hoofed heel of a satyr crushes
  The chestnut-husk at the chestnut-root.

And Pan by noon and Bacchus by night,
  Fleeter of foot than the fleet-foot kid,
Follows with dancing and fills with delight
  The Maenad and the Bassarid;
And soft as lips that laugh and hide
The laughing leaves of the trees divide,
And screen from seeing and leave in sight
  The god pursuing, the maiden hid.

The ivy falls with the Bacchanal's hair
  Over her eyebrows hiding her eyes;
The wild vine slipping down leaves bare
  Her bright breast shortening into sighs;
The wild vine slips with the weight of its leaves,
But the berried ivy catches and cleaves
To the limbs that glitter, the feet that scare
  The wolf that follows, the fawn that flies.

from ATALANTA IN CALYDON

Man

Before the beginning of years,
  There came to the making of man
Time, with a gift of tears;
  Grief, with a glass that ran;
Pleasure, with pain for leaven;
  Summer, with flowers that fell;
Remembrance fallen from heaven,
  And madness risen from hell;
Strength without hands to smite;
  Love that endures for a breath;
Night, the shadow of light,
  And life, the shadow of death.

And the high gods took in hand
  Fire, and the falling of tears,
And a measure of sliding sand
  From under the feet of the years;

And froth and drift of the sea;
  And dust of the laboring earth;
And bodies of things to be
  In the houses of death and of birth;
And wrought with weeping and laughter,
  And fashioned with loathing and love,
With life before and after
  And death beneath and above,
For a day and a night and a morrow,
  That his strength might endure for a span
With travail and heavy sorrow,
  The holy spirit of man.

From the winds of the north and the south
  They gathered as unto strife;
They breathed upon his mouth,
  They filled his body with life;
Eyesight and speech they wrought
  For the veils of the soul therein,
A time for labor and thought,
  A time to serve and to sin;
They gave him light in his ways,
  And love, and a space for delight,
And beauty and length of days,
  And night, and sleep in the night.
His speech is a burning fire;
  With his lips he travaileth;
In his heart is a blind desire,
  In his eyes foreknowledge of death;
He weaves, and is clothed with derision;
  Sows, and he shall not reap;
His life is a watch or a vision
  Between a sleep and a sleep.

from ATALANTA IN CALYDON

Swinburne's star continued to rise. His POEMS AND BALLADS, published a year after ATALANTA IN CALYDON, took the literary world by storm. At thirty Swinburne was a sensation; he was not only a poet, but a controversy. His verses spoke vaguely of liberty and rebellion, but the vagueness was concealed by a superabundant imagery and a verbal furiousness. The moralists were quick to use such words as "vicious" and "libidinous"; they were alarmed to find the limp lilies of the Pre-Raphaelites grafted on the evil flowers of Baudelaire. But Swinburne's celebration of "the roses and raptures of vice" is a poetic naughtiness rather than actual depravity; it is, as Edward Thomas pointed out, "from the lips outward. In the spirit of gay and amateur perversity he flatters sin with appellations of virtue, as George Herbert gave his religious poetry the unction of love."

Nowhere are Swinburne's paganism and pantheism more effectively presented than in THE GARDEN OF PROSERPINE. Here, in a tribute to the queen of the lower world, Swinburne speaks not only as the beauty-intoxicated Englishman, but as a pagan Roman. Here, more than in most poems, his archaic speech is not perverse but richly appropriate.

The Garden of Proserpine

Here, where the world is quiet;
  Here, where all trouble seems
Dead winds' and spent waves' riot
  In doubtful dreams of dreams;
I watch the green field growing
For reaping folk and sowing,
For harvest-time and mowing,
  A sleepy world of streams.

I am tired of tears and laughter,
  And men that laugh and weep;
Of what may come hereafter
  For men that sow to reap:
I am weary of days and hours,
Blown buds of barren flowers,
Desires and dreams and powers
  And everything but sleep.

Here life has death for neighbor,
  And far from eye or ear
Wan waves and wet winds labor,
  Weak ships and spirits steer;
They drive adrift, and whither
They wot not who make thither;
But no such winds blow hither,
  And no such things grow here.

No growth of moor or coppice,
  No heather-flower or vine,
But bloomless buds of poppies,
  Green grapes of Proserpine,
Pale beds of blowing rushes,
Where no leaf blooms or blushes
Save this whereout she crushes
  For dead men deadly wine.

Pale, without name or number,
  In fruitless fields of corn,
They bow themselves and slumber
  All night till light is born;
And like a soul belated,
In hell and heaven unmated,
By cloud and mist abated
  Comes out of darkness morn.

Though one were strong as seven,
  He too with death shall dwell,
Nor wake with wings in heaven,
  Nor weep for pains in hell;
Though one were fair as roses,
His beauty clouds and closes;
And well though love reposes,
  In the end it is not well.

Pale, beyond porch and portal,
  Crowned with calm leaves, she stands
Who gathers all things mortal
  With cold immortal hands;
Her languid lips are sweeter
Than love's who fears to greet her,
To men that mix and meet her
  From many times and lands.

She waits for each and other,
  She waits for all men born;
Forgets the earth her mother,
  The life of fruits and corn;
And spring and seed and swallow
Take wing for her and follow
Where summer song rings hollow
  And flowers are put to scorn.

There go the loves that wither,
  The old loves with wearier wings;
And all dead years draw thither,
  And all disastrous things;
Dead dreams of days forsaken,
Blind buds that snows have shaken,
Wild leaves that winds have taken,
  Red strays of ruined springs.

We are not sure of sorrow;
  And joy was never sure;
Today will die tomorrow;
  Time stoops to no man's lure;
And love, grown faint and fretful,
With lips but half regretful
Sighs, and with eyes forgetful
  Weeps that no loves endure.

From too much love of living,
  From hope and fear set free,
We thank with brief thanksgiving
  Whatever gods may be
That no life lives for ever;
That dead men rise up never;
That even the weariest river
  Winds somewhere safe to sea.

Then star nor sun shall waken,
  Nor any change of light:
Nor sound of waters shaken,
  Nor any sound or sight:
Nor wintry leaves nor vernal,
Nor days nor things diurnal;
Only the sleep eternal
  In an eternal night.

In his thirties, Swinburne began a series of dramas in imitation of the Elizabethans. CHASTELARD, the first of a trilogy of plays centering about the tragedy of Queen Mary, was written at twenty-eight; the concluding MARY STUART was not published until sixteen years later. Swinburne's debt to the Elizabethans was acknowledged not only by his plays but by the sonnets he wrote in praise of Shakespeare, Marlowe, Webster, and other playwrights of the period.

William Shakespeare

Not if men's tongues and angels' all in one
Spake, might the word be said that might speak Thee.
Streams, winds, woods, flowers, fields, mountains, yea, the sea,
What power is in them all to praise the sun?
His praise is this,—he can be praised of none.
Man, woman, child, praise God for him; but he
Exults not to be worshipped, but to be.

He is; and, being, beholds his work well done.
All joy, all glory, all sorrow, all strength, all mirth,
Are his: without him, day were night on earth.
Time knows not his from time's own period.
All lutes, all harps, all viols, all flutes, all lyres,
Fall dumb before him ere one string suspires.
All stars are angels; but the sun is God.

Christopher Marlowe

Crowned, girdled, garbed, and shod with light and fire,
Son first-born of the morning, sovereign star!
Soul nearest ours of all, that wert most far,
Most far off in the abysm of time, thy lyre
Hung highest above the dawn-enkindled quire
Where all ye sang together, all that are,
And all the starry songs behind thy car
Rang sequence, all our souls acclaim thee sire.

"If all the pens that ever poets held
Had fed the feeling of their masters' thoughts,"
And as with rush of hurtling chariots
The flight of all their spirits were impelled
Toward one great end, thy glory—nay, not then,
Not yet might'st thou be praised enough of men.

In SONGS BEFORE SUNRISE Swinburne hailed the Italian patriot, Mazzini, and announced another revolt, a protest against political restraint rather than moral conventions. POEMS AND BALLADS: SECOND SERIES continued "the noble pleasure of praising" and glorified Victor Hugo. But in his early forties it was evident that Swinburne's ambitions and dissipations were too much for him. His friend Theodore Watts-Dunton came to the rescue and took charge of him the last thirty years of his life. Max Beerbohm's NO 2. THE PINES is a brilliant if irreverent account of Swinburne's declining days. The poet softened into a mild little country gentleman; he grew deaf; he adored babies. But he continued to write with never-abating energy. The old fire was gone, but not the gift of phrase and the mastery of sound. He died, after an attack of pneumonia, at the home of Watts-Dunton, April 10, 1909.

Song

Love laid his sleepless head
On a thorny rosy bed;
And his eyes with tears were red,
And pale his lips as the dead.

And fear and sorrow and scorn
Kept watch by his head forlorn,
Till the night was overworn,
And the world was merry with morn.

And Joy came up with the day,
And kissed Love's lips as he lay,
And the watchers ghostly and gray
Sped from his pillow away.

And his eyes as the dawn grew bright,
And his lips waxed ruddy as light:
Sorrow may reign for a night,
But day shall bring back delight.

The Sea

I will go back to the great sweet mother,
  Mother and lover of men, the sea.
I will go down to her, I and none other,
  Close with her, kiss her and mix her with me;
Cling to her, strive with her, hold her fast.
O fair white mother, in days long past
Born without sister, born without brother,
  Set free my soul as thy soul is free.

O fair green-girdled mother of mine,
  Sea, that art clothed with the sun and the rain,
Thy sweet hard kisses are strong like wine,
  Thy large embraces are keen like pain.
Save me and hide me with all thy waves,
Find me one grave of thy thousand graves,
Those pure cold populous graves of thine,
  Wrought without hand in a world without stain.

I shall sleep, and move with the moving ships,
  Change as the winds change, veer in the tide;
My lips will feast on the foam of thy lips,
  I shall rise with thy rising, with thee subside;
Sleep, and not know if she be, if she were,
Filled full with life to the eyes and hair,
As a rose is fulfilled to the roseleaf tips
  With splendid summer and perfume and pride.

This woven raiment of nights and days,
  Were it once cast off and unwound from me,
Naked and glad would I walk in thy ways,
  Alive and aware of thy ways and thee;
Clear of the whole world, hidden at home,
Clothed with the green and crowned with the foam,
A pulse of the life of thy straits and bays,
  A vein in the heart of the streams of the sea.

from THE TRIUMPH OF TIME

It is fitting that some of Swinburne's best poetry should be about the sea, for his is a rise and fall of crashing sounds which first stimulate and then engulf the reader. Swinburne delighted in sensations rather than passion, in shocks and hurrying waves of excitement. Too often the reader, swept by Swinburne's echoing vowels and consonants, is swept away from the subject. This is not surprising, for, in spite of his imposing erudition, Swinburne was not a thinker. His mind, as Max Beerbohm wittily concluded, "rose ever away from reason to rhapsody. Neither was he human. . . . He was a singing bird that could build no nest. He was a youth who could not afford to age."

THOMAS HARDY

[1840–1928]

A SUCCESSFUL novelist, Thomas Hardy wrote nothing but poetry after his fifty-seventh year, and continued to publish verse until the day of his death, thirty years later. He was born June 2, 1840, in Dorsetshire; the Wessex landscape was the beloved background of his work. His father was a stonemason, and the boy was apprenticed to an architect; at twenty-three he won a prize offered by the Royal Institute of British Architects. But Hardy, doubtful of sermons in stones, saw no future for himself in the profession. He had already written some poetry, for which he had found no publisher. Engaged to be married, and encouraged by Meredith, he turned to the more profitable trade of storytelling and wrote his first novel, DESPERATE REMEDIES, at the age of thirty. During the next twenty-five years Hardy published a dozen challenging novels of character and environment. Readers were fascinated by his dispassionate naturalism, but the more conservative critics were suspicious of his rough honesty. In 1895 JUDE THE OBSCURE was attacked as "immoral," and Hardy was so deeply offended that, as he said, "it cured him of all interest in novel-writing."

Hardy had often deplored the necessity that made him write the novels, which he referred to as "pot-boilers." Now he considered himself free to return to poetry, his first love and his last. After his fifty-eighth year, nine volumes of poems were published, including THE DYNASTS, a huge epic-drama of the Napoleonic Wars in one hundred and thirty scenes, which has been called "the biggest and most consistent exhibition of fatalism in literature."

Fatalism was the keynote of Hardy's work. It was his answer to the pastoral idealism of Wordsworth, the indomitable optimism of Browning, and the unthinking pantheism of Swinburne. Hardy knew nature too intimately to believe that it was benign. He saw the grim warfare of the farmer, the tragedies of drought and disease, the continual struggle and inevitable defeat of plant and man. If the universe was governed at all, it was governed by accident. God, maintained Hardy, had ceased to be concerned with man; if He thought of this world at all, He thought of it as one of His failures.

It was neither cruelty nor kindness that ruled, but chance. "Crass Casualty obstructs the sun and rain," Hardy concluded grimly in the poem significantly entitled HAP.

But Hardy could not regard a pitiless universe without pity. Dubious about human values, he was stirred by the strivings of humanity. Man was noblest in defeat, and in nobility there was hope. On the darkest of days, Hardy heard that hope in a storm-tossed thrush, "frail, gaunt and small," who had chosen to fling his song and his soul through unrelieved gloom.

The Darkling Thrush

I leaned upon a coppice gate
  When frost was specter-gray,
And winter's dregs made desolate
  The weakening eye of day.
The tangled bine-stems scored the sky
  Like strings from broken lyres,
And all mankind that haunted nigh
  Had sought their household fires.

The land's sharp features seemed to be
  The Century's corpse outleant;
His crypt the cloudy canopy,
  The wind his death-lament.
The ancient pulse of germ and birth
  Was shrunken hard and dry,
And every spirit upon earth
  Seemed fervorless as I.

At once a voice burst forth among
  The bleak twigs overhead
In a full-hearted evensong
  Of joy unlimited;
An aged thrush, frail, gaunt and small,
  In blast-beruffled plume,
Had chosen thus to fling his soul
  Upon the growing gloom.

So little cause for carolings
  Of such ecstatic sound
Was written on terrestrial things
  Afar or nigh around,

That I could think there trembled through
  His happy good-night air
Some blessed hope, whereof he knew
  And I was unaware.

Hardy wrote with objective power in every form and on almost every subject. His was an ungainly force, a dogged and appealing clumsiness. Only a few of his poems are autobiographical. One of the best of these, AFTERWARDS, was written during the latter part of his life and reveals his close scrutiny of little things. THE IMPERCIPIENT, a much earlier poem, is a scarcely less veiled disclosure of his philosophy.

Afterwards

When the Present has latched its postern behind my tremulous stay,
  And the May month flaps its glad green leaves like wings,
Delicate-filmed as new-spun silk, will the neighbors say,
  "He was a man who used to notice such things"?

If it be in the dusk when, like an eyelid's soundless blink,
  The dewfall-hawk comes crossing the shades to alight
Upon the wind-warped upland thorn, a gazer may think,
  "To him this must have been a familiar sight."

If I pass during some nocturnal blackness, mothy and warm,
  When the hedgehog travels furtively over the lawn,
One may say, "He strove that such innocent creatures should come to no harm,
  But he could do little for them; and now he is gone."

If, when hearing that I have been stilled at last, they stand at the door,
  Watching the full-starred heavens that winter sees,
Will this thought rise on those who will meet my face no more,
  "He was one who had an eye for such mysteries"?

And will any say when my bell of quittance is heard in the gloom,
  And a crossing breeze cuts a pause in its outrollings,
Till they rise again, as they were a new bell's boom,
  "He hears it not now, but used to notice such things"?

The Impercipient

AT A CATHEDRAL SERVICE

That with this bright believing band
  I have no claim to be,
That faiths by which my comrades stand
  Seem fantasies to me,
And mirage-mists their Shining Land,
  Is a strange destiny.

Why thus my soul should be consigned
  To infelicity,
Why always I must feel as blind
  To sights my brethren see,
Why joys they've found I cannot find,
  Abides a mystery.

Since heart of mine knows not that ease
  Which they know; since it be
That He who breathes All's Well to these
  Breathes no All's-Well to me,
My lack might move their sympathies
  And Christian charity!

I am like a gazer who should mark
  An inland company
Standing upfingered, with, "Hark! hark!
  The glorious distant sea!"
And feel, "Alas, 'tis but yon dark
  And wind-swept pine to me!"

Yet I would bear my shortcomings
  With meet tranquillity,
But for the charge that blessed things
  I'd liefer not have be.
O, doth a bird deprived of wings
  Go earth-bound wilfully!

. . . . .

Enough. As yet disquiet clings
  About us. Rest shall we.

Hardy was twice married. His domestic life was amusingly but cruelly lampooned by W. Somerset Maugham in CAKES AND ALE, OR THE SKELETON IN THE CUPBOARD. In 1910 he was given the Order of Merit, but his pleasure in that honor did not lessen his pride in being asked to preside at little ceremonies in his own village. He died in his eighty-eighth year, January 11, 1928. His ashes were placed in Westminster Abbey. But his heart, as requested in his will, was buried in the Wessex countryside he loved so well.

WILFRID SCAWEN BLUNT

[1840–1922]

IF WILFRID SCAWEN BLUNT was not the great poet some of his contemporaries thought him, he was a success in more than a literary way. T. Earle Welby puts the case for Blunt nicely if incompletely: "To have married Byron's granddaughter, bred Arab horses, and been admired by Henley is to have made a great deal of life."

Blunt was born to be a rebellious and even romantic figure. His father was a famous soldier, and the son entered the diplomatic service at eighteen. After a career which took him from Athens to Madrid, and from Lisbon to South America, Blunt married the daughter of the Earl of Lovelace and retired from the service. He was then thirty. Two years later he inherited Crabbet Park, a handsome estate in Sussex, and established a stable for the breeding of Arab horses. This interest took him to Arabia, where he became a passionate sympathizer with the Mohammedan cause. He devoted much time to the Islamic movement, in direct opposition to British policy. He identified himself with all minorities. He spoke up for the Egyptians and condemned the war against the Boers.

At forty-seven Blunt was arrested for helping the Irish insurgents and was sentenced to prison for two months. The experience is recorded in a series of protesting sonnets entitled IN VINCULIS.

The Deeds That Might Have Been

There are wrongs done in the fair face of heaven
Which cry aloud for vengeance, and shall cry;
Loves beautiful in strength whose wit has striven
Vainly with loss and man's inconstancy;
Dead children's faces watched by souls that die;
Pure streams defiled; fair forests idly riven;
A nation suppliant in its agony
Calling on justice, and no help is given.

All these are pitiful. Yet, after tears,
Come rest and sleep and calm forgetfulness,
And God's good providence consoles the years.
Only the coward heart which did not guess,
The dreamer of brave deeds that might have been,
Shall cureless ache with wounds forever green.

from IN VINCULIS

At eighty Blunt published MY DIARIES, a work so candid, so critical of British diplomacy, that the publisher withdrew it. Blunt had already brought out three volumes of poetry; to the fourth edition of one of them he added this note: "No life is perfect that has not been lived—youth in feeling—manhood in battle—old age in meditation." Having experienced all, he died content in his eighty-third year, September 11, 1922.

Blunt's verse is more emotional than classical. But his sonnets—particularly the sequences ESTHER: A YOUNG MAN'S TRAGEDY and THE LOVE SONNETS OF PROTEUS—are as effectively simple as they are sincere. The ESTHER poems have the moving force of a personal outcry.

FROM

Esther

He who has once been happy is for aye
  Out of destruction's reach. His fortune then
Holds nothing secret; and Eternity,
  Which is a mystery to other men,

Has like a woman given him its joy.
  Time is his conquest. Life, if it should fret,
Has paid him tribute. He can bear to die,
  He who has once been happy! When I set
The world before me and survey its range,
  Its mean ambitions, its scant fantasies,
The shreds of pleasure which for lack of change
  Men wrap around them and call happiness,
The poor delights which are the tale and sum
Of the world's courage in its martyrdom;

When I hear laughter from a tavern door,
  When I see crowds agape and in the rain
Watching on tiptoe and with stifled roar
  To see a rocket fired or a bull slain,
When misers handle gold, when orators
  Touch strong men's hearts with glory till thev weep,
When cities deck their streets for barren wars
  Which have laid waste their youth, and when I keep
Calmly the count of my own life and see
  On what poor stuff my manhood's dreams were fed
Till I too learned what dole of vanity
  Will serve a human soul for daily bread,
—Then I remember that I once was young
And lived with Esther the world's gods among.

The sonnets to Juliet in the PROTEUS volume are only a little less impassioned than those to Esther. At least one of them, a late nineteenth-century echo of Drayton's lines beginning "Since there's no help, come, let us kiss and part" (see page 250), is worthy to stand beside its famous sixteenth-century model.

Farewell

Juliet, farewell. I would not be forgiven
Even if I forgave. These words must be
The last between us two in Earth or Heaven,
The last and bitterest. You are henceforth free
For ever from my bitter words and me.
You shall not at my hand be further vexed
With either love, reproach or jealousy
(So help me Heaven), in this world or the next.

Our souls are single for all time to come
And for eternity, and this farewell
Is as the trumpet note, the crack of doom,
Which heralds an eternal silence. Hell
Has no more fixed and absolute decree.
And Heaven and Hell may meet,—yet never we.

from THE LOVE SONNETS OF PROTEUS

ARTHUR O'SHAUGHNESSY

[1844–1881]

ARTHUR O'SHAUGHNESSY is known for a single famous poem, and that one is never quoted in the form in which it was written. The "singer of one song" was born in London, March 14, 1844, and was employed in various clerical capacities by the British Museum; he ended up in its zoological department, where he specialized in icthyology. O'Shaughnessy was, for a while, one of Rossetti's undistinguished disciples. Frail in health, he rarely left his native city, had no experiences outside of books, and died of influenza in his thirty-seventh year.

Most of O'Shaughnessy's poetry is facile, the kind of verse which is easier to write than to read. Even the continually reprinted ODE was once a garrulous string of verses. The anthologist F. T. Palgrave deserves at least part of the credit for the fame of the lines, Palgrave having cut down an overwritten poem of nine stanzas to an almost perfect three. It is Palgrave's condensed version that is quoted, one of the most musical and most imaginative poems about poetry ever written.

Ode

We are the music-makers,
  And we are the dreamers of dreams,
Wandering by lone sea-breakers,
  And sitting by desolate streams;
World-losers and world-forsakers,
  On whom the pale moon gleams:
Yet we are the movers and shakers
  Of the world for ever, it seems.

With wonderful deathless ditties
We build up the world's great cities,
  And out of a fabulous story
  We fashion an empire's glory:
One man with a dream, at pleasure,
  Shall go forth and conquer a crown;
And three with a new song's measure
  Can trample an empire down.

We, in the ages lying
  In the buried past of the earth,
Built Nineveh with our sighing,
  And Babel itself with our mirth;
And o'erthrew them with prophesying
  To the old of the new world's worth;
For each age is a dream that is dying,
  Or one that is coming to birth.

GERARD MANLEY HOPKINS

[1844–1889]

Gerard Manley Hopkins, perhaps the most difficult and certainly one of the most original poets of the century, was born at Stratford, Essex, June 11, 1844. He was educated at Balliol College, Oxford, where his writing was commended and where he was strongly influenced by Walter Pater and Pater's highly colored style. In his twenty-third year Hopkins became a Roman Catholic and burned his early verses. Eleven years later he was ordained to the priesthood. After serving as a missionary in Liverpool, he was given a church in Oxford. A Jesuit, he taught Rhetoric and Greek at University College in Dublin. There he spent the last five years of his life.

Although Hopkins wrote a great deal of spiritual-sensual poetry, none of his poems appeared during his lifetime. His manuscripts were left to his friend Robert Bridges, later poet laureate, and it was not until thirty years after Hopkins' death that his extraordinary verse was published. A second edition, including some additional poems, appeared in 1931, and Hopkins was belatedly discovered. He was attacked as an eccentric and hailed as an originator.

The younger men admired, and many of them imitated, his metrical experiments, his breathless pace in which grammar was sacrificed for the sake of speed, his way of telescoping ideas by cutting off every nonessential word. Hopkins luxuriated in extravagance; to him the world was not only colorful but prodigal, overflowing with a divine largess. He delighted in "couple-colored" oddities, the rose-moles along the sides of trout, freckles and finches' wings, all things contrary, "counter, original, spare, strange," all the entrancing superfluities of creation.

Pied Beauty

Glory be to God for dappled things—
  For skies of couple-color as a brinded cow;
    For rose-moles all in stipple upon trout that swim;
Fresh-firecoal chestnut-falls; finches' wings;
  Landscape plotted and pieced—fold, fallow, and plow;
    And all trades, their gear and tackle and trim.

All things counter, original, spare, strange;
  Whatever is fickle, freckled (who knows how?)
    With swift, slow; sweet, sour; adazzle, dim;
He fathers-forth whose beauty is past change:
        Praise Him.

Hopkins saw the whole world "barbarous in beauty." Even the inanimate "azurous hung hills" expressed the "brute beauty and valor" of existence and woke "Man's mounting spirit in his bone-house." Hopkins spoke of Swinburne's "delirium-tremendous imagination," but Hopkins' imagination was far more reckless and opulent. To him everything was "charged with the grandeur of God."

God's Grandeur

The world is charged with the grandeur of God.
  It will flame out, like shining from shook foil;
  It gathers to a greatness, like the ooze of oil
Crushed. Why do men then now not reck his rod?

Generations have trod, have trod, have trod;
  And all is seared with trade; bleared, smeared with toil;
  And wears man's smudge and shares man's smell: the soil
Is bare now, nor can foot feel, being shod.

And for all this, nature is never spent;
  There lives the dearest freshness deep down things;
And though the last lights off the black West went
  Oh, morning, at the brown brink eastward, springs—
Because the Holy Ghost over the bent
  World broods with warm breast and with ah! bright wings.

It was not an erratic wildness in Hopkins but a daring purpose which broke down the traditional poetic idiom and reformed it into a new speech. Hopkins crowded metaphors with almost more associations than they could bear; he leaped, with the agility of lightning, from one image to another. Readers often have difficulty following the extraordinary rush of language, in which sounds, sights, textures, and ideas seem thrown pell-mell. But there is order in Hopkins' speed, a definite if seemingly kaleidoscopic design in the swiftness of his "terrible sincerity."

Hopkins' passionate devoutness was an answer not only to Hardy's atheism, but to the skeptical spirit of an age floundering between a religion it had discarded and a science it feared to accept. Unhampered by the confusion about him, unconcerned with publication, Hopkins composed the finest religious poems written since the seventeenth century.

Heaven: Haven

A NUN TAKES THE VEIL

I have desired to go
  Where springs not fail,
To fields where flies no sharp and sided hail,
  And a few lilies blow.

And I have asked to be
  Where no storms come,
Where the green swell is in the havens dumb,
  And out of the swing of the sea.

The Habit of Perfection

Elected Silence, sing to me
And beat upon my whorlèd ear,
Pipe me to pastures still, and be
The music that I care to hear.

Shape nothing, lips; be lovely-dumb;
It is the shut, the curfew sent
From there where all surrenders come
Which only makes you eloquent.

Be shellèd, eyes, with double dark
And find the uncreated light:
This ruck and reel which you remark
Coils, keeps, and teases simple sight.

Palate, the hatch of tasty lust,
Desire not to be rinsed with wine:
The can must be so sweet, the crust
So fresh that come in fasts divine!

Nostrils, your careless breath that spend
Upon the stir and keep of pride,
What relish shall the censers send
Along the sanctuary side!

O feel-of-primrose hands, O feet
That want the yield of plushy sward,
But you shall walk the golden street
And you unhouse and house the Lord.

And, Poverty, be thou the bride
And now the marriage feast begun,
And lily-colored clothes provide
Your spouse not labored-at nor spun.

Unlike such equally affirmative spirits as Wordsworth and Whitman, Hopkins can never be a popular poet. He cannot be a companion to the ordinary individual, for he shows no appreciation of the struggles of the average man. But within the scope of his vision and the range of his genius, he is magnificent.

ROBERT BRIDGES

[1844–1930]

THE sixteenth poet laureate of England, Robert Bridges, was a noted surgeon who abandoned his practice at thirty-six, and a lyric poet who published a long philosophical poem, by some considered his most important work, at the age of eighty-five. He was born at Walmer, October 23, 1844, was educated at Corpus Christi College, Oxford, and became a general practitioner in London. Almost at the same time he joined the staff at St. Bartholomew's Hospital, from which he retired, after a serious illness in 1881, to devote himself entirely to literature.

Although Bridges published eight plays and many small volumes of verse, all of them had a small circulation. The poet was almost unknown to the public until the appearance of his POETICAL WORKS, at which time he was sixty-eight. The following year, he was appointed poet laureate, succeeding the innocuous Alfred Austin.

Bridges' failure to achieve popularity is easy enough to understand. His ideas were direct and his emotions simple, but his preoccupation with meters made him construct lines that were too subtle for wide enjoyment. Even a poem on a dead child was forced into an involved metrical pattern.

So I lay thee there, thy sunken eyelids closing—
  Go lie thou there in the coffin, thy last little bed!—
      Propping thy wise, sad head,
Thy firm, pale hands across thy chest disposing.

Most readers considered Bridges a cold classicist; they respected him, but they could not love him. Nevertheless, under the archaic diction and technical experiments there is a persistently sweet strain of music.

I love all beauteous things,
  I seek and adore them;
God hath no better praise,
And man in his hasty days
  Is honored for them.

Serenity and fastidiousness mark his work, a quiet if somewhat severe contemplation of beauty. Praising Bridges' delight in beauty, Charles Williams adds, "It is a delight which may require a certain similarity of temperament or a certain prolonged discipline before it can be accepted, especially from a reader used to more violent effects." But no discipline is needed to enjoy the dexterously muted melodies.

Nightingales

Beautiful must be the mountains whence ye come,
And bright in the fruitful valleys the streams wherefrom
Ye learn your song:
Where are those starry woods? O might I wander there,
Among the flowers, which in that heavenly air
Bloom the year long!

Nay, barren are those mountains and spent the streams:
Our song is the voice of desire, that haunts our dreams,
A throe of the heart,
Whose pining visions dim, forbidden hopes profound,
No dying cadence nor long sigh can sound,
For all our art.

Alone, aloud in the raptured ear of men
We pour our dark nocturnal secret; and then,
As night is withdrawn
From these sweet-springing meads and bursting boughs of May,
Dream, while the innumerable choir of day
Welcome the dawn.

London Snow

When men were all asleep the snow came flying,
In large white flakes falling on the city brown,
Stealthily and perpetually settling and loosely lying,
Hushing the latest traffic of the drowsy town;
Deadening, muffling, stifling its murmurs failing;
Lazily and incessantly floating down and down;
Silently sifting and veiling road, roof and railing;
Hiding difference, making unevenness even,
Into angles and crevices softly drifting and sailing.

All night it fell, and when full inches seven
It lay in the depth of its uncompacted lightness,
The clouds blew off from a high and frosty heaven;
And all woke earlier for the unaccustomed brightness
Of the winter dawning, the strange unheavenly glare:
The eye marveled—marveled at the dazzling whiteness;
The ear hearkened to the stillness of the solemn air;
No sound of wheel rumbling nor of foot falling,
And the busy morning cries came thin and spare.
Then boys I heard, as they went to school, calling;
They gathered up the crystal manna to freeze
Their tongues with tasting, their hands with snow-balling;
Or rioted in a drift, plunging up to the knees;
Or peering up from under the white-mossed wonder,
"O look at the trees!" they cried. "O look at the trees!"
With lessened load, a few carts creak and blunder,
Following along the white deserted way,
A country company long dispersed asunder:
When now already the sun, in pale display
Standing by Paul's high dome, spread forth below
His sparkling beams, and awoke the stir of the day.
For now doors open, and war is waged with the snow;
And trains of somber men, past tale of number,
Tread long brown paths, as toward their toil they go:
But even for them awhile no cares encumber
Their minds diverted; the daily word is unspoken,
The daily thoughts of labor and sorrow slumber
At the sight of the beauty that greets them, for the charm they
have broken.

At seventy-four Bridges edited the poems of Gerard Manley Hopkins (see page 977), poems which were the very opposite of Bridges' restrained consciousness and deliberate harmonies. At eighty-five he published THE TESTAMENT OF BEAUTY, a work which was compared to Wordsworth's PRELUDE, and which, wrote Robert Hillyer, "combines with the philosopher's learning and reasoning the persuasion of beauty itself." A year after the publication of his impressive and possibly major work, Bridges died, following a short illness, April 21, 1930.

W. E. HENLEY

[1849–1903]

NO ONE ever sang more courageously of life than William Ernest Henley, who was a cripple for more than forty years. At the age of twelve in Gloucester, where he was born, it was discovered that the boy was suffering from a tubercular disease of the bone. One leg was amputated, and some years later the doctors advised the amputation of the other. Henley, who was then twenty-four, went to the Edinburgh Infirmary, was treated by Lister, the founder of antiseptic surgery, and, after twenty months, the disease was checked and the foot saved.

One of Henley's most constant visitors at the hospital was Robert Louis Stevenson. A year his junior and, later, his best friend, Stevenson is clearly pictured in APPARITION, one of the sketches and sonnets entitled IN HOSPITAL.

Apparition

Thin-legged, thin-chested, slight unspeakably,
Neat-footed and weak-fingered; in his face—
Lean, large-boned, curved of beak and touched with race,
Bold-lipped, rich-tinted, mutable as the sea,
The brown eyes radiant with vivacity—
There shines a brilliant and romantic grace,
A spirit intense and rare, with trace on trace
Of passion, impudence and energy.
Valiant in velvet, light in ragged luck,
Most vain, most generous, sternly critical,
Buffoon and poet, lover and sensualist;
A deal of Ariel, just a streak of Puck,
Much Antony, of Hamlet most of all,
And something of the Shorter-Catechist.

It was in the Edinburgh hospital that Henley wrote many of his best-known verses. The "bludgeonings of chance"—a Hardyesque phrase—could not defeat his tough spirit. He said it by implication in a score of lyrics, explicitly in INVICTUS (literally "Unconquered") that grim defiance from the black Pit of Hell.

Invictus

Out of the night that covers me,
  Black as the Pit from pole to pole,
I thank whatever gods may be
  For my unconquerable soul.

In the fell clutch of circumstance
  I have not winced nor cried aloud.
Under the bludgeonings of chance
  My head is bloody, but unbowed.

Beyond this place of wrath and tears
  Looms but the horror of the shade,
And yet the menace of the years
  Finds, and shall find me, unafraid.

It matters not how strait the gate,
  How charged with punishments the scroll,
I am the master of my fate:
  I am the captain of my soul.

Two years after leaving the hospital Henley went to London and became an editor on a magazine. He made many gratifying discoveries among the younger writers, but drove himself ruthlessly. Editorial work kept him from expressing himself more fully in verse. "After spending the better part of my life in the pursuit of poetry," he wrote in self-exculpation, "I found myself so utterly unmarketable that I had to own myself beaten in art, and to addict myself to journalism." Later, however, the impulse to write poetry was still strong, and Henley found that, "after all, the lyrical instinct had slept, not died."

The lyrical instinct triumphed. The early gusto was succeeded by a delicate music and, as in MARGARITAE SORORI (a poem written in memory of his wife's sister Margaret), a grave and dignified unrhymed measure.

The Blackbird

The nightingale has a lyre of gold,
  The lark's is a clarion call,
And the blackbird plays but a boxwood flute,
  But I love him best of all.

For his song is all of the joy of life,
  And we in the mad, spring weather,
We two have listened till he sang
  Our hearts and lips together.

Madam Life

Madam Life's a piece in bloom
  Death goes dogging everywhere:
She's the tenant of the room,
  He's the ruffian on the stair.

You shall see her as a friend,
  You shall bilk him once and twice;
But he'll trap you in the end,
  And he'll stick you for her price.

With his kneebones at your chest,
  And his knuckles in your throat,
You would reason—plead—protest!
  Clutching at her petticoat.

But she's heard it all before,
  Well she knows you've had your fun,
Gingerly she gains the door,
  And your little job is done.

Margaritae Sorori

A late lark twitters from the quiet skies;
And from the west,
Where the sun, his day's work ended,
Lingers as in content,

There falls on the old, gray city
An influence luminous and serene,
A shining peace.

The smoke ascends
In a rosy-and-golden haze. The spires
Shine, and are changed. In the valley
Shadows rise. The lark sings on. The sun,
Closing his benediction,
Sinks, and the darkening air
Thrills with a sense of the triumphing night—
Night with her train of stars
And her great gift of sleep.

So be my passing!
My task accomplished and the long day done,
My wages taken, and in my heart
Some late lark singing,
Let me be gathered to the quiet west,
The sundown splendid and serene,
Death.

Henley continued busy and belligerent until forty-five, when the death of his five-year-old daughter broke his heart. He wrote for several years more, but the spirit had gone out of him. He was at work on a preface for the Tudor Bible when he died, July 12, 1903.

ROBERT LOUIS STEVENSON

[1850–1894]

HENLEY'S etching of the "thin-legged, thin-chested" Robert Louis Stevenson portrayed the youth with diagnostic accuracy, for Stevenson was a consumptive. His life was a pitiful attempt to find a climate in which he could survive.

The man whom Henley pictured as a combination of lover and sensualist, a happy Ariel and a melancholy Hamlet, a mischievous Puck and a Calvinist preacher, was born November 13, 1850, in Edinburgh. An only child, frail from birth, he received little regular schooling. It was hoped that he would become a lighthouse engineer, following the family profession, but poor health made this impossible. The ancestral love of the sea was in him. He studied law dutifully and went so far as to be called to the bar in his twenty-sixth year, but he never practiced. Instead, he began to write, enjoying himself in rhyme and training himself as narrator and essayist by sedulously studying the masters of prose. When it was apparent that his disease was crippling him, Stevenson gladly responded to the sea call and went abroad for warmth and sunshine.

In France Stevenson met Mrs. Fanny Osbourne, an American widow, followed her to California, and, after almost succumbing to the rigors of the journey, married her in his thirtieth year. The couple were poor; they lived in a shabby mining camp. But Stevenson made the place bright with "bird-song at morning and star-shine at night."

Romance

I will make you brooches and toys for your delight
Of bird-song at morning and star-shine at night.
I will make a palace fit for you and me,
Of green days in forests and blue days at sea.

I will make my kitchen, and you shall keep your room,
Where white flows the river and bright blows the broom,
And you shall wash your linen and keep your body white
In rainfall at morning and dewfall at night.

And this shall be for music when no one else is near,
The fine song for singing, the rare song to hear!
That only I remember, that only you admire,
Of the broad road that stretches and the roadside fire.

Although Stevenson had written tales and travel books which had been well received, it was not until the publication of TREASURE ISLAND in 1883 that he became popular. Three years later his fame was definitely established with THE STRANGE CASE OF DR. JEKYLL AND MR. HYDE. At thirty-five he published A CHILD'S GARDEN OF VERSES with some misgiving; but the collection Stevenson hesitated to offer to the public has grown to be a universal favorite, second only to Mother Goose in its appeal to every generation.

Escape at Bedtime

The lights from the parlor and kitchen shone out
  Through the blinds and the windows and bars;
And high overhead and all moving about,
  There were thousands of millions of stars.
There ne'er were such thousands of leaves on a tree,
  Nor of people in church or the park,
As the crowds of the stars that looked down upon me,
  And that glittered and winked in the dark.

The Dog, and the Plough, and the Hunter, and all,
  And the star of the sailor, and Mars,
These shone in the sky, and the pail by the wall
  Would be half full of water and stars.
They saw me at last, and they chased me with cries,
  And they soon had me packed into bed;
But the glory kept shining and bright in my eyes,
  And the stars going round in my head.

Stevenson's serious poetry is unpretentious, but its quiet romanticism has a warm and heartening glow. Lucid without being brilliant, precise without being stiff, it retains its old charm.

Bright Is the Ring of Words

Bright is the ring of words
  When the right man rings them,
Fair is the fall of songs
  When the singer sings them.
Still they are caroled and said—
  On wings they are carried—
After the singer is dead
  And the maker buried.

Low as the singer lies
  In the field of heather,
Songs of his fashion bring
  The swains together.

And when the west is red
  With the sunset embers,
The lover lingers and sings
  And the maid remembers.

Ditty

TO AN AIR FROM BACH

The cock shall crow
    In the morning grey,
The bugles blow
    At the break of day:
The cock shall sing and the merry bugles ring,
And all the little brown birds sing upon the spray.

The thorn shall blow
    In the month of May,
And my love shall go
    In her holiday array:
But I shall lie in the kirkyard nigh
While all the little brown birds sing upon the spray.

The Celestial Surgeon

If I have faltered more or less
In my great task of happiness;
If I have moved among my race
And shown no glorious morning face;
If beams from happy human eyes
Have moved me not; if morning skies,
Books, and my food, and summer rain
Knocked on my sullen heart in vain:—
Lord, Thy most pointed pleasure take
And stab my spirit broad awake;
Or, Lord, if too obdurate I,
Choose Thou, before that spirit die,
A piercing pain, a killing sin,
And to my dead heart run them in!

Fighting his ever-progressing disease, Stevenson traveled through America. A winter at Saranac Lake in the Adirondack Mountains gave him a respite, but the following year he grew worse and craved the sea again. He left San Francisco for a voyage among the islands of the South Sea, and what was intended to be an excursion became a voluntary exile. Death found him in Samoa, December 3, 1894. Sixty natives carried him to a peak on the Pacific, and there a tablet was placed carved with the lines from his REQUIEM which Stevenson always intended as his epitaph.

Requiem

Under the wide and starry sky,
Dig the grave and let me lie.
Glad did I live and gladly die,
 And I laid me down with a will.

This be the verse you grave for me:
Here he lies where he longed to be;
Home is the sailor, home from sea,
 And the hunter home from the hill.

EDWIN MARKHAM

[1852–1940]

ONE of the most indignant poems of social protest was written by a quiet teacher, Edwin Markham, born in Oregon City, Oregon, April 23, 1852. Markham grew up in California, worked on a cattle ranch, entered the State Normal School at San José, and became a superintendent of schools. Social consciousness was awakening. The world of aristocracy was at war with the world of wealth; in the conflict the worker was the victim. Seeing Millet's painting of a bowed, broken toiler, Markham made the French peasant a symbol of all workers, and wrote THE MAN WITH THE HOE. The poem was immediately successful upon its appearance in the San Francisco EXAMINER the last year of the nineteenth century. It was copied in every part of the world. It caught up the passion for social justice that was waiting to be expressed and was hailed as "the battle cry of the next thousand years." Not in protest against toil but against the exploitation of labor, Markham saw the well-to-do farmer as the Yeoman; but here in the Millet picture, he wrote, "is his opposite: the Hoeman, the landless workman of the world."

The Man With the Hoe

Bowed by the weight of centuries he leans
Upon his hoe and gazes on the ground,
The emptiness of ages in his face,
And on his back the burden of the world.
Who made him dead to rapture and despair,
A thing that grieves not and that never hopes,
Stolid and stunned, a brother to the ox?
Who loosened and let down this brutal jaw?
Whose was the hand that slanted back this brow?
Whose breath blew out the light within this brain?

Is this the Thing the Lord God made and gave
To have dominion over sea and land;
To trace the stars and search the heavens for power;
To feel the passion of Eternity?
Is this the dream He dreamed who shaped the suns
And marked their ways upon the ancient deep?
Down all the caverns of Hell to their last gulf
There is no shape more terrible than this—
More tongued with censure of the world's blind greed—
More filled with signs and portents for the soul—
More packt with danger to the universe.

What gulfs between him and the seraphim!
Slave of the wheel of labor, what to him
Are Plato and the swing of Pleiades?
What the long reaches of the peaks of song,
The rift of dawn, the reddening of the rose?
Through this dread shape the suffering ages look;
Time's tragedy is in that aching stoop;
Through this dread shape humanity betrayed,
Plundered, profaned, and disinherited,
Cries protest to the Judges of the World,
A protest that is also prophecy.

O masters, lords and rulers in all lands,
Is this the handiwork you give to God,
This monstrous thing distorted and soul-quenched?
How will you ever straighten up this shape;
Touch it again with immortality;
Give back the upward looking and the light;
Rebuild in it the music and the dream;
Make right the immemorial infamies,
Perfidious wrongs, immedicable woes?

O masters, lords and rulers in all lands,
How will the Future reckon with this man?
How answer his brute question in that hour
When whirlwinds of rebellion shake all shores?
How will it be with kingdoms and with kings—
With those who shaped him to the thing he is—
When this dumb terror shall rise to judge the world,
After the silence of the centuries?

Once established as a writer, Markham produced a great quantity of verse; but it was unoriginal in subject, undistinguished in style. Readers had come to the regretful conclusion that Markham was the poet of a single poem, when suddenly the author of THE MAN WITH THE HOE published LINCOLN, THE MAN OF THE PEOPLE. Less magniloquent than its predecessor, the Lincoln poem is more compact in thought, more restrained in utterance. The central image is powerful and the concluding figure is as appropriate as it is eloquent, a truly noble climax.

The poem, selected from more than two hundred tributes to the martyr-President, was read at the dedication ceremonies of the Lincoln Memorial at Washington, D. C., May 30, 1922.

Lincoln, the Man of the People

When the Norn Mother saw the Whirlwind Hour
Greatening and darkening as it hurried on,
She left the Heaven of Heroes and came down
To make a man to meet the mortal need.
She took the tried clay of the common road—
Clay warm yet with the genial heat of earth,
Dasht through it all a strain of prophecy;
Tempered the heap with thrill of human tears;

Then mixt a laughter with the serious stuff.
Into the shape she breathed a flame to light
That tender, tragic, ever-changing face;
And laid on him a sense of the Mystic Powers,
Moving—all husht—behind the mortal veil.
Here was a man to hold against the world,
A man to match the mountains and the sea.

The color of the ground was in him, the red earth;
The smack and tang of elemental things:
The rectitude and patience of the cliff;
The good-will of the rain that loves all leaves;
The friendly welcome of the wayside well;
The courage of the bird that dares the sea;
The gladness of the wind that shakes the corn;
The pity of the snow that hides all scars;
The secrecy of streams that make their way
Under the mountain to the rifted rock;
The tolerance and equity of light
That gives as freely to the shrinking flower
As to the great oak flaring to the wind—
To the grave's low hill as to the Matterhorn
That shoulders out the sky. Sprung from the West,
He drank the valorous youth of a new world.
The strength of virgin forests braced his mind,
The hush of spacious prairies stilled his soul.
His words were oaks in acorns; and his thoughts
Were roots that firmly gript the granite truth.

Up from log cabin to the Capitol,
One fire was on his spirit, one resolve—
To send the keen ax to the root of wrong,
Clearing a free way for the feet of God,
The eyes of conscience testing every stroke,
To make his deed the measure of a man.
He built the rail-pile as he built the State,
Pouring his splendid strength through every blow:
The grip that swung the ax in Illinois
Was on the pen that set a people free.

So came the Captain with the mighty heart.
And when the judgment thunders split the house,
Wrenching the rafters from their ancient rest,
He held the ridgepole up, and spiked again
The rafters of the Home. He held his place—

Held the long purpose like a growing tree—
Held on through blame and faltered not at praise.
And when he fell in whirlwind, he went down
As when a lordly cedar, green with boughs,
Goes down with a great shout upon the hills,
And leaves a lonesome place against the sky.

In his late forties Markham came East and made his home on Staten Island. Rugged and patriarchal, he overcame criticism and illness. He grew more beautiful with age; someone said that Markham in his seventies looked like a composite picture of all the New England poets. A more cautious admirer observed him as "a deity dispossessed and declining on a suburban Olympus." His life spanned the continent. Born near one ocean, Markham died facing the other, at eighty-eight, March 7, 1940.

OSCAR WILDE

[1856–1900]

CULTIVATED affectation and whispered scandal increased Wilde's renown as a playwright and poet; a criminal trial ruined it. He was a notoriously spoiled child of society until his fortieth year; at forty-three he was an almost unrecognizable derelict. Son of a distinguished but profligate Irish surgeon and a highly affected mother, Oscar Fingal O'Flahertie Wills Wilde was born October 16, 1856, in Dublin, Ireland. He was educated at Trinity College, Dublin, and at Magdalen College, Oxford, where he won the Newdigate Prize at twenty-one for his poem RAVENNA. Even as an undergraduate he had become celebrated as an "artist in attitudes." He wore a languishing look and long hair; his clothes were oddly cut and carefully cobwebby, "with a tender bloom like cold gravy"; he said he despaired of living up to his blue china. By the time he had left Oxford he had become the recognized leader of the Aesthetic Movement. PUNCH, England's most famous humorous weekly, never tired of caricaturing him and his velveteen breeches. A few years later his bizarre cult was immortally burlesqued in W. S. Gilbert's PATIENCE.

At twenty-six Wilde made a spectacular lecture tour through the

United States. The Americans refused to take his dandyism seriously, but they enjoyed quoting his statement to the customs authorities that he had "nothing to declare except his genius" and that he was disappointed by the Atlantic Ocean.

At twenty-eight Wilde married and, for a while, seemed to adjust himself to normal domesticity. But he remarked that "women spoil every romance by trying to make it last forever," and, after a short period of virtue, Wilde began dallying with "the raptures and roses of vice." He wrote a great deal of rococo prose, a few glittering period plays in which banter takes the place of ideas, several charming if overwritten fairy tales, and a novel, THE PICTURE OF DORIAN GRAY, which is a cross between an allegory and a leer, a work which may well be described as satyrical.

As a poet, Wilde sinks beneath the burden of his baroque manner. The language of his verse is tinsel, the thinking is tawdry. One of his earliest poems is among his best. REQUIESCAT ("May she rest in peace") was written in memory of Wilde's sister who died in childhood. It is interesting to compare the lines with Matthew Arnold's poem by the same name, on page 924.

Requiescat

Tread lightly, she is near
  Under the snow,
Speak gently, she can hear
  The daisies grow.

All her bright golden hair
  Tarnished with rust,
She that was young and fair
  Fallen to dust.

Lily-like, white as snow,
  She hardly knew
She was a woman, so
  Sweetly she grew.

Coffin-board, heavy stone
  Lie on her breast;
I vex my heart alone,
  She is at rest.

Peace, peace; she cannot hear
  Lyre or sonnet;
All my life's buried here.
  Heap earth upon it.

Wilde was in his fortieth year when the Marquis of Queensberry accused him of undue intimacy with the latter's son, Lord Alfred Douglas. Wilde was unwisely advised to bring suit for libel against the Marquis, lost the suit, was faced with arrest, and was tried for statutory offenses under the criminal law. Found guilty, he was sentenced to two years at hard labor. His prison experiences are recorded in the prose of DE PROFUNDIS, a defense which is also a confession, and THE BALLAD OF READING GAOL, in many ways his most sincere work.

FROM

The Ballad of Reading Gaol

Yet each man kills the thing he loves,
  By each let this be heard,
Some do it with a bitter look,
  Some with a flattering word,
The coward does it with a kiss,
  The brave man with a sword!

Some kill their love when they are young,
  And some when they are old;
Some strangle with the hands of Lust,
  Some with the hands of Gold:
The kindest use a knife, because
  The dead so soon grow cold.

Some love too little, some too long,
  Some sell, and others buy;
Some do the deed with many tears,
  And some without a sigh:
For each man kills the thing he loves,
  Yet each man does not die.

He does not die a death of shame
  On a day of dark disgrace,

Nor have a noose about his neck,
  Nor a cloth upon his face,
Nor drop feet foremost through the floor
  Into an empty space.

He did not wring his hands nor weep,
  Nor did he peak or pine,
But he drank the air as though it held
  Some healthful anodyne;
With open mouth he drank the sun
  As though it had been wine!

And I and all the souls in pain,
  Who tramped the other ring,
Forgot if we ourselves had done
  A great or little thing,
And watched with gaze of dull amaze
  The man who had to swing.

And strange it was to see him pass
  With a step so light and gay,
And strange it was to see him look
  So wistfully at the day,
And strange it was to think that he
  Had such a debt to pay.

. . . . . .

For oak and elm have pleasant leaves
  That in the spring-time shoot:
But grim to see is the gallows-tree,
  With its adder-bitten root,
And, green or dry, a man must die
  Before it bears its fruit!

The loftiest place is that seat of grace
  For which all worldlings try:
But who would stand in hempen band
  Upon a scaffold high,
And through a murderer's collar take
  His last look at the sky?

It is sweet to dance to violins
  When Love and Life are fair:
To dance to flutes, to dance to lutes
  Is delicate and rare:
But it is not sweet with nimble feet
  To dance upon the air!

So with curious eyes and sick surmise
  We watched him day by day,
And wondered if each one of us
  Would end the self-same way,
For none can tell to what red Hell
  His sightless soul may stray.

At last the dead man walked no more
  Amongst the Trial Men,
And I knew that he was standing up
  In the black dock's dreadful pen,
And that never would I see his face
  In God's sweet world again.

Like two doomed ships that pass in storm
  We had crossed each other's way:
But we made no sign, we said no word,
  We had no word to say;
For we did not meet in the holy night,
  But in the shameful day.

A prison wall was round us both,
  Two outcast men we were:
The world had thrust us from its heart,
  And God from out His care:
And the iron gin that waits for Sin
  Had caught us in its snare.

After his release from prison, Wilde changed his name, moved to the Continent, and drank himself to death. He died of cerebral meningitis, November 30, 1900. He was buried according to the rites of the Roman Catholic Church, in the cemetery of Bagneux, on the outskirts of Paris. Lord Alfred Douglas was chief mourner.

SIR WILLIAM WATSON

[1858–1935]

AUTHOR of odes that were once considered Wordsworthian and elegies that were favorably compared to Tennyson's IN MEMORIAM, William Watson is remembered for only a few epigrams and one short lyric. He was born in Yorkshire, August 2,

1858, and began writing in his childhood. After several volumes had appeared, it became the custom to refer to Watson's poetry as "lofty" and "dignified"; few critics had the bad grace to say that it was derivative and rather dull. Queen Victoria voiced her admiration for LACRYMAE MUSARUM, Watson's elegy on Tennyson; Gladstone suggested that the author be made poet laureate. Watson, together with Rudyard Kipling and the "impossible" Swinburne, was seriously considered for the laureateship; but the authorities, unable to come to an agreement, awarded the honor to the unknown Alfred Austin, an ultraconservative journalist.

After a too-promising start, Watson's career ended abruptly. He was snubbed by a prime minister for some tactless verses; his contemporaries were embarrassed by the poet's garrulous rhymes; the younger men were either scornful or silent. At sixty he was almost forgotten. At seventy he was so desperately in need that a committee had to raise funds for him. He died in obscurity August 13, 1935.

Miscast in the role of prophet, Watson was one of the last of the Royal Purple tradition. Never careless, he was often too pompous, too intent upon wrapping himself in the oversize mantles of Milton, Wordsworth, and Tennyson. The shorter poems, and particularly the EPIGRAMS, are more certainly his own.

Two Epigrams

LOVE

Love, like a bird, hath perched upon a spray
  For thee and me to hearken what he sings.
Contented, he forgets to fly away;
  But hush! Remind not Eros of his wings.

THE POET

The Poet gathers fruit from every tree,
Yea, grapes from thorns and figs from thistles he.
Plucked by his hand, the basest weed that grows
Towers to a lily, reddens to a rose.

Watson's ambitious WORDSWORTH'S GRAVE and THE PRINCE'S QUEST are seldom read; his many volumes are no longer printed. But the lighthearted song beginning "April, April" continues to be uncritically quoted.

Song

April, April,
Laugh thy girlish laughter;
Then, the moment after,
Weep thy girlish tears,
April, that mine ears
Like a lover greetest,
If I tell thee, sweetest,
All my hopes and fear.
April, April,
Laugh thy golden laughter,
But, the moment after,
Weep thy golden tears!

FRANCIS THOMPSON

[1859–1907]

A SEVENTEENTH-CENTURY mystic thrust into the embattled commercialism of the late nineteenth century, Francis Thompson withdrew from a world in which he could not compete into a world of religious fantasy where he was comforted if not secure. He was born December 18, 1859, in Lancashire. Son of a doctor, he was educated to succeed his father. But, after making vague declarations that he hoped to be a priest, and after failing three times to pass his medical examinations, it was apparent that he was not interested in medicine. The family was outraged, and Thompson, at twenty-five, cut himself adrift and went to London. No one was less capable of supporting himself in the crowded metropolis. For at least four years he sold matches at street corners, ran errands, called cabs, and sank to an incredible level of poverty. His father sent him a few shillings a week in care of the reading room at the British Museum, but Thompson became so shabby that he was refused admittance. Literally starving, he was rescued by a prostitute who took him to her room, fed him, and gave him shelter.

Thompson now began to write; his first poem was penned on blue paper used to wrap sugar. He submitted an article and some verse to Wilfrid Meynell, editor of MERRY ENGLAND, but Meynell's letter of acceptance failed to locate Thompson. When Thompson was finally found and urged to come to the editorial office, he looked like a wild and hounded thing. His shoes were broken; there was no shirt under his closely buttoned ragged coat. Finally, according to Francis Meynell, Wilfrid Meynell's son, "he was persuaded, though with difficulty, to come off the streets; and even to give up for many years the laudanum he had been taking. For the remaining nineteen years of his life he had an existence at any rate three-quarters protected from the physical tragedies of his starved and homeless young manhood."

Meynell induced Thompson to spend two years at Stonington Priory to cure him of the effects of the drug; it was while he was living with the Franciscan monks that Thompson wrote the ecstatic essay on Shelley and the even more rhapsodic THE HOUND OF HEAVEN. The title was probably derived from Shelley, who in PROMETHEUS UNBOUND speaks of "Heaven's wingéd hound." In a turbulent vision, Thompson saw man as the human quarry, the frightened spirit running to hide in nature, and God as the divine hunter, pursuer and rescuer. Thompson employed every device to heighten the effect of the extraordinary pursuit: a riotous pace and an elaborately ornamented speech, archaic phrases and new words—some of them coined by Thompson—and a headlong extravagance of style.

The Hound of Heaven

I fled Him, down the nights and down the days;
  I fled Him, down the arches of the years;
I fled Him, down the labyrinthine ways
  Of my own mind; and in the mist of tears
I hid from Him, and under running laughter.
        Up vistaed hopes I sped;
        And shot, precipitated,
Adown Titanic glooms of chasmed fears,
  From those strong Feet that followed, followed after.
        But with unhurrying chase,
        And unperturbéd pace,
    Deliberate speed, majestic instancy,
        They beat—and a Voice beat
        More instant than the Feet—
    "All things betray thee, who betrayest Me."

I pleaded, outlaw-wise,
By many a hearted casement, curtained red,
Trellised with intertwining charities
(For, though I knew His love Who followéd,
Yet was I sore adread
Lest, having Him, I must have naught beside);
But, if one little casement parted wide,
The gust of His approach would clash it to:
Fear wist not to evade, as Love wist to pursue.
Across the margent of the world I fled,
And troubled the gold gateways of the stars,
Smiting for shelter on their clanged bars;
Fretted to dulcet jars
And silvern chatter the pale ports o' the moon.
I said to Dawn: Be sudden—to Eve: Be soon;
With thy young skiey blossoms heap me over
From this tremendous Lover—
Float thy vague veil about me, lest He see!
I tempted all His servitors, but to find
My own betrayal in their constancy,
In faith to Him their fickleness to me,
Their traitorous trueness, and their loyal deceit.
To all swift things for swiftness did I sue;
Clung to the whistling mane of every wind.
But whether they swept, smoothly fleet,
The long savannahs of the blue;
Or whether, Thunder-driven,
They clanged his chariot 'thwart a heaven,
Plashy with flying lightnings round the spurn o' their feet:—
Fear wist not to evade as Love wist to pursue.
Still with unhurrying chase,
And unperturbéd pace,
Deliberate speed, majestic instancy,
Came on the following Feet,
And a Voice above their beat—
"Naught shelters thee, who wilt not shelter Me."

I sought no more that after which I strayed
In face of man or maid;
But still within the little children's eyes
Seems something, something that replies,
They at least are for me, surely for me!
I turned me to them very wistfully;
But just as their young eyes grew sudden fair
With dawning answers there,

Their angel plucked them from me by the hair.
"Come then, ye other children, Nature's–share
With me" (said I) "your delicate fellowship;
        Let me greet you lip to lip,
        Let me twine with you caresses,
          Wantoning
        With our Lady-Mother's vagrant tresses,
          Banqueting
        With her in her wind-walled palace,
        Underneath her azured daïs,
        Quaffing, as your taintless way is,
          From a chalice
Lucent-weeping out of the dayspring."
          So it was done:
I in their delicate fellowship was one–
Drew the bolt of Nature's secrecies.
        I knew all the swift importings
        On the willful face of skies;
        I knew how the clouds arise
        Spumed of the wild sea-snortings;
          All that's born or dies
        Rose and drooped with; made them shapers
Of mine own moods, or wailful or divine;
        With them joyed and was bereaven.
        I was heavy with the even,
        When she lit her glimmering tapers
        Round the day's dead sanctities.
        I laughed in the morning's eyes.
I triumphed and I saddened with all weather,
        Heaven and I wept together,
And its sweet tears were salt with mortal mine;

Against the red throb of its sunset-heart
        I laid my own to beat,
        And share commingling heat;
But not by that, by that, was eased my human smart.
In vain my tears were wet on Heaven's gray cheek.
For ah! we know not what each other says,
        These things and I; in sound *I* speak–
Their sound is but their stir, they speak by silences.
Nature, poor stepdame, cannot slake my drouth;
        Let her, if she would owe me,
Drop yon blue bosom-veil of sky, and show me
        The breasts o' her tenderness:

Never did any milk of hers once bless
My thirsting mouth.
Nigh and nigh draws the chase,
With unperturbéd pace,
Deliberate speed, majestic instancy;
And past those noiséd Feet
A Voice comes yet more fleet—
"Lo! naught contents thee, who content'st not Me."

Naked I wait Thy love's uplifted stroke!
My harness piece by piece Thou hast hewn from me,
And smitten me to my knee;
I am defenseless utterly.
I slept, methinks, and woke,
And, slowly gazing, find me stripped in sleep.
In the rash lustihead of my young powers,
I shook the pillaring hours
And pulled my life upon me; grimed with smears,
I stand amid the dust o' the mounded years—
My mangled youth lies dead beneath the heap.
My days have crackled and gone up in smoke,
Have puffed and burst as sun-starts on a stream.
Yea, faileth now even dream
The dreamer, and the lute the lutanist;
Even the linked fantasies, in whose blossomy twist
I swung the earth a trinket at my wrist,
Are yielding; cords of all too weak account
For earth with heavy griefs so overplused.
Ah! is Thy love indeed
A weed, albeit an amaranthine weed,
Suffering no flowers except its own to mount?
Ah! must—
Designer infinite!—
Ah! must Thou char the wood ere Thou canst limn with it?
My freshness spent its wavering shower i' the dust;
And now my heart is as a broken fount,
Wherein tear-drippings stagnate, spilt down ever
From the dank thoughts that shiver
Upon the sighful branches of my mind.
Such is; what is to be?
The pulp so bitter, how shall taste the rind?
I dimly guess what Time in mists confounds;
Yet ever and anon a trumpet sounds
From the hid battlements of Eternity;
Those shaken mists a space unsettle, then

Round the half-glimpsed turrets slowly wash again.
But not ere him who summoneth
I first have seen, enwound
With glooming robes purpureal, cypress-crowned;
His name I know, and what his trumpet saith.
Whether man's heart or life it be which yields
Thee harvest, must Thy harvest-fields
Be dunged with rotten death?

Now of that long pursuit
Comes on at hand the bruit;
That Voice is round me like a bursting sea:
"And is thy earth so marred,
Shattered in shard on shard?
Lo, all things fly thee, for thou fliest Me!
Strange, piteous, futile thing!
Wherefore should any set thee love apart?
Seeing none but I makes much of naught" (He said),
"And human love needs human meriting:
How hast thou merited—
Of all man's clotted clay the dingiest clot?
Alack, thou knowest not
How little worthy of any love thou art!
Whom wilt thou find to love ignoble thee
Save Me, save only Me?
All which I took from thee I did but take,
Not for thy harms,
But just that thou might'st seek it in My arms.
All which thy child's mistake
Fancies as lost, I have stored for thee at home:
Rise, clasp My hand, and come!"

Halts by me that footfall:
Is my gloom, after all,
Shade of His hand, outstretched caressingly?
"Ah, fondest, blindest, weakest,
I am He Whom thou seekest!
Thou dravest love from thee, who dravest Me."

"To be the poet of the return to Nature is somewhat," wrote Thompson. "But I would be the poet of the return to God." That desire was not fulfilled without difficulty, and it accounts for the obstacles readers may find in Thompson's poetry. He was obviously indebted to Crashaw (see page 466) and Crashaw's metaphysical involvements. Thompson often confused glitter with gold, sometimes achieving a baroque magnificence, sometimes falling from the grand manner into the grand-opera manner. But the best of his work is clear enough; it glows with a "honey of wild flame."

To a Snowflake

What heart could have thought you?
Past our devisal
(O filigree petal!)
Fashioned so purely,
Fragilely, surely,
From what Paradisal
Imagineless metal,
Too costly for cost?
Who hammered you, wrought you,
From argentine vapor?—
"God was my shaper.
Passing surmisal,
He hammered, He wrought me,
From curled silver vapor,
To lust of his mind:—
Thou couldst not have thought me!
So purely, so palely,
Tinily, surely,
Mightily, frailly,
Insculped and embossed,
With His hammer of wind,
And His graver of frost."

A posthumous poem contains Thompson's most moving lines. It is a reminiscence of the time Thompson slept on benches and saw from the depths "the traffic of Jacob's ladder pitched between Heaven and Charing Cross." Wilfrid Meynell, who found the poem among Thompson's papers, spoke of "these triumphing stanzas" in which we see "in retrospect, as did he, those days and nights of human dereliction he spent beside London's River, and in the shadow—but all radiance to him—of Charing Cross."

In No Strange Land

"THE KINGDOM OF GOD IS WITHIN YOU"

O world invisible, we view thee,
O world intangible, we touch thee,
O world unknowable, we know thee,
Inapprehensible, we clutch thee!

Does the fish soar to find the ocean,
The eagle plunge to find the air—
That we ask of the stars in motion
If they have rumor of thee there?

Not where the wheeling systems darken,
And our benumbed conceiving soars!—
The drift of pinions, would we hearken,
Beats at our own clay-shuttered doors.

The angels keep their ancient places;—
Turn but a stone, and start a wing!
'Tis ye, 'tis your estranged faces,
That miss the many-splendored thing.

But (when so sad thou canst not sadder)
Cry—and upon thy so sore loss
Shall shine the traffic of Jacob's ladder
Pitched betwixt Heaven and Charing Cross.

Yea, in the night, my Soul, my daughter,
Cry—clinging Heaven by the hems;
And lo, Christ walking on the water
Not of Gennesareth, but Thames!

In his mid-forties Thompson's health, never robust, failed him. He contracted tuberculosis and died in London, November 13, 1907.

FIVE AMERICAN FOLK SONGS

MOST American folk songs are importations. Brought over by the settlers, influenced by a new environment, changed to reflect another scene and setting, they still show their origins. Under different titles, and celebrating another set of characters, the story songs of Vermont and the hillbilly tunes of the Appalachians are largely adaptations of such English and Scottish border ballads as BARBARA ALLEN, THE HANGMAN'S SONG, THE TWO SISTERS, and LORD RANDAL.

But a few—and perhaps the best—of American ballads are genuinely native, as original in theme as they are racy in idiom. Beginning as reports of local events or current beliefs or merely play songs, they have become part of the national life. The five most vivid are also the most popular: DIXIE, MY OLD KENTUCKY HOME, FRANKIE AND JOHNNY, CASEY JONES, and JOHN HENRY. Unlike most folk songs, the authorship of at least two of them is known.

DIXIE, the battle cry of the South, was not written for a marching song but for a minstrel show. To complete the irony, its author was not a Southern patriot, but a professional entertainer from Ohio.

Daniel Decatur Emmett was born in 1815, in Mt. Vernon, Ohio. His father was a blacksmith, and the boy's character was hammered out, Emmett liked to say, on the anvil. From thirteen to seventeen he worked on small-town newspapers; at eighteen he got into the army as a fife player; at nineteen he traveled with circus bands. In his mid-thirties, he organized the first colored minstrel troop, after consulting a dictionary to satisfy himself that the word "minstrel" was not too inappropriate. His organization was immediately successful and widely imitated, and Emmett was soon prosperous enough to afford a manager and talk of retiring.

One morning—it was September 18, 1859—Emmett told his wife that the show needed a new "walk-around" with a lively melody and words that could be picked up easily. Emmett started improvising on his violin, kept it up all day, and finally had the tune with most of the words. His wife liked it. So did the rest of the nation.

Dixie

I wish I was in de land ob cotton,
Old times dar am not forgotten;
Look away! Look away! Look away! Dixie land!
In Dixie land whar I was born in,
Early on one frosty mornin'
Look away! Look away! Look away! Dixie land!

Missus married Will de weaber;
William was a gay deceaber;
When he put his arm around 'er,
He looked as fierce as a forty-pounder.

While missus libbed, she libbed in clover,
When she died, she died all over;
So here's a health to de nex' ole missus,
An' all de gals dat want to kiss us.

Now ef you want to drive 'way sorrow,
Come an' hear dis song tomorrow;
Den hoe it down an' scratch your grabble—
To Dixie's land I'm boun' to trabble.

Chorus

Den I wish I was in Dixie. Hooray! Hooray!
In Dixie land I'll take my stand, an' lib an' die in Dixie.
Away! Away! Away down south in Dixie!
Away! Away! Away down south in Dixie!

Some of the simplest American songs are also the most melancholy—and most of them were written and composed by Stephen Collins Foster. Foster was born, patriotically enough, on July 4, 1826. Son of a prosperous Pittsburgh merchant related by marriage to President Buchanan, the child was a natural musician. At twelve he played on several instruments; at thirteen he composed a song which was widely circulated. At seventeen he went into business with his brother in Cincinnati, Ohio, and became more prolific than ever. His melodies were highly singable, his words were easily remembered; they were repeated and parodied until they became the most popular songs of the period. There was something of the primitive singer in Foster, but the simplicity was often spoiled by Foster's canny knowledge of the nostalgic demands of the public. He was an uncultured Schubert, a commercialized Burns. He mixed pathos with bathos, and let himself slip from true sentiment into bald sentimentality. But the best of his songs combine picturesqueness and genuine emotion.

Although Foster wrote more than one hundred and thirty ballads and innumerable dance tunes, his last days were spent in abject poverty. He was only thirty-eight when he died in the charity ward of Bellevue, New York City, January 13, 1864.

Seventy-seven years after his death, Foster was established as a national classic. MY OLD KENTUCKY HOME was enthusiastically sung at the annual Kentucky Derby. A postage stamp was issued in Foster's honor. The radio blared forth his melodies in determined repetition and distorted tempi. A bronze portrait bust was unveiled in the Hall of Fame for Great Americans. The man who had been regarded as an intemperate tunesmith had become the acknowledged singer of the people.

My Old Kentucky Home

The sun shines bright in the old Kentucky home;
  'Tis summer, the darkeys are gay;
The corn-top's ripe, and the meadow's in the bloom,
  While the birds make music all the day.
The young folks roll on the little cabin floor,
  All merry, all happy and bright;
By-'n'-by hard times comes a-knocking at the door:—
  Then my old Kentucky home, good-night!

    Weep no more, my lady,
    O, weep no more to-day!
  We will sing one song for the old Kentucky home,
    For the old Kentucky home, far away.

They hunt no more for the 'possum and the coon,
  On the meadow, the hill, and the shore;
They sing no more by the glimmer of the moon,
  On the bench by the old cabin door.

The day goes by like a shadow o'er the heart,
With sorrow, where all was delight;
The time has come when the darkeys have to part:—
Then my old Kentucky home, good-night!

The head must bow, and the back will have to bend,
Wherever the darkey may go;
A few more days, and the trouble all will end,
In the field where the sugar-canes grow.
A few more days for to tote the weary load—
No matter, 'twill never be light;
A few more days till we totter on the road:—
Then my old Kentucky home, good-night!

Weep no more, my lady,
O, weep no more to-day!
We will sing one song for the old Kentucky home,
For the old Kentucky home, far away.

Although it is impossible to ascertain the authorship of FRANKIE AND JOHNNY, the date can be approximated. Some researchers maintain that the song dates back to 1850 and that the scene of the sordid tragedy was Natchez-under-the-Hill. But John Huston has shown, if he has not conclusively proved, that the time was 1899, the locale St. Louis, and the heroine an actual Frankie Baker who shot her "mack," or *maquereau,* in a jealous brawl.

By 1935 the song had taken so firm a hold on the popular imagination that two dramas, a moving picture, and a ballet had been built about the tale, and more than twenty versions were in existence, some melodramatic, some ribald, and several unprintable.

Frankie and Johnny

Frankie and Johnny were lovers, O Lordy, how they could love!
Swore to be true to each other, true as the stars above.
He was her man, but he done her wrong.

Frankie she was a good woman, just like everyone knows.
She spent a hundred dollars for a suit of Johnny's clothes.
He was her man, but he done her wrong.

Frankie and Johnny went walking, Johnny in a brand new suit.
"Oh, good Lord," says Frankie, "don't my Johnny look cute?"
He was her man, but he done her wrong.

Frankie went down to Memphis, she went on the evening train.
She paid one hundred dollars for Johnny a watch and chain.
He was her man, but he done her wrong.

Frankie lived in the crib-house, crib-house had only two doors;
Gave all her money to Johnny, he spent it on those parlor whores.
He was her man, but he done her wrong.

Frankie went down to the corner to buy a glass of beer,
Says to the fat bartender, "Has my lovingest man been here?
He was my man, but he's doing me wrong."

"Ain't going to tell you no story; ain't going to tell you no lie,
I seen your man 'bout an hour ago with a girl named Nellie Bly.
If he's your man, he's doing you wrong."

Frankie went down to the pawnshop, she didn't go there for fun;
She hocked all of her jewelry, bought a pearl-handled forty-four gun
For to get her man who was doing her wrong.

Frankie went down to the hotel, she rang that hotel bell.
"Stand back, all you chippies, or I'll blow you all to hell.
I want my man, who's doing me wrong."

Frankie threw back her kimono, she took out her forty-four,
Root-a-toot-toot three times she shot right through that hotel door
She was after her man who was doing her wrong.

Johnny grabbed off his Stetson, "Oh, good Lord, Frankie, don't shoot!"
But Frankie pulled the trigger and the gun went root-a-toot-toot.
He was her man, but she shot him down.

"Roll me over easy; roll me over slow;
Roll me over on my left side, for the bullet is hurting me so.
I was her man, but I done her wrong."

Oh, bring on your rubber-tired hearses; bring on your rubber-tired hacks;
They're taking Johnny to the cemetery, and they ain't a-bringing him back.
He was her man, but he done her wrong.

Now it was not murder in the second degree, it was not murder in the third.
The woman simply dropped her man, like a hunter drops his bird.
He was her man and he done her wrong.

"Oh, put me in that dungeon. Oh, put me in that cell.
Put me where the northeast wind blows from the southwest corner of hell.
I shot my man 'cause he done me wrong."

Frankie walked up the scaffold, as calm as a girl can be,
And turning her eyes to heaven she said, "Good Lord, I'm coming to thee.
He was my man, and I done him wrong."

This story has got no moral, this story has got no end.
This story only goes to show that there ain't no good in men.
He was her man, but he done her wrong.

The American heritage of folk heroes includes not only the trampling giants of tall stories, but hard-living, loud-laughing pioneers. These heroes have grown larger with time: Dan'l Boone, Davy Crockett, Jean Lafitte, Buffalo Bill, and Johnny Appleseed, as well as such mythical workers as Paul Bunyan, Mike Fink, Casey Jones, and John Henry. Since these characters live in an atmosphere of free braggadocio, it is natural that their songs are full of swaggering and artless robustiousness. The ballad of CASEY JONES is typical in its casual beginning, its tragic denouement, and unexpectedly rowdy end.

The fabled brave engineer was a real person, John Luther Jones, of Cayce (pronounced Casey), Kentucky, and the much-sung collision actually happened, April 30, 1900. A tablet erected to Jones's memory at Cayce states: "While running the Illinois Central Fast Mail, and by no fault of his, his engine bolted through three freight cars. . . . Casey died with his hand clenched to the brake helve, and his was the only life lost." Contrary to the song, however, Mrs. Jones's children did not have "another papa on the Salt Lake Line."

Casey Jones[1]

Come all you rounders if you want to hear
The story of a brave engineer;
Casey Jones was the rounder's name,
On a six-eight wheeler, boys, he won his fame.

Caller called Casey at half-past four,
He kissed his wife at the station door,
Mounted to the cabin with orders in his hand,
And took his farewell trip to the Promised Land.

> Casey Jones, mounted to the cabin,
> Casey Jones, with his orders in his hand!
> Casey Jones, mounted to the cabin,
> Took his farewell trip into the Promised Land.

Put in your water and shovel in your coal,
Put your head out the window, watch them drivers roll,
I'll run her till she leaves the rail,
'Cause we're eight hours late with the western mail!

He looked at his watch and his watch was slow,
Looked at the water and the water was low,
Turned to his fireboy and then he said,
"We're goin' to reach 'Frisco, but we'll all be dead!"

Casey pulled up that Reno Hill,
Tooted for the crossing with an awful shrill,
The switchman knew by the engine's moans
That the man at the throttle was Casey Jones.

He pulled up short two miles from the place,
Number Four stared him right in the face,
Turned to his fireboy, said, "You'd better jump,
'Cause there's two locomotives that's a-goin' to bump!"

Casey said, just before he died,
"There's two more roads I'd like to ride."
Fireboy said, "What could they be?"
"The Southern Pacific and the Santa Fe."

1 *The original version, copyright 1909 by Newton & Seibert; copyright renewed 1936; Shapiro, Bernstein & Company, proprietors.*

Mrs. Jones sat on her bed a-sighin',
Got a message that Casey was dyin',
Said, "Go to bed, children, and hush your cryin',
'Cause you got another papa on the Salt Lake Line."

Casey Jones! Got another papa!
Casey Jones, on the Salt Lake Line!
Casey Jones! Got another papa!
You got another papa on the Salt Lake Line!

Among the heroes of extravagant exploits, none is greater than John Henry. This steel-driving Negro who pitted his strength against the modern steam-drill and "died with his hammer in his hand" is a mythical American of the machine age. Many parts of the country have claimed John Henry. There are records of his prowess in a dozen states; one account in West Virginia specifically pictures him as six feet two, two hundred and thirty pounds, straight as an arrow, and "black as a kittle in hell."

John Henry

John Henry was a little baby,
    Setting on his mammy's knee,
Said "The Big Bend Tunnel on the C. & O. Road
    Is gonna be the death of me,
        Lawd, gonna be the death of me."

One day his captain told him,
    How he had bet a man
That John Henry could beat his steam drill down,
    Cause John Henry was the best in the land,
        John Henry was the best in the land.

John Henry walked in the tunnel,
    His captain by his side;
The mountain so tall, John Henry so small,
    He laid down his hammer and he cried,
        Laid down his hammer and he cried.

John Henry kissed his hammer;
    White man turned on the steam;
Shaker held John Henry's steel;
    Was the biggest race the world had ever seen,
        Lawd, biggest race the world ever seen.

John Henry on the right side
    The steam drill on the left,
"Before I'll let your steam drill beat me down,
    I'll hammer my fool self to death,
        Hammer my fool self to death."

Captain heard a mighty rumbling,
    Said, "The mountain must be caving in."
John Henry said to the captain,
    "It's my hammer sucking de wind,
        My hammer sucking de wind."

John Henry said to his captain,
    "A man ain't nothin' but a man,
But before I'll let dat steam drill beat me down,
    I'll die wid my hammer in my hand,
        Lawd, die wid my hammer in my hand."

John Henry hammering on the mountain,
    The whistle blew for half-past two,
The last words his captain heard him say,
    "I've done hammered my insides in two,
        Lawd, I've hammered my insides in two."

The hammer that John Henry swung
    It weighed over twelve pound,
He broke a rib in his left-hand side
    And his intrels fell on the ground,
        Lawd, his intrels fell on the ground.

They took John Henry to the river,
    And buried him in the sand,
And every locomotive come a-roaring by,
    Says, "There lies that steel-drivin' man,
        Lawd, there lies that steel-drivin' man!"

A folk song is made by the blurring changes rung by its singers, whether they are craft-conscious musicians or unself-conscious slaves, cowboys, lumberjacks, and guttersnipes. The future of the folk song is, therefore, unlimited. The spread of mechanized music may temporarily discourage folk singing; but the pleasure of personal performance is one that cannot be satisfied by vicarious mediums. It is possible that the radio may well encourage further variations and spread the range of words and ideas. Its very scope and diffusion may create a new tradition and make national what is now regional.

Meanwhile, the folk songs grow in number and vigor, around the hearth and in the backwoods with brusque camaraderie.

FOUR NEGRO SPIRITUALS

THE Negro spirituals, which many musicians consider America's purest melodies, are a blend of savagely rhythmic chants and placid Christian hymns. The stirring combination, first heard in the 1820's, was like nothing previously created in the new world. To the Negroes, the Bible seemed a replica of their own tragic history. The sufferings of the Israelites in Egypt were their own; the punishment of the wealthy masters was identified with their half-hopeless hopes. They sang of Jordan and Jericho, but it was their own walls that were to come tumbling down; it was a black Moses who was to say to the Pharaohs of the Southland, "Let my people go."

It was not until after the Civil War that the songs began to be written down. Today there are more than a hundred collections of the "black and unknown bards of long ago," as James Weldon Johnson called them, and new versions are constantly being discovered. They are of varying literary merit. But the best of them express not only a deep emotional sincerity but a robust poetic quality as well. Some of the happiest effects in the spirituals are the sudden shifts in mood, the childlike responses that make the imagery at once homely and daring. Thus the railroad—an apocalyptic wonder to the plantation slaves—becomes the iron steed on which King Jesus rides, the modern Elijah's chariot on which all the congregation, the "little chillun," are urged to get on board. To the barefoot blacks, a pair of shoes was as precious as the spotless robe which, in some free hereafter, they would wear to walk all over God's heaven.

Joshua Fit de Battle of Jericho

Joshua fit de battle of Jericho,
Jericho, Jericho,
Joshua fit de battle of Jericho,
And de walls come tumbling down.

You may talk about yo' king of Gideon
Talk about yo' man of Saul,
Dere's none like good old Joshua
At de battle of Jericho.

Up to de walls of Jericho,
He marched with spear in hand;
"Go blow dem ram horns," Joshua cried,
"Kase de battle am in my hand."

Den de lamb ram sheep-horns begin to blow,
Trumpets begin to sound,
Joshua commanded de chillun to shout,
And de walls come tumbling down.

Dat morning,
Joshua fit de battle of Jericho,
Jericho, Jericho,
Joshua fit de battle of Jericho,
And de walls come tumbling down.

Steal Away

Steal away, steal away, steal away to Jesus.
Steal away, steal away home,
I ain't got long to stay here.

My Lord, He calls me,
He calls me by the thunder,
The trumpet sounds within-a my soul;
I ain't got long to stay here.

Steal away, steal away, steal away to Jesus,
Steal away, steal away home,
I ain't got long to stay here.

Green trees a-bending,
Po' sinner stands a-trembling
The trumpet sounds within-a my soul;
I ain't got long to stay here.

Steal away, steal away, steal away to Jesus.
Steal away, steal away home,
I ain't got long to stay here.

The Crucifixion

They crucified my Lord,
  And He never said a mumbaling word.
They crucified my Lord,
  And He never said a mumbaling word.
Not a word—not a word—not a word.

They nailed Him to the tree,
  And He never said a mumbaling word.
They nailed Him to the tree,
  And He never said a mumbaling word.
Not a word—not a word—not a word.

They pierced Him in the side,
  And He never said a mumbaling word.
They pierced Him in the side,
  And He never said a mumbaling word.
Not a word—not a word—not a word.

The blood came twinkaling down,
  And He never said a mumbaling word.
The blood came twinkaling down,
  And He never said a mumbaling word.
Not a word—not a word—not a word.

He bowed His head and died,
  And He never said a mumbaling word.
He bowed His head and died,
  And He never said a mumbaling word.
Not a word—not a word—not a word.

Strictly speaking, WATER-BOY is not a spiritual, but a work song. It is said to have originated toward the end of the nineteenth century, and it has been credited to a Negro convict in Georgia. Working in the chain gang under the pitiless sun, he calls for the boy who carries the water. As the boy delays coming and the convict continues to break stone, the singer reviews his life, particularly his devotion to gambling which has brought him to the present pass. The convict's boasting of his strength with the hammer seems to be an unconscious echo of JOHN HENRY.

Water-Boy

Water-Boy, where are yo' hidin'?
If yo' don't-a come, I'm gwineter tell-a yo' Mammy.

Dere ain't no hammer dat's on-a dis mountain,
Dat ring-a like mine, boys, dat ring-a like mine.
Done bus' dis rock, boys, f'om hyah to Macon,
All de way to de jail, boys, yes, back to de jail.

Yo' Jack-o'-Di'monds, yo' Jack-o'-Di'monds,
I know yo' of old, boys, yas, I know yo' of old.
Yo' robbed ma pocket, yas, robba ma pocket,
Done robba ma pocket of silver an' gold.

Water-Boy, where are yo' hidin'?
If yo' don't-a come, I'm gwineter tell-a yo' Mammy.
Oh, Water-Boy!

XV

The World of the Twentieth Century

A. E. HOUSMAN

[1859–1936]

A PESSIMISM darker than Omar-FitzGerald's and even more intense than Hardy's was voiced by a cloistered scholar, a professor of Latin, who wrote blithely about murder and suicide, personal betrayal and cosmic injustice.

Alfred Edward Housman was born in a village in Worcestershire, near Shropshire, the county which became the scene of his poetry. Educated at St. John's College, Oxford, he failed in an important examination. The setback destroyed his hope of an immediate scholastic appointment at a large university and forced him to accept the work of a civil servant (actually a kind of clerkship) in the Patent Office. He worked ten years in this uncongenial position.

Early in youth Housman was drawn toward paganism. He was, he said, a deist at thirteen and an atheist before he was twenty-one. During his ten years' clerkship, he devoted every spare hour to a study of the classics, and in 1892 he was made professor of Latin at University College, London. He remained there twenty years. In 1911 he went to Cambridge University and taught and lectured there almost until the day of his death, April 30, 1936.

Housman's withdrawal from the world had become proverbial. His brother, Laurence Housman, explains what seemed to be an antisocial feeling. In MY BROTHER, A. E. HOUSMAN, Laurence Housman quotes a passage from T. E. Lawrence's SEVEN PILLARS OF WISDOM:

> There was my craving to be liked—so strong and nervous that never could I open myself friendly to another. The terror of failure in an effort so important made me shrink from trying. . . . There was a craving to be famous, and a horror of being known to like being known. Contempt for my passion for distinction made me refuse every offered honor.

Laurence Housman tells us that his brother wrote in the margin against this passage: "This is me."

Housman's inverted "passion for distinction" made him disguise his work as well as himself. He originally intended to call A SHROPSHIRE LAD, his first and most famous book, POEMS BY TERENCE HEARSAY. The rejected title explains the personal reference in the often-quoted EPILOGUE, which sums up Housman's central philosophy.

Epilogue

"Terence, this is stupid stuff;
You eat your victuals fast enough;
There can't be much amiss, 'tis clear,
To see the rate you drink your beer.
But oh, good Lord, the verse you make,
It gives a chap the belly-ache.
The cow, the old cow, she is dead;
It sleeps well, the horned head:
We poor lads, 'tis our turn now
To hear such tunes as killed the cow.
Pretty friendship 'tis to rhyme
Your friends to death before their time
Moping melancholy mad:
Come, pipe a tune to dance to, lad."

Why, if 'tis dancing you would be,
There's brisker pipes than poetry.
Say, for what were hop-yards meant,
Or why was Burton built on Trent?
Oh, many a peer of England brews
Livelier liquor than the Muse,

And malt does more than Milton can
To justify God's ways to man.
Ale, man, ale's the stuff to drink
For fellows whom it hurts to think:
Look into the pewter pot
To see the world as the world's not.
And faith, 'tis pleasant till 'tis past:
The mischief is that 'twill not last.
Oh, I have been to Ludlow fair
And left my necktie God knows where,
And carried half way home, or near,
Pints and quarts of Ludlow beer:
Then the world seemed none so bad,
And I myself a sterling lad;
And down in lovely muck I've lain,
Happy till I woke again.
Then I saw the morning sky:
Heigho, the tale was all a lie;
The world, it was the old world yet,
I was I, my things were wet,
And nothing now remained to do
But begin the game anew.

Therefore, since the world has still
Much good, but much less good than ill,
And while the sun and moon endure
Luck's a chance, but trouble's sure,
I'd face it as a wise man would,
And train for ill and not for good.
'Tis true, the stuff I bring for sale
Is not so brisk a brew as ale:
Out of a stem that scored the hand
I wrung it in a weary land.
But take it: if the smack is sour,
The better for the embittered hour;
It should do good to heart and head
When your soul is in my soul's stead;
And I will friend you, if I may,
In the dark and cloudy day.

There was a king reigned in the East:
There, when kings will sit to feast,
They get their fill before they think
With poisoned meat and poisoned drink.
He gathered all that springs to birth

From the many-venomed earth;
First a little, thence to more,
He sampled all her killing store;
And easy, smiling, seasoned sound,
Sat the king when healths went round.
They put arsenic in his meat
And stared aghast to watch him eat;
They poured strychnine in his cup
And shook to see him drink it up:
They shook, they stared as white's their shirt:
Them it was their poison hurt.
—I tell the tale that I heard told.
Mithridates, he died old.

After A SHROPSHIRE LAD became popular, Housman was surprised when critics referred to his poetry as having a "classical" origin. He insisted that, although he may have been unconsciously influenced by the Greeks and Latins, the chief sources of the book were Scottish Border ballads, Shakespeare's songs, and Heine's lyrics. The combination is apparent in everything Housman published, even in the posthumous work. It explains Housman's deceptive simplicity and sparsely decorated verse, a verse whose sweetness is strengthened by its severity.

With Rue My Heart Is Laden

With rue my heart is laden
  For golden friends I had,
For many a rose-lipt maiden
  And many a lightfoot lad.

By brooks too broad for leaping
  The lightfoot boys are laid;
The rose-lipt girls are sleeping
  In fields where roses fade.

Loveliest of Trees

Loveliest of trees, the cherry now
Is hung with bloom along the bough,
And stands about the woodland ride
Wearing white for Eastertide.

Now, of my threescore years and ten,
Twenty will not come again,
And take from seventy springs a score,
It only leaves me fifty more.

And since to look at things in bloom
Fifty springs are little room,
About the woodlands I will go
To see the cherry hung with snow.

When I Was One-and-Twenty

When I was one-and-twenty
 I heard a wise man say,
"Give crowns and pounds and guineas
 But not your heart away;
Give pearls away and rubies
 But keep your fancy free."
But I was one-and-twenty,
 No use to talk to me.

When I was one-and-twenty
 I heard him say again,
"The heart out of the bosom
 Was never given in vain;
'Tis paid with sighs a-plenty
 And sold for endless rue."
And I am two-and-twenty,
 And oh, 'tis true, 'tis true.

Is My Team Ploughing

"Is my team ploughing,
 That I was used to drive
And hear the harness jingle
 When I was man alive?"

Aye, the horses trample,
 The harness jingles now;
No change though you lie under
 The land you used to plough.

"Is football playing
  Along the river shore,
With lads to chase the leather,
  Now I stand up no more?"

Aye, the ball is flying,
  The lads play heart and soul;
The goal stands up, the keeper
  Stands up to keep the goal.

"Is my girl happy,
  That I thought hard to leave,
And has she tired of weeping
  As she lies down at eve?"

Aye, she lies down lightly,
  She lies not down to weep:
Your girl is well contented.
  Be still, my lad, and sleep.

"Is my friend hearty,
  Now I am thin and pine;
And has he found to sleep in
  A better bed than mine?"

Aye, lad, I lie easy,
  I lie as lads would choose;
I cheer a dead man's sweetheart.
  Never ask me whose.

I Hoed and Trenched and Weeded

I hoed and trenched and weeded,
  And took the flowers to fair:
I brought them home unheeded;
  The hue was not the wear.

So up and down I sow them
  For lads like me to find,
When I shall lie below them,
  A dead man out of mind.

Some seeds the birds devour,
  And some the season mars,
But here and there will flower
  The solitary stars,

And fields will yearly bear them
  As light-leaved spring comes on,
And luckless lads will wear them
  When I am dead and gone.

In a world of infidelity and unreason, Housman insists, only death has dignity. The heart out of the bosom is given in vain; lightfoot lads drink and die, and there is small joy in their brief athleticism. It is a merry-mournful tune that Housman sings, but it is the more memorable for its undiluted acid sharpness.

To an Athlete Dying Young

The time you won your town the race
We chaired you through the market-place;
Man and boy stood cheering by,
And home we brought you shoulder-high.

Today, the road all runners come,
Shoulder-high we bring you home,
And set you at your threshold down,
Townsman of a stiller town.

Smart lad, to slip betimes away
From fields where glory does not stay,
And early though the laurel grows
It withers quicker than the rose.

Eyes the shady night has shut
Cannot see the record cut,
And silence sounds no worse than cheers
After earth has stopped the ears:

Now you will not swell the rout
Of lads that wore their honors out,
Runners whom renown outran
And the name died before the man.

So set, before its echoes fade,
The fleet foot on the sill of shade,
And hold to the low lintel up
The still-defended challenge-cup.

And round that early-laureled head
Will flock to gaze the strengthless dead,
And find unwithered on its curls
The garland briefer than a girl's.

Echoing Hardy, and opposed to Wordsworth, Housman has no illusions about the goodness of existence. Nature is evil, he tells us; the countryside riots in haphazard cruelty. Man is "a stranger and afraid in a world he never made." The sensible person trains for ill and not for good. Injustice is a constant, and there is no hope from heaven: "High heaven and earth ail from the prime foundation."

The troubles of our proud and angry dust
  Are from eternity, and shall not fail.

Yet Housman adds a note of stoicism, a reply to the overwhelming iniquities.

Bear them we can, and if we can we must.
  Shoulder the sky, my lad, and drink your ale.

Be Still, My Soul, Be Still

Be still, my soul, be still; the arms you bear are brittle,
  Earth and high heaven are fixt of old and founded strong.
Think rather,—call to thought, if now you grieve a little,
  The days when we had rest, O soul, for they were long.

Men loved unkindness then, but lightless in the quarry
  I slept and saw not; tears fell down, I did not mourn;
Sweat ran and blood sprang out and I was never sorry:
  Then it was well with me, in days ere I was born.

Now, and I muse for why and never find the reason,
  I pace the earth, and drink the air, and feel the sun.
Be still, be still, my soul; it is but for a season:
  Let us endure an hour and see injustice done.

Ay, look: high heaven and earth ail from the prime foundation;
  All thoughts to rive the heart are here, and all are vain:
Horror and scorn and hate and fear and indignation—
  Oh, why did I awake? When shall I sleep again?

When I Watch the Living Meet

When I watch the living meet,
  And the moving pageant file
Warm and breathing through the street
  Where I lodge a little while,

If the heats of hate and lust
  In the house of flesh are strong,
Let me mind the house of dust
  Where my sojourn shall be long.

In the nation that is not
  Nothing stands that stood before;
There revenges are forgot,
  And the hater hates no more;

Lovers lying two and two
  Ask not whom they sleep beside,
And the bridegroom all night through
  Never turns him to the bride.

Fortitude can be learned, Housman assures us grimly. "Luck's a chance, but trouble's sure," he repeats, like a cheerful prophet of doom. The pessimism would be unbearable but for Housman's brisk measures and his unfailing artistry. The reader is diverted from a pervading hopelessness by the poet's brief but graphic revelations of the English countryside, by the quick play of his irony, and by the exquisite lyricism which frames it all.

The scrupulous craftsmanship may be gathered from the fact that twenty-six years passed between Housman's first book and his second, significantly if inaccurately entitled LAST POEMS. (A third volume, MORE POEMS, was published the year of his death.) Housman's notebooks show how carefully he worked for the exact word. Laurence Housman discloses that, in the superb description of the clock striking the quarters in EIGHT O'CLOCK, the word "tossed" was arrived at only after Housman had tried and rejected "loosed," "spilt," "cast," "told," "dealt," and "pitched."

Eight o'Clock

He stood, and heard the steeple
  Sprinkle the quarters on the morning town.
One, two, three, four, to market-place and people
  It tossed them down.

Strapped, noosed, nighing his hour,
  He stood and counted them and cursed his luck;
And then the clock collected in the tower
  Its strength, and struck.

Housman's criticisms were chiefly confined to controversies about literature and, in particular, the process of creation. Contemptuous of careless work, he wrote occasional prose that is full of the same edged phrasing which distinguishes his poetry. He epitomized Swinburne's verbosity by declaring, "Swinburne has now said not only all he has to say about everything, but all he has to say about nothing." His chief scorn was directed against pretentious scholarship, and one of his victims drew this devastating sentence: "Nature, not content with denying to Mr. X the faculty of thinking, has endowed him with the faculty of writing."

It has been said that, because of his severely disciplined tone and his epigrammatic line, Housman may well be considered the greatest Latin poet who ever wrote in English.

GEORGE SANTAYANA

[1863–1952]

SUPERFICIALLY George Santayana seems to have little in common with A. E. Housman, but, unknown to each other, they shared the same classical point of view if not the same ironic skepticism. "My own moral philosophy," wrote Santayana, "may not seem very robust or joyous. The owl hooting from his wintry bough cannot be chanticleer crowing in the barnyard, yet he is sacred to Minerva."

A Spaniard by birth (Madrid, December 16, 1863), son of Spanish parents, Santayana was taken to Boston at the age of nine. Educated at the Boston Latin School and Harvard, he began teaching philosophy at Harvard in his mid-twenties. In the 1900's his students—among whom were T. S. Eliot, Conrad Aiken, and Felix Frankfurter—considered him an inspired teacher, but Santayana actively disliked the academic tradition. Shortly before his fiftieth birthday he received an inheritance, resigned his professorship, and went abroad. He lived for a while in Oxford and Paris and finally settled in Rome.

Santayana's work, as befits a philosopher, is concerned with moral values. Writing chiefly on aesthetics and religious philosophy, Santayana remained a writer for the few until the appearance of THE LAST PURITAN, published in his seventy-second year. THE LAST PURITAN is a novel which, widely discussed, anticipated John P. Marquand's caustic examinations of the New England spirit. It was Santayana's one popular success, but readers were by no means united in their approval. Robert Hillyer spoke of the author

. . . who alone
Among philosophers still seeks their Stone;
Whose irony, in golden prose alloyed
With doubt, yet yields not to the acid Freud;
Who, after years of rightful fame defrauded,
Wrote one bad book at last—and all applauded.

Santayana apologized for his poetry by saying that English was not his native language and that he was, at best, an apprentice in a great school. "I never drank in in childhood the homely cadences and ditties which in pure spontaneous poetry set the essential key. . . . Moreover, I am city-bred, and that companionship with nature, those rural notes which for English poets are almost inseparable from poetic feeling, fail me altogether. . . . My approach to language is literary, my images are only metaphors, and sometimes it seems to me that I resemble my countryman Don Quixote, when in his airy flights he was merely perched on a high horse and a wooden Pegasus."

Santayana's modesty is becoming but misleading. His verse is not, as he insists, "thin in texture," but richly woven. His sonnets are particularly warm in phrase and deep in feeling. More affirmative than most of his writing they are among the finest contemporary examples of the form.

O World

O world, thou choosest not the better part!
It is not wisdom to be only wise,
And on the inward vision close the eyes,
But it is wisdom to believe the heart.
Columbus found a world, and had no chart,
Save one that faith deciphered in the skies;
To trust the soul's invincible surmise
Was all his science and his only art.
Our knowledge is a torch of smoky pine
That lights the pathway but one step ahead
Across a void of mystery and dread.
Bid, then, the tender light of faith to shine
By which alone the mortal heart is led
Unto the thinking of the thought divine.

Deem Not, Because You See Me

Deem not, because you see me in the press
Of this world's children run my fated race,
That I blaspheme against a proffered grace,
Or leave unlearned the love of holiness.
I honor not that sanctity the less
Whose aureole illumines not my face,
But dare not tread the secret, holy place
To which the priest and prophet have access.
For some are born to be beatified
By anguish, and by grievous penance done;
And some, to furnish forth the age's pride,
And to be praised of men beneath the sun;
And some are born to stand perplexed aside
From so much sorrow—of whom I am one.

With You a Part of Me

With you a part of me hath passed away;
For in the peopled forest of my mind
A tree made leafless by this wintry wind
Shall never don again its green array.

Chapel and fireside, country road and bay,
Have something of their friendliness resigned;
Another, if I would, I could not find,
And I am grown much older in a day.
But yet I treasure in my memory
Your gift of charity, and young heart's ease,
And the dear honor of your amity;
For these once mine, my life is rich with these.
And I scarce know which part may greater be—
What I keep of you, or you rob from me.

What Riches Have You?

What riches have you that you deem me poor,
Or what large comfort that you call me sad?
Tell me what makes you so exceeding glad:
Is your earth happy or your heaven sure?
I hope for heaven, since the stars endure
And bring such tidings as our fathers had.
I know no deeper doubt to make me mad,
I need no brighter love to keep me pure.
To me the faiths of old are daily bread;
I bless their hope, I bless their will to save,
And my deep heart still meaneth what they said.
It makes me happy that the soul is brave,
And, being so much kinsman to the dead,
I walk contented to the peopled grave.

WILLIAM BUTLER YEATS

[1865–1939]

SHELLEY's remark that "poets are the unacknowledged legislators of the world" is usually regarded as a flight of youthful rhetoric. Yet, besides being a poet and playwright, William Butler Yeats was a senator and served the Irish Free State from 1922 to 1928.

Yeats was born June 13, 1865, at Sandymount, near Dublin. His family was distinguished in the arts; his father was a well-known painter, and Yeats studied at the Royal Dublin Society. But, when he began contributing to the Irish periodicals, it was apparent that his medium was not the brush but the pen. In his early twenties Yeats went to London, joined the Rhymers' Club, which specialized in the latest aestheticism, and imitated the Pre-Raphaelites. But the affectations of the moment could not hold him. His devotion to Ireland was so intense that he returned to the varying aspects of its counties, to integrate himself with the problems of his own land, and express a life that had never been given full expression. With the collaboration of a few others, Yeats was responsible for the renascence of culture in Ireland; he helped to establish not only the Gaelic League but also the Irish Literary Theater. It was to be a communal adventure based upon native material. In his late twenties Yeats wrote enthusiastically: "I would have Ireland re-create the ancient arts, the arts as they were understood in Judea, in India, in Scandinavia, in Greece and Rome, in every ancient land as they were understood when they moved a whole people, and not a few people who have grown up in a leisure class and made this understanding their business."

To further this aim Yeats wrote dramas and lyrics centering about Irish legendry. He re-created folklore, published eloquent essays, and perfected a poetry of vague music and delicate nostalgia.

The Lake Isle of Innisfree

I will arise and go now, and go to Innisfree,
And a small cabin build there, of clay and wattles made;
Nine bean rows will I have there, a hive for the honey bee,
    And live alone in the bee-loud glade.

And I shall have some peace there, for peace comes dropping slow,
Dropping from the veils of the morning to where the cricket sings;
There midnight's all a glimmer, and noon a purple glow,
    And evening full of the linnet's wings.

I will arise and go now, for always night and day
I hear lake water lapping with low sounds by the shore;
While I stand on the roadway, or on the pavements gray,
    I hear it in the deep heart's core.

To his admirers it seemed that Yeats had found himself in a set of charming abstractions and lovely, though rather facile, symbols.

But at fifty Yeats turned against his own idiom. Freeing himself from shadowy waters and a wavering music, he dealt with actualities; his lines became subtler and, at the same time, more precise. Even when he employed mythological themes, he changed them from remote fantasies into the semblance of an immediate experience. In complete contrast to his early Pre-Raphaelite leanings, when he "hid his face amid a crowd of stars," he began to express his delight "in the whole man—blood, imagination, intellect, running together."

Leda and the Swan

A sudden blow: the great wings beating still
Above the staggering girl, her thighs caressed
By the dark webs, her nape caught in his bill,
He holds her helpless breast upon his breast.

How can those terrified vague fingers push
The feathered glory from her loosening thighs?
And how can body, laid in that white rush,
But feel the strange heart beating where it lies?

A shudder in the loins engenders there
The broken wall, the burning roof and tower
And Agamemnon dead.
                                        Being so caught up,
So mastered by the brute blood of the air,
Did she put on his knowledge with his power
Before the indifferent beak could let her drop?

Yeats continued to pursue that delight "in the whole man" and express it in some of the richest poetry of the period. He who had loved "symbols, popular beliefs, and old scraps of verse that made Ireland romantic to herself" declared that "the new Ireland, overwhelmed by responsibility, begins to long for psychological truths." His intellectual power increased. In A DIALOGUE OF SELF AND SOUL he wrote:

I am content to follow to its source,
Every event in action or in thought;
Measure the lot; forgive myself the lot!
When such as I cast out remorse

So great a sweetness flows into the breast
We must laugh and we must sing,
We are blest by everything,
Everything we look upon is blest.

The language became more and more straightforward. Quietly but fiercely it probed for "psychological truth." It faced personal disappointment and national despair.

An Irish Airman Foresees His Death

I know that I shall meet my fate
Somewhere among the clouds above;
Those that I fight I do not hate,
Those that I guard I do not love;
My country is Kiltartan Cross,
My countrymen Kiltartan's poor,
No likely end could bring them loss
Or leave them happier than before.
Nor law, nor duty bade me fight,
Nor public men, nor cheering crowds,
A lonely impulse of delight
Drove to this tumult in the clouds;
I balanced all, brought all to mind,
The years to come seemed waste of breath,
A waste of breath the years behind
In balance with this life, this death.

AMONG SCHOOL CHILDREN is an integration and a summary. In this candid yet complex poem, so different from the early musical verse, the "sixty-year-old smiling public man" remembers his own youth and the woman he loved in young manhood, the magnificent and unattainable Maud Gonne. In a blend of disillusion and self-mockery he questions the certainty of all philosophies—"Old clothes upon old sticks to scare a bird"—and the figure reminds him of himself in age, "a comfortable kind of scarecrow."

Among School Children

I

I walk through the long schoolroom questioning;
A kind old nun in a white hood replies;
The children learn to cipher and to sing,
To study reading-books and history,
To cut and sew, be neat in everything
In the best modern way—the children's eyes
In momentary wonder stare upon
A sixty-year-old smiling public man.

II

I dream of a Ledaean body, bent
Above a sinking fire, a tale that she
Told of a harsh reproof, or trivial event
That changed some childish day to tragedy—
Told, and it seemed that our two natures blent
Into a sphere from youthful sympathy,
Or else, to alter Plato's parable,
Into the yolk and the white of one shell.

III

And thinking of that fit of grief or rage
I look upon one child or t'other there
And wonder if she stood so at that age—
For even daughters of the swan can share
Something of every paddler's heritage—
And had that color upon cheek or hair,
And thereupon my heart is driven wild:
She stands before me as a living child.

IV

Her present image floats into the mind—
Did Quattrocento finger fashion it
Hollow of cheek as though it drank the wind
And took a mess of shadows for its meat?

And I though never of Ledaean kind
Had pretty plumage once—enough of that,
Better to smile on all that smile, and show
There is a comfortable kind of scarecrow.

V

What youthful mother, a shape upon her lap
Honey of generation had betrayed,
And that must sleep, shriek, struggle to escape
As recollection or the drug decide,
Would think her son, did she but see that shape
With sixty or more winters on its head,
A compensation for the pang of his birth,
Or the uncertainty of his setting forth?

VI

Plato thought nature but a spume that plays
Upon a ghostly paradigm of things;
Solider Aristotle played the taws
Upon the bottom of a king of kings;
World-famous golden-thighed Pythagoras
Fingered upon a fiddle-stick or strings
What a star sang and careless Muses heard:
Old clothes upon old sticks to scare a bird.

VII

Both nuns and mothers worship images,
But those the candles light are not as those
That animate a mother's reveries,
But keep a marble or a bronze repose.
And yet they too break hearts—O Presences
That passion, piety or affection knows,
And that all heavenly glory symbolize—
O self-born mockers of man's enterprise;

VIII

Labor is blossoming or dancing where
The body is not bruised to pleasure soul,
Nor beauty born out of its own despair,
Nor blear-eyed wisdom out of midnight oil.

O chestnut tree, great rooted blossomer,
Are you the leaf, the blossom or the bole?
O body swayed to music, O brightening glance,
How can we know the dancer from the dance?

In old age Yeats lost faith in the average man whom he had once championed. He revolted against the middle classes who "fumble in the greasy till, and add the half-pence to the pence." Long ago he had given up his dream of a culturally awakened Ireland—

Romantic Ireland's dead and gone,
It's with O'Leary in the grave.

Yeats yearned for "an aristocratic order" and inveighed against "the vulgarity and the materialism whereon England has founded her worst life and the whole life she sends us." His poetry began to express anger and impotence. In his seventies, lashed by the chaotic forces that threatened from without and frustrated by the loss of power within, he offered this quatrain as a "final apology":

You think it horrible that Lust and Rage
Should dance attendance upon my old age;
They were not such a plague when I was young.
What else have I to spur me into song?

Yeats spent much of his time during his last years in southern Europe. He died, after a brief illness, at Roquebrune, near Nice, January 28, 1939. He had already written his own epitaph:

Cast a cold eye
On life, on death.
Horseman, pass by.

Tributes to Yeats's living power increased after his death. Books of interpretation and dozens of critical essays reappraised his varying work. The most rounded poem was written by W. H. Auden, IN MEMORY OF W. B. YEATS (see page 1204), a poem which ends:

Follow, poet, follow right
To the bottom of the night,
With your unconstraining voice
Still persuade us to rejoice . . .

In the deserts of the heart
Let the healing fountain start,
In the prison of his days
Teach the free man how to praise.

RUDYARD KIPLING

[1865–1936]

COMING out of India, Rudyard Kipling swept into English literature like a salt sea gale. He burst through doors that had been tightly sealed by the Victorians and threw open the preciously decorated Pre-Raphaelite windows. Challenging the vogue of the sentimentally archaic, Kipling exalted the world of prosaic things. An uncrowned laureate of machinery, he sang of the grimy by-products of science and of all those who did the work of the world: engineers, road builders, explorers, stokers, sailors, and soldiers.

Born December 30, 1865, at Bombay, India, of English parents, Kipling was taken to England at the age of six. He attended the United Service College at Westward Ho!, in North Devon, a place that is pictured in STALKY & CO., a book which many readers find highly amusing, but which Edmund Wilson considers "a hair-raising picture of the sadism of the English public school."

When Kipling returned to India, he became sub-editor of the LAHORE CIVIL AND MILITARY GAZETTE. At twenty-one he published his first volume, a collection of verse; at twenty-two he produced his first narrative, PLAIN TALES FROM THE HILLS. According to Wilson, Kipling took the part of the natives and the Tommies because they were victimized, and he, too, had been a victim of cruelty. Whether or not the theory is tenable, Kipling added a new province to English literature. As Somerset Maugham wrote: "Rudyard Kipling was the first to blaze the trail through new-found country, and no one has invested it with more glamor, no one has made it more exciting. . . . He not only created characters, he created men."

Fuzzy-Wuzzy

We've fought with many men acrost the seas,
  An' some of 'em was brave an' some was not:
The Paythan an' the Zulu an' Burmese;
  But the Fuzzy was the finest o' the lot.
We never got a ha'porth's change of 'im:
  'E squatted in the scrub an' 'ocked our 'orses,
'E cut our sentries up at Sua*kim,*
  An' 'e played the cat an' banjo with our forces.
    So 'ere's *to* you, Fuzzy-Wuzzy, at your 'ome in the Sowdan;
    You're a pore benighted 'eathen but a first-class fightin' man;
    We gives you your certifikit, an' if you want it signed
    We'll come an' 'ave a romp with you whenever you're inclined.

We took our chanst among the Kyber 'ills,
  The Boers knocked us silly at a mile,
The Burman guv us Irriwaddy chills,
  An' a Zulu *impi* dished us up in style:
But all we ever got from such as they
  Was pop to what the Fuzzy made us swaller;
We 'eld our bloomin' own, the papers say,
  But man for man the Fuzzy knocked us 'oller.
    Then 'ere's *to* you, Fuzzy-Wuzzy, an' the missis and the kid;
    Our orders was to break you, an' of course we went an' did.
    We sloshed you with Martinis, an' it wasn't 'ardly fair;
    But for all the odds agin you, Fuzzy-Wuz, you bruk the square.

'E 'asn't got no papers, of 'is own,
  'E 'asn't got no medals nor rewards,
So we must certify the skill 'e's shown
  In usin' of 'is long two-'anded swords;
When 'e's 'oppin' in an' out among the bush
  With 'is coffin-'eaded shield an' shovel-spear,
A 'appy day with Fuzzy on the rush
  Will last a 'ealthy Tommy for a year.
    So 'ere's *to* you, Fuzzy-Wuzzy, an' your friends which are no more,
    If we 'adn't lost some messmates we would 'elp you to deplore;
    But give an' take's the gospel, an' we'll call the bargain fair,
    For if you 'ave lost more than us, you crumpled up the square!

'E rushes at the smoke when we let drive,
  An', before we know, 'e's 'ackin' at our 'ead;
'E's all 'ot sand an' ginger when alive,
  An' 'e's generally shammin' when 'e's dead.
'E's a daisy, 'e's a ducky, 'e's a lamb!
'E's a injia-rubber idiot on the spree,
'E's the on'y thing that doesn't care a damn
  For the Regiment o' British Infantree.
    So 'ere's *to* you, Fuzzy-Wuzzy, at your 'ome in the Sowdan;
    You're a pore benighted 'eathen but a first-class fightin' man;
    An 'ere's *to* you, Fuzzy-Wuzzy, with your 'ayrick 'ead of 'air—
    You big black boundin' beggar—for you bruk a British square.

Danny Deever

"What are the bugles blowin' for?" said Files-on-Parade.
"To turn you out, to turn you out," the Color-Sergeant said.
"What makes you look so white, so white?" said Files-on-Parade.
"I'm dreadin' what I've got to watch," the Color-Sergeant said.
  For they're hangin' Danny Deever, you can 'ear the Dead March play,
  The regiment's in 'ollow square—they're hangin' him today;
  They've taken of his buttons off an' cut his stripes away,
  An' they're hangin' Danny Deever in the mornin'.

"What makes the rear-rank breathe so 'ard?" said Files-on-Parade.
"It's bitter cold, it's bitter cold," the Color-Sergeant said.
"What makes that front-rank man fall down?" says Files-on-Parade.
"A touch of sun, a touch of sun," the Color-Sergeant said.
  They are hangin' Danny Deever, they are marchin' of 'im round.
  They 'ave 'alted Danny Deever by 'is coffin on the ground:
  An 'e'll swing in 'arf a minute for a sneakin' shootin' hound—
  O they're hangin' Danny Deever in the mornin'!

" 'Is cot was right-'and cot to mine," said Files-on-Parade.
" 'E's sleepin' out an' far tonight," the Color-Sergeant said.
"I've drunk 'is beer a score o' times," said Files-on-Parade.
" 'E's drinkin' bitter beer alone," the Color-Sergeant said.
  They are hangin' Danny Deever, you must mark 'im to 'is place,
  For 'e shot a comrade sleepin'—you must look 'im in the face;
  Nine 'undred of 'is county an' the regiment's disgrace,
  While they're hangin' Danny Deever in the mornin'.

"What's that so black agin the sun?" said Files-on-Parade.
"It's Danny fightin' 'ard for life," the Color-Sergeant said.
"What's that that whimpers over'ead?" said Files-on-Parade.
"It's Danny's soul that's passin' now," the Color-Sergeant said.
For they're done with Danny Deever, you can 'ear the quickstep play,
The regiment's in column, an' they're marchin' us away;
Ho! the young recruits are shakin', an' they'll want their beer today,
After hangin' Danny Deever in the mornin'.

Mandalay

By the old Moulmein Pagoda, lookin' eastward to the sea,
There's a Burma girl a-settin', an' I know she thinks o' me;
For the wind is in the palm-trees, an' the temple bells they say:
"Come you back, you British soldier; come you back to Mandalay!"
Come you back to Mandalay,
Where the old Flotilla lay:
Can't you 'ear their paddles chunkin' from Rangoon to Mandalay?
On the road to Mandalay,
Where the flyin'-fishes play,
An' the dawn comes up like thunder outer China 'crost the Bay!

'Er petticut was yaller an' 'er little cap was green,
An' 'er name was Supi-yaw-let—jes' the same as Theebaw's Queen,
An' I seed her fust a-smokin' of a whackin' white cheroot,
An' a-wastin' Christian kisses on an 'eathen idol's foot:
Bloomin' idol made o' mud—
What they called the Great Gawd Budd—
Plucky lot she cared for idols when I kissed 'er where she stud!
On the road to Mandalay—

When the mist was on the rice-fields an' the sun was droppin' slow,
She'd git 'er little banjo an' she'd sing *"Kulla-lo-lo!"*
With 'er arm upon my shoulder an' her cheek agin my cheek
We useter watch the steamers an' the *hathis* pilin' teak.
Elephints a-pilin' teak
In the sludgy, squdgy creek,
Where the silence 'ung that 'eavy you was 'arf afraid to speak!
On the road to Mandalay—

But that's all shove be'ind me—long ago an' fur away,
An' there ain't no 'busses runnin' from the Bank to Mandalay;
An' I'm learnin' 'ere in London what the ten-year sodger tells:
"If you've 'eard the East a-callin', why, you won't 'eed nothin' else."
No! you won't 'eed nothin' else
But them spicy garlic smells
An' the sunshine an' the palm-trees an' the tinkly temple-bells!
On the road to Mandalay—

I am sick o' wastin' leather on these gritty pavin'-stones,
An' the blasted Henglish drizzle wakes the fever in my bones;
'Tho' I walks with fifty 'ousemaids outer Chelsea to the Strand,
An' they talks a lot o' lovin', but wot do they understand?
Beefy face an' grubby 'and—
Law! wot *do* they understand?
I've a neater, sweeter maiden in a cleaner, greener land!
On the road to Mandalay—

Ship me somewheres east of Suez where the best is like the worst,
Where there aren't no Ten Commandments, an' a man can raise a thirst:
For the temple-bells are callin', an' it's there that I would be—
By the old Moulmein Pagoda, lookin' lazy at the sea—
On the road to Mandalay,
Where the old Flotilla lay,
With our sick beneath the awnings when we went to Mandalay!
Oh, the road to Mandalay,
Where the flyin'-fishes play,
An' the dawn comes up like thunder outer China 'crost the Bay!

Famous at twenty-seven, Kipling traveled around the world. He married an American, Caroline Balestier, and lived for a few years in Brattleboro, Vermont. It is probable that Kipling would have remained in America, where he wrote several of his most popular works, if a quarrel with his brother-in-law had not driven him back to England. Suspicious and apprehensive, he became antisocial. His daughter had died, and the loss of a son during the First World War embittered him. He secluded himself in the Sussex village of Burwash.

In his later work Kipling identified himself with the lords and masters, governors of Empire. His heartiness became exaggerated, his imperialism brazenly militant. Yet RECESSIONAL, Kipling's most famous poem, was a daring rebuke. Written at the time of Queen Victoria's Diamond Jubilee, Kipling reminded the British Empire of man's impermanent grandeur: "Lo, all our pomp of yesterday is one with Nineveh and Tyre!" The very title, indicating the hymn sung at the close of a service, was a warning and a prophecy.

Recessional

God of our fathers, known of old,
  Lord of our far-flung battle-line,
Beneath whose awful hand we hold
  Dominion over palm and pine—
Lord God of Hosts, be with us yet,
Lest we forget—lest we forget!

The tumult and the shouting dies;
  The captains and the kings depart:
Still stands Thine ancient sacrifice,
  An humble and a contrite heart.
Lord God of Hosts, be with us yet,
Lest we forget—lest we forget!

Far-called, our navies melt away;
  On dune and headland sinks the fire:
Lo, all our pomp of yesterday
  Is one with Nineveh and Tyre!
Judge of the Nations, spare us yet,
Lest we forget—lest we forget!

If, drunk with sight of power, we loose
  Wild tongues that have not Thee in awe,
Such boastings as the Gentiles use,
  Or lesser breeds without the Law—
Lord God of Hosts, be with us yet,
Lest we forget—lest we forget!

For heathen heart that puts her trust
  In reeking tube and iron shard,
All valiant dust that builds on dust,
  And, guarding, calls not Thee to guard,
For frantic boast and foolish word—
Thy Mercy on Thy People, Lord!

In his forty-second year Kipling received the Nobel Prize for literature. A few years later it became the fashion to belittle Kipling's work. It was implied that he, like one of his own titles, was "The Light That Failed"; in 1935 a deprecating editorial referred to him as "the forgotten man of English literature." He died January 18, 1936, a few weeks after his seventieth birthday.

Although it is conceded that Kipling was a master of the modern short story, his poetry has been variously judged. His verse has suffered from its very ease as well as from the extremes of praise and disapproval. A new generation is beginning to re-estimate his peculiar combination of pounding rhythms and delicate accents, of exuberance and nostalgia. It is significant that A CHOICE OF KIPLING'S VERSE was unexpectedly and enthusiastically compiled by T. S. Eliot in 1941.

L'Envoi

What is the moral? Who rides may read.
When the night is thick and the tracks are blind
A friend at a pinch is a friend indeed,
But a fool to wait for the laggard behind.
Down to Gehenna or up to the Throne,
He travels the fastest who travels alone.

White hands cling to the tightened rein,
Slipping the spur from the booted heel,
Tenderest voices cry "Turn again!"
Red lips tarnish the scabbarded steel.
High hopes faint on a warm hearth stone—
He travels the fastest who travels alone.

One may fall but he falls by himself—
Falls by himself with himself to blame.
One may attain and to him is pelf—
Loot of the city in Gold or Fame.
Plunder of earth shall be all his own
Who travels the fastest and travels alone.

Wherefore the more ye be holpen and stayed,
Stayed by a friend in the hour of toil,
Sing the heretical song I have made—
His be the labor and yours be the spoil.
Win by his aid and the aid disown—
He travels the fastest who travels alone!

In spite of a critical minority, it seems likely that Kipling will outlive most of his generation as a people's poet; he will be rediscovered again and again. The best of his lines are refreshingly outspoken, brimming with vitality. His story poems have the natural force which characterizes true narrative verse. Kipling may well have written the popular measures of one age and the remembered ballads of another.

ERNEST DOWSON

[1867–1900]

DEAD at thirty-two, Dowson's life was as luckless as his career was frail. It was a brief career of wine and roses—roses flung riotously but unhappily—as though in a disordered dream. He wrote his own autobiography in the eight lines entitled VITAE SUMMA BREVIS SPEM NOS VETAT INCOHARE LONGAM, a quotation from Horace's first book of ODES: "The shortness of life prevents us from entertaining far-off hopes."

Vitae Summa Brevis Spem Nos Vetat Incohare Longam

They are not long, the weeping and the laughter,
  Love and desire and hate;
I think they have no portion in us after
        We pass the gate.

They are not long, the days of wine and roses:
  Out of a misty dream
Our path emerges for a while, then closes
        Within a dream.

Dowson was born at Belmont Hill, in Kent, August 2, 1867. His family was an eminent one; his great-uncle was Prime Minister of New Zealand. Although Dowson attended Queen's College, Oxford, he left without finishing his studies, went to London, and joined the Rhymers' Club. Alternating between fits of religion and dissipation, he lived recklessly. He fell idealistically in love with a waitress, daughter of a restaurant keeper, but she understood neither his verse nor his reticence. She was his "Cynara," and it was to her that he wrote his universally known poem with a Latin title that she found even more inexplicable than the man who adored her with such virginal devotion. The title was from Dowson's favorite Horace, from the beginning of the fourth book of ODES: "I am not what I was under the reign of the lovely Cynara."

Non Sum Qualis Eram Bonae Sub Regno Cynarae

Last night, ah, yesternight, betwixt her lips and mine
There fell thy shadow, Cynara! thy breath was shed
Upon my soul between the kisses and the wine;
And I was desolate and sick of an old passion,
  Yea, I was desolate and bowed my head:
I have been faithful to thee, Cynara! in my fashion.

All night upon mine heart I felt her warm heart beat,
Night-long within mine arms in love and sleep she lay;
Surely the kisses of her bought red mouth were sweet;
But I was desolate and sick of an old passion,
  When I awoke and found the dawn was gray:
I have been faithful to thee, Cynara! in my fashion.

I have forgot much, Cynara! gone with the wind,
Flung roses, roses riotously with the throng,
Dancing, to put thy pale, lost lilies out of mind;
But I was desolate and sick of an old passion,
  Yea, all the time, because the dance was long:
I have been faithful to thee, Cynara! in my fashion.

I cried for madder music and for stronger wine,
But when the feast is finished and the lamps expire,
Then falls thy shadow, Cynara! the night is thine;
And I am desolate and sick of an old passion,
  Yea, hungry for the lips of my desire:
I have been faithful to thee, Cynara! in my fashion.

The puzzled and finally impatient "Cynara" ran away and married a waiter. Dowson, feeling that his life was ruined, became irresponsible. Instead of drinking haphazardly, he drank deliberately. His father had left him an old dock, and Dowson hid there, in cabmen's shelters, living in utmost squalor. "He drifted about in whatever company came his way," wrote Arthur Symons; "he let heedlessness develop into a curious disregard of personal tidiness."

Dowson tried to forget his misery in France. But, though he made friends with innkeepers, he got into fights with the fishermen who came in to drink. It was too late to toughen his fragile spirit by contact with rough animal life. His VILLANELLE OF THE POET'S ROAD is not only an exquisite use of an old French form, but also a confession of Dowson's frustrated desire.

Villanelle of the Poet's Road

Wine and woman and song,
  Three things garnish our way:
Yet is day over long.

Lest we do our youth wrong,
  Gather them while we may:
Wine and woman and song.

Three things render us strong,
  Vine leaves, kisses and bay:
Yet is day over long.

Unto us they belong,
  Us the bitter and gay,
Wine and woman and song.

We, as we pass along,
  Are sad that they will not stay;
Yet is day over long.

Fruits and flowers among,
  What is better than they:
Wine and woman and song?
Yet is day over long.

Venus had rejected his garlands. Now, toward the end of his life, Dowson lit a candle to the Virgin. He died, a convert to the Roman Catholic Church, February 23, 1900.

Much of the literature of the 1890's seems written on plush; but Dowson's intensity rose above decadence. Limited by his temperament, defeated by life, Dowson left a few unique things. "In a subdued way," wrote Donald Davidson in BRITISH POETRY OF THE EIGHTEEN-NINETIES, "he was an English Poe, half angel, half Bohemian—a saint of the gutter, a Catullus lost in the wilderness of English respectability."

EDWIN ARLINGTON ROBINSON

[1869–1935]

After Whitman had celebrated "the divine average," poetry in America became more concerned with the common man. Edwin Arlington Robinson went further; he devoted himself not only to the ordinary individual, but also to the misfits and the outcasts, those who were unable to maintain themselves in a world of ruthless efficiency. Robinson protested against acquisitiveness and success at any cost; he almost made a fetish of failure. This was perhaps inevitable, for Robinson's own life was, except for a few short intervals, a dignified and losing battle.

Robinson was born December 22, 1869, in the village of Head Tide, Maine, and, while still a child, moved to the near-by town of Gardiner. At twenty-one he entered Harvard College and left it two years later. At twenty-seven he issued a privately printed collection of verse. But he feared to market himself as a poet, and there seemed little future for him as a breadwinner. "This itch for authorship," he wrote, "is worse than the devil and spoils a man for anything else." He went to New York, tried to earn a living as an inspector in the New York subway, and almost starved. At thirty-five he was rescued from poverty by President Theodore Roosevelt, who gave him a clerkship in the New York Custom House. But if Robinson was relieved, he was not elated. He remained sympathetic to the cheated dreamers, the bewildered mediocrities. He created an entire gallery of American figures like Richard Cory, who, hiding his despair, "glittered when he walked," and Miniver Cheevy, the incompetent "child of scorn," with his futile dream of escape.

Richard Cory

Whenever Richard Cory went down town,
  We people on the pavement looked at him:
He was a gentleman from sole to crown,
  Clean favored, and imperially slim.

And he was always quietly arrayed,
  And he was always human when he talked;
But still he fluttered pulses when he said,
  "Good-morning," and he glittered when he walked.

And he was rich—yes, richer than a king—
  And admirably schooled in every grace:
In fine, we thought that he was everything
  To make us wish that we were in his place.

So on we worked, and waited for the light,
  And went without the meat, and cursed the bread;
And Richard Cory, one calm summer night,
  Went home and put a bullet through his head.

Miniver Cheevy

Miniver Cheevy, child of scorn,
  Grew lean while he assailed the seasons;
He wept that he was ever born,
  And he had reasons.

Miniver loved the days of old
  When swords were bright and steeds were prancing;
The vision of a warrior bold
  Would set him dancing.

Miniver sighed for what was not,
  And dreamed, and rested from his labors;
He dreamed of Thebes and Camelot,
  And Priam's neighbors.

Miniver mourned the ripe renown
That made so many a name so fragrant;
He mourned Romance, now on the town,
And Art, a vagrant.

Miniver loved the Medici,
Albeit he had never seen one;
He would have sinned incessantly
Could he have been one.

Miniver cursed the commonplace
And eyed a khaki suit with loathing;
He missed the medieval grace
Of iron clothing.

Miniver scorned the gold he sought,
But sore annoyed was he without it;
Miniver thought, and thought, and thought,
And thought about it.

Miniver Cheevy, born too late,
Scratched his head and kept on thinking;
Miniver coughed, and called it fate,
And kept on drinking.

Reuben Bright

Because he was a butcher and thereby
Did earn an honest living (and did right)
I would not have you think that Reuben Bright
Was any more a brute than you or I;
For when they told him that his wife must die,
He stared at them and shook with grief and fright,
And cried like a great baby half that night,
And made the women cry to see him cry.

And after she was dead, and he had paid
The singers and the sexton and the rest,
He packed a lot of things that she had made
Most mournfully away in an old chest
Of hers, and put some chopped-up cedar boughs
In with them, and tore down the slaughter-house.

Success came late to Robinson. Until his late fifties he had been a poet admired only by the few. TRISTRAM, published in his fifty-eighth year, made him famous. Strangely enough, the romantic mysticism of this book-length poem—part of an Arthurian cycle—was far less characteristic of the author than the earthy New England portraits. The unexpected, and even unlooked-for, triumph was actually harmful. Robinson began to fear the future, to feel that everything he wrote would be pitted against TRISTRAM. For seven years he drove himself to write an annual volume in a vain effort to live up to the standard set for him. Three times he was awarded the Pulitzer Prize. Nevertheless, he refused to be feted; he doomed himself to solitude. Distrusting most men and fearing almost all women, he became a laconic, lonely man, a man obsessed by defeat and in love with death.

Robinson had schooled himself so severely that he could express the depths of isolation even in so restricted, and usually artificial, a form as the villanelle—witness THE HOUSE ON THE HILL.

The House on the Hill

They are all gone away,
  The House is shut and still,
There is nothing more to say.

Through broken walls and gray
  The winds blow bleak and shrill;
They are all gone away.

Nor is there one today
  To speak them good or ill:
There is nothing more to say.

Why is it then we stray
  Around that sunken sill?
They are all gone away,

And our poor fancy-play
  For them is wasted skill:
There is nothing more to say.

There is ruin and decay
  In the House on the Hill:
They are all gone away,
There is nothing more to say.

Robinson lived most of his summers at the MacDowell colony, in Peterboro, New Hampshire, where he was the center of adulation. He divided his winters between Boston and New York. Except for occasional evenings of conviviality, he withdrew from an oppressive world. In his mid-sixties he became seriously ill. When he was finally taken to the New York Hospital, it was impossible to operate successfully. He died April 6, 1935.

Although much was made of Robinson's pessimism, even the darkest of his monologues are enlivened by the sparkle of imagination and the flicker of wit. The compact lyrics read like extended epigrams; the longer poems are lit with shrewd humor. Sometimes the humor is unaffectedly tender, as in MR. FLOOD'S PARTY, that touching picture of a battered derelict nursing his companionable jug and putting it down with trembling care, "knowing that most things break."

Mr. Flood's Party

Old Eben Flood, climbing alone one night
Over the hill between the town below
And the forsaken upland hermitage
That held as much as he should ever know
On earth again of home, paused warily.
The road was his with not a native near;
And Eben, having leisure, said aloud,
For no man else in Tilbury Town to hear:

"Well, Mr. Flood, we have the harvest moon
Again, and we may not have many more;
The bird is on the wing, the poet says,
And you and I have said it here before.
Drink to the bird." He raised up to the light
The jug that he had gone so far to fill,
And answered huskily: "Well, Mr. Flood,
Since you propose it, I believe I will."

Alone, as if enduring to the end
A valiant armor of scarred hopes outworn,
He stood there in the middle of the road
Like Roland's ghost winding a silent horn.

Below him, in the town among the trees,
Where friends of other days had honored him,
A phantom salutation of the dead
Rang thinly till old Eben's eyes were dim.

Then, as a mother lays her sleeping child
Down tenderly, fearing it may awake,
He set the jug down slowly at his feet
With trembling care, knowing that most things break;
And only when assured that on firm earth
It stood, as the uncertain lives of men
Assuredly did not, he paced away,
And with his hand extended paused again:

"Well, Mr. Flood, we have not met like this
In a long time; and many a change has come
To both of us, I fear, since last it was
We had a drop together. Welcome home!"
Convivially returning with himself,
Again he raised the jug up to the light;
And with an acquiescent quaver said:
"Well, Mr. Flood, if you insist, I might.

"Only a very little, Mr. Flood—
For auld lang syne. No more, sir; that will do."
So, for the time, apparently it did,
And Eben evidently thought so too;
For soon amid the silver loneliness
Of night he lifted up his voice and sang,
Secure, with only two moons listening,
Until the whole harmonious landscape rang—

'For auld lang syne." The weary throat gave out,
The last word wavered; and the song being done,
He raised again the jug regretfully
And shook his head, and was again alone.
There was not much that was ahead of him,
And there was nothing in the town below—
Where strangers would have shut the many doors
That many friends had opened long ago.

Robinson's letters have been published, but they reveal little of the man. His spiritual autobiography as well as his philosophy is in RICHARD CORY, in MINIVER CHEEVY, even—and perhaps especially—in MR. FLOOD'S PARTY.

EDGAR LEE MASTERS

[1869–1950]

AFTER three books of innocuous verse, two of which were published under pseudonyms, and seven plays, all of which were failures, Edgar Lee Masters seemed defeated as a writer and devoted himself to the practice of law. A few years later, at forty-five, he wrote SPOON RIVER ANTHOLOGY, a landmark in contemporary literature.

Born August 23, 1869, in Garnett, Kansas, Edgar Lee Masters was taken to Illinois as a child. His father, a man of "dark pugnacity," lost money, and the boy's schooling was haphazard; at sixteen he had to do odd jobs for a living. He worked as printer's devil, harvest hand, and clerk in a drugstore, and spent his savings on books. He attended Knox College, thought of being a teacher, but entered his father's law office. In his twenty-second year he was admitted to the bar.

Masters had published verse since youth; by the time he was twenty-four he had written some four hundred poems. His work showed little besides promise, energy, and a confused worship of Poe, Whitman, Shelley, Milton, and Swinburne. Suddenly the poet emerged in a new and surprising manner. Employing the loose, unrhymed line of Whitman and the concise summaries of THE GREEK ANTHOLOGY, Masters presented a collection of free-verse biographies, some of them imaginary, but many based upon people he knew in Illinois. He called it SPOON RIVER ANTHOLOGY, and even those who were repelled by its brute realism had to acknowledge its honesty. A critical examination of village life, the book was a forerunner of Sinclair Lewis' MAIN STREET and the ensuing fiction which challenged smugness and complacent hypocrisy.

In SPOON RIVER ANTHOLOGY the intrigues as well as the monotony of small-town life are synthesized; but, although hatred and disgust dominate the mood, pity is not lacking. The prologue begins in a key of regret, a tender parody of Villon's lines beginning "Where are the snows of yesteryear?"

Where are Elmer, Herman, Bert, Tom and Charley,
The weak of will, the strong of arm, the clown, the boozer, the fighter?
All, all, are sleeping on the hill.

One of the most affecting pages in SPOON RIVER ANTHOLOGY vivifies the tragedy of Abraham Lincoln's requited but unfulfilled love for Ann Rutledge, the New Salem tavernkeeper's daughter. Lincoln was twenty-five; she was a little more than twenty. "The earth was their footstool," wrote Carl Sandburg in ABRAHAM LINCOLN: THE PRAIRIE YEARS, "the sky was a sheaf of blue dreams; the rise of the blood-gold rim of a full moon in the evening was almost too much to live, see, and remember." But before they could be married she died of fever, and Lincoln carried the scars of that burning throughout his life. "He was a changed man keeping to himself the gray mystery of that change."

Ann Rutledge

Out of me unworthy and unknown
The vibrations of deathless music:
"With malice toward none, with charity for all."
Out of me the forgiveness of millions toward millions,
And the beneficent face of a nation
Shining with justice and truth.
I am Ann Rutledge who sleep beneath these weeds,
Beloved in life of Abraham Lincoln,
Wedded to him, not through union,
But through separation.
Bloom forever, O Republic,
From the dust of my bosom!

SPOON RIVER ANTHOLOGY is primarily not a book of verse but a book of characters; as such it has been relished by people who do not usually read poetry. It is full of forthright strength and angry energy; even its tenderness is rugged, never soft and not too sympathetic. But a hunger for beauty struggles through the desperation and cruelty.

Fiddler Jones

The earth keeps some vibration going
There in your heart, and that is you.
And if the people find you can fiddle,
Why, fiddle you must, for all your life.
What do you see, a harvest of clover?

Or a meadow to walk through to the river?
The wind's in the corn; you rub your hands
For beeves hereafter ready for market;
Or else you hear the rustle of skirts
Like the girls when dancing at Little Grove.
To Cooney Potter a pillar of dust
Or whirling leaves meant ruinous drouth;
They looked to me like Red-Head Sammy
Stepping it off, to "Toor-a-Loor."
How could I till my forty acres
Not to speak of getting more,
With a medley of horns, bassoons and piccolos
Stirred in my brain by crows and robins
And the creak of a wind-mill—only these?
And I never started to plow in my life
That some one did not stop in the road
And take me away to a dance or picnic.
I ended up with forty acres;
I ended up with a broken fiddle—
And a broken laugh, and a thousand memories,
And not a single regret.

SPOON RIVER ANTHOLOGY is Masters' lonely eminence. The many volumes written before and after that work are a disheartening array, heavily rhetorical, platitudinous, verbose. The industry is unflagging; between his sixty-sixth and sixty-ninth years Masters published nine volumes—a long autobiography, a novel, three biographies, and four collections of poems. Of his fifty books, only one seems likely to survive. That one remains not so much for its poetry as for its authentic portrait of a man and his bitter times. Its cumulative epitaphs compose a living American document, harsh, unhappy, but desperately honest. Self-doomed to unhappiness, Masters died after a long illness in 1950.

CHARLOTTE MEW

[1869–1928]

ALMOST unknown to the world of men, and little known even in the world of letters, Charlotte Mew wrote two small volumes of firm and distinguished poetry. She was born November 15, 1869, daughter of an architect who died when she was an infant. The struggle with poverty began in childhood; she and her sister Anne never had quite enough funds for comfort. She was happiest in the countryside, but, unable to live there, she was forced to seek a meager living in London. One of her happiest excursions was a week end in Wessex where she was the guest of Thomas Hardy, who said: "She is the least pretentious but undoubtedly the best woman poet of our day." In her late fifties, through the joint efforts of Hardy, Masefield, and others, she was granted a civil-list pension. But, though this kept her alive, her spirit sank beneath the weight of personal maladjustments and private griefs. She never married. The death of her mother made her more of a recluse than ever. After the death of her sister, there was no one to whom she could turn. A severe illness sent her to a nursing home in her sixtieth year. Feeling there was nothing to live for, she committed suicide at the hospital, March 24, 1928.

In an obituary note, Sidney Cockerell wrote, "Charlotte and Anne Mew had more than a little in them of what made another Charlotte and Anne, and their sister Emily, what they were. They were indeed like two Brontë sisters reincarnate." It will never be known how much of her work Charlotte Mew destroyed in a critical passion for perfection. Her published pieces number no more than sixty. Yet these are not only the intensification but the distillation of emotion. The few long poems are probingly meditative; even the lyrics are grave and sonorous.

Sea Love

Tide be runnin' the great world over:
  'Twas only last June month I mind that we
Was thinkin' the toss and the call in the breast of the lover
  So everlastin' as the sea.

Here's the same little fishes that sputter and swim,
  Wi' the moon's old glim on the gray, wet sand;
An' him no more to me nor me to him
  Than the wind goin' over my hand.

I Have Been Through the Gates

His heart, to me, was a place of palaces and pinnacles and shining towers;
I saw it then as we see things in dreams,—I do not remember how long I slept;
I remember the trees, and the high, white walls, and how the sun was always on the towers;
The walls are standing today, and the gates: I have been through the gates, I have groped, I have crept
Back, back. There is dust in the streets, and blood; they are empty; darkness is over them;
His heart is a place with the lights gone out, forsaken by great winds and the heavenly rain, unclean and unswept,
Like the heart of the holy city, old, blind, beautiful Jerusalem,
Over which Christ wept.

Charlotte Mew had a gift for making her personal outcry impersonal. BESIDE THE BED is a human experience, but the transformation into verse gives it an unearthly solemnity. It is one of the shortest but one of the most beautiful of dirges.

Beside the Bed

Someone has shut the shining eyes, straightened and folded
The wandering hands quietly covering the unquiet breast:
So, smoothed and silenced you lie, like a child, not again to be questioned or scolded:
But, for you, not one of us believes that this is rest.

Not so to close the windows down can cloud and deaden
The blue beyond: or to screen the wavering flame subdue its breath:
Why, if I lay my cheek to your cheek, your gray lips, like dawn, would quiver and redden,
Breaking into the old, odd smile at this fraud of death.

Because all night you have not turned to us or spoken
It is time for you to wake; your dreams were never very deep:
I, for one, have seen the thin bright, twisted threads of them dimmed suddenly and broken.
This is only a most piteous pretense of sleep!

THE FARMER'S BRIDE, the title poem of Charlotte Mew's first book, is half lyric, half narrative. It is a little masterpiece, of which Harold Monro wrote: "The outline of THE FARMER'S BRIDE would have resolved itself in the mind of Mrs. Browning into a poem of at least two thousand lines; Browning might have worked it up to six thousand . . . Charlotte Mew tells the whole touching story in forty-six lines."

The Farmer's Bride

Three Summers since I chose a maid,
Too young maybe—but more's to do
At harvest-time than bide and woo.
  When us was wed she turned afraid
Of love and me and all things human;
Like the shut of a winter's day.
Her smile went out, and 'twasn't a woman—
  More like a little frightened fay.
    One night, in the Fall, she runned away.

"Out 'mong the sheep, her be," they said,
'Should properly have been abed;
But sure enough she wasn't there
Lying awake with her wide brown stare.
So over seven-acre field and up-along across the down
We chased her, flying like a hare
Before our lanterns. To Church-Town
  All in a shiver and a scare
We caught her, fetched her home at last
  And turned the key upon her, fast.

She does the work about the house
As well as most, but like a mouse:
  Happy enough to chat and play
  With birds and rabbits and such as they,
  So long as men-folk keep away.
"Not near, not near!" her eyes beseech
When one of us comes within reach.
  The women say that beasts in stall
  Look round like children at her call.
  I've hardly heard her speak at all.

Shy as a leveret, swift as he,
Straight and slight as a young larch tree,

Sweet as the first wild violets, she
To her wild self. But what to me?

The short days shorten and the oaks are brown,
  The blue smoke rises to the low gray sky,
One leaf in the still air falls slowly down,
  A magpie's spotted feathers lie
On the black earth spread white with rime,
The berries redden up to Christmas-time.
  What's Christmas-time without there be
  Some other in the house than we!

  She sleeps up in the attic there
  Alone, poor maid. 'Tis but a stair
Betwixt us. Oh! my God! the down,
The soft young down of her, the brown,
The brown of her—her eyes, her hair, her hair . . .

W. H. DAVIES

[1870–1940]

"A GENUINE innocent, writing odds and ends of verse about odds and ends of things," is the way Bernard Shaw described W. H. Davies in his preface to THE AUTOBIOGRAPHY OF A SUPER-TRAMP. William Henry Davies lived up to the characterization. He was born in a public house, incongruously called Church House, in Monmouthshire, April 20, 1870. His parents were Welsh countrymen, and the boy educated himself. He became a cattleman, a berry picker, and, as the title of his autobiography indicates, a panhandler. He came to the United States, remained there six years, rode the rails, and had his right foot cut off by a train in Canada. Returning to England in his early thirties, he supported himself by peddling and, when necessary, begging.

It was not until his thirty-fifth year that Davies decided to be a poet, and had his book set up in a printer's shop with money he had, somehow, saved. As a poet, he was as fecund as he was determined. Between 1906 and the year of his death, Davies issued twenty-three volumes—five of autobiography, eighteen of verse—

and more than six hundred poems. His birdlike simplicities and almost mindless fluency made it difficult for the critics to separate what was good, bad, and indifferent in his blithe verse. He was called "a Welsh Herrick," and many of his lines justified the appellation. Davies sang ingenuously and tirelessly of a fair world, of happy mornings and evenings full of pleasant reverie.

Sing out, my Soul, thy songs of joy;
  Such as a happy bird will sing
Beneath a rainbow's lovely arch
  In early spring.

Davies regarded with an air of continual surprise the objects which everyone takes for granted. His sense of wonder was unfailing. Glowworms and lovely ladies, staring sheep and the moon "with her white fleet of stars," were observed as rapturously as though no one had noticed them before. A butterfly on a stone, or the juxtaposition of a rainbow and a cuckoo, was all Davies needed for a full life.

Leisure

What is this life if, full of care,
We have no time to stand and stare.

No time to stand beneath the boughs
And stare as long as sheep or cows.

No time to see, when woods we pass,
Where squirrels hide their nuts in grass.

No time to see, in broad daylight,
Streams full of stars, like skies at night.

No time to turn at Beauty's glance,
And watch her feet, how they can dance.

No time to wait till her mouth can
Enrich that smile her eyes began.

A poor life this if, full of care,
We have no time to stand and stare.

The Example

Here's an example from
  A Butterfly;
That on a rough, hard rock
  Happy can lie;
Friendless and all alone
On this unsweetened stone.

Now let my bed be hard,
  No care take I;
I'll make my joy like this
  Small Butterfly,
Whose happy heart has power
To make a stone a flower.

Davies had superintended four constantly enlarging editions of his COLLECTED POEMS and was planning another assembly when he died at seventy, September 26, 1940.

Although Davies, more than any poet of the twentieth century, recalls Herrick, he was indebted to other forerunners, mostly Elizabethan. Another influence, less obvious but more integral, was that of Blake; many of Davies' shorter lyrics are echoes, perhaps unconscious, of SONGS OF INNOCENCE. Even more direct though far less deep than his inspired source, Davies remained a charming rather than a great poet. He could not frame burning images and prophetic visions. He was content with quiet pictures and miniature panoramas, a Blake in words of one syllable.

Ambition

I had Ambition, by which sin
  The angels fell;
I climbed and, step by step, O Lord,
  Ascended into Hell.

Returning now to peace and quiet,
  And made more wise,
Let my descent and fall, O Lord,
  Be into Paradise.

RALPH HODGSON

[1872–1962]

BORN in Yorkshire in 1872, Ralph Hodgson was a contradiction in his own terms. He was so reticent that he refused to be interviewed or to prepare the shortest statement for works of reference; yet he waged a violent campaign to end the custom of docking dogs' tails and clipping their ears. Known to a small circle as a person of few words and a writer of a few poems, he was celebrated in a larger sphere, the sporting world, as a breeder and judge of bull terriers. In youth he worked as a pressman in London and was employed as draftsman on an evening paper. In his early thirties, with the artist Claud Lovat Fraser, he founded The Sign of Flying Fame for the publication of pamphlets, broadsides, and chapbooks.

At fifty-three Hodgson went to Japan as lecturer on English literature at Sendai University, about two hundred miles from Tokyo. He remained there several years, but in 1939, with his American wife, he came to the United States. After trying various retreats, he bought a place—half farm, half bird sanctuary—near Canton, Ohio, and revived the project of a small press, which he called Packington's Pound; late "Flying Fame," London. This time he furnished and hand-colored his own illustrations.

Hodgson's poetry adheres to the tradition in form, but its spirit has its own singularity. One or two of the longer poems, particularly THE SONG OF HONOR, may carry overtones of Christopher Smart's A SONG TO DAVID. The lyrics, however, are altogether Hodgson's, fresh without freakishness, original without straining for originality. EVE takes one of the oldest symbols in literature, the mother of mankind, and translates it into a new world in terms of a young English girl. TIME, YOU OLD GYPSY MAN employs another familiar symbol to create one of the most haunting of modern lyrics.

Eve

Eve, with her basket, was
Deep in the bells and grass,
Wading in bells and grass
Up to her knees.

Picking a dish of sweet
Berries and plums to eat,
Down in the bells and grass
Under the trees.

Mute as a mouse in a
Corner the cobra lay,
Curled round a bough of the
Cinnamon tall. . . .
Now to get even and
Humble proud heaven and
Now was the moment or
Never at all.

"Eva!" Each syllable
Light as a flower fell,
"Eva!" he whispered the
Wondering maid,
Soft as a bubble sung
Out of a linnet's lung,
Soft and most silverly
"Eva!" he said.

Picture that orchard sprite;
Eve, with her body white,
Supple and smooth to her
Slim finger tips;
Wondering, listening,
Listening, wondering,
Eve with a berry
Half-way to her lips.

Oh, had our simple Eve
Seen through the make-believe!
Had she but known the
Pretender he was!
Out of the boughs he came,
Whispering still her name,
Tumbling in twenty rings
Into the grass.

Here was the strangest pair
In the world anywhere,
Eve in the bells and grass
Kneeling, and he

Telling his story low. . . .
Singing birds saw them go
Down the dark path to
The Blasphemous Tree.

Oh, what a clatter when
Titmouse and Jenny Wren
Saw him successful and
Taking his leave!
How the birds rated him,
How they all hated him!
How they all pitied
Poor motherless Eve!

Picture her crying
Outside in the lane,
Eve, with no dish of sweet
Berries and plums to eat,
Haunting the gate of the
Orchard in vain. . . .
Picture the lewd delight
Under the hill tonight—
"Eva!" the toast goes round,
"Eva!" again.

Time, You Old Gypsy Man

Time, you old gypsy man,
  Will you not stay,
Put up your caravan
  Just for one day?

All things I'll give you
Will you be my guest,
Bells for your jennet
Of silver the best,
Goldsmiths shall beat you
A great golden ring,
Peacocks shall bow to you,
Little boys sing,
Oh, and sweet girls will
Festoon you with may.

Time, you old gypsy,
Why hasten away?

Last week in Babylon,
Last night in Rome,
Morning, and in the crush
Under Paul's dome;
Under Paul's dial
You tighten your rein—
Only a moment,
And off once again;
Off to some city
Now blind in the womb,
Off to another
Ere that's in the tomb.

Time, you old gypsy man,
  Will you not stay,
Put up your caravan
  Just for one day?

Silver Wedding

In the middle of the night
He started up
At a cry from his sleeping Bride—
A bat from some ruin
In a heart he'd never searched,
Nay, hardly seen inside:

"Want me and take me
For the woman that I am
And not for her that died,
The lovely chit nineteen
I one time was,
And am no more," she cried

WALTER DE LA MARE

[1873–1956]

IT HAS BEEN said that Walter de la Mare wrote more for antiquity than for posterity, and it is true that he dwelt in an enchanted past rather than in a disturbing present. His is the domain of vanished childhood, of impossible dreams, of lovely ghosts from a romantic and forgotten world. His poetry is conceived in the mood of memory. Sadly it recalls the little truants, "the children magic hath stolen away," silver reeds in a silver stream, a bird sliding through the frosty air, a beautiful lady of the West Country.

> But beauty vanishes; beauty passes;
> However rare—rare it be.
> And when I crumble, who will remember
> This lady of the West Country?

The sense of loss runs through de la Mare's verse like a persistent refrain. The word "gone" beats through his bell-like lines; he loves all that is irrecoverable, "all that's past," he says in one of his most poignant lyrics.

All That's Past

Very old are the woods;
  And the buds that break
Out of the briar's boughs,
  When March winds wake,
So old with their beauty are—
  Oh, no man knows
Through what wild centuries
  Roves back the rose.

Very old are the brooks;
  And the rills that rise
Where snows sleep cold beneath
  The azure skies

Sing such a history
  Of come and gone,
Their every drop is as wise
  As Solomon.

Very old are we men;
  Our dreams are tales
Told in dim Eden
  By Eve's nightingales;
We wake and whisper awhile,
  But, the day gone by,
Silence and sleep like fields
  Of amaranth lie.

Walter de la Mare was born at Charlton in Kent, April 25, 1873, descended from a Huguenot family, and related to Browning. Educated at St. Paul's School in London, he was unable to attend college. At eighteen he went into business, remaining in the English branch of the Standard Oil Company for twenty years. His first volume, SONGS OF CHILDHOOD, was not published until he was almost thirty, and it appeared under the anagrammatic pseudonym of "Walter Ramal." Since that publication de la Mare has composed and edited more than forty volumes—novels, short stories, and anthologies, as well as books of poems—most of which explore a strange limbo, a veiled borderland, half juvenile, half supernatural.

The Song of Shadows

Sweep thy faint strings, Musician,
  With thy long lean hand;
Downward the starry tapers burn,
  Sinks soft the waning sand;
The old hound whimpers couched in sleep,
  The embers smolder low;
Across the walls the shadows
  Come, and go.

Sweep softly thy strings, Musician,
  The minutes mount to hours;
Frost on the windless casement weaves
  A labyrinth of flowers;

Ghosts linger in the darkening air,
  Hearken at the open door;
Music hath called them, dreaming,
  Home once more.

"Nature itself," wrote de la Mare, "resembles a veil over some further reality of which the imagination in its visionary moments seems to achieve a more direct evidence." It is in the "visionary moments" that de la Mare triumphs; the area just beyond realism is his true home. Nowhere is this better exemplified than in THE LISTENERS. In this poem the traditional adventure story takes on new significance. It can be interpreted in many ways, as the record of an actual quest or as a symbol, as a fable of man's eternal attempt to answer life's riddle or as a courageous challenge to terror. But no contemporary poem is more provocative, more purely a work of the imagination, a work that does not explain but never fails to illumine.

The Listeners

"Is there anybody there?" said the Traveler,
  Knocking on the moonlit door;
And his horse in the silence champed the grasses
  Of the forest's ferny floor.
And a bird flew up out of the turret,
  Above the Traveler's head:
And he smote upon the door again a second time;
  "Is there anybody there?" he said.
But no one descended to the Traveler;
  No head from the leaf-fringed sill
Leaned over and looked into his gray eyes,
  Where he stood perplexed and still.
But only a host of phantom listeners
  That dwelt in the lone house then
Stood listening in the quiet of the moonlight
  To that voice from the world of men:
Stood thronging the faint moonbeams on the dark stair
  That goes down to the empty hall,
Hearkening in an air stirred and shaken
  By the lonely Traveler's call.
And he felt in his heart their strangeness,
  Their stillness answering his cry,

While his horse moved, cropping the dark turf,
'Neath the starred and leafy sky;
For he suddenly smote on the door, even
Louder, and lifted his head:—
"Tell them I came, and no one answered,
That I kept my word," he said.
Never the least stir made the listeners,
Though every word he spake
Fell echoing through the shadowiness of the still house
From the one man left awake:
Aye, they heard his foot upon the stirrup,
And the sound of iron on stone,
And how the silence surged softly backward,
When the plunging hoofs were gone.

TRUMBULL STICKNEY

[1874–1904]

BORN June 20, 1874, in Geneva, Switzerland, of New England parents, Trumbull Stickney was something of a prodigy in childhood. Entering Harvard at seventeen, he was graduated with high classical honors, went abroad, and studied at the Sorbonne. The University of Paris awarded him a degree never before conferred on an American. At twenty-nine he returned to the United States as instructor of Greek at Harvard. A year later, barely thirty, he died of a tumor on the brain.

The early published verse as well as the posthumous poems indicate what Stickney might have accomplished with fuller life and experience. Unknown to all but a few, Stickney's lines are proud, stoical with "wise denials," and stern peace. Only a sonnet or two survives, still sonorous with the music of a vanished day.

Live Blindly and Upon the Hour

Live blindly and upon the hour. The Lord,
Who was the Future, died full long ago.
Knowledge which is the Past is folly. Go,
Poor child. and be not to thyself abhorred.

Around thine earth sun-wingéd winds do blow
And planets roll; a meteor draws his sword;
The rainbow breaks his seven-colored chord
And the long strips of river-silver flow:
Awake! Give thyself to the lovely hours.
Drinking their lips, catch thou the dream in flight
About their fragile hairs' aërial gold.
Thou art divine, thou livest—as of old
Apollo springing naked to the light,
And all his island shivered into flowers.

Mount Lykaion

Alone on Lykaion since man hath been
Stand on the height two columns, where at rest
Two eagles hewn of gold sit looking East
Forever; and the sun goes up between.
Far down around the mountain's oval green
An order keeps the falling stones abreast.
Below within the chaos last and least
A river like a curl of light is seen.
Beyond the river lies the even sea,
Beyond the sea another ghost of sky—
O God, support the sickness of my eye
Lest the far space and long antiquity
Suck out my heart, and on this awful ground
The great wind kill my little shell with sound.

from SONNETS FROM GREECE

G. K. CHESTERTON

[1874–1936]

IT WAS Chesterton's misfortune that, as a poet, he was considered a master of paradox. His gift for brilliant contradiction was his undoing. He exploited it from the beginning and allowed it to dictate a philosophy of words rather than ideas, a rational irrationalism. Objecting with impartial violence to both capitalism and socialism, he championed a fictitious medievalism and advocated a New Order which was nothing more than an old disorder.

Born in London, May 29, 1874, educated at St. Paul's School and the Slade School of Art, Gilbert Keith Chesterton was a journalist most of his life. Nothing bored him; everything bothered him, profitably. By the time he was sixty-two—he died June 14, 1936—he had written fantastic novels and serious plays, narrative poems and detective stories combining murder with sermonizing, solid biographies and whimsical essays that changed into parables, art criticisms and faintly disguised religious tracts; a total of more than one hundred works. The titles often furnished the clue: THE POET AND THE LUNATICS, THE SCANDAL OF FATHER BROWN, THE MAN WHO WAS THURSDAY, THE CLUB OF QUEER TRADES, and, most characteristically, TREMENDOUS TRIFLES.

The poetry sometimes escapes into quieter territory than the topsy-turvy land which Chesterton cultivated with such gusto. In verse the epigrams do not turn upon themselves so tirelessly and so tiresomely; the twist of thought is natural, witty and graceful. Hearing the phrase "vile dust," Chesterton imagines the earth in protest, the dead stones speaking, and the body of man remembering the day of Creation:

When God to all his paladins
By his own splendor swore
To make a fairer face than heaven,
Of dust and nothing more.

Chesterton delighted to beat the strong gongs of rhyme, notably in the long and booming LEPANTO. But his finest lines are in such restrained lyrics as A PRAYER IN DARKNESS and the tersely ironic ELEGY IN A COUNTRY CHURCHYARD, with its grim reply to Gray's resigned poem, on page 555.

A Prayer in Darkness

This much, O heaven—if I should brood or rave,
Pity me not; but let the world be fed,
Yea, in my madness if I strike me dead,
Heed you the grass that grows upon my grave.

If I dare snarl between this sun and sod,
  Whimper and clamor, give me grace to own,
  In sun and rain and fruit in season shown,
The shining silence of the scorn of God.

Thank God the stars are set beyond my power,
  If I must travail in a night of wrath;
  Thank God my tears will never vex a moth,
Nor any curse of mine cut down a flower.

Men say the sun was darkened: yet I had
  Thought it beat brightly, even on—Calvary:
  And He that hung upon the Torturing Tree
Heard all the crickets singing, and was glad.

Elegy in a Country Churchyard

The men that worked for England
They have their graves at home;
And bees and birds of England
About the cross can roam.

But they that fought for England,
Following a falling star,
Alas, alas, for England
They have their graves afar.

And they that rule in England
In stately conclave met,
Alas, alas, for England
They have no graves as yet.

AMY LOWELL

[1874–1925]

EXTRAORDINARILY prolific, Amy Lowell the poet was always breathlessly in the rear of Amy Lowell the propagandist. She flourished in controversy and lived on attack.

She was born February 9, 1874, in Brookline, Massachusetts.

There were famous pioneers, traders, and teachers in her family. James Russell Lowell, the New England poet, was her grandfather's cousin; her brother Percival was the astronomer who mapped out the much-disputed canals on Mars; another brother, Abbott Lawrence, was president of Harvard University. She had nursed vague hopes for the stage; but a glandular defect which made her seem even larger than she was precluded such a career—"I'm nothing but a disease," she complained with wry jocularity.

At twenty-eight she determined to be a poet, and for nine years she studied the classics and the works of her contemporaries; she experimented in every form. Her first book, published in her thirty-eighth year, was obviously imitative; she was still learning her craft.

At the beginning of the First World War, Amy Lowell went to London and "captured" the Imagist movement from Ezra Pound—Pound subsequently referred to the members as "Amygists." She reorganized the group, made it a fighting word, and stormed up and down the country on a crusade of furious emancipation. Smoking her famous cigars, she tyrannized over editors and brought every kind of influence into play—wealth, charm, family background, good fellowship, cajolery, and dictatorial commands—to carry forward her powerful offensive. The air seethed with loud efforts to "free" poetry from the shackles of rhyme, regular rhythm, and other traditional assets. But Amy Lowell could not be held by strictures—not even her own; she tried every poetic device and brilliantly violated the Imagist "manifesto." Her own poetry extended beyond the artificial tenets of the *vers libre* school, and her most colorful poem, PATTERNS, is a proof of her practice rather than her theories.

Patterns

I walk down the garden-paths,
And all the daffodils
Are blowing, and the bright blue squills.
I walk down the patterned garden-paths
In my stiff, brocaded gown.
With my powdered hair and jeweled fan,
I too am a rare
Pattern. As I wander down
The garden-paths.

My dress is richly figured,
And the train
Makes a pink and silver stain
On the gravel, and the thrift
Of the borders.
Just a plate of current fashion,
Tripping by in high-heeled, ribboned shoes.
Not a softness anywhere about me,
Only whalebone and brocade.
And I sink on a seat in the shade
Of a lime-tree. For my passion
Wars against the stiff brocade.
The daffodils and squills
Flutter in the breeze
As they please.
And I weep;
For the lime-tree is in blossom
And one small flower has dropped upon my bosom.

And the plashing of waterdrops
In the marble fountain
Comes down the garden-paths.
The dripping never stops.
Underneath my stiffened gown
Is the softness of a woman bathing in a marble basin,
A basin in the midst of hedges grown
So thick, she cannot see her lover hiding,
But she guesses he is near,
And the sliding of the water
Seems the stroking of a dear
Hand upon her.
What is Summer in a fine brocaded gown!
I should like to see it lying in a heap upon the ground.
All the pink and silver crumpled up on the ground.

I would be the pink and silver as I ran along the paths,
And he would stumble after,
Bewildered by my laughter.
I should see the sun flashing from his sword-hilt and the buckles
on his shoes.
I would choose
To lead him in a maze along the patterned paths,
A bright and laughing maze for my heavy-booted lover.
Till he caught me in the shade,
And the buttons of his waistcoat bruised my body as he clasped me,

Aching, melting, unafraid.
With the shadows of the leaves and the sundrops,
And the plopping of the waterdrops,
All about us in the open afternoon—
I am very like to swoon
With the weight of this brocade,
For the sun sifts through the shade.

Underneath the fallen blossom
In my bosom
Is a letter I have hid.
It was brought to me this morning by a rider from the Duke.
"Madam, we regret to inform you that Lord Hartwell
Died in action Thursday sen'night."
As I read it in the white, morning sunlight,
The letters squirmed like snakes.
"Any answer, Madam?" said my footman.
"No," I told him.
"See that the messenger takes some refreshment.
"No, no answer."
And I walked into the garden,
Up and down the patterned paths,
In my stiff, correct brocade.
The blue and yellow flowers stood up proudly in the sun,
Each one.
I stood upright too,
Held rigid to the pattern
By the stiffness of my gown;
Up and down I walked,
Up and down.

In a month he would have been my husband.
In a month, here, underneath this lime,
We would have broke the pattern;
He for me, and I for him,
He as Colonel, I as Lady,
On this shady seat.
He had a whim
That sunlight carried blessing.
And I answered, "It shall be as you have said."
Now he is dead.

In Summer and in Winter I shall walk
Up and down
The patterned garden-paths

In my stiff, brocaded gown.
The squills and daffodils
Will give place to pillared roses, and to asters, and to snow.
I shall go
Up and down
In my gown.
Gorgeously arrayed,
Boned and stayed.
And the softness of my body will be guarded from embrace
By each button, hook, and lace.
For the man who should loose me is dead,
Fighting with the Duke in Flanders,
In a pattern called a war.
Christ! What are patterns for?

A sick woman, Amy Lowell worked relentlessly. The labor on the two-volume biography of Keats may not have killed her, but it hastened her end. In her late forties she ruptured the small blood vessels of her eyes and suffered irremediable pains in the head and groin. After having been unsuccessfully operated upon more than once, she died of a paralytic stroke May 12, 1925. The following year her WHAT'S O'CLOCK was posthumously awarded the Pulitzer Prize.

Her ten volumes of poems, once so challenging a part of every "advanced" library, now look prim. The storm of controversy seems a tempest about technique in a shopworn teapot. But if Amy Lowell's poetry suffered because she had "everything except genius," if her "school," like most schools, is dated and academic, her spirit is not dead.

ROBERT FROST

[1875–1963]

THE most penetrating interpreter of modern New England, author of books whose areas seemed defined by their titles—NORTH OF BOSTON, MOUNTAIN INTERVAL, NEW HAMPSHIRE—Robert Frost was born in the Far West, in San Francisco, March 26, 1875. Both his parents had been schoolteachers, and both had been born in the East, where his forefathers had lived for eight generations.

His father died when Frost was ten, and his mother brought her children back to their paternal grandfather in Lawrence, Massachusetts. Here young Frost went to school and became a bobbin boy in one of the mills. At seventeen he entered Dartmouth, but remained there only a few months. He married at twenty, went to Harvard, and, after wrestling with the curriculum, left it within two years. He said he had stopped learning and might as well teach. Never a pedagogue but an "awakener," Frost taught in country schools and academies. He also made shoes, edited a weekly paper, and wrote poetry. In 1900 he began to farm at Derry, New Hampshire.

Eleven years later, confessing himself beaten as a farmer, Frost sold his acres and, with wife and four children, sailed for England. In England Frost encountered, for the first time, the world of writers and publishers. He did not like it, although his first two books were published in England. In 1915 Frost returned to America. He was now in his fortieth year, unknown and without funds.

Suddenly, with the American publication of NORTH OF BOSTON, Frost was famous. Critics of every school united to praise these stern bucolics, so different from the traditional English pastorals. Here was the very blood and sinew of a country, an embodiment of New England which transcended boundaries. This was poetic realism, but it was as teasing-tender as it was severe. The very opening lines were a racy invitation:

> I'm going out to clean the pasture spring;
> I'll only stop to rake the leaves away
> (And wait to watch the water clear, I may):
> I sha'n't be gone long.—You come too.

This was unquestionably a poetry of personal experience, but it was, nevertheless, full of symbols. The symbolic element was no less significant for being taken from the business of everyday life and for being conveyed by innuendo and understatement.

> Something there is that doesn't love a wall

says Frost, and the reader is free to accept the statement as a literal fact or as an implied protest against barriers. Philosophy and understatement continually play through Frost's talk-flavored blank verse. Even his most dramatic monologues are illuminated by the humor of reservation, of philosophic banter. BIRCHES begins with pure observation:

observation gives way to imagination; and the poem develops into something which is both a fantasy and a philosophy. THE DEATH OF THE HIRED MAN almost conceals its pathos in asides about self-respect and the way to build a load of hay, in unforgettable differences as to the definition of "home," in the sheer fancy of a moon falling down the west, "dragging the whole sky with it to the hills."

Birches

When I see birches bend to left and right
Across the line of straighter darker trees,
I like to think some boy's been swinging them.
But swinging doesn't bend them down to stay.
Ice-storms do that. Often you must have seen them
Loaded with ice a sunny winter morning
After a rain. They click upon themselves
As the breeze rises, and turn many-colored
As the stir cracks and crazes their enamel.
Soon the sun's warmth makes them shed crystal shells
Shattering and avalanching on the snow-crust—
Such heaps of broken glass to sweep away
You'd think the inner dome of heaven had fallen.
They are dragged to the withered bracken by the load,
And they seem not to break; though once they are bowed
So low for long, they never right themselves:
You may see their trunks arching in the woods
Years afterwards, trailing their leaves on the ground
Like girls on hands and knees that throw their hair
Before them over their heads to dry in the sun.
But I was going to say when Truth broke in
With all her matter-of-fact about the ice-storm
I should prefer to have some boy bend them
As he went out and in to fetch the cows—
Some boy too far from town to learn baseball,
Whose only play was what he found himself,
Summer or winter, and could play alone.
One by one he subdued his father's trees
By riding them down over and over again
Until he took the stiffness out of them,
And not one but hung limp, not one was left
For him to conquer. He learned all there was
To learn about not launching out too soon
And so not carrying the tree away

Clear to the ground. He always kept his poise
To the top branches, climbing carefully
With the same pains you use to fill a cup
Up to the brim, and even above the brim.
Then he flung outward, feet first, with a swish,
Kicking his way down through the air to the ground.

So was I once myself a swinger of birches;
And so I dream of going back to be.
It's when I'm weary of considerations,
And life is too much like a pathless wood
Where your face burns and tickles with the cobwebs
Broken across it, and one eye is weeping
From a twig's having lashed across it open.
I'd like to get away from earth awhile
And then come back to it and begin over.
May no fate willfully misunderstand me
And half grant what I wish and snatch me away
Not to return. Earth's the right place for love:
I don't know where it's likely to go better.
I'd like to go by climbing a birch tree,
And climb black branches up a snow-white trunk
Toward heaven, till the tree could bear no more,
But dipped its top and set me down again.
That would be good both going and coming back.
One could do worse than be a swinger of birches.

The Death of the Hired Man

Mary sat musing on the lamp-flame at the table
Waiting for Warren. When she heard his step,
She ran on tip-toe down the darkened passage
To meet him in the doorway with the news
And put him on his guard. "Silas is back."
She pushed him outward with her through the door
And shut it after her. "Be kind," she said.
She took the market things from Warren's arms
And set them on the porch, then drew him down
To sit beside her on the wooden steps.

"When was I ever anything but kind to him?
But I'll not have the fellow back," he said.
"I told him so last haying, didn't I?

'If he left then,' I said, 'that ended it.'
What good is he? Who else will harbor him
At his age for the little he can do?
What help he is there's no depending on.
Off he goes always when I need him most.
'He thinks he ought to earn a little pay,
Enough at least to buy tobacco with,
So he won't have to beg and be beholden.'
'All right,' I say, 'I can't afford to pay
Any fixed wages, though I wish I could.'
'Someone else can.' 'Then someone else will have to.'
I shouldn't mind his bettering himself
If that was what it was. You can be certain,
When he begins like that, there's someone at him
Trying to coax him off with pocket-money,—
In haying time, when any help is scarce.
In winter he comes back to us. I'm done."

"Sh! not so loud: he'll hear you," Mary said.

"I want him to: he'll have to soon or late."

"He's worn out. He's asleep beside the stove.
When I came up from Rowe's I found him here,
Huddled against the barn-door fast asleep,
A miserable sight, and frightening, too—
You needn't smile—I didn't recognize him—
I wasn't looking for him—and he's changed.
Wait till you see."

"Where did you say he'd been?"

"He didn't say. I dragged him to the house,
And gave him tea and tried to make him smoke.
I tried to make him talk about his travels,
Nothing would do: he just kept nodding off."

"What did he say? Did he say anything?"

"But little."

"Anything? Mary, confess
He said he'd come to ditch the meadow for me."

"Warren!"

"But did he? I just want to know."

"Of course he did. What would you have him say?
Surely you wouldn't grudge the poor old man
Some humble way to save his self-respect.
He added, if you really care to know,
He meant to clear the upper pasture, too.
That sounds like something you have heard before?
Warren, I wish you could have heard the way
He jumbled everything. I stopped to look
Two or three times—he made me feel so queer—
To see if he was talking in his sleep.
He ran on Harold Wilson—you remember—
The boy you had in haying four years since.
He's finished school, and teaching in his college.
Silas declares you'll have to get him back.
He says they two will make a team for work:
Between them they will lay this farm as smooth!
The way he mixed that in with other things.
He thinks young Wilson a likely lad, though daft
On education—you know how they fought
All through July under the blazing sun,
Silas up on the cart to build the load,
Harold along beside to pitch it on."

"Yes, I took care to keep well out of earshot."

"Well, those days trouble Silas like a dream.
You wouldn't think they would. How some things linger!
Harold's young college boy's assurance piqued him.
After so many years he still keeps finding
Good arguments he sees he might have used.
I sympathize. I know just how it feels
To think of the right thing to say too late.
Harold's associated in his mind with Latin.
He asked me what I thought of Harold's saying
He studied Latin like the violin
Because he liked it—that an argument!
He said he couldn't make the boy believe
He could find water with a hazel prong—
Which showed how much good school had ever done him.
He wanted to go over that. But most of all
He thinks if he could have another chance
To teach him how to build a load of hay—"

"I know, that's Silas' one accomplishment.
He bundles every forkful in its place,

And tags and numbers it for future reference,
So he can find and easily dislodge it
In the unloading. Silas does that well.
He takes it out in bunches like birds' nests.
You never see him standing on the hay
He s trying to lift, straining to lift himself."

"He thinks if he could teach him that, he'd be
Some good perhaps to someone in the world.
He hates to see a boy the fool of books.
Poor Silas, so concerned for other folk,
And nothing to look backward to with pride,
And nothing to look forward to with hope,
So now and never any different."

Part of a moon was falling down the west,
Dragging the whole sky with it to the hills.
Its light poured softly in her lap. She saw
And spread her apron to it. She put out her hand
Among the harp-like morning-glory strings,
Taut with the dew from garden bed to eaves,
As if she played unheard the tenderness
That wrought on him beside her in the night.
"Warren," she said, "he has come home to die:
You needn't be afraid he'll leave you this time."

"Home," he mocked gently.

"Yes, what else but home?
It all depends on what you mean by home.
Of course he's nothing to us, any more
Than was the hound that came a stranger to us
Out of the woods, worn out upon the trail."

"Home is the place where, when you have to go there,
They have to take you in."

"I should have called it
Something you somehow haven't to deserve."

Warren leaned out and took a step or two,
Picked up a little stick, and brought it back
And broke it in his hand and tossed it by.
"Silas has better claim on us, you think,
Than on his brother? Thirteen little miles

As the road winds would bring him to his door.
Silas has walked that far no doubt today.
Why didn't he go there? His brother's rich,
A somebody—director in the bank."

"He never told us that."

"We know it though."

"I think his brother ought to help, of course.
I'll see to that if there is need. He ought of right
To take him in, and might be willing to—
He may be better than appearances.
But have some pity on Silas. Do you think
If he'd had any pride in claiming kin
Or anything he looked for from his brother,
He'd keep so still about him all this time?"

"I wonder what's between them."

"I can tell you.
Silas is what he is—we wouldn't mind him—
But just the kind that kinsfolk can't abide.
He never did a thing so very bad.
He don't know why he isn't quite as good
As anyone. He won't be made ashamed
To please his brother, worthless though he is."

"I can't think Si ever hurt anyone."

"No, but he hurt my heart the way he lay
And rolled his old head on that sharp-edged chair-back
He wouldn't let me put him on the lounge.
You must go in and see what you can do.
I made the bed up for him there tonight.
You'll be surprised at him—how much he's broken.
His working days are done; I'm sure of it."

"I'd not be in a hurry to say that."

"I haven't been. Go, look, see for yourself.
But, Warren, please remember how it is:
He's come to help you ditch the meadow.
He has a plan. You mustn't laugh at him.
He may not speak of it, and then he may.
I'll sit and see if that small sailing cloud
Will hit or miss the moon."

It hit the moon.
Then there were three there, making a dim row,
The moon, the little silver cloud, and she.

Warren returned—too soon, it seemed to her,
Slipped to her side, caught up her hand and waited.

"Warren?" she questioned.

"Dead," was all he answered.

After returning to America Frost went back to the hills of his ancestors. But he was no longer allowed to farm in privacy, and, once again, he found himself teaching. He managed to avoid the classroom and act as a "poetic radiator" on lecture platforms and as "poet in residence" at the University of Michigan, Amherst, Harvard, and Dartmouth. He received the Pulitzer Prize in 1924, 1931, 1937, and 1942, the only American author to win that coveted award four times.

NORTH OF BOSTON had established the author as a dramatic poet; his power as a lyric poet came as a surprise, only a few critics remembering that Frost's first book, A BOY'S WILL, was a collection of lyrics. Like the monologues, the later lyrics are distinguished by inner seriousness and outer humor. They dispense with irrelevant ornaments; many of them are as spare as the New England mountains against which they are placed—"a further range" in every sense. Saying less than they imply, they stir the mind and lift the heart. Never have experience and intuition been more sensitively combined.

Fire and Ice

Some say the world will end in fire,
Some say in ice.
From what I've tasted of desire
I hold with those who favor fire.
But if it had to perish twice,
I think I know enough of hate
To say that for destruction ice
Is also great
And would suffice.

Tree at My Window

Tree at my window, window tree,
My sash is lowered when night comes on;
But let there never be curtain drawn
Between you and me.

Vague dream-head lifted out of the ground,
And thing next most diffuse to cloud,
Not all your light tongues talking aloud
Could be profound.

But, tree, I have seen you taken and tossed,
And if you have seen me when I slept,
You have seen me when I was taken and swept
And all but lost.

That day she put our heads together,
Fate had her imagination about her,
Your head so much concerned with outer,
Mine with inner, weather.

Stopping by Woods on a Snowy Evening

Whose woods these are I think I know.
His house is in the village though;
He will not see me stopping here
To watch his woods fill up with snow.

My little horse must think it queer
To stop without a farmhouse near
Between the woods and frozen lake
The darkest evening of the year.

He gives his harness bells a shake
To ask if there is some mistake.
The only other sound's the sweep
Of easy wind and downy flake.

The woods are lovely, dark and deep,
But I have promises to keep,
And miles to go before I sleep,
And miles to go before I sleep.

Frost's style, appealing to readers of every class, unites opposites. It is colloquial yet elevated, simple yet elusive. The fact has a way of turning into a fancy, and the playfulness sets off the profundities. Such a poem as TWO TRAMPS IN MUD-TIME turns a small autobiographical experience into a complete philosophy of life. The language is the language of everyday; the scene is an ordinary one; the images are familiar and exact without being commonplace. But it is the tone—part earnestness, part raillery—which is not only persuasive but immediately convincing.

Two Tramps in Mud-Time

Out of the mud two strangers came
And caught me splitting wood in the yard.
And one of them put me off my aim
By hailing cheerily "Hit them hard!"
I knew pretty well why he dropped behind
And let the other go on a way.
I knew pretty well what he had in mind:
He wanted to take my job for pay.

Good blocks of beech it was I split,
As large around as the chopping-block;
And every piece I squarely hit
Fell splinterless as a cloven rock.
The blows that a life of self-control
Spares to strike for the common good
That day, giving a loose to my soul,
I spent on the unimportant wood.

The sun was warm but the wind was chill.
You know how it is with an April day:
When the sun is out and the wind is still,
You're one month on in the middle of May.
But if you so much as dare to speak,
A cloud comes over the sunlit arch,
A wind comes off a frozen peak,
And you're two months back in the middle of March.

A bluebird comes tenderly up to alight
And fronts the wind to unruffle a plume,
His song so pitched as not to excite
A single flower as yet to bloom.

It is snowing a flake: and he half knew
Winter was only playing possum.
Except in color he isn't blue,
But he wouldn't advise a thing to blossom.

The water for which we may have to look
In summertime with a witching-wand,
In every wheelrut's now a brook,
In every print of a hoof a pond.
Be glad of water, but don't forget
The lurking frost in the earth beneath
That will steal forth after the sun is set
And show on the water its crystal teeth.

The time when most I loved my task
These two must make me love it more
By coming with what they came to ask.
You'd think I never had felt before
The weight of an ax-head poised aloft,
The grip on earth of outspread feet,
The life of muscles rocking soft
And smooth and moist in vernal heat.

Out of the woods two hulking tramps
(From sleeping God knows where last night
But not long since in the lumber camps).
They thought all chopping was theirs of right.
Men of the woods and lumber-jacks,
They judged me by their appropriate tool.
Except as a fellow handled an ax,
They had no way of knowing a fool.

Nothing on either side was said.
They knew they had but to stay their stay
And all their logic would fill my head:
As that I had no right to play
With what was another man's work for gain.
My right might be love but theirs was need.
And where the two exist in twain
Theirs was the better right—agreed.

But yield who will to their separation,
My object in life is to unite
My avocation and my vocation
As my two eyes make one in sight.

Only where love and need are one,
And the work is play for mortal stakes,
Is the deed ever really done
For Heaven and the future's sakes.

At sixty-seven Frost published A WITNESS TREE, a further proof that with the years his gifts had not declined, but had grown in firmness, clarity, and wisdom. Never had the poet written more succinctly, especially in the philosophic lyrics, laconic but loving. The new poems bore Frost's characteristic tone with surprising vigor: a reflective intensity, seasoned in experience, fresh in emotion.

Come In

As I came to the edge of the woods,
Thrush music—hark!
Now if it was dusk outside,
Inside it was dark.

Too dark in the woods for a bird
By sleight of wing
To better its perch for the night,
Though it still could sing.

The last of the light of the sun
That had died in the west
Still lived for one song more
In a thrush's breast.

Far in the pillared dark
Thrush music went—
Almost like a call to come in
To the dark and lament.

But no, I was out for stars:
I would not come in.
I meant not even if asked,
And I hadn't been.

"A poem," wrote Frost in a foreword to his COLLECTED POEMS, "begins in delight and ends in wisdom. The figure is the same as for love." Later, considering the quality of surprise in poetry, he added: "For me the initial delight is in the surprise of remembering something I didn't know I knew." The sentence may well explain Frost's hold upon his readers. They have not only learned something new; they have recalled, with a new significance, something old. They have remembered something they had forgotten they knew—and loved.

CARL SANDBURG
[1878–1967]

MORE ambitiously than any poet since Whitman, Carl Sandburg ranged over America. He celebrated steel mills and cornfields; he rhapsodized Chicago, "Hog Butcher for the World," and wrote nocturnes in a deserted brickyard. Born Charles August Sandburg, January 6, 1878, at Galesburg, Illinois, he was entitled to be known as the laureate of industrial America, for his was a life of many labors. At thirteen he went to work delivering milk. Before he was twenty he had earned a living as porter in a barbershop, sceneshifter, truck handler, dishwasher, turner's apprentice, and harvest hand. At twenty-one he enlisted in the Sixth Illinois Volunteers and was in Puerto Rico during the Spanish-American War. On his return to the United States, Sandburg entered Lombard College in his native Galesburg, became editor of the college paper, captain of the basketball team, and janitor of the gymnasium. After leaving college he was a salesman, advertising manager, and, for many years, a journalist.

Unknown as a poet until his thirty-ninth year, Sandburg startled the literary world with CHICAGO POEMS. It was alternately attacked and praised for its revolutionary ardor, its loosely vigorous language, and its unflinching realism. It was soon apparent, however, that Sandburg was using the common American speech, even slang, with surety, and that he was fulfilling Whitman's demand for "limber, lasting, fierce words." It also became evident that his fermenting violence was an overcompensation for a streak of mysticism, and that his toughness usually broke down into unashamed tenderness.

Cool Tombs

When Abraham Lincoln was shoveled into the tombs, he forgot the copperheads and the assassin . . . in the dust, in the cool tombs.

And Ulysses Grant lost all thought of con men and Wall Street, cash and collateral turned ashes . . . in the dust, in the cool tombs.

Pocahontas' body, lovely as a poplar, sweet as a red haw in November or a pawpaw in May, did she wonder? does she remember? . . . in the dust, in the cool tombs?

Take any streetful of people buying clothes and groceries, cheering a hero or throwing confetti and blowing tin horns . . . tell me if the lovers are losers . . . tell me if any get more than the lovers . . . in the dust . . . in the cool tombs.

Grass

Pile the bodies high at Austerlitz and Waterloo.
Shovel them under and let me work–
I am the grass; I cover all.

And pile them high at Gettysburg
And pile them high at Ypres and Verdun.
Shovel them under and let me work.
Two years, ten years, and passengers ask the conductor:
What place is this?
Where are we now?

I am the grass.
Let me work.

"Poetry," declared Sandburg, in one of his thirty-eight tentative definitions of poetry, "is a series of explanations of life, fading off into horizons too swift for explanation." And again, "Poetry is the opening and closing of a door, leaving those who look through to guess about what is seen during a moment." Sandburg lived up to his definitions. Even the most straightforward of his poems are allusive and somewhat enigmatic. Combining satire and sentiment, they leave the reader "to guess about what is seen during a moment."

Losers

If I should pass the tomb of Jonah
I would stop there and sit for a while;
Because I was swallowed one time deep in the dark
And came out alive after all.

If I pass the burial spot of Nero
I shall say to the wind, "Well, well!"—
I who have fiddled in a world on fire,
I who have done so many stunts not worth the doing.

I am looking for the grave of Sinbad too.
I want to shake his ghost-hand and say,
"Neither of us died very early, did we?"

And the last sleeping-place of Nebuchadnezzar—
When I arrive there I shall tell the wind:
"You ate grass; I have eaten crow—
Who is better off now or next year?"

Jack Cade, John Brown, Jesse James,
There too I could sit down and stop for a while.
I think I could tell their headstones:
"God, let me remember all good losers."

I could ask people to throw ashes on their heads
In the name of that sergeant at Belleau Woods.
Walking into the drumfires, calling his men,
"Come on, you . . . Do you want to live forever?"

After his early forties Sandburg spent most of his time traveling about the United States, examining folkways and assembling documents for his monumental work on Lincoln. In his fiftieth year he published THE AMERICAN SONGBAG, a collection of two hundred and eighty songs and ballads gathered from convicts and cowboys, work gangs and "play-parties," and from all people who sing "because they must." About one hundred of the songs had never been printed before. Six volumes were necessary to complete the ABRAHAM LINCOLN biography. The first two volumes, THE PRAIRIE YEARS, were printed in 1926; the last four volumes, THE WAR YEARS, appeared thirteen years later. His autobiographical ALWAYS THE YOUNG STRANGERS was published in 1953.

Sandburg's affirmations grew stronger with age. His passionate advocacy of the common man reaches its height in THE PEOPLE, YES. Written in his fifty-eighth year, the work is not only a combination of homely glories, "a synthesis of hyacinths and biscuits," but an omnibus of history and tall tales, gossip and prophecy. Here are the people, cheated and misled, but, beneath their skepticism, as wise as they are strong.

The People Will Live On

The people will live on.
The learning and blundering people will live on.
They will be tricked and sold and again sold
And go back to the nourishing earth for rootholds,
The people so peculiar in renewal and comeback,
You can't laugh off their capacity to take it.
The mammoth rests between his cyclonic dramas.

The people so often sleepy, weary, enigmatic,
is a vast huddle with many units saying:
"I earn my living.
I make enough to get by
and it takes all my time.
If I had more time
I could do more for myself
and maybe for others.
I could read and study
and talk things over
and find out about things.
It takes time.
I wish I had the time."

The people is a tragic and comic two-face:
hero and hoodlum: phantom and gorilla twist-
ing to moan with a gargoyle mouth: "They
buy me and sell me . . . it's a game . . .
sometime I'll break loose . . ."

Once having marched
Over the margins of animal necessity,
Over the grim line of sheer subsistence
Then man came
To the deeper rituals of his bones,
To the lights lighter than any bones,
To the time for thinking things over,
To the dance, the song, the story,
Or the hours given over to dreaming,
Once having so marched.

Between the finite limitations of the five senses
and the endless yearnings of man for the beyond
the people hold to the humdrum bidding of work and food
while reaching out when it comes their way
for lights beyond the prison of the five senses,
for keepsakes lasting beyond any hunger or death.
This reaching is alive.
The panderers and liars have violated and smutted it.
Yet this reaching is alive yet
for lights and keepsakes.

The people know the salt of the sea
and the strength of the winds
lashing the corners of the earth.
The people take the earth
as a tomb of rest and a cradle of hope.
Who else speaks for the Family of Man?
They are in tune and step
with constellations of universal law.

The people is a polychrome,
a spectrum and a prism
held in a moving monolith,
a console organ of changing themes,
a clavilux of color poems
wherein the sea offers fog
and the fog moves off in rain
and the labrador sunset shortens
to a nocturne of clear stars
serene over the shot spray
of northern lights.

The steel mill sky is alive.
The fire breaks white and zigzag
shot on a gun-metal gloaming.

Man is a long time coming.
Man will yet win.
Brother may yet line up with brother:

This old anvil laughs at many broken hammers.
There are men who can't be bought.
The fireborn are at home in fire.
The stars make no noise.
You can't hinder the wind from blowing.
Time is a great teacher.
Who can live without hope?

In the darkness with a great bundle of grief
the people march.
In the night, and overhead a shovel of stars for
keeps, the people march:
"Where to? what next?"

from THE PEOPLE, YES

JOHN MASEFIELD

[1878–1967]

EXCEPT during one short period Masefield wrote in a mood of reminiscence. Although his rhymed narratives were considered "ultrarealistic" and shocked many of his compatriots, Masefield was a traditionalist in love with the past and devoted to the spirit of romance, especially on the high seas. He was born June 1, 1878, in Herefordshire, son of a lawyer, but the growing boy refused to remain at a desk. At fourteen he shipped on a merchantman and became a wanderer for ten years. His ventures took him to America, where he worked in a Yonkers carpet factory (as recounted forty years later in IN THE MILL) and in a Greenwich Village saloon. He discovered Chaucer, and the robust humanity of the fourteenth-century poet inspired him to put his own way of life into verse. His sympathies were naturally not with "the princes and prelates and periwigged charioteers," but with:

The men of the tattered battalion which fights till it dies,
Dazed with the dust of the battle, the din and the cries,
The men with the broken heads and the blood running in their
eyes . . .

The sailor, the stoker of steamers, the man with the clout,
The chantyman bent at the halliards putting a tune to
the shout,
The drowsy man at the wheel and the tired look-out.

SALT WATER BALLADS is a collection of lyrics which are sometimes raffish, sometimes sentimental, written in the sailor's speech, and, considering that it was published in the poet's mid-twenties, curiously nostalgic.

Sea-Fever

I must go down to the seas again, to the lonely sea and the sky,
And all I ask is a tall ship and a star to steer her by,
And the wheel's kick and the wind's song and the white sail's
shaking,
And a gray mist on the sea's face and a gray dawn breaking.

I must go down to the seas again, for the call of the running tide
Is a wild call and a clear call that may not be denied;
And all I ask is a windy day with the white clouds flying,
And the flung spray and the blown spume, and the sea-gulls crying.

I must go down to the seas again to the vagrant gypsy life.
To the gull's way and the whale's way where the wind's like a
whetted knife;
And all I ask is a merry yarn from a laughing fellow-rover,
And quiet sleep and a sweet dream when the long trick's over.

In his thirties Masefield excited readers with a series of narrative poems or rhymed yarns about "common characters" who suffered violently, sinned and reformed, and mixed profanity with ecstasy. They were followed by REYNARD THE FOX, a poem about hunting by a man who did not hunt—the sympathy being with the fox—a poem that became a transcription of the spirit of rural England. It is said that this poem convinced the authorities that Masefield was entitled to the laureateship; succeeding Robert Bridges, he received the honor in 1930.

After becoming poet laureate, Masefield wrote with increasing determination and lessening power. Before he was sixty he had published more than seventy-five books of poems, plays, novels, essays, adaptations, studies of Shakespeare, public addresses, and stories for boys. The later verse is prolix and undistinguished, but the tediousness is forgotten in the stimulation of the early high-spirited and courageous syllables.

Tomorrow

Oh yesterday the cutting edge drank thirstily and deep,
The upland outlaws ringed us in and herded us as sheep,
They drove us from the stricken field and bayed us into keep;
        But tomorrow,
    By the living God, we'll try the game again!

Oh yesterday our little troop was ridden through and through,
Our swaying, tattered pennons fled, a broken, beaten few,
And all a summer afternoon they hunted us and slew;
        But tomorrow,
    By the living God, we'll try the game again!

And here upon the turret-top the bale-fire glowers red,
The wake-lights burn and drip about our hacked, disfigured dead,
And many a broken heart is here and many a broken head;
        But tomorrow,
    By the living God, we'll try the game again!

VACHEL LINDSAY

[1879–1931]

A MISSIONARY who preached the Gospel through a saxophone, an evangelist who spoke in terms of sheer fantasy, a patriot who saw America as a perpetual county fair, "every soul resident in the earth's one circus tent"—this was Vachel Lindsay, disciple of beauty and ballyhoo.

He was born November 10, 1879, in Springfield, Illinois, a city whose possibilities suggested a visionary future for the United States, a place that would restore lost Atlantis and rebuild Jerusalem on its green and pleasant soil.

Art was to be Lindsay's career; he studied drawing at the Art Institute of Chicago and the New York School of Art. But, after imitating Blake and Beardsley, he devoted himself to crusades. He lectured for the Anti-Saloon League, preached a "Gospel of Beauty" in the South, and tramped through the Middle West, exchanging a pamphlet of poems, RHYMES TO BE TRADED FOR BREAD, for food and a night's lodging. Restlessness was his demon, so he made it into a religion. He was Saint Francis and Johnny Appleseed in one.

In his first book, GENERAL WILLIAM BOOTH ENTERS INTO HEAVEN, Lindsay announced a new fusion. Uniting the old Greek chant with what he termed the "Higher Vaudeville," he combined religion and ragtime. He brought over into verse the blare of street-corner Salvationists, the syncopation of dance bands, the noise and nervous energy of whole communities. It was a new thing in American poetry, semibarbaric but deeply emotional, brilliantly colored, richly musical, and tremendously effective.

General William Booth Enters into Heaven

(TO BE SUNG TO THE TUNE OF "THE BLOOD OF THE LAMB" WITH INDICATED INSTRUMENTS)

I

(*Bass drum beaten loudly.*)
Booth led boldly with his big bass drum—
(Are you washed in the blood of the Lamb?)
The Saints smiled gravely and they said: "He's come."
(Are you washed in the blood of the Lamb?)
Walking lepers followed, rank on rank,
Lurching bravos from the ditches dank,
Drabs from the alleyways and drug fiends pale—
Minds still passion-ridden, soul-powers frail:—
Vermin-eaten saints with moldy breath,
Unwashed legions with the ways of Death—
(Are you washed in the blood of the Lamb?)

(*Banjos.*)
Every slum had sent its half-a-score
The round world over. (Booth had groaned for more.)
Every banner that the wide world flies
Bloomed with glory and transcendent dyes.

Big-voiced lasses made their banjos bang,
Tranced, fanatical they shrieked and sang:—
"Are you washed in the blood of the Lamb?"
Hallelujah! it was queer to see
Bull-necked convicts with that land make free.
Loons with trumpets blowed a blare, blare, blare
On, on upward thro' the golden air!
(Are you washed in the blood of the Lamb?)

II

(Bass drum slower and softer.)
Booth died blind and still by faith he trod,
Eyes still dazzled by the ways of God.
Booth led boldly, and he looked the chief,
Eagle countenance in sharp relief,
Beard a-flying, air of high command
Unabated in that holy land.

(Sweet flute music.)
Jesus came from out the court-house door,
Stretched his hands above the passing poor.
Booth saw not, but led his queer ones there
Round and round the mighty court-house square.
Yet in an instant all that blear review
Marched on spotless, clad in raiment new.
The lame were straightened, withered limbs uncurled
And blind eyes opened on a new, sweet world.

(Bass drum louder.)
Drabs and vixens in a flash made whole!
Gone was the weasel-head, the snout, the jowl!
Sages and sibyls now, and athletes clean,
Rulers of empires, and of forests green!

(Grand chorus of all instruments. Tambourines to the foreground.)
The hosts were sandaled, and their wings were fire!
(Are you washed in the blood of the Lamb?)
But their noise played havoc with the angel-choir.
(Are you washed in the blood of the Lamb?)
Oh, shout Salvation! it was good to see
Kings and Princes by the Lamb set free.
The banjos rattled and the tambourines
Jing-jing-jingled in the hands of Queens.

(Reverently sung, no instruments.)
And when Booth halted by the curb for prayer
He saw his Master thro' the flag-filled air.
Christ came gently with a robe and crown
For Booth the soldier, while the throng knelt down.
He saw King Jesus. They were face to face,
And he knelt a-weeping in that holy place.
Are you washed in the blood of the Lamb?

His reputation established with his first volume, Lindsay quickened the tempo and broadened his effects. He exploited his own dynamic personality and depended largely on exaggeration. His vision of America became a motley Nirvana, a congregation of pioneers and baseball players, Presidents and "movie queens," a country where such incongruous figures as William Jennings Bryan and John L. Sullivan, Andrew Jackson and P. T. Barnum, were enshrined not merely as symbols but as demigods.

Lindsay's comedy was only partly planned. The half-conscious humor made THE CONGO both grandiose and absurd; it turned THE KALLYOPE YELL from a college cheer into a rhapsody, and lifted THE DANIEL JAZZ into a grotesque extravaganza.

The Daniel Jazz

Beginning with a strain of "Dixie."

Darius the Mede was a king and a wonder.
His eye was proud, and his voice was thunder.
He kept bad lions in a monstrous den.
He fed up the lions on Christian men.

With a touch of "Alexander's Ragtime Band."

Daniel was the chief hired man of the land.
He stirred up the jazz in the palace band.
He whitewashed the cellar. He shovelled in the coal.
And Daniel kept a-praying:—"Lord save my soul."
Daniel kept a-praying "Lord save my soul."
Daniel kept a-praying "Lord save my soul."

Daniel was the butler, swagger and swell.
He ran up stairs. He answered the bell.
And he would let in whoever came a-calling:—
Saints so holy, scamps so appalling.
"Old man Ahab leaves his card.
Elisha and the bears are a-waiting in the yard.
Here comes Pharaoh and his snakes a-calling.

Here comes Cain and his wife a-calling.
Shadrach, Meshach and Abednego for tea.
Here comes Jonah and the whale,
And the Sea!
Here comes St. Peter and his fishing pole.
Here comes Judas and his silver a-calling.
Here comes old Beelzebub a-calling."
And Daniel kept a-praying:—"Lord save my soul."
Daniel kept a-praying:—"Lord save my soul."
Daniel kept a-praying:—"Lord save my soul."

His sweetheart and his mother were Christian and meek.
They washed and ironed for Darius every week.
One Thursday he met them at the door:—
Paid them as usual, but acted sore.

He said:—"Your Daniel is a dead little pigeon.
He's a good hard worker, but he talks religion."
And he showed them Daniel in the lions' cage.
Daniel standing quietly, the lions in a rage.
His good old mother cried:—
"Lord save him."
And Daniel's tender sweetheart cried:—
"Lord save him."

And she was a golden lily in the dew.
And she was as sweet as an apple on the tree
And she was as fine as a melon in the corn-field,
Gliding and lovely as a ship on the sea,
Gliding and lovely as a ship on the sea.

And she prayed to the Lord:—
"Send Gabriel. Send Gabriel."

King Darius said to the lions:—
"Bite Daniel. Bite Daniel.
Bite him. Bite him. Bite him!"

Thus roared the lions:—
"We want Daniel, Daniel, Daniel,
We want Daniel, Daniel, Daniel.
Grrrrrrrrrrrrrrrrrrrrrrrrrrrrrrrrrrrrrrrrrrrrrrrrr *Here the audience roars.*
Grrrrrrrrrrrrrrrrrrrrrrrrrrrrrrrrrrrrrrrrrrrrrrrrr"

And Daniel did not frown,
Daniel did not cry.

He kept on looking at the sky.
And the Lord said to Gabriel:—
"Go chain the lions down,
Go chain the lions down.
Go chain the lions down."

The audience sings this with the leader, to the old negro tune.

And *Gabriel* chained the lions,
And *Gabriel* chained the lions,
And *Gabriel* chained the lions,
And Daniel got out of the den,
And Daniel got out of the den,
And Daniel got out of the den.
And Darius said:—"You're a Christian child,"
Darius said:—"You're a Christian child,"
Darius said:—"You're a Christian child,"
And gave him his job again,
And gave him his job again,
And gave him his job again.

The golden dream could not be carried over into reality; it broke into bits of leaden memories. Lindsay began to grow ashamed of his "roaring, epic, ragtime tune"; he suddenly became sentimental and resuscitated the coy lace-valentine rhymes of his youth. He distrusted his hearers when they applauded, and despised them when he felt they were being entertained without being uplifted.

Baffled at fifty, desperately tired, Lindsay tried to retreat. He had traded too long upon fantasy. His creative strength was gone; he had exhausted himself and his audiences. At fifty-two the most demanded poet-performer of his day was no longer in demand. His faith shaken, his following lost, he considered himself a failure. On the night of December 5, 1931, he drank a bottle of Lysol, and died in the house in which he was born.

HAROLD MONRO

[1879–1932]

IT IS not easy to be charming and bizarre at the same time, but Harold Monro accomplished this remarkable fusion. His life was a mixture of fantasy and practicality, and his work reflected his life.

Born in Brussels of Scottish parents in 1879, Monro was taken to England as a child. Educated at Radley and Caius College, Cambridge, he became an author, editor, and publisher. In his thirty-third year, with the help of Alida Klemantaski, whom he later married, he founded the Poetry Bookshop, which became a center for the younger men and was responsible for the publication of the biennial GEORGIAN POETRY. Fashions changed, but Monro remained an influence until his death, March 16, 1932.

"The test of intellect is more important than tests of prosody or tradition," wrote Monro. "The passing event and its effect on the mind is everything." He endeavored to arrest the passing event, to capture the most trivial aspects of ordinary life, the creak of a door, the kettle puffing "a tentacle of breath," a piece of paper in the wastebasket shoving another piece, the "independent" pencil breaking its own point, the "ruminating" clock stirring its slow body, the minutes "pricking" their ears and running about. Making the inanimate not only animate but articulate, Monro shaped an odd verse that is both whimsical and metaphysical.

Solitude

When you have tidied all things for the night,
And while your thoughts are fading to their sleep,
You'll pause a moment in the late firelight,
Too sorrowful to weep.

The large and gentle furniture has stood
In sympathetic silence all the day
With that old kindness of domestic wood;
Nevertheless the haunted room will say:
"Someone must be away."

The little dog rolls over half awake,
Stretches his paws, yawns, looking up at you,
Wags his tail very slightly for your sake,
That you may feel he is unhappy too.

A distant engine whistles, or the floor
Creaks, or the wandering night-wind bangs a door.

Silence is scattered like a broken glass.
The minutes prick their ears and run about,

Then one by one subside again and pass
Sedately in, monotonously out.

You bend your head and wipe away a tear.
Solitude walks one heavy step more near.

WALLACE STEVENS

[1879–1955]

WALLACE STEVENS has been placed in more categories than any other contemporary poet. He has been called a symbolist, an unrealist, a platonist, an impressionist, an abstractionist whose poetry is "beyond good and evil, beyond hope and despair, beyond thought of any kind." The poet himself might not object to the comparison with the abstract painters, for one of his recent volumes was entitled THE MAN WITH THE BLUE GUITAR and was, by implication, a kind of homage to Picasso.

Stevens was born October 2, 1879, in Reading, Pennsylvania, of Dutch and German descent. Educated at Harvard, he was admitted to the bar in his twenty-fifth year, and practiced law in New York. Twelve years later he moved to Connecticut, specialized in insurance law, and, in 1934, became vice-president of the Hartford Accident and Indemnity Company.

"Wallace Stevens is a rhetorician," wrote Howard Baker, poet and teacher, "a persuasive artificer of the poetic line. . . . His poetry gets part of its loftiness from brilliant epithets and daring images." Stevens himself asks:

Is the function of the poet here mere sound,
Subtler than the ornatest prophecy
To stuff the ear?

There are no explicit answers in Stevens. Everything is implied; if anything is stated, it is stated in terms of something else. All the arts are wittily confused in a luxuriance which Stevens once called "the essential gaudiness of poetry." Thus, one of his most fanciful and delicately rounded poems, PETER QUINCE AT THE CLAVIER, appeals to all the senses. Sight and sound, taste and touch, contribute to make a comparison (always implied) between love and music, innocence and sensuality, the body's death and beauty's deathlessness. The four contrasting sections suggest the four movements of a symphony: the stately presentation of the main theme, the meditative slow movement, the mischievous scherzo, and the grave recapitulation of the finale.

Peter Quince at the Clavier

I

Just as my fingers on these keys
Make music, so the self-same sounds
On my spirit make a music, too.

Music is feeling, then, not sound;
And thus it is that what I feel,
Here in this room, desiring you,

Thinking of your blue-shadowed silk,
Is music. It is like the strain
Waked in the elders by Susanna:

Of a green evening, clear and warm,
She bathed in her still garden, while
The red-eyed elders, watching, felt

The basses of their beings throb
In witching chords, and their thin blood
Pulse pizzicati of Hosanna.

II

In the green water, clear and warm,
Susanna lay,
She searched
The touch of springs,
And found
Concealed imaginings.
She sighed,
For so much melody.

Upon the bank, she stood
In the cool
Of spent emotions.
She felt, among the leaves,
The dew
Of old devotions.

She walked upon the grass,
Still quavering.
The winds were like her maids
On timid feet,
Fetching her woven scarves,
Yet wavering.

A breath upon her hand
Muted the night.
She turned—
A cymbal crashed,
And roaring horns.

III

Soon, with a noise like tambourines,
Came her attendant Byzantines.

They wondered why Susanna cried
Against the elders by her side;

And as they whispered, the refrain
Was like a willow swept by rain.

Anon, their lamps' uplifted flame
Revealed Susanna and her shame.

And then, the simpering Byzantines
Fled, with a noise like tambourines.

IV

Beauty is momentary in the mind—
The fitful tracing of a portal;
But in the flesh it is immortal.

The body dies; the body's beauty lives.
So evenings die, in their green going,
A wave, interminably flowing.
So gardens die, their meek breath scenting
The cowl of Winter, done repenting.
So maidens die, to the auroral
Celebration of a maiden's choral.

Susanna's music touched the bawdy strings
Of those white elders; but, escaping,
Left only Death's ironic scraping.
Now, in its immortality, it plays
On the clear viol of her memory,
And makes a constant sacrament of praise.

Stevens' seventy-fifth birthday was marked by the publication of his COLLECTED POEMS, a book of more than five hundred pages. His explorations of the relation between the world of reality and the world of the imagination had always been appreciated, but his admirers were a small and rather exclusive group. By 1954, however, his scrupulously studied but evocative style had won a generation of readers, as well as honors, and had established a poetry of peculiar authority, "not ideas about the thing but the thing itself."

The Poems of Our Climate

I

Clear water in a brilliant bowl,
Pink and white carnations. The light
In the room more like a snowy air,
Reflecting snow. A newly-fallen snow
At the end of winter when afternoons return.
Pink and white carnations—one desires
So much more than that. The day itself
Is simplified: a bowl of white,
Cold, a cold porcelain, low and round,
With nothing more than the carnations there.

II

Say even that this complete simplicity
Stripped one of all one's torments, concealed
The evilly compounded, vital I
And made it fresh in a world of white,

A world of clear water, brilliant-edged,
Still one would want more, one would need more,
More than a world of white and snowy scents.

III

There would still remain the never-resting mind,
So that one would want to escape, come back
To what had been so long composed.
The imperfect is our paradise.
Note that, in this bitterness, delight,
Since the imperfect is so hot in us,
Lies in flawed words and stubborn sounds.

JAMES STEPHENS

[1882–1950]

JAMES STEPHENS' most characteristic poetry sounds as though it were dictated by a wise old elf interrupted by an irresponsible gamin. Actually, Stephens is a man who, playing with light diablerie in youth, is concerned in maturity with nothing less than essential truths. He was born in 1882 in Dublin. Too poor to receive a formal education, he wandered over Ireland and was "discovered" by the poet and economist George Russell ("Æ"). Stephens' INSURRECTIONS, published in his twenty-seventh year, received immediate praise for its mixture of anger and sensitivity. The inherent impishness grew more dominating in subsequent volumes. Like a grown-up child, the poet delighted to contemplate a world peopled with romantic pirates and dancing centaurs, a heaven with God's beard swinging "far out of sight behind the world's curve." His universe sometimes was overcast, as a lonely God roamed to "the fringes of the infinite," hoping to hide from the very thought of Space. But it was usually brisk with merriment, with madcap angels sowing poppy seeds, and an old reprobate squirming with laughter on God's throne for a moment, then tumbling down—

> Scraping old moons, and twisting, heels and head,
> A chuckle in the void.

Stephens' later philosophy is the expression of an Irish seer. It is universal—and debatable. But there is no arguing with the early "chuckle in the void." The poet died December 26, 1950.

What Thomas an Buile Said in a Pub

I saw God. Do you doubt it?
  Do you dare to doubt it?
I saw the Almighty Man. His hand
Was resting on a mountain, and
He looked upon the World and all about it:
I saw Him plainer than you see me now,
  You mustn't doubt it.

He was not satisfied;
  His look was all dissatisfied.
His beard swung on a wind far out of sight
Behind the world's curve, and there was light
Most fearful from His forehead, and He sighed,
"That star went always wrong, and from the start
  I was dissatisfied."

He lifted up His hand–
  I say He heaved a dreadful hand
Over the spinning Earth. Then I said, "Stay,
You must not strike it, God; I'm in the way;
And I will never move from where I stand."
He said, "Dear child, I feared that you were dead,"
  And stayed His hand.

WILLIAM CARLOS WILLIAMS

[1883–1963]

It is probable that the impartial exactness which marked the medical career of Dr. William Carlos Williams had its effect upon his poetry. He was born September 17, 1883, in Rutherford, New Jersey, where he always lived and practiced. Educated in New York, Switzerland, and the University of Pennsylvania, he was graduated in medicine in his twenty-fourth year. At twenty-six he published his first volume, and he pursued the dual career of poet and doctor thereafter.

When his COMPLETE COLLECTED POEMS appeared, it was evident

that at fifty-five Williams had progressed from an early preciosity to a full acceptance of the American idiom and the emotion "which clusters about common things." Williams regarded the objects of his scrutiny with such impartial affection that it was said no one could love anything as much as Williams loved everything. But there is no denying a power which gains impressiveness with further reading. In a lean colloquial speech Williams depicts the everyday world in small but vivid details. He cuts away ornate decoration and stresses not only the significance of the object but the emotion behind the object.

Tract

I will teach you my townspeople
how to perform a funeral—
for you have it over a troop
of artists—
unless one should scour the world—
you have the ground sense necessary.

See! the hearse leads.
I begin with a design for a hearse.
For Christ's sake not black—
nor white either—and not polished!
Let it be weathered—like a farm wagon—
with gilt wheels (this could be
applied fresh at small expense)
or no wheels at all:
a rough dray to drag over the ground.

Knock the glass out!
My God—glass, my townspeople!
For what purpose? Is it for the dead
to look out or for us to see
how well he is housed or to see
the flowers or the lack of them—
or what?

To keep the rain and snow from him?
He will have a heavier rain soon:
pebbles and dirt and what not.
Let there be no glass—

and no upholstery! phew!
and no little brass rollers
and small easy wheels on the bottom—
my townspeople what are you thinking of!

A rough plain hearse then
with gilt wheels and no top at all.
On this the coffin lies
by its own weight.

No wreaths please—
especially no hot-house flowers!
Some common memento is better,
something he prized and is known by:
his old clothes—a few books perhaps—
God knows what! You realize
how we are about these things,
my townspeople—
something will be found—anything—
even flowers if he had come to that.
So much for the hearse.

For heaven's sake though see to the driver!
Take off the silk hat! In fact
that's no place at all for him
up there unceremoniously
dragging our friend out to his own dignity!
Bring him down—bring him down!
Low and inconspicuous! I'd not have him ride
on the wagon at all—damn him—
the undertaker's understrapper!
Let him hold the reins
and walk at the side
and inconspicuously too!

Then briefly as to yourselves:
Walk behind—as they do in France,
seventh class, or, if you ride,
Hell take curtains! Go with some show
of inconvenience; sit openly—
to the weather as to grief.
Or do you think you can shut grief in?

What—from us? We who have perhaps
nothing to lose? Share with us
share with us—it will be money
in your pockets.

Go now
I think you are ready.

The Hounded Lovers

Where shall we go?
Where shall we go
who are in love?

Juliet went
to Friar Laurence's cell,
but we have no rest.

Rain water lies
on the hard-packed ground,
reflecting
the morning sky,

But where shall we go?
We cannot resolve ourselves
into a dew

Or sink into the earth.
Shall we postpone it
to Eternity?

The dry heads
of the goldenrod,
turned to stiff ghosts,

Jerk at their dead
stalks, signalling hieroglyphs
of grave warning.

Where shall we go?
The movement of benediction
does not turn back
the cold wind.

SARA TEASDALE

[1884–1933]

A FRANK and unhappy refrain ran through Sara Teasdale's verse. "Why am I unsatisfied?" she asked herself and the world, and replied with another question:

> O beauty, are you not enough?
> Why am I crying after love?

Her life was a sad and finally tragic pursuit of the answer. The physical facts are few. Sara Teasdale was born August 8, 1884, in St. Louis, Missouri. She traveled sporadically in Europe, meanwhile longing for America; but, once back, was restless at home. The poet Vachel Lindsay fell in love with her, but, though she was more than half in love with him, his exuberance frightened her even more than his eccentricities. At thirty she married a businessman, Ernst Filsinger, a devotee who should have been the perfect husband. But her health was never robust, and her temperament was too nervous. Unable to share her life with anyone, she retreated into a spinsterlike privacy. She did not resent the man; she resented marriage.

> My heart has grown rich with the passing of years,
> I have less need now than when I was young
> To share myself with every comer,
> Or shape my thoughts into words with my tongue.

The natural opposite of Anna Wickham, Sara Teasdale voiced no revolt. She was content to be a solitary. One day, fifteen years after her marriage, without a word to her most intimate friends, she went to Reno and obtained a divorce. In her mid-forties she was more alone than she had ever been, more alone than she wanted to be. She was not, as she had assured herself, "self-complete as a flower or a stone." Her poems grew more and more autumnal. Unlike the facile early stanzas, once so popular, the later lyrics are serene in their confession of love and loss.

> That what we never have, remains;
> It is the things we have that go.

The poetry began to sound premonitions of the end. The nostalgic strain of her youth was echoed in a somber key, the music more and more restrained.

Let It Be Forgotten

Let it be forgotten, as a flower is forgotten,
  Forgotten as a fire that once was singing gold,
Let it be forgotten for ever and ever,
  Time is a kind friend, he will make us old.

If anyone asks, say it was forgotten
  Long and long ago,
As a flower, as a fire, as a hushed footfall
  In a long-forgotten snow.

The death of Vachel Lindsay increased her sense of loss. Weakened by an attack of pneumonia, she suffered a nervous breakdown. A year and a month after Lindsay's suicide, she took an overdose of sleeping tablets and died January 28, 1933.

Until the last six years of her life Sara Teasdale wrote too easily and too much. The best of her poetry is characterized by the title of her ripest book, FLAME AND SHADOW. "The poet," she wrote to a friend, "should try to give his poem the quiet swiftness of flame, so that the reader will feel and not think while he is reading. But the thinking will come afterwards." There is no new trick of utterance, little surprise, and seemingly little thought in Sara Teasdale's melodious lines. The thinking comes afterwards.

I Shall Not Care

When I am dead and over me bright April
  Shakes out her rain-drenched hair,
Though you should lean above me broken-hearted,
  I shall not care.

I shall have peace, as leafy trees are peaceful
  When rain bends down the bough;
And I shall be more silent and cold-hearted
  Than you are now.

D. H. LAWRENCE

[1885–1930]

NO MAN ever tried to run away from himself more desperately than David Herbert Lawrence. "I wish I were going to Thibet," he wrote to a friend on the eve of one of his travels, "or Kamschatka—or Tahiti—to the ultima, ultima Thule . . . I feel sometimes I shall go mad because there is nowhere to go, no 'new world.' One of these days I shall be departing in some rash fashion to some foolish place."

Lawrence was born September 11, 1885, in Eastwood, a colliery town in Nottinghamshire. His father was a miner who drank himself into beating his wife and bullying David, the youngest of three sons. As a result Lawrence's affections were fixed upon his mother, an almost crippling attachment which is disclosed in Lawrence's best novel, the autobiographical SONS AND LOVERS. In youth he was a clerk, a teacher in a country school, and, in his twenty-sixth year, a novelist. At twenty-six, shortly after the death of his mother, which shook the foundations of his health, he fell in love with a married woman. She was Frieda von Richtofen, sister of a famous German flier, seven years his senior, mother of three children. They eloped, lived abroad, and, two years later, were married. But there was little peace for them in England. The First World War had started; the Lawrences, victims of spy-hunting fever, were hounded from place to place.

Lawrence's long pilgrimage began. He denounced the "artificial complexities of civilization" and left England, never to live there again. He became Poe's own "weary, wayworn wanderer," but for him there was no mothering "native shore." He tried living in Florence, Sicily, France, Ceylon, Australia, Tahiti, Mexico, New Mexico, back to Florence—always "departing in some rash fashion to some foolish place," always seeking the lost security, "the ultima, ultima Thule." He hated groups and colonies, but he was always trying to start a colony of his own; the pagan in him was opposed by the fanatical Puritan with an itch to reform.

An exhibition of his paintings was raided; three of his novels were censored and suppressed. Tubercular and self-tormented, Lawrence fought to the end. He died at forty-five on the French Riviera, March 2, 1930.

Sex and society were Lawrence's demonic preoccupations. Obsessed with the evils of civilization, he yearned for a primitive way of life, agitated for a state that, somehow, joined anarchy with dictatorship, and worshiped the unconscious. He made a fetish of instinct; he wrote of self-division and sex renewal as though his throat were "choked in its own crimson." Never before has there been such an exaltation and terror of passion, such a dependence on "the hot blood's blindfold art."

Love on the Farm

What large, dark hands are those at the window
Grasping in the golden light
Which weaves its way through the evening wind
    At my heart's delight?

Ah, only the leaves! But in the west
I see a redness suddenly come
Into the evening's anxious breast—
    'Tis the wound of love goes home!

The woodbine creeps abroad
Calling low to her lover:
    The sunlit flirt who all the day
    Has poised above her lips in play
    And stolen kisses, shallow and gay
    Of pollen, now has gone away—
        She woos the moth with her sweet, low word,
And when above her his moth-wings hover
Then her bright breast she will uncover
And yield her honey-drop to her lover.

Into the yellow, evening glow
Saunters a man from the farm below;
Leans, and looks in at the low-built shed
Where the swallow has hung her marriage bed.
    The bird lies warm against the wall.
    She glances quick her startled eyes
    Towards him, then she turns away
    Her small head, making warm display
    Of red upon the throat. Her terrors sway

Her out of the nest's warm, busy ball,
Whose plaintive cry is heard as she flies
In one blue stoop from out the sties
Into the twilight's empty hall.

Oh, water-hen, beside the rushes,
Hide your quaintly scarlet blushes,
Still your quick tail, lie still as dead,
Till the distance folds over his ominous tread!
The rabbit presses back her ears,
Turns back her liquid, anguished eyes
And crouches low; then with wild spring
Spurts from the terror of his oncoming;
To be choked back, the wire ring
Her frantic effort throttling:
Piteous brown ball of quivering fears!
Ah, soon in his large, hard hands she dies,
And swings all loose from the swing of his walk!
Yet calm and kindly are his eyes
And ready to open in brown surprise
Should I not answer to his talk
Or should he my tears surmise.

I hear his hand on the latch, and rise from my chair
Watching the door open; he flashes bare
His strong teeth in a smile, and flashes his eyes
In a smile like triumph upon me; then careless-wise
He flings the rabbit soft on the table board
And comes toward me: ah! the uplifted sword
Of his hand against my bosom! and oh, the broad
Blade of his glance that asks me to applaud
His coming! With his hand he turns my face to him
And caresses me with his fingers that still smell grim
Of rabbit's fur! God, I am caught in a snare!
I know not what fine wire is round my throat;
I only know I let him finger there
My pulse of life, and let him nose like a stoat
Who sniffs with joy before he drinks the blood.

And down his mouth comes to my mouth! and down
His bright dark eyes come over me, like a hood
Upon my mind! his lips meet mine, and a flood
Of sweet fire sweeps across me, so I drown
Against him, die, and find death good.

During his lifetime Lawrence published thirty-seven books; about ten more appeared posthumously—a body of strangely powerful work and a long record of suffering, anger, and ecstasy. In furious but eloquent prose and verse he lashed out against the stupidity of the intelligence; he extolled a fluid "vitalism," a sex-fearful, sex-driven mindlessness. Lawrence had an uncanny way of creating tension in a casual scene and precipitating a crisis with the turn of a dramatic phrase. His early impassioned, curiously feminine lyrics achieve as much intensity as the later tortured prose.

A Youth Mowing

There are four men mowing down by the Isar;
I can hear the swish of the scythe-strokes, four
Sharp breaths taken; yea, and I
Am sorry for what's in store.

The first man out of the four that's mowing
Is mine, I claim him once and for all;
Though it's sorry I am, on his young feet, knowing
None of the trouble he's led to stall.

As he sees me bringing the dinner, he lifts
His head as proud as a deer that looks
Shoulder-deep out of the corn; and wipes
His scythe-blade bright, unhooks

The scythe-stone and over the stubble to me.
Lad, thou hast gotten a child in me,
Laddie, a man thou'lt ha'e to be,
Yea, though I'm sorry for thee.

Somewhat disguised portraits of Lawrence appear in Kay Boyle's REST CURE, Aldous Huxley's POINT COUNTER POINT, in which Lawrence is "Mark Rampion," and Osbert Sitwell's MIRACLE ON SINAI. In the ten years following his death more than ten volumes of reminiscence, biography, and analysis of Lawrence were published. Harry T. Moore's more recent THE LIFE AND WORKS OF D. H. LAWRENCE is a comprehensive as well as an authoritative résumé.

EZRA POUND

[1885–]

AN ANGRY expatriate who, in his twenties, began scolding his mother country from the vantage point of Europe, Ezra Pound was born in Hailey, Idaho, October 30, 1885. At fifteen he entered the University of Pennsylvania and was graduated at twenty from Hamilton College. After a brief pedagogical career as "instructor with professorial functions," Pound simultaneously left the academic life and America. He lived in London, Paris, and various towns in Italy; except for a short and bellicose visit in 1939 he never returned to the United States. At forty he established himself on the Italian Riviera; at fifty-six he delivered broadsides over the official Fascist radio.

In May, 1945, when he was sixty, he was taken prisoner and indicted for treason. Brought to Washington, Pound escaped trial when four psychiatrists testified that the poet was of unsound mind. In 1946 he was committed to St. Elizabeth's Hospital as an insane person. His CANTOS, over which much good ink and bad blood had been spilled, remained unfinished. Pound had written seventy-one of the contemplated one hundred, one group (*The Pisan Cantos*) had been awarded the Bollingen Prize. The award roused a storm of protests, for it had been conferred by the Fellows of the Library of Congress and was assumed to have semiofficial approval. As a result, Pound became more of a controversial figure than ever.

Pound's work had several metamorphoses. It influenced many; its stress upon the exact word as opposed to a decorative generality was responsible for the Imagists. Yeats acknowledged that his change from a rhetorical to a colloquial speech was largely due to Pound, even though later in life Yeats declared that Pound had "more style than form . . . a style constantly interrupted, broken, twisted into nervous obsession, nightmare, stammering confusion," and that he wrote like "a brilliant improvisator translating at sight from an unknown Greek masterpiece."

But, though Pound changed his manner with his point of view, the poetry survives. Even the early verse is interesting; it blends the old poetic diction with a fiercely living speech.

Ballad of the Goodly Fere[1]

SIMON ZELOTES SPEAKETH IT SOMEWHILE AFTER THE CRUCIFIXION

Ha' we lost the goodliest fere o' all
For the priests and the gallows tree?
Aye, lover he was of brawny men,
O' ships and the open sea.

When they came wi' a host to take Our Man
His smile was good to see,
"First let these go!" quo' our Goodly Fere,
"Or I'll see ye damned," says he.

Aye, he sent us out through the crossed high spears,
And the scorn of his laugh rang free,
"Why took ye not me when I walked about
Alone in the town?" says he.

Oh we drank his "Hale" in the good red wine
When we last made company,
No capon priest was the Goodly Fere
But a man o' men was he.

I ha' seen him drive a hundred men
Wi' a bundle o' cords swung free,
When they took the high and holy house
For their pawn and treasury.

They'll no get him a' in a book I think
Though they write it cunningly;
No mouse of the scrolls was the Goodly Fere
But aye loved the open sea.

If they think they ha' snared our Goodly Fere
They are fools to the last degree.
"I'll go to the feast," quo' our Goodly Fere,
"Though I go to the gallows tree."

"Ye ha' seen me heal the lame and the blind,
And wake the dead," says he,
"Ye shall see one thing to master all:
'Tis how a brave man dies on the tree."

1 *Mate, companion.*

A son of God was the Goodly Fere
That bade us his brothers be.
I ha' seen him cow a thousand men.
I ha' seen him upon the tree.

He cried no cry when they drave the nails
And the blood gushed hot and free,
The hounds of the crimson sky gave tongue
But never a cry cried he.

I ha' seen him cow a thousand men
On the hills o' Galilee,
They whined as he walked out calm between,
Wi' his eyes like the gray o' the sea.

Like the sea that brooks no voyaging
With the winds unleashed and free,
Like the sea that he cowed at Gennesaret
Wi' twey words spoke' suddenly.

A master of men was the Goodly Fere,
A mate of the wind and sea,
If they think they ha' slain our Goodly Fere

They are fools eternally.
I ha' seen him eat o' the honey-comb
Sin' they nailed him to the tree.

At one time Pound let it be known that, when the CANTOS were completed, the work would have a monumental structure "like that of a Bach fugue"; at another time readers were told that it was a huge COMMEDIA, Pound having yet to construct the PARADISO which was to follow his INFERNO and PURGATORIO. In the CANTOS everything is derived and juxtaposed with a kind of inverted pedantry: Chinese ideograms and dialectics about Social Credit, magnificent seascapes and sniggering jokes, Greek myths and elliptical attacks on usury. No poem of the period succeeded so completely in splitting the critics far apart from each other. "The CANTOS form an unparalleled history of a world seen from the shores which are the home of our civilization," wrote Ford Madox Ford. "About the poems," demurred Edward Fitzgerald, "there hangs a dismal mist of unresolved confusion."

Canto I

And then went down to the ship,
Set keel to breakers, forth on the godly sea, and
We set up mast and sail on that swart ship,
Bore sheep aboard her, and our bodies also
Heavy with weeping, and winds from sternward
Bore us out onward with bellying canvas,
Circe's this craft, the trim-coifed goddess.
Then sat we amidships, wind jamming the tiller,
Thus with stretched sail, we went over sea till day's end.
Sun to his slumber, shadows o'er all the ocean,
Came we then to the bounds of deepest water,
To the Kimmerian lands, and peopled cities
Covered with close-webbed mist, unpierced ever
With glitter of sun-ray
Nor with stars stretched, nor looking back from heaven
Swartest night stretched over wretched men there.
The ocean flowing backward, came we then to the place
Aforesaid by Circe.
Here did they rites, Perimedes and Eurylochus,
And drawing sword from my hip
I dug the ell-square pitkin;
Poured we libations unto each the dead,
First mead and then sweet wine, water mixed with white flour.
Then prayed I many a prayer to the sickly death's-heads;
As set in Ithaca, sterile bulls of the best
For sacrifice, heaping the pyre with goods,
A sheep to Tiresias only, black and a bell-sheep.
Dark blood flowed in the fosse,
Souls out of Erebus, cadaverous dead, of brides
Of youths and of the old who had borne much;
Souls stained with recent tears, girls tender,
Men many, mauled with bronze lance heads,
Battle spoil, bearing yet dreory [1] arms,
These many crowded about me; with shouting,
Pallor upon me, cried to my men for more beasts;
Slaughtered the herds, sheep slain of bronze;
Poured ointment, cried to the gods,
To Pluto the strong, and praised Proserpine;
Unsheathed the narrow sword.

[1] Dreory: Anglo-Saxon for "bloody."

I sat to keep off the impetuous impotent dead,
Till I should hear Tiresias.
But first Elpenor came, our friend Elpenor,
Unburied, cast on the wide earth,
Limbs that we left in the house of Circe,
Unwept, unwrapped in sepulchre, since toils urged other.
Pitiful spirit. And I cried in hurried speech:
"Elpenor, how art thou come to this dark coast?
"Cam'st thou afoot, outstripping seamen?"
            And he in heavy speech:
"Ill fate and abundant wine. I slept in Circe's ingle.
"Going down the long ladder unguarded,
"I fell against the buttress,
"Shattered the nape-nerve, the soul sought Avernus.
"But thou, O King, I bid remember me, unwept, unburied,
"Heap up mine arms, be tomb by sea-board, and inscribed:
" 'A man of no fortune and with a name to come.'
"And set my oar up, that I swung mid fellows."

And Anticlea came, whom I beat off, and then Tiresias Theban,
Holding his golden wand, knew me, and spoke first:
"A second time? why? man of ill star,
"Facing the sunless dead and this joyless region?
"Stand from the fosse, leave me my bloody bever
"For soothsay."
            And I stepped back,
And he strong with the blood, said then: "Odysseus
"Shalt return through spiteful Neptune, over dark seas,
"Lose all companions." And then Anticlea came.
Lie quiet Divus. I mean that is Andreas Divus,
In officina Wecheli, 1538, out of Homer.
And he sailed, by Sirens and thence outward and away
And unto Circe.
            Venerandam,
In the Cretan's phrase, with the golden crown, Aphrodite,
Cypri munimenta sortita est, mirthful, oricalchi, with golden
Girdles and breast bands, thou with dark eyelids
Bearing the golden bough of Argicida.

ELINOR WYLIE

[1885–1928]

ELINOR WYLIE characterized herself in her love of patrician delicacies, fine filigree, mother-of-pearl, exquisite lacquers, silver trickery, a hummingbird's wing in hammered gold. Her quality, her very features, were depicted when she made a catalogue of what she considered beautiful people:

A tall throat, round as a column;
A mournful mouth, small and solemn,
Having, to confound the mourner,
Irony in either corner . . .

The eyes large and wide apart.
They carry a dagger in the heart
So keen and clean it never rankles . . .
They wear small bones in wrists and ankles.

Thomas Browne, she announced, was her spiritual brother and Shelley her *alter ego*. Beauty for her was innocent and ruthless; neither good nor evil, it had "the hard heart of a child." She studied herself in the carefully polished mirror of her verse. Sometimes the results of the scrutiny were disguised; sometimes they were purposely revealing, as in the last poem from the sequence WILD PEACHES, which, with her permission, was renamed PURITAN SONNET.

Puritan Sonnet

Down to the Puritan marrow of my bones
There's something in this richness that I hate.
I love the look, austere, immaculate,
Of landscapes drawn in pearly monotones.
There's something in my very blood that owns
Bare hills, cold silver on a sky of slate,
A thread of water, churned to milky spate
Streaming through slanted pastures fenced with stones.

I love those skies, thin blue or snowy gray,
Those fields sparse-planted, rendering meager sheaves;
That spring, briefer than apple-blossom's breath,
Summer, so much too beautiful to stay,
Swift autumn, like a bonfire of leaves,
And sleepy winter, like the sleep of death.

She was born Elinor Hoyt September 7, 1885, in Somerville, New Jersey, of, as she liked to say, "pure Pennsylvania stock." Her grandfather was Governor of Pennsylvania, and her father became Solicitor General during the administration of Theodore Roosevelt. At twenty she married Philip Hichborn, son of a rear admiral, and had a child; three years later she eloped with Horace Wylie. The couple lived in England until Wylie obtained his divorce; the outbreak of the First World War forced them back to America. In 1923 she divorced her second husband and married the poet William Rose Benét.

A small volume of poems, chiefly juvenilia, had been privately printed in England in 1912, but Elinor Wylie was thirty-six before NETS TO CATCH THE WIND, her first representative book of poems, appeared. The verse was delicate but firm; it had the clarity as well as the coldness of crystal. It was, like the woman herself, fastidious and subtle. Technically it was seldom less than brilliant; never has the texture of a winter day, the very silence of snow, been so skillfully communicated as in VELVET SHOES.

Velvet Shoes

Let us walk in the white snow
  In a soundless space;
With footsteps quiet and slow,
  At a tranquil pace,
  Under veils of white lace.

I shall go shod in silk,
  And you in wool,
White as a white cow's milk,
  More beautiful
  Than the breast of a gull.

We shall walk through the still town
In a windless peace;
We shall step upon white down,
Upon silver fleece,
Upon softer than these.

We shall walk in velvet shoes:
Wherever we go
Silence will fall like dews
On white silence below.
We shall walk in the snow.

Each successive volume increased Elinor Wylie's dexterity; the increase in depth was not evident until the last. In her forty-first year she went alone to England for an extended period of rest and novel writing. Two years later she suffered an almost fatal accident. Slightly paralyzed, she recovered sufficiently to return to America for the Christmas holiday and prepare the manuscript of ANGELS AND EARTHLY CREATURES for the press. On December 15, 1928, she made the final arrangement of her book. The following day she was dead.

Let No Charitable Hope

Now let no charitable hope
Confuse my mind with images
Of eagle and of antelope;
I am in nature none of these.

I was, being human, born alone;
I am, being woman, hard beset;
I live by squeezing from a stone
The little nourishment I get.

In masks outrageous and austere
The years go by in single file;
But none has merited my fear,
And none has quite escaped my smile.

Toward the last Elinor Wylie recognized the dangers of her own technique. She studied to disdain

The frail, the overfine
That tapers to a line
Knotted about the brain.

She endeavored to unite the elegance of the Elizabethans and the intellectual passion of the metaphysicians. It is significant that the title of her first book was a quotation from Webster and the last was from Donne.

WILLIAM ROSE BENÉT

[1886–1950]

ALL the Benéts were poets at heart, and most of them were poets in practice. Of Spanish origin, the family had come to Florida in the eighteenth century. The grandfather was an army man; the father followed the same career, but in him "burned a reverence for the word." He read verse to his children, and they—William Rose, Stephen Vincent, and Laura—published no less than thirty volumes of poetry.

William Rose Benét was born February 2, 1886, at Fort Hamilton in New York Harbor. He was expected to enter West Point and follow the career of his father and grandfather, but he attended the Sheffield Scientific School at Yale and was graduated in his twenty-second year. It was as a poet, however, not as a scientist, that he made his way. He was assistant editor of THE CENTURY MAGAZINE and helped found THE SATURDAY REVIEW OF LITERATURE. He was four times married, the second time to Elinor Wylie, the dedicatee of his most representative poems, MAN POSSESSED.

Although Benét has written voluminously, he is most himself in narrative verse. His early poetry is rich and exotic, but somewhat too highly spiced. The later work controls its wayward fantasy and restrains its cantering rhymes. The native scene emerges distinctly, and American myths from Harlem to the Wild West take on new vigor. The saga of JESSE JAMES, for example, is condensed in verse which is something like an old-fashioned dime novel and something like the Robin Hood story translated by Hollywood.

Jesse James

A DESIGN IN RED AND YELLOW FOR A NICKEL LIBRARY

Jesse James was a two-gun man,
(Roll on, Missouri!)
Strong-arm chief of an outlaw clan,
(From Kansas to Illinois!)
He twirled an old Colt forty-five;
(Roll on, Missouri!)
They never took Jesse James alive.
(Roll, Missouri, roll!)

Jesse James was King of the Wes';
(Cataracts in the Missouri!)
He'd a di'mon' heart in his lef' breas';
(Brown Missouri rolls!)
He'd a fire in his heart no hurt could stifle;
(Thunder, Missouri!)
Lion eyes an' a Winchester rifle.
(Missouri, roll down!)

Jesse James rode a pinto hawse;
Come at night to a water-cawse;
Tetched with the rowel that pinto's flank;
She sprung the torrent from bank to bank.

Jesse rode through a sleepin' town;
Looked the moonlit street both up an' down;
Crack-crack-crack, the street ran flames
An' a great voice cried, "I'm Jesse James!"

Hawse an' afoot they're after Jess!
(Roll on, Missouri!)
Spurrin' an' spurrın'—but he's gone Wes'.
(Brown Missouri rolls!)
He was ten foot tall when he stood in his boots;
(Lightnin' like the Missouri!)
More'n a match fer sich galoots.
(Roll, Missouri, roll!)

Jesse James rode outa the sage;
Roun' the rocks come the swayin' stage;
Straddlin' the road a giant stan's
An' a great voice bellers, "Throw up yer han's!"

Jesse raked in the di'mon' rings,
The big gold watches an' the yuther things;
Jesse divvied 'em then an' thar
With a cryin' child had lost her mar.

. . . .

They're creepin'; they're crawlin'; they're stalkin' Jess;
(Roll on, Missouri!)
They's a rumor he's gone much further Wes';
(Roll, Missouri, roll!)
They's word of a cayuse hitched to the bars
(Ruddy clouds on Missouri!)
Of a golden sunset that busts into stars.
(Missouri, roll down!)

Jesse James rode hell fer leather;
He was a hawse an' a man together;
In a cave in a mountain high up in air
He lived with a rattlesnake, a wolf, an' a bear.

Jesse's heart was as sof' as a woman;
Fer guts an' stren'th he was sooper-human;
He could put six shots through a woodpecker's eye
And take in one swaller a gallon o' rye.

They sought him here an' they sought him there,
(Roll on, Missouri!)
But he strides by night through the ways of the air;
(Brown Missouri rolls!)
They say he was took an' they say he is dead,
(Thunder, Missouri!)
But he ain't—he's a sunset overhead!
(Missouri down to the sea!)

Jesse James was a Hercules.
When he went through the woods he tore up the trees.
When he went on the plains he smoked the groun'
An' the hull lan' shuddered fer miles aroun'.

Jesse James wore a red bandanner
That waved on the breeze like the Star Spangled Banner;
In seven states he cut up dadoes.
He's gone with the buffler an' the desperadoes.

Yes, Jesse James was a two-gun man
        (Roll on, Missouri!)
The same as when this song began;
        (From Kansas to Illinois!)
An' when you see a sunset bust into flames
        (Lightnin' light the Missouri!)
Or a thunderstorm blaze—that's Jesse James!
        (Hear that Missouri roll!)

At fifty-five Benét published THE DUST WHICH IS GOD, a semi-autobiographical poem of 559 pages, a book which, offered as a novel, is a personal revelation and a picture of a period. It was awarded the Pulitzer Prize for the best book of poetry published in 1941. A few years later Benét suffered his first heart attack. He survived, however, and published two more collections of his vigorous verse before his death May 4, 1950.

H. D.

[1886–1961]

H. D. MAY not have been "the perfect Imagist," but she was the only one of the group who consistently put into practice the theory of pure imagery. Born Hilda Doolittle in Bethlehem, Pennsylvania, September 10, 1886, she entered Bryn Mawr in 1904, but was forced to leave after two years because of poor health. In her twenties she went abroad, met Ezra Pound, and, with him, helped to establish the Imagist movement. She married Richard Aldington, one of the members of the group, but separated from her husband at the end of the First World War and subsequently divorced him. She lived in England and Switzerland; except for a short visit, she never returned to the United States. To Amy Lowell's disappointment, she refused to be dragged into the *vers libre* controversy; she preferred to remain semianonymous, and signed her work only with her initials.

H. D.'s early poetry was so definitely sculptured that it arrested emotion at the source. The language was exact but chill; beauty seemed fixed in a frozen gesture. In HYMEN, however, and in the succeeding volumes H. D. added sensuousness to precision. As her work grew more formal it became more flexible in music, warmer in emotion. She wrote almost entirely of the classical world, but her insight brought ancient figures to life and made the remote immediate.

Never More Will the Wind

Never more will the wind
Cherish you again,
Never more will the rain.

Never more
Shall we find you bright
In the snow and wind.

The snow is melted,
The snow is gone,
And you are flown:

Like a bird out of our hand,
Like a light out of our heart,
You are gone.

from HYMEN

Lethe

Nor skin nor hide nor fleece
    Shall cover you,
Nor curtain of crimson nor fine
Shelter of cedar-wood be over you,
    Nor the fir-tree
    Nor the pine.

Nor sight of whin nor gorse
    Nor river-yew,
Nor fragrance of flowering bush,

Nor wailing of reed-bird to waken you.
    Nor of linnet
    Nor of thrush.

Nor word nor touch nor sight
    Of lover, you
Shall long through the night but for this:
The roll of the full tide to cover you
    Without question,
    Without kiss.

RUPERT BROOKE

[1887–1915]

RUPERT BROOKE's beauty, exquisite but masculine, was a legend even in his own day. He stood six feet tall, athletically built, his finely modeled head topped with a crown of shining hair. "A golden young Apollo," said Edward Thomas; "to look at, he was part of the youth of the world."

Son of an assistant master at Rugby, Rupert Brooke was born at the famous school for boys August 3, 1887. Educated at Rugby and King's College, Cambridge, he published his first book at twenty-four, a book of influences but radiant with Brooke's own pleasure in the senses. He was never halfhearted, never blasé. His intellectual appetite was enormous, his physical enthusiasm inexhaustible. "I want to walk a thousand miles," he wrote to a friend, "and write one thousand plays, and sing one thousand poems, and drink one thousand pots of beer, and kiss one thousand girls." He delighted, said Walter de la Mare, "in things for themselves, not merely for their beauty. . . . The theme of his poetry is the life of the mind, the senses, the feelings—life here and now." He was, in the most inclusive sense, the great lover.

The Great Lover

I have been so great a lover: filled my days
So proudly with the splendor of Love's praise,
The pain, the calm, and the astonishment,
Desire illimitable, and still content,

And all dear names men use, to cheat despair,
For the perplexed and viewless streams that bear
Our hearts at random down the dark of life.
Now, ere the unthinking silence on that strife
Steals down, I would cheat drowsy Death so far,
My night shall be remembered for a star
That outshone all the suns of all men's days.
Shall I not crown them with immortal praise
Whom I have loved, who have given me, dared with me
High secrets, and in darkness knelt to see
The inenarrable godhead of delight?
Love is a flame:—we have beaconed the world's night.
A city:—and we have built it, these and I.
An emperor:—we have taught the world to die.
So, for their sakes I loved, ere I go hence,
And the high cause of Love's magnificence,
And to keep loyalties young, I'll write those names
Golden for ever, eagles, crying flames,
And set them as a banner, that men may know,
To dare the generations, burn, and blow
Out on the wind of Time, shining and streaming. . . .

These I have loved:
White plates and cups, clean-gleaming,
Ringed with blue lines; and feathery, faëry dust;
Wet roofs, beneath the lamp-light; the strong crust
Of friendly bread; and many-tasting food;
Rainbows; and the blue bitter smoke of wood;
And radiant raindrops couching in cool flowers;
And flowers themselves, that sway through sunny hours,
Dreaming of moths that drink them under the moon;
Then, the cool kindliness of sheets, that soon
Smooth away trouble; and the rough male kiss
Of blankets; grainy wood; live hair that is
Shining and free; blue-massing clouds; the keen
Unpassioned beauty of a great machine;
The benison of hot water; furs to touch;
The good smell of old clothes; and other such—
The comfortable smell of friendly fingers,
Hair's fragrance, and the musty reek that lingers
About dead leaves and last year's ferns. . . .
Dear names,
And thousand others throng to me! Royal flames;
Sweet water's dimpling laugh from tap or spring;

Holes in the ground; and voices that do sing:
Voices in laughter, too; and body's pain,
Soon turned to peace; and the deep-panting train;
Firm sands; the little dulling edge of foam
That browns and dwindles as the wave goes home;
And washen stones, gay for an hour; the cold
Graveness of iron; moist black earthen mold;
Sleep; and high places; footprints in the dew;
And oaks; and brown horse-chestnuts, glossy-new;
And new-peeled sticks; and shining pools on grass;—
All these have been my loves. And these shall pass,
Whatever passes not, in the great hour,
Nor all my passion, all my prayers, have power
To hold them with me through the gate of Death.
They'll play deserter, turn with the traitor breath,
Break the high bond we made, and sell Love's trust
And sacramental covenant to the dust.
—Oh, never a doubt but, somewhere, I shall wake,
And give what's left of love again, and make
New friends now strangers. . . .
But the best I've known
Stays here, and changes, breaks, grows old, is blown
About the winds of the world, and fades from brains
Of living men, and dies.
Nothing remains.

O dear my loves, O faithless, once again
This one last gift I give: that after men
Shall know, and later lovers, far-removed
Praise you, "All these were lovely"; say, "He loved."

Shortly after the outbreak of the First World War Brooke entered the Royal Naval Division and took part in the unsuccessful defense of Antwerp. A few months later, on his way to the Dardanelles, he contracted blood poison and died April 23, 1915. He was buried on the island of Skyros, in his twenty-eighth year.

Ardor intensified the least of Brooke's activities. "He flung himself into the world," wrote Walter de la Mare, "as a wasp pounces into a cake shop, Hotspur into the fighting." As a soldier he was no less fervent than as a poet. In the sonnet which begins "If I should die, think only this of me," Brooke expressed a patriotism which lifts itself above nationalism, "all evil shed away, a pulse in the eternal mind."

The Soldier

If I should die, think only this of me;
  That there's some corner of a foreign field
That is for ever England. There shall be
  In that rich earth a richer dust concealed;
A dust whom England bore, shaped, made aware,
  Gave, once, her flowers to love, her ways to roam,
A body of England's breathing English air,
  Washed by the rivers, blest by suns of home.

And think, this heart, all evil shed away,
  A pulse in the eternal mind, no less
    Gives somewhere back the thoughts by England given;
Her sights and sounds; dreams happy as her day;
  And laughter, learnt of friends; and gentleness,
    In hearts at peace, under an English heaven.

EDITH SITWELL

[1887–1964]

THE Sitwells precipitated themselves upon a postwar England with eruptive satires, impudent burlesques, and megaphonic challenges. There were three of them—Osbert, Sacheverell, and Edith, the most gifted of the family—and they throve upon their well-advertised eccentricities. In prose and verse, as well as personal performances, they ridiculed the ingenuousness of the Georgians and mocked the nostalgia of their more wistful contemporaries. Gibing at the outworn patterns of class and the bankruptcy of an aristocratic culture, they purposely distorted statement and suggestion, cause and effect. For a literature of rhetoric they substituted a literature of nerves.

Descended from a line of Norman chiefs who reputedly accompanied William the Conqueror, Edith Sitwell was born at Scarborough, Yorkshire, in 1887. Her grandfather was the Earl of Londesborough, and her father was the fourth baronet of his line.

Oldest of the three Sitwell coadjutors, she was privately educated, traveled extensively, and left the imposing six-hundred-year-old estate to live in London. She wrote fluently: strange verse, orthodox biographies, criticisms of modern verse and appreciation of eighteenth-century styles.

Most of Miss Sitwell's poetry achieves its extraordinary effect by mixed syncopated rhythms, ironic overtones, and a skillful confusion of visual and tactile images. An AUBADE—or morning song—begins:

Jane, Jane,
Tall as a crane,
The morning light creaks down again.

Comb your cockscomb-ragged hair;
Jane, Jane, come down the stair.

Each dull blunt wooden stalactite
Of rain creaks, hardened by the light,

Sounding like an overtone
From some lonely world unknown . .

The light would show (if it could harden)
Eternities of kitchen-garden,

Cockscomb flowers that none will pluck,
And wooden flowers that 'gin to cluck.

Thus Miss Sitwell, seeing the early-morning world through the eyes of the kitchenmaid, pictures the overhanging rain hardening into a "dull blunt wooden stalactite," the "eternities" of kitchen garden always in need of weeding, and flowers that "cluck," since most of them are lorded over by the proud cockscombs. Character as well as scene is established by such a method, extreme but logical, just as a kind of adult nonsense is achieved by the jazz rhythms of a jingle which clangs its way into the mind:

When
Sir
Beelzebub called for his syllabub in the hotel in Hell
Where Proserpine fell,
Blue as the gendarmerie were the waves of the sea,
(Rocking and shocking the bar-maid.)
Nobody comes to give him his rum but the
Rim of the sky hippopotamus-glum . . .

Miss Sitwell's later work seldom depends on startling shifts of tone and kaleidoscopic images in surrealist nursery rhymes. The human drama becomes her concern, and she considers it with deep understanding and in simple terms. Her STILL FALLS THE RAIN is her most forceful. Using toward the climax two lines from the end of Marlowe's DOCTOR FAUSTUS (see page 328,) she dramatically combines the world of legend with the world of frightful actuality, and brings Gethsemane to bombed London.

Still Falls the Rain

(THE RAIDS, 1940: NIGHT AND DAWN)

Still falls the Rain—
Dark as the world of man, black as our loss—
Blind as the nineteen hundred and forty nails upon the Cross

Still falls the Rain
With a sound like the pulse of the heart that is changed to the hammer beat
In the Potter's Field, and the sound of the impious feet

On the Tomb:
Still falls the Rain
In the Field of Blood where the small hopes breed and the human brain
Nurtures its greed, that worm with the brow of Cain.

Still falls the Rain
At the feet of the Starved Man hung upon the Cross,
Christ that each day, each night, nails there, have mercy on us—
On Dives and on Lazarus:
Under the Rain the sore and the gold are as one.

Still falls the Rain—
Still falls the Blood from the Starved Man's wounded Side:
He bears in His Heart all wounds,—those of the light that died,
The last faint spark
In the self-murdered heart, the wounds of the sad uncomprehending dark,
The wounds of the baited bear,—
The blind and weeping bear whom the keepers beat
On his helpless flesh . . . the tears of the hunted hare.

Still falls the Rain—
Then—"O Ile leape up to my God! Who pulles me doune?—
See, see where Christ's blood streames in the firmament."
It flows from the Brow we nailed upon the tree
Deep to the dying, to the thirsting heart
That holds the fires of the world,—dark-smirched with pain
As Caesar's laurel crown.

Then sounds the voice of One who, like the heart of man,
Was once a child who among beasts has lain—
"Still do I love, still shed my innocent light, my Blood, for thee."

ROBINSON JEFFERS

[1887–1962]

To Robinson Jeffers the earth was hopelessly prostrate; people were "all compelled, all unhappy, all helpless"; human nature was "ignoble in its quiet times, mean in its pleasures, slavish in the mass"; civilization was a transient sickness, and consciousness a walking disease. There was only the alleviation of a "divinely superfluous beauty," of moments when a tragic deed might "shine terribly against the dark magnificence of things," and there was always death, the beautiful though capricious savior, "the gay child with the gypsy eyes." God is cruel; but Jeffers, like a pessimistic Francis Thompson, acknowledges there is no escaping him.

The world's God is treacherous and full of unreason; a torturer, but also
The only foundation and the only fountain.
Who fights him eats his own flesh and perishes of hunger.

In lines of uncompromising negation but indubitable force, Jeffers praises stoical defeat and desperate energy; he regards an unnecessary, and almost irrelevant, humanity with pity if not with active sympathy.

Unmeasured power, incredible passion, enormous craft: no thought apparent but burns darkly

Smothered with its own smoke in the human brain-vault: no thought
outside: a certain measure in phenomena:
The fountains of the boiling stars, the flowers on the foreland, the
ever-returning roses of dawn.

Robinson Jeffers was born January 10, 1887, in Pittsburgh, Pennsylvania. Son of a theologian and a mother twenty-three years younger than the father, Jeffers was brought up on the classics. His father took him through Europe on walking trips, and the boy attended schools in Switzerland and Germany for three years. His academic education was completed at Southern California in medicine and at the University of Washington in forestry.

A legacy left by a cousin made it possible for Jeffers to give all his time to writing; his first and most uncharacteristic volume, FLAGONS AND APPLES, was published at his own expense. At twenty-six he married Una Call Kuster and planned to go to England. But the news of the war turned them back to California, and when they reached Carmel, Jeffers said that "it was evident that we had come without knowing it to our inevitable place." There Jeffers remained. Years later, with his own hands and with the help of his twin sons, he built a house not of ivory but of headland boulders. Nevertheless, it was a tower in which he could immure himself and escape the world.

From 1912 on, Jeffers published twenty volumes of verse which announced a powerful if somewhat monotonous pessimism, a fearful hatred of life and an obsession with "self-destructive" love. "The calm to look for is the calm at the whirlwind's heart," he assured a war-torn world in BE ANGRY AT THE SUN. But all of his poems are not complacent preludes to Doomsday. Again and again Jeffers praises a violent individualism, and writes melodramatically about the tragic struggle toward self-realization, bitter recognition, and the ennobling power of pain.

Post Mortem

Happy people die whole, they are all dissolved in a moment, they
have had what they wanted,
No hard gifts; the unhappy
Linger a space, but pain is a thing that is glad to be forgotten; but
one who has given

His heart to a cause or a country,
His ghost may spaniel it a while, disconsolate to watch it. I was wondering how long the spirit
That sheds this verse will remain
When the nostrils are nipped, when the brain rots in its vault or bubbles in the violence of fire
To be ash in metal. I was thinking
Some stalks of the wood whose roots I married to the earth of this place will stand five centuries;
I held the roots in my hand,
The stems of the trees between two fingers; how many remote generations of women
Will drink joy from men's loins,
And dragged from between the thighs of what mothers will giggle at my ghost when it curses the axmen,
Gray impotent voice on the sea-wind,
When the last trunk falls? The women's abundance will have built roofs over all this foreland;
Will have buried the rock foundations
I laid here: the women's exuberance will canker and fail in its time and like clouds the houses
Unframe, the granite of the prime
Stand from the heaps: come storm and wash clean: the plaster is all run to the sea and the steel
All rusted; the foreland resumes
The form we loved when we saw it. Though one at the end of the age and far off from this place
Should meet my presence in a poem,
The ghost would not care but be here, long sunset shadow in the seams of the granite, and forgotten
The flesh, a spirit for the stone.

If most values are inconsequential in a universe which flees "the contagion of consciousness," the protesting mortal may learn hardihood from the rocks; he can draw courage, though no comfort, from the merciless air. There still is "the leopard-footed evening," and, for pure contemplation, the wings of hawks, the storm dances of gulls, the heartbreaking beauty which remains when there is no heart to break for it. And, sometimes, there is a brief joy of the written word, the "honey of peace in old poems."

To the Stone-Cutters

Stone-cutters fighting time with marble, you foredefeated
Challengers of oblivion,
Eat cynical earnings, knowing rock splits, records fall down,
The square-limbed Roman letters
Scale in the thaws, wear in the rain. The poet as well
Builds his monument mockingly;
For man will be blotted out, the blithe earth die, the brave sun
Die blind and blacken to the heart:
Yet stones have stood for a thousand years, and pained thoughts
    found
The honey of peace in old poems.

MARIANNE MOORE

[1887–   ]

Although Marianne Moore was born in St. Louis, Missouri, November 15, 1887, most of her life was spent in the eastern section of the United States. She received her B.A. from Bryn Mawr in 1909; taught stenography at the Indian School at Carlisle, Pennsylvania, from 1911 to 1915; and, after that, supported herself as a librarian, editor, and poet. As a poet she was daring but exceptionally modest; a few of her friends had to "pirate" some of her poems in order to have her first volume published in 1921. Three years later she received the Dial Award of two thousand dollars for "distinguished service for American Letters."

From that time on Miss Moore never lacked honors. Her SELECTED POEMS (1935) carried an introductory tribute by T. S. Eliot. WHAT ARE YEARS? (1941) received salvos of critical praise because of Miss Moore's fastidious discriminations, her odd but precious images, her extraordinarily skillful interweaving of curious quotations, obscure data, and fascinating references—a highly dexterous kind of poetic montage.

COLLECTED POEMS (1951) again proved that no poet owed more to more sources than Miss Moore, yet no contemporary author was more original. The book won all three of the most coveted awards:

the National Book Award, the Bollingen Prize, and the Pulitzer Prize. Among pages of brilliantly bizarre and queerly patterned verse, the volume contained "What Are Years?" and "In Distrust of Merits," which was ranked by many as the most eloquent poem of the Second World War. In the face of this national acclaim Miss Moore, consistently modest, declared: "I can see no reason for calling my work poetry except that there is no other category in which to put it. Anyone could do what I do, and I am, therefore, the more grateful that those whose judgment I trust should regard it as poetry."

What Are Years?

What is our innocence,
what is our guilt? All are
naked, none is safe. And whence
is courage: the unanswered question,
the resolute doubt—
dumbly calling, deadly listening—that
in misfortune, even death,
encourages others
and in its defeat, stirs

the soul to be strong? He
sees deep and is glad, who
accedes to mortality
and in his imprisonment, rises
upon himself as
the sea in a chasm, struggling to be
free and unable to be,
in its surrounding
finds its continuing.

So he who strongly feels,
behaves. The very bird,
grown taller as he sings, steels
his form straight up. Though he is captive,
his mighty singing
says, satisfaction is a lowly
thing, how pure a thing is joy.
This is mortality,
this is eternity.

In Distrust of Merits

Strengthened to live, strengthened to die for
  medals and positioned victories?
They're fighting, fighting, fighting the blind
  man who thinks he sees,—
who cannot see that the enslaver is
enslaved; the hater, harmed. O shining O
    firm star, O tumultuous
      ocean lashed till small things go
    as they will, the mountainous
      wave makes us who look, know

depth. Lost at sea before they fought! O
  star of David, star of Bethlehem,
O black imperial lion
  of the Lord—emblem
of a risen world—be joined at last, be
joined. There is hate's crown beneath which all is
    death; there's love's without which none
      is king; the blessed deeds bless
    the halo. As contagion
      of sickness makes sickness,

contagion of trust can make trust. They're
  fighting in deserts and caves, one by
one, in battalions and squadrons;
  they're fighting that I
may yet recover from the disease, *my*
self; some have it lightly, some will die. "Man's
    wolf to man?" And we devour
      ourselves? The enemy could not
    have made a greater breach in our
      defenses. One pilot-

ing a blind man can escape him, but
  Job disheartened by false comfort knew,
that nothing is so defeating
  as a blind man who
can see. O alive who are dead, who are
proud not to see, O small dust of the earth

that walks so arrogantly,
trust begets power and faith is
an affectionate thing. We
vow, we make this promise

to the fighting—it's a promise—"We'll
never hate black, white, red, yellow, Jew,
Gentile, Untouchable." We are
not competent to
make our vows. With set jaw they are fighting,
fighting, fighting,—some we love whom we know,
some we love but know not—that
hearts may feel and not be numb.
It cures me; or am I what
I can't believe in? Some

in snow, some on crags, some in quicksands,
little by little, much by much, they
are fighting fighting fighting that where
there was death there may
be life. "When a man is prey to anger,
he is moved by outside things; when he holds
his ground in patience patience
patience, that is action or
beauty," the soldier's defense
and hardest armor for

the fight. The world's an orphan's home. Shall
we never have peace without sorrow?
without pleas of the dying for
help that won't come? O
quiet form upon the dust, I cannot
look and yet I must. If these great patient
dyings—all these agonies
and woundbearings and blood shed—
can teach us how to live, these
dyings were not wasted.

Hate-hardened heart, O heart of iron,
iron is iron till it is rust.
There never was a war that was
not inward; I must
fight till I have conquered in myself what
causes war, but I would not believe it.

I inwardly did nothing,
  O Iscariotlike crime!
Beauty is everlasting
  and dust is for a time.

T. S. ELIOT

[1888–1965]

More than any other contemporary, Thomas Stearns Eliot influenced poetry on both sides of the Atlantic. A naturalized Englishman, he came of Puritan New England stock and was born in St. Louis, Missouri, September 26, 1888. He was educated at Harvard, of which a distant relative, Charles W. Eliot, was president, and concluded his studies at the Sorbonne and Oxford. In his mid-twenties he settled in London, taught at a boys' school, worked in a bank, became an assistant editor, and, in his infrequent leisure periods, wrote poetry and critical essays. His first collection created a small sensation. PRUFROCK, published in 1917, was immediately hailed as a new manner in English literature and belittled as an echo of Laforgue and the French symbolists to whom Eliot was indebted. The subject matter was strange; the technique was puzzling; the style—alternately sonorous and discordant, elaborately obscure and conversationally simple—was harshly criticized and widely imitated. The unprepared reader may have been shocked, but he was shocked awake.

The title poem, THE LOVE SONG OF J. ALFRED PRUFROCK, was written while Eliot was still an undergraduate at Harvard. One of his first, and still one of his most famous poems, it is a highly allusive picture of decadence against the background of a sterile society. Concentrating upon moments of intensity, omitting all but the most vital commentary, Eliot portrays a tired world through the eyes of an ultrafastidious and futile dilettante. The title sets the mood for the poem with its contrast between the alluring LOVE SONG and the unromantic business signature of J. ALFRED PRUFROCK. The irony is stressed by the quotation from Dante: "If I thought my answer were to one who could possibly return to this world, then this flame would shake no more. But since, if what I hear is true, that none ever did return alive from these depths, I answer you without fear of misrepresentation." The discord suggested by the title is continued in the opening stanza with its inviting promise:

Let us go then, you and I,
When the evening is spread out against the sky—

And then the shock, the reminder of the world's desperate illness:

Like a patient etherized upon a table.

The poem proceeds on this double level. The startling but logical images, the bizarre but suggestive epithets, carry on the contrary movement and emphasize the ambivalence of the central character. An inhibited, culture-ridden, prematurely old young man ("grown slightly bald"), Prufrock loses himself between intensities and trivialities, between great emotions and the futility of days spent in small talk—"In the room the women come and go, talking of Michelangelo"—and a life "measured out with coffee spoons." He is aware of passion everywhere about him, but he cannot rouse himself to it.

Do I dare
Disturb the universe?

. . . .

I know the voices dying with a dying fall
Beneath the music from a farther room.
So how should I presume?

Prufrock can live only in terms of art, images of the past, escapes from responsible action. He procrastinates and isolates himself, a modern Hamlet. But he does not flatter himself even here.

No! I am not Prince Hamlet, nor was meant to be;
Am an attendant lord, one that will do
To swell a progress, start a scene or two . . .
Full of high sentence, but a bit obtuse;
At times, indeed, almost ridiculous—
Almost, at times, the Fool.

The mockery of the prefatory quotation from Dante is now fully revealed as each verse presents the defeat of the irresolute Prufrock, too priggish for pathos, too sunk in his depths ever to "return alive" to this world.

The Love Song of J. Alfred Prufrock

S'io credesse che mia risposta fosse
A persona che mai tornasse al mondo,
Questa fiamma staria senza piu scosse.
Ma perciocche giammai di questo fondo
Non torno vivo alcun, s'i'odo il vero,
Senza tema d'infamia ti rispondo.

Let us go then, you and I,
When the evening is spread out against the sky
Like a patient etherized upon a table;
Let us go, through certain half-deserted streets,
The muttering retreats
Of restless nights in one-night cheap hotels
And sawdust restaurants with oyster-shells:
Streets that follow like a tedious argument
Of insidious intent
To lead you to an overwhelming question. . . .
Oh, do not ask, "What is it?"
Let us go and make our visit.

In the room the women come and go
Talking of Michelangelo.

The yellow fog that rubs its back upon the window-panes,
The yellow smoke that rubs its muzzle on the window-panes,
Licked its tongue into the corners of the evening,
Lingered upon the pools that stand in drains,
Let fall upon its back the soot that falls from chimneys,
Slipped by the terrace, made a sudden leap,
And seeing that it was a soft October night,
Curled once about the house, and fell asleep.

And indeed there will be time
For the yellow smoke that slides along the street,
Rubbing its back upon the window-panes;
There will be time, there will be time
To prepare a face to meet the faces that you meet;
There will be time to murder and create,
And time for all the works and days of hands
That lift and drop a question on your plate;

Time for you and time for me,
And time yet for a hundred indecisions,
And for a hundred visions and revisions,
Before the taking of a toast and tea.

In the room the women come and go
Talking of Michelangelo.

And indeed there will be time
To wonder, "Do I dare?" and, "Do I dare?"
Time to turn back and descend the stair,
With a bald spot in the middle of my hair—
(They will say: "How his hair is growing thin!")
My morning coat, my collar mounting firmly to the chin,
My necktie rich and modest, but asserted by a simple pin—
(They will say: "But how his arms and legs are thin!")
Do I dare
Disturb the universe?
In a minute there is time
For decisions and revisions which a minute will reverse.

For I have known them all already, known them all:
Have known the evenings, mornings, afternoons,
I have measured out my life with coffee spoons;
I know the voices dying with a dying fall
Beneath the music from a farther room.
    So how should I presume?

And I have known the eyes already, known them all—
The eyes that fix you in a formulated phrase,
And when I am formulated, sprawling on a pin,
When I am pinned and wriggling on the wall,
Then how should I begin
To spit out all the butt-ends of my days and ways?
    And how should I presume?

And I have known the arms already, known them all—
Arms that are braceleted and white and bare
(But in the lamplight, downed with light brown hair!)
Is it perfume from a dress
That makes me so digress?
Arms that lie along a table, or wrap about a shawl,
    And should I then presume?
    And how should I begin?

. . . .

Shall I say, I have gone at dusk through narrow streets
And watched the smoke that rises from the pipes
Of lonely men in shirt-sleeves, leaning out of windows? . . .

I should have been a pair of ragged claws
Scuttling across the floors of silent seas.

. . . .

And the afternoon, the evening, sleeps so peacefully!
Smoothed by long fingers,
Asleep . . . tired . . . or it malingers,
Stretched on the floor, here beside you and me.
Should I, after tea and cakes and ices,
Have the strength to force the moment to its crisis?
But though I have wept and fasted, wept and prayed,
Though I have seen my head (grown slightly bald) brought in upon
a platter,
I am no prophet—and here's no great matter;
I have seen the moment of my greatness flicker,
And I have seen the eternal Footman hold my coat, and snicker,
And in short, I was afraid.

And would it have been worth it, after all,
After the cups, the marmalade, the tea,
Among the porcelain, among some talk of you and me,
Would it have been worth while,
To have bitten off the matter with a smile,
To have squeezed the universe into a ball
To roll it toward some overwhelming question,
To say: "I am Lazarus, come from the dead,
Come back to tell you all, I shall tell you all"—
If one, settling a pillow by her head,
Should say: "That is not what I meant at all;
That is not it, at all."

And would it have been worth it, after all,
Would it have been worth while,
After the sunsets and the dooryards and the sprinkled streets,
After the novels, after the teacups, after the skirts that trail along
the floor—
And this, and so much more?—
It is impossible to say just what I mean!
But as if a magic lantern threw the nerves in patterns on a screen:
Would it have been worth while
If one, settling a pillow or throwing off a shawl,

And turning toward the window, should say:
"That is not it at all,
That is not what I meant, at all."

. . . .

No! I am not Prince Hamlet, nor was meant to be;
Am an attendant lord, one that will do
To swell a progress, start a scene or two,
Advise the prince; no doubt, an easy tool,
Deferential, glad to be of use,
Politic, cautious, and meticulous;
Full of high sentence, but a bit obtuse;
At times, indeed, almost ridiculous—
Almost, at times, the Fool.

I grow old. . . . I grow old. . . .
I shall wear the bottoms of my trousers rolled.

Shall I part my hair behind? Do I dare to eat a peach?
I shall wear white flannel trousers, and walk upon the beach.
I have heard the mermaids singing, each to each.

I do not think that they will sing to me.

I have seen them riding seaward on the waves
Combing the white hair of the waves blown back
When the wind blows the water white and black.
We have lingered in the chambers of the sea
By sea-girls wreathed with seaweed red and brown
Till human voices wake us, and we drown.

Most of Eliot's predecessors were divided between an allegiance to the past and a loyalty to the present scene. Eliot superimposed the past upon the present—usually an idealized past against a vulgar present—and interpreted modernity by quoting Donne, Webster, Wagner, without supplying quotation marks. His colleagues were searching for security in the midst of roaring industry, reclaimed farms, teeming prairies, sky-searching cities. Eliot uncovered death-in-life everywhere. He explored a land of drought, of vacant lots cluttered with old newspapers, of musty parlors and filthy alleys, of cheap boardinghouses and rivers sweating oil. The result of his exploration was THE WASTE LAND, which, with its extension of the death wish, characterized a whole period. THE HOLLOW MEN pictured a still more hopeless state of desolation. In bitter but precise phrases, here, as David Daiches wrote, "is an impressive symbolic picture of an age without belief, without value, without meaning." It is an exhausted world in which men gather on stony soil in a valley of dying stars, a world of "shape without form, gesture without motion," a world that ends:

Not with a bang but a whimper.

Eliot had reached an impasse. Having found the limits of emptiness, he groped back to an established faith. In his fortieth year he became an English citizen and declared himself a "classicist in literature, royalist in politics, and Anglo-Catholic in religion." The turning point is seen at its best in JOURNEY OF THE MAGI. Here Eliot turns away from ignominy to a contemplation of glory. After the hope of a new birth, it is impossible to remain at ease in disbelief or half-faith, "in the old dispensation." Salvation is glimpsed in a miraculous vision of the past, but the terms are the terms of the present.

Journey of the Magi

"A cold coming we had of it,
Just the worst time of the year
For a journey, and such a long journey:
The ways deep and the weather sharp,
The very dead of winter."
And the camels galled, sore-footed, refractory,
Lying down in the melting snow.
There were times we regretted
The summer palaces on slopes, the terraces,
And the silken girls bringing sherbet.
Then the camel men cursing and grumbling
And running away, and wanting their liquor and women,
And the night-fires going out, and the lack of shelters,
And the cities hostile and the towns unfriendly
And the villages dirty and charging high prices:
A hard time we had of it.
At the end we preferred to travel all night,
Sleeping in snatches,
With the voices singing in our ears, saying
That this was all folly.

Then at dawn we came down to a temperate valley,
Wet, below the snow line, smelling of vegetation;
With a running stream and a water-mill beating the darkness,
And three trees on the low sky,
And an old white horse galloped away in the meadow.
Then we came to a tavern with vine-leaves over the lintel,
Six hands at an open door dicing for pieces of silver,
And feet kicking the empty wine-skins.
But there was no information, and so we continued
And arriving at evening, not a moment too soon
Finding the place; it was (you may say) satisfactory.

All this was a long time ago, I remember,
And I would do it again, but set down
This set down
This: were we led all that way for
Birth or Death? There was a Birth, certainly,
We had evidence and no doubt. I had seen birth and death,
But had thought they were different; this Birth was
Hard and bitter agony for us, like Death, our death.
We returned to our places, these Kingdoms,
But no longer at ease here, in the old dispensation,
With an alien people clutching their gods.
I should be glad of another death.

Eliot's mother had written a poetic drama, SAVONAROLA; at forty-six Eliot wrote a poetic play about another martyr, Thomas Becket and entitled it MURDER IN THE CATHEDRAL. Its pious affirmation was accentuated by ASH WEDNESDAY, considered by many to be one of the best of modern religious poems. The religious note was extended and intensified in FOUR QUARTETS (1943), which ranged in tone from the flatly colloquial to the raptly mystical and revolved about the conflicts between time and timelessness. Five years later Eliot was awarded the Nobel Prize for his work "as a trail-blazing pioneer of modern poetry." His play THE COCKTAIL PARTY, produced in New York in 1950, received a somewhat puzzled but generally enthusiastic press. It was followed three years later by THE CONFIDENTIAL CLERK, an intellectual farce, part Euripides and part Gilbert and Sullivan, packed with nimble repartee. Even those who were confused by the ambiguities acknowledged the playwright's extraordinary compressions and allusiveness. In his sixties Eliot was the most discussed as well as the most widely quoted poet of his day.

JOHN CROWE RANSOM

[1888–   ]

INFLUENCED by T. S. Eliot but retaining his own Southern inflection, John Crowe Ransom fashioned a verse that was both bland and tart. Its characteristic tone, a grave gaiety, is heard even when the poet announces a death:

> Here lies a lady of beauty and high degree.
> Of chills and fever she died, of fever and chills,
> The delight of her husband, her aunts, an infant of three,
> And of medicos marveling sweetly on her ills.

Such mock seriousness identifies Ransom's idiom. Sometimes it grows so broadly pedantic that it approaches parody, but it is customarily balanced between philosophic irony and whimsical fantasy.

Lady Lost

This morning, there flew up the lane
A timid lady-bird to our bird-bath
And eyed her image dolefully as death;
This afternoon, knocked on our windowpane
To be let in from the rain.

And when I caught her eye
She looked aside, but at the clapping thunder
And sight of the whole earth blazing up like tinder
Looked in on us again most miserably,
Indeed as if she would cry.

So I will go out into the park and say,
"Who has lost a delicate brown-eyed lady
In the West End Section? Or has anybody
Injured some fine woman in some dark way,
Last night or yesterday?

"Let the owner come and claim possession,
No questions will be asked. But stroke her gently

With loving words, and she will evidently
Resume her full soft-haired white-breasted fashion,
And her right home and her right passion."

A minister's son, John Crowe Ransom was born April 30, 1888, in Pulaski, Tennessee. Educated at Vanderbilt University, he was a Rhodes scholar at Oxford, and returned to Tennessee to teach. He remained on the faculty of Vanderbilt University for more than twenty years, headed a group of controversial writers, and established THE FUGITIVE, a magazine of regional experiment. In his fiftieth year, he went to Kenyon College, Ohio, where he founded THE KENYON REVIEW.

A patrician agrarian, Ransom sweetens the soil and plows old ground for new crops. He localizes subjects as old as poetry itself. PIAZZA PIECE is typical. The setting is native; one can almost detect a Southern accent in the dialogue of the elderly suitor and the young charmer in her bower of roses. But the dying roses suggest the transiency of beauty, the "spectral" singing reminds us that the moon is a dead body—and the gray man in a dustcoat and the young belle become two figures in one of the oldest allegories: *Tod und das Mädchen,* Death and the Lady.

Piazza Piece

—I am a gentleman in a dustcoat trying
To make you hear. Your ears are soft and small
And listen to an old man not at all;
They want the young men's whispering and sighing.
But see the roses on your trellis dying
And hear the spectral singing of the moon—
For I must have my lovely lady soon.
I am a gentleman in a dustcoat trying.

—I am a lady young in beauty waiting
Until my truelove comes, and then we kiss.
But what gray man among the vines is this
Whose words are dry and faint as in a dream?
Back from my trellis, sir, before I scream!
I am a lady young in beauty waiting.

CONRAD AIKEN

[1889–   ]

CONRAD AIKEN's poetry is a long hymn to chaos, but it is a softly cushioned chaos set in a charmingly iridescent void. His tone poems (miscalled "symphonies") are heavy with blurred harmonies and a somewhat too cultivated vagueness. All the rough edges of reality are smoothed down through subtly diminished cadences in a kind of whispered incantation. It is a sweet mellifluousness, a little like Chopin's languid nocturnes and more than a little like the subaqueous, wavering melodies of Debussy:

> The profound gloom of bells among still trees,
> Like a rolling of huge boulders beneath seas.

Conrad Potter Aiken was born August 5, 1889, in Savannah, Georgia, of New England parents. Taken north as a child after the tragic deaths of his mother and father, he studied at Middlesex School in Massachusetts, and, at eighteen, entered Harvard, where he became class poet and close friend of T. S. Eliot. His studies had been interrupted by a trip abroad and, after graduating with the class of 1912, Aiken, with an independent income, was able to travel freely. In his early thirties he determined to live in England and made his home in the Sussex coast town of Rye. A few years later he returned to America as tutor in English at Harvard. For the next ten years Aiken alternated between both sides of the Atlantic. In his early fifties he apparently decided to settle down with his third wife on the Massachusetts shore, "the proud possessor of an eight-acre plantation of poison ivy in the midmost jungle of Cape Cod."

Aiken's passion for music is exceeded only by his preoccupation with psychoanalysis. The attempted fusion of the two has made his poetry distinctive but undisciplined. Too ready to respond to every twitch of the unconscious, Aiken's verse is nebular in structure, atmospheric, indefinite.

> There is a fountain in a wood
> Where wavering lies a moon:
> It plays to the slowly falling leaves
> A sleepy tune.

But indefiniteness is part of the charm of Aiken's verse. Few modern lyrics can match the hypnotic movement of THIS IS THE SHAPE OF THE LEAF. The poet takes a set of detached images and gives them a resonance which is abstract and yet poignant.

This Is the Shape of the Leaf

This is the shape of the leaf, and this of the flower,
And this the pale bole of the tree
Which watches its bough in a pool of unwavering water
In a land we never shall see.

The thrush on the bough is silent, the dew falls softly,
In the evening is hardly a sound. . . .
And the three beautiful pilgrims who come here together
Touch lightly the dust of the ground.

Touch it with feet that trouble the dust but as wings do,
Come shyly together, are still,
Like dancers who wait in a pause of the music, for music
The exquisite silence to fill . . .

This is the thought of the first, and this of the second,
And this the grave thought of the third:
"Linger we thus for a moment, palely expectant,
And silence will end, and the bird

"Sing the pure phrase, sweet phrase, clear phrase in the twilight
To fill the blue bell of the world;
And we, who on music so leaflike have drifted together,
Leaflike apart shall be whirled

"Into what but the beauty of silence, silence forever? . . ."
. . . This is the shape of the tree,
And the flower, and the leaf, and the three pale beautiful pilgrims:
This is what you are to me.

from PRIAPUS AND THE POOL

For many years Aiken continued to explore the dim reaches of self-analysis, particularly "the process of vicarious wish fulfillment by which civilized man enriches his circumscribed life." Nowhere were his investigations better rewarded than in SENLIN: A BIOGRAPHY, best of all in the section generally known as MORNING SONG. Here the poet dispenses with muffled chords and cloudy minors to evoke the immensities beneath the overfamiliar and just beyond the casual fact.

Morning Song

It is morning, Senlin says, and in the morning
When the light drips through the shutters like the dew,
I arise, I face the sunrise,
And do the things my fathers learned to do.
Stars in the purple dusk above the rooftops
Pale in a saffron mist and seem to die,
And I myself on a swiftly tilting planet
Stand before a glass and tie my tie.

Vine-leaves tap my window,
Dew-drops sing to the garden stones,
The robin chirps in the chinaberry tree
Repeating three clear tones.

It is morning. I stand by the mirror
And tie my tie once more.
While waves far off in a pale rose twilight
Crash on a white sand shore.
I stand by a mirror and comb my hair:
How small and white my face!—
The green earth tilts through a sphere of air
And bathes in a flame of space.
There are houses hanging above the stars
And stars hung under a sea . . .
And a sun far off in a shell of silence
Dapples my walls for me. . . .

It is morning, Senlin says, and in the morning
Should I not pause in the light to remember God?
Upright and firm I stand on a star unstable,
He is immense and lonely as a cloud.
I will dedicate this moment before my mirror
To him alone, for him I will comb my hair.
Accept these humble offerings, clouds of silence!
I will think of you as I descend the stair.

Vine-leaves tap my window,
The snail-track shines on the stones;
Dew-drops flash from the chinaberry tree
Repeating two clear tones.

It is morning, I awake from a bed of silence,
Shining I rise from the starless waters of sleep.
The walls are about me still as in the evening,
I am the same, and the same name still I keep.
The earth revolves with me, yet makes no motion,
The stars pale silently in a coral sky.
In a whistling void I stand before my mirror,
Unconcerned, and tie my tie.

There are horses neighing on far-off hills
Tossing their long white manes,
And mountains flash in the rose-white dusk,
Their shoulders black with rains. . . .
It is morning, I stand by the mirror
And surprise my soul once more;
The blue air rushes above my ceiling,
There are suns beneath my floor. . . .

. . . It is morning, Senlin says, I ascend from darkness
And depart on the winds of space for I know not where;
My watch is wound, a key is in my pocket,
And the sky is darkened as I descend the stair.
There are shadows across the windows, clouds in heaven,
And a god among the stars; and I will go
Thinking of him as I might think of daybreak
And humming a tune I know. . . .

Vine-leaves tap at the window,
Dew-drops sing to the garden stones,
The robin chirps in the chinaberry tree
Repeating three clear tones.

from SENLIN: A BIOGRAPHY

By the time he was fifty-two Aiken had published four novels, four collections of short stories, two books of criticism, and eighteen volumes of poetry. His SELECTED POEMS received the Pulitzer Prize award for 1930. A rapturous study of his work by Houston Peterson was aptly entitled THE MELODY OF CHAOS. His dreamlike autobiography, punningly entitled USHANT, appeared in 1952.

W. J. TURNER

[1889–1947]

Almost unknown in America, and read in England chiefly as a music critic, W. J. Turner has appeared in anthologies of modern verse because of one small lyric. It is a lyric of escape, of incantation; the spell is worked not only by the faraway associations but by the very sounding of exotic syllables: Chimborazo, Cotopaxi, Popocatepetl.

Romance

When I was but thirteen or so
  I went into a golden land,
Chimborazo, Cotopaxi
  Took me by the hand.

My father died, my brother too,
  They passed like fleeting dreams,
I stood where Popocatepetl
  In the sunlight gleams.

I dimly heard the master's voice
  And boys far-off at play—
Chimborazo, Cotopaxi
  Had stolen me away.

I walked in a great golden dream
  To and fro from school—
Shining Popocatepetl
  The dusty streets did rule.

I walked home with a gold dark boy
  And never a word I'd say;
Chimborazo, Cotopaxi
  Had taken my speech away.

I gazed entranced upon his face
  Fairer than any flower—
O shining Popocatepetl,
  It was thy magic hour.

The houses, people, traffic seemed
  Thin fading dreams by day;
Chimborazo, Cotopaxi,
  They had stolen my soul away!

Walter James Turner was born in 1889 in Melbourne, Australia, where his father was organist in St. Paul's Pro-Cathedral. Educated at Scotch College, Melbourne, Turner went to Europe at seventeen, studied in Germany, and traveled for almost five years through the Continent and South Africa. At twenty-seven he became music critic of THE NEW STATESMAN; at thirty he wrote dramatic criticism for THE LONDON MERCURY; at thirty-two he was literary editor of THE DAILY HERALD. Before he was fifty, Turner had published two plays, a fantastic novel, seven volumes of essays, fifteen books of verse, and the best critical biographies of Berlioz and Mozart. He was planning still larger works when he died in his fifty-eighth year.

EDNA ST. VINCENT MILLAY

[1892–1950]

AT NINETEEN Edna St. Vincent Millay, born February 22, 1892, in Rockland, Maine, wrote an extraordinary poem of more than two hundred lines. Entitled RENASCENCE, it began as nonchalantly, and almost as aimlessly, as a child's rhyme:

All I could see from where I stood
Was three long mountains and a wood;
I turned and looked another way,
And saw three islands in a bay.

Imperceptible, with scarcely a change in tone, the poem reached a climax of exaltation:

God, I can push the grass apart
And lay my finger on Thy heart!

Nothing Miss Millay wrote subsequently recaptured that ecstasy; only the later sonnets compensated with a sad wisdom for the dazzled innocence. The sonnets, scattered through ten books and gathered in one volume in Miss Millay's fiftieth year, range from Elizabethan rhetoric to contemporary plain speaking. Even the thinnest of them are craftsmanlike exercises, and the best of them are superb uses of the form.

Pity Me Not

Pity me not because the light of day
At close of day no longer walks the sky;
Pity me not for beauties passed away
From field and thicket as the year goes by;
Pity me not the waning of the moon,
Nor that the ebbing tide goes out to sea,
Nor that a man's desire is hushed so soon,
And you no longer look with love on me.

This have I known always: love is no more
Than the wide blossom which the wind assails,
Than the great tide that treads the shifting shore,
Strewing fresh wreckage gathered in the gales.
Pity me that the heart is slow to learn
What the swift mind beholds at every turn.

Miss Millay attended Vassar and, after her graduation in 1917, supported herself by writing short stories under pseudonyms and by acting with the Provincetown Players. Her Greenwich Village days are reflected in the arch cleverness and flippant protests of A FEW FIGS FROM THISTLES. The serious poet triumphs in SECOND APRIL, published in Miss Millay's twenty-ninth year. Disillusion takes the place of banter; the fears of age and death—Miss Millay's foreboding leitmotifs—sound their warnings. In 1923 she was awarded the Pulitzer Prize and, in the same year, married Eugen Jan Boissevain and moved to the Berkshires. There she became a recluse and something of a legend; she died there October 19, 1950.

Her critics often accused her of forcing her emotion and simulating passion "at the pitch of romantic extravagance." But, for the most part, the artistry is admirable. At its best, real feeling dominates, more than verbally inspired; delight and despair sometimes combine in an effortless nobility. The lapses in taste, the seemingly fatal blemishes, are forgotten in her triumphs.

On Hearing a Symphony of Beethoven

Sweet sounds, oh, beautiful music, do not cease!
Reject me not into the world again.
With you alone is excellence and peace,
Mankind made plausible, his purpose plain.
Enchanted in your air benign and shrewd,
With limbs a-sprawl and empty faces pale,
The spiteful and the stingy and the rude
Sleep like the scullions in the fairy-tale.
This moment is the best the world can give:
The tranquil blossom on the tortured stem.
Reject me not, sweet sounds! oh, let me live,
Till Doom espy my towers and scatter them,
A city spell-bound under the aging sun.
Music my rampart, and my only one.

Many of the sonnets are lyrical in effect, and many of the early lyrics are as direct and unaffected as a girl singing to please herself. The later work is quite different. Experience brings no happiness to the mature poet. A crepuscular light throws long shadows over the landscape. The key is the key of loss. "Gone, gone again is summer, the lovely." "Now goes under, and I watch it go under, the sun that will not rise again." "When evening darkens the water and the stream is dull."

Autumn is no less on me that a rose
Hugs the brown bough and sighs before it goes.

The music darkens with unhappy knowledge, with the mutations of love and the permanence of death.

Dirge Without Music

I am not resigned to the shutting away of loving hearts in the hard
 ground.
So it is, and so it will be, for so it has been, time out of mind:
Into the darkness they go, the wise and the lovely. Crowned
With lilies and with laurel they go; but I am not resigned.

Lovers and thinkers, into the earth with you.
Be one with the dull, the indiscriminate dust.
A fragment of what you felt, of what you knew,
A formula, a phrase remains,—but the best is lost.

The answers quick and keen, the honest look, the laughter, the love,—
They are gone. They have gone to feed the roses. Elegant and curled
Is the blossom. Fragrant is the blossom. I know. But I do not approve.
More precious was the light in your eyes than all the roses in the world.

Down, down, down into the darkness of the grave
Gently they go, the beautiful, the tender, the kind;
Quietly they go, the intelligent, the witty, the brave.
I know. But I do not approve. And I am not resigned.

Although this poet's work has been liberally, and at times hysterically, applauded, one sonnet has been insufficiently praised. TO JESUS ON HIS BIRTHDAY is the utterance of a frustrated idealist. Discarding the note of personal romanticism, she speaks with a bitterness and broken pride, a human cry against disappointing humanity. It is a declaration which has the ring of timelessness.

To Jesus on His Birthday

For this your mother sweated in the cold,
For this you bled upon the bitter tree:
A yard of tinsel ribbon bought and sold;
A paper wreath; a day at home for me.
The merry bells ring out, the people kneel;
Up goes the man of God before the crowd;
With voice of honey and with eyes of steel
He drones your humble gospel to the proud.
Nobody listens. Less than the wind that blows
Are all your words to us you died to save.
O Prince of Peace! O Sharon's dewy Rose!
How mute you lie within your vaulted grave.
The stone the angel rolled away with tears
Is back upon your mouth these thousand years.

ARCHIBALD MACLEISH

[1892–]

THE last thing that Archibald MacLeish would have predicted was that he would become executive librarian of the Library of Congress and a recognized, though often anonymous, voice of government. A champion of the advance guard in literature, he admired originality wherever he found it. Before he achieved his own idiom, he experimented with every modern device and never grudged to pay tribute to his predecessors.

Archibald MacLeish, lawyer, teacher, soldier, editor, and always a poet, was born May 7, 1892, at Glencoe, Illinois. His father, "a cold, tall rigorous man of beautiful speech," was a Chicago merchant born in Scotland; his mother, who had taught at Vassar and was his father's third wife, came from a Connecticut seafaring family. MacLeish attended Hotchkiss School, hated it, and went to Yale, where he distinguished himself in athletics. His prowess on the football and swimming teams did not prevent him from winning a Phi Beta Kappa key. Being graduated at twenty-three, he entered the Harvard Law School and, in the second year, led his class. At twenty-four he married. At twenty-five he joined a hospital unit, went to France, was transferred to the field artillery, and had the rank of captain when the First World War ended.

Upon his return to the United States after the armistice, MacLeish taught for a year in the Harvard Law School, entered a Boston attorney's office, and practiced for three years. Suddenly, in 1923, he closed his desk and, armed with an independent income, went abroad with his wife and two children. For five years he traveled about Europe, visited Persia, and spent a summer in Normandy. In early 1929 he went to Mexico, following the route of Cortez from the coast inland. The result of his journey (plus the reading of Bernal Díaz del Castillo's TRUE HISTORY OF THE CONQUEST OF NEW SPAIN) was CONQUISTADOR, which won the Pulitzer Prize for 1933.

The chief characteristic of MacLeish's poetry is its employment of old devices for new ends. Alliteration and assonance take on fresh values in his vivid lines; brusque phrases alternating with long suspended sentences create a surprising tension. No modern poet has used repetition—that dangerous contrivance—with such effectiveness.

Even the formal sonnet has a new sound and dramatic power, as in the imaginative THE END OF THE WORLD.

The End of the World

Quite unexpectedly as Vasserot
The armless ambidextrian was lighting
A match between his great and second toe
And Ralph the lion was engaged in biting
The neck of Madame Sossman while the drum
Pointed, and Teeny was about to cough
In waltz-time swinging Jocko by the thumb–
Quite unexpectedly the top blew off.

And there, there overhead, there, there, hung over
Those thousands of white faces, those dazed eyes,
There in the starless dark, the poise, the hover,
There with vast wings across the canceled skies,
There in the sudden blackness, the black pall
Of nothing, nothing, nothing–nothing at all.

Suspense and imagination emphasize MacLeish's later work, from THE POT OF EARTH, written at thirty-one, to THE LAND OF THE FREE, a "sound track" published in his forty-sixth year. A poem should not only state and suggest, it should act, says MacLeish:

A poem should not mean
But be.

Such poems as EPISTLE TO BE LEFT IN THE EARTH and IMMORTAL AUTUMN have lives of their own. They transcend commentary; they have implications that look forward and backward in time.

Epistle to Be Left in the Earth

. . . It is colder now
there are many stars
we are drifting
North by the Great Bear
the leaves are falling

The water is stone in the scooped rocks
                                        to southward
Red sun gray air
                    the crows are
Slow on their crooked wings
                            the jays have left us
Long since we passed the flares of Orion
Each man believes in his heart he will die
Many have written last thoughts and last letters
None know if our deaths are now or forever
None know if this wandering earth will be found

We lie down and the snow covers our garments
I pray you
        you (if any open this writing)
Make in your mouths the words that were our names
I will tell you all we have learned
                                    I will tell you everything
The earth is round
                    there are springs under the orchards
The loam cuts with a blunt knife
                                    beware of
Elms in thunder
                    the lights in the sky are stars
We think they do not see
                            we think also
The trees do not know nor the leaves of the grasses
                                                    hear us
The birds too are ignorant
                            Do not listen
Do not stand at dark in the open windows
We before you have heard this
                                they are voices
They are not words at all but the wind rising
Also none among us has seen God
(. . . We have thought often
The flaws of sun in the late and driving weather
Pointed to one tree but it was not so)
As for the nights I warn you the nights are dangerous
The wind changes at night and the dreams come

It is very cold
                there are strange stars near Arcturus

Voices are crying an unknown name in the sky

Immortal Autumn

I speak this poem now with grave and level voice
In praise of autumn of the far-horn-winding fall
I praise the flower-barren fields the clouds the tall
Unanswering branches where the wind makes sullen noise

I praise the fall it is the human season now
No more the foreign sun does meddle at our earth
Enforce the green and thaw the frozen soil to birth
Nor winter yet weigh all with silence the pine bough

But now in autumn with the black and outcast crows
Share we the spacious world the whispering year is gone
There is more room to live now the once secret dawn
Comes late by daylight and the dark unguarded goes

Between the mutinous brave burning of the leaves
And winter's covering of our hearts with his deep snow
We are alone there are no evening birds we know
The naked moon the tame stars circle at our eaves

It is the human season on this sterile air
Do words outcarry breath the sound goes on and on
I hear a dead man's cry from autumn long since gone

I cry to you beyond this bitter air.

PUBLIC SPEECH, issued in MacLeish's forty-fourth year, marked a turning point. The poet determinedly faced the material of his day and the problems of the American scene. A few years later he wrote the first, and still the most important, verse play for radio, THE FALL OF THE CITY, and followed it, in 1938, with the equally impressive anti-Fascist AIR RAID. In 1939 he was appointed librarian of the Library of Congress. In 1941, continuing to serve as librarian, he became director of the Office of Facts and Figures. After World War II, MacLeish taught at Harvard; his COLLECTED POEMS received the Pulitzer Prize award in 1953.

It was charged that, having discovered the power of suggestion, poets were forcing it beyond the limits of intelligibility. MacLeish kept his symbols under control; even the private allusions were always part of a communication. Some critics found YOU, ANDREW MARVELL puzzling in purpose and willfully obscure in title. But the intention is as clear as the poem itself, one of the most beautiful of contemporary lyrics. A lyric of gradual cadences and slow tension, the suspense is achieved by the varying pictures of night's ominous approach and the colorful associations of exotic places; it is heightened by the lack of punctuation, sustained by the cumulative intensity of the one long sentence. And the title? The poet gently reminds us that another poet, Andrew Marvell (see page 480), warned his "coy mistress" of the "always rising of the night" and "the deserts of vast eternity"—

> But at my back I always hear
> Time's winged chariot hurrying near.

The "shadow of the night comes on . . ." And the deeper sense is suggested by the persistent echo in time.

You, Andrew Marvell

And here face down beneath the sun
And here upon earth's noonward height
To feel the always coming on
The always rising of the night

To feel creep up the curving east
The earthly chill of dusk and slow
Upon those under lands the vast
And ever-climbing shadow grow

And strange at Ecbatan the trees
Take leaf by leaf the evening strange
The flooding dark about their knees
The mountains over Persia change

And now at Kermanshah the gate
Dark empty and the withered grass
And through the twilight now the late
Few travelers in the westward pass

And Baghdad darken and the bridge
Across the silent river gone
And through Arabia the edge
Of evening widen and steal on

And deepen on Palmyra's street
The wheel rut in the ruined stone
And Lebanon fade out and Crete
High through the clouds and overblown

And over Sicily the air
Still flashing with the landward gulls
And loom and slowly disappear
The sails above the shadowy hulls

And Spain go under and the shore
Of Africa the gilded sand
And evening vanish and no more
The low pale light across that land

Nor now the long light on the sea—

And here face downward in the sun
To feel how swift how secretly
The shadow of the night comes on. . . .

MacLeish is not only a poet but an interpreter of the spirit which animates poetry. This is attested by his prose, in particular by an excerpt from a recent essay: "In that great unfinished definition of poetry in which Aristotle distinguished poetry from history he said: History draws things which have happened, but poetry things which may possibly happen. . . . The possibility of which Aristotle speaks is human possibility. In this time in which everything is possible except the spirit to desire and the love to choose, poetry becomes again the one deliverer of the people."

WILFRED OWEN

[1893–1918]

Dead at twenty-five, Wilfred Owen left a few lyrics and sonnets that must be reckoned among the most moving poems produced by any war. Born March 18, 1893, at Oswestry, England, Owen was educated at Birkenhead Institute and London University, and spent some time in France as a private tutor. At the outbreak of the war he joined a rifle corps and, although his health had been impaired since childhood, fought steadily for two years until he was invalided home. A year later he returned to the front, and was awarded the Military Cross for gallantry. A month after receiving the honor, and a week before the armistice, Owen was killed in action, November 4, 1918. His one book was not published until nearly two years after his death.

Unknown at the time of his death, Owen influenced poets that followed him twenty years later. His peculiar suspensions, consonances and dissonances, were adopted by such postwar poets as W. H. Auden and Stephen Spender. Owen's efforts to find substitutes for rhyme—substitutes which, because of their unexpectedness, would enrich the verse—are best illustrated in STRANGE MEETING, perhaps the most powerfully projected of all war poems.

Strange Meeting

It seemed that out of the battle I escaped
Down some profound dull tunnel, long since scooped
Through granites which Titanic wars had groined.
Yet also there encumbered sleepers groaned,
Too fast in thought or death to be bestirred.
Then, as I probed them, one sprang up, and stared
With piteous recognition in fixed eyes,
Lifting distressful hands as if to bless.
And by his smile, I knew that sullen hall;
By his dead smile I knew I stood in Hell.
With a thousand pains that vision's face was grained;
Yet no blood reached there from the upper ground,
And no guns thumped, or down the flues made moan.
"Strange, friend," I said, "here is no cause to mourn."
"None," said the other, "save the undone years,
The hopelessness. Whatever hope is yours,
Was my life also; I went hunting wild
After the wildest beauty in the world,
Which lies not calm in eyes, or braided hair,
But mocks the steady running of the hour,
And if it grieves, grieves richlier than here.
For by my glee might many men have laughed,
And of my weeping something has been left,
Which must die now. I mean the truth untold,
The pity of war, the pity war distilled.

Now men will go content with what we spoiled,
Or, discontent, boil bloody, and be spilled.
They will be swift with swiftness of the tigress,
None will break ranks, though nations trek from progress
Courage was mine, and I had mystery,
Wisdom was mine, and I had mastery;
To miss the march of this retreating world
Into vain citadels that are not walled.
Then when much blood had clogged their chariot-wheels
I would go up and wash them from sweet wells,
Even with truths that lie too deep for taint.
I would have poured my spirit without stint
But not through wounds; not on the cess of war.
Foreheads of men have bled where no wounds were.
I am the enemy you killed, my friend.
I knew you in this death; for so you frowned
Yesterday through me as you jabbed and killed.
I parried; but my hands were loath and cold.
Let us sleep now. . . ."

While Owen was recuperating at an English hospital in 1917, he met Siegfried Sassoon. With characteristic modesty Owen considered himself "not worthy to light Sassoon's pipe," but he surpassed his fellow soldier-poet in the ability to project the feeling of shock and dark emptiness. It was Sassoon who, having discovered Owen, said in his introduction to the posthumous POEMS: "He never wrote his poems (as so many war poets did) to make the effect of a personal gesture. He pitied others; he did not pity himself."

Anthem for Doomed Youth

What passing-bells for these who die as cattle?
Only the monstrous anger of the guns.
Only the stuttering rifles' rapid rattle
Can patter out their hasty orisons.
No mockeries for them; no prayers nor bells,
Nor any voice of mourning save the choirs,—
The shrill, demented choirs of wailing shells;
And bugles calling for them from sad shires.

What candles may be held to speed them all?
Not in the hands of boys, but in their eyes
Shall shine the holy glimmers of good-bys.
The pallor of girls' brows shall be their pall;
Their flowers the tenderness of patient minds,
And each slow dusk a drawing-down of blinds.

"It is impossible," wrote Edmund Blunden in the enlarged edition of Owen's POEMS published in 1931, "to become deeply acquainted with Owen's work and not be haunted by comparisons between his genius and his premature death and the wonder and tragedy of his admired Keats." Keats had been Owen's idol in youth. At eighteen he made a pilgrimage to Keats's house at Teignmouth, and spoke of the sea which seemed to share his grief for one "whose name was writ in water." But Owen's full poetic power was not manifest until the last year of his life. The poems written in the shadow of his death survive him, Sassoon wrote, "as his true and splendid testament." The poem FUTILITY is his own unplanned tragic epitaph.

Futility

Move him into the sun–
Gently its touch awoke him once,
At home, whispering of fields unsown.
Always it woke him, even in France.
Until this morning and this snow.
If anything might rouse him now
The kind old sun will know.

Think how it wakes the seeds–
Woke, once, the clay of a cold star.
Are limbs, so dear-achieved, are sides
Full-nerved,–still warm,–too hard to stir?
Was it for this the clay grew tall?
–Oh, what made fatuous sunbeams toil
To break earth's sleep at all?

MARK VAN DOREN

[1894-   ]

ONE of a country doctor's five sons, Mark Van Doren was born July 13, 1894, in Hope, Illinois. Graduating at twenty from the University of Illinois, he went to New York and undertook advanced work at Columbia. After the First World War, in which he served in the infantry, he received his doctor's degree and began teaching at Columbia. He was literary editor of THE NATION from 1924 to 1928.

Although Van Doren has distinguished himself as a critic, his chief concern has been the writing of poetry. Six volumes of his verse appeared before the Pulitzer Prize was awarded to his COLLECTED POEMS: 1922–1938 in 1940. In the same year Van Doren began to preside over the radio program INVITATION TO LEARNING.

Van Doren's influences are strictly native. The early verse owes something to Robert Frost; the later A WINTER DIARY brings Whittier to the present scene. But Van Doren's accent, quiet and cool, is his own. His persuasive individuality is communicated in a tone which is alternately straightforward and semimystical.

Proper Clay

Their little room grew light with cries;
He woke and heard them thread the dark,
He woke and felt them like the rays
Of some unlawful dawn at work:

Some random sunrise, lost and small,
That found the room's heart, vein by vein.
But she was whispering to the wall,
And he must see what she had seen.

He asked her gently, and she wept.
"Oh, I have dreamed the ancient dream.
My time was on me, and I slept;
And I grew greater than I am;

"And lay like dead; but when I lived,
Three wingéd midwives wrapped the child.
It was a god that I had loved,
It was a hero I had held.

"Stretch out your mortal hands, I beg.
Say common sentences to me.
Lie cold and still, that I may brag
How close I am to proper clay.

"Let this within me hear the truth.
Speak loud to it." He stopped her lips.
He smoothed the covers over both.
It was a dream perhaps, perhaps . . .

Yet why this radiance round the room?
And why this trembling at her waist?
And then he smiled. It was the same
Undoubted flesh that he had kissed;

She lay unchanged from what she was,
She cried as ever woman cried.
Yet why this light along his brows?
And whence the music no one made?

E. E. CUMMINGS

[1894–1962]

A NOSE-THUMBING satirist and a lyrical sentimentalist, irresponsible clown and angry critic, Edward Estlin Cummings delighted in being the Peck's Bad Boy of American poetry.

He was born October 14, 1894, in Cambridge, Massachusetts, where his father taught English at Harvard and later became minister of Old South Church in Boston. Educated at Harvard, Cummings served in the ambulance corps during the First World War and, because of a censor's error, spent three months in a detention camp, an experience recorded in THE ENORMOUS ROOM. He was almost thirty upon the appearance of his first volume of poems, TULIPS AND CHIMNEYS, a book that was original to the point of eccentricity. Perhaps the chief surprise was the incongruous mixture of archaic diction and contemporary slang, of soft affectations and a violently disrupted typography. Taking a cue from the advertiser's layout, Cummings confronted the eye with broken lines of verse, often by words broken up by irrelevant punctuation. Sometimes these displays arrested the attention of the reader; sometimes they merely annoyed him.

At his best Cummings does not rely upon typographical oddities. His subject matter is traditional; the beauty of spring, the redness of roses, the pleasure of love, the pain of death.

since feeling is first
who pays any attention
to the syntax of things
will never wholly kiss you;

wholly to be a fool
while Spring is in the world
my blood approves.

Cummings' work is seemingly a set of nondescript, and sometimes obscene, variations on familiar, even banal, themes. Once past the barrier of his singular style, the reader will discover a surprisingly old-fashioned sensual romanticist.

O Sweet Spontaneous Earth

O sweet spontaneous
earth how often have
the
doting
            fingers of
prurient philosophers pinched
and
poked
thee
, has the naughty thumb
of science prodded
thy
        beauty   , how
often have religions taken
thee upon their scraggy knees
squeezing and

buffeting thee that thou mightest conceive
gods
        (but
true
to the incomparable
couch of death thy
rhythmic
lover

        thou answerest

them only with
                spring)

The emphasis on visual effects may be explained by the fact that Cummings is a painter as well as a writer. One of his volumes was entitled CIOPW, indicating that its contents consisted of drawings and paintings in Charcoal, Ink, Oil, Pencil, and Watercolor. Cummings has also published plays and a ballet, TOM. But it is as a lyrical poet, not as a draftsman or a thinker, that he will arouse—and probably hold—an audience.

Somewhere I Have Never Travelled

somewhere i have never travelled, gladly beyond
any experience, your eyes have their silence:
in your most frail gesture are things which enclose me,
or which i cannot touch because they are too near

your slightest look easily will unclose me
though i have closed myself as fingers,
you open always petal by petal myself as Spring opens
(touching skilfully, mysteriously) her first rose

or if your wish be to close me, i and
my life will shut very beautifully, suddenly,
as when the heart of this flower imagines
the snow carefully everywhere descending;

nothing which we are to perceive in this world equals
the power of your intense fragility: whose texture
compels me with the color of its countries,
rendering death and forever with each breathing

(i do not know what it is about you that closes
and opens; only something in me understands
the voice of your eyes is deeper than all roses)
nobody, not even the rain, has such small hands

At sixty Cummings collected some six hundred of his odd, impudent, ingenious and sometimes inspired pieces in an imposing volume, POEMS: 1923–1954. Although the uncritical poet still relied heavily on rhetoric and roses, he gave the standard platitudes about love, spring, and death new verbal twists. The tone continued to alternate between tender-minded stock sentiments and tough-talking arrogance, but the soft romanticisms were offset by a hard integrity and many moments of sudden magic.

STEPHEN VINCENT BENÉT

[1898–1943]

GENERAL STEPHEN VINCENT BENÉT, chief of ordnance of the United States Army, wrote a TREATISE ON MILITARY LAW which became a standard authority. Two generations later his grandson, bearing his grandfather's name, wrote JOHN BROWN'S BODY, an epic of the Civil War.

Stephen Vincent Benét was born July 22, 1898, in Bethlehem, Pennsylvania, and spent his boyhood in California and Georgia, where his father was stationed at various government arsenals. He entered Yale at seventeen and in the same year published his first volume, a book of dramatic portraits in verse entitled FIVE MEN AND POMPEY. After getting his degree, he engaged briefly in the advertising business, but soon began to support himself by writing. Dissatisfied with the imitativeness of his early work Benét started to explore American backgrounds. One of the first of his attempts in the new manner, THE BALLAD OF WILLIAM SYCAMORE, begins:

My father, he was a mountaineer,
His fist was a knotty hammer;
He was quick on his feet as a running deer,
And he spoke with a Yankee stammer.

Resolutely indigenous, the poem ends:

Go play with the towns you have built of blocks
The towns where you would have bound me!
I sleep in my earth like a tired fox,
And my buffalo have found me.

THE MOUNTAIN WHIPPOORWILL is an extension of the native ballad, vigorous and harshly resonant. Best of Benét's story poems, this fantasy, roughened with the tang of earth, is not confined to the Georgia which furnishes the setting.

The Mountain Whippoorwill

OR, HOW HILL-BILLY JIM WON THE GREAT FIDDLERS' PRIZE

Up in the mountains, it's lonesome all the time,
(Sof' win' slewin' thu' the sweet-potato vine.)

Up in the mountains, it's lonesome for a child,
(Whippoorwills a-callin' when the sap runs wild.)

Up in the mountains, mountains in the fog,
Everythin's as lazy as an old houn' dog.

Born in the mountains, never raised a pet,
Don't want nuthin' an' never got it yet.

Born in the mountains, lonesome-born,
Raised runnin' ragged thu' the cockleburrs and corn.

Never knew my pappy, mebbe never should.
Think he was a fiddle made of mountain laurel-wood.

Never had a mammy to teach me pretty-please.
Think she was a whippoorwill, a-skitin' thu' the trees.

Never had a brother ner a whole pair of pants,
But when I start to fiddle, why, yuh got to start to dance!

Listen to my fiddle—Kingdom Come—Kingdom Come!
Hear the frogs a-chunkin' "Jug o' rum, Jug o' rum!"
Hear that mountain whippoorwill be lonesome in the air,
An' I'll tell yuh how I travelled to the Essex County Fair.

Essex County has a mighty pretty fair,
All the smarty fiddlers from the South come there.

Elbows flyin' as they rosin up the bow
For the First Prize Contest in the Georgia Fiddlers' Show.

Old Dan Wheeling, with his whiskers in his ears,
King-pin fiddler for nearly twenty years.

Big Tom Sargent, with his blue wall-eye,
An' Little Jimmy Weezer that can make a fiddle cry.

All sittin' roun', spittin' high an' struttin' proud,
(Listen, little whippoorwill, yuh better bug yore eyes!)
Tun-a-tun-a-tunin' while the jedges told the crowd
Them that got the mostest claps 'd win the bestest prize.

Everybody waitin' for the first tweedle-dee,
When in comes a-stumblin'—hill-billy me!

Bowed right pretty to the jedges an' the rest,
Took a silver dollar from a hole inside my vest,

Plunked it on the table an' said, "There's my callin' card!
An' anyone that licks me—well, he's got to fiddle hard!"

Old Dan Wheeling, he was laughin' fit to holler,
Little Jimmy Weezer said, "There's one dead dollar!"

Big Tom Sargent had a yaller-toothy grin,
But I tucked my little whippoorwill spang underneath my chin,
An' petted it an' tuned it till the jedges said, "Begin!"

Big Tom Sargent was the first in line;
He could fiddle all the bugs off a sweet-potato vine.

He could fiddle down a possum from a mile-high tree,
He could fiddle up a whale from the bottom of the sea.

Yuh could hear hands spankin' till they spanked each other raw,
When he finished variations on "Turkey in the Straw."

Little Jimmy Weezer was the next to play;
He could fiddle all night, he could fiddle all day.

He could fiddle chills, he could fiddle fever,
He could make a fiddle rustle like a lowland river.

He could make a fiddle croon like a lovin' woman.
An' they clapped like thunder when he'd finished strummin'.

Then came the ruck of the bob-tailed fiddlers,
The let's-go-easies, the fair-to-middlers.

They got their claps an' they lost their bicker,
An' they all settled back for some more corn-licker.

An' the crowd was tired of their no-count squealing,
When out in the center steps Old Dan Wheeling.

He fiddled high and he fiddled low,
(Listen, little whippoorwill, yuh got to spread yore wings!)
He fiddled and fiddled with a cherrywood bow,
(Old Dan Wheeling's got bee-honey in his strings).

He fiddled the wind by the lonesome moon,
He fiddled a most almighty tune.

He started fiddling like a ghost.
He ended fiddling like a host.

He fiddled north an' he fiddled south,
He fiddled the heart right out of yore mouth.

He fiddled here an' he fiddled there.
He fiddled salvation everywhere.

When he was finished, the crowd cut loose,
(Whippoorwill, they's rain on yore breast.)
An' I sat there wonderin' "What's the use?"
(Whippoorwill, fly home to yore nest.)

But I stood up pert an' I took my bow,
An' my fiddle went to my shoulder, so.

An'—they wasn't no crowd to get me fazed—
But I was alone where I was raised.

Up in the mountains, so still it makes yuh skeered
Where God lies sleepin' in his big white beard.

An' I heard the sound of the squirrel in the pine,
An' I heard the earth a-breathin' thu' the long night-time.

They've fiddled the rose, and they've fiddled the thorn,
But they haven't fiddled the mountain-corn.

They've fiddled sinful an' fiddled moral,
But they haven't fiddled the breshwood-laurel.

They've fiddled loud, and they've fiddled still,
But they haven't fiddled the whippoorwill.

I started off with a *dump-diddle-dump,*
(Oh, hell's broke loose in Georgia!)
Skunk-cabbage growin' by the bee-gum stump.
(Whippoorwill, yo're singin' now!)

My mother was a whippoorwill pert,
My father, he was lazy,
But I'm hell broke loose in a new store shirt
To fiddle all Georgia crazy.

Swing yore partners—up an' down the middle!
Sashay now—oh, listen to that fiddle!
Flapjacks flippin' on a red-hot griddle,
An' hell's broke loose,
Hell's broke loose,
Fire on the mountains—snakes in the grass.
Satan's here a-bilin'—oh, Lordy, let him pass!
Go down Moses, set my people free;
Pop goes the weasel thu' the old Red Sea!
Jonah sittin' on a hickory-bough,
Up jumps a whale—an' where's yore prophet now?
Rabbit in the pea-patch, possum in the pot,
Try an' stop my fiddle, now my fiddle's gettin' hot!

Whippoorwill, singin' thu' the mountain hush,
Whippoorwill, shoutin' from the burnin' bush,
Whippoorwill, cryin' in the stable-door,
Sing tonight as yuh never sang before!
Hell's broke loose like a stompin' mountain-shoat,
Sing till yuh bust the gold in yore throat!
Hell's broke loose for forty miles aroun'
Bound to stop yore music if yuh don't sing it down.
Sing on the mountains, little whippoorwill,
Sing to the valleys, an' slap 'em with a hill,
For I'm struttin' high as an eagle's quill,
An' hell's broke loose,
Hell's broke loose,
Hell's broke loose in Georgia!

They wasn't a sound when I stopped bowin',
(Whippoorwill, yuh can sing no more.)
But, somewhere or other, the dawn was growin',
(Oh, mountain whippoorwill!)

An' I thought, "I've fiddled all night an' lost,
Yo're a good hill-billy, but yuh've been bossed."

So I went to congratulate old man Dan,
—But he put his fiddle into my han'—
An' then the noise of the crowd began!

A Guggenheim fellowship gave Benét the leisure necessary to complete his chief work, JOHN BROWN'S BODY, which revealed the impact of the Civil War on a set of diverse characters. The book, which Hervey Allen said was "exhaustingly alive," received the Pulitzer Prize award for 1929.

As versatile in poetry as his brother, William Rose Benét (see page 1131), Stephen Vincent Benét had a more pronounced gift for fiction. Before he was forty, he was the author of five novels and three collections of short stories. One of his tall tales, THE DEVIL AND DANIEL WEBSTER, attained the eminence of a contemporary classic; it was made into a play, an opera, and a moving picture. He died, at the very peak of his career of a heart attack, in his forty-fifth year.

HART CRANE

[1899–1932]

THE experimenter risks the apathy of the public and the dialectics of the professional critic. Modern poetry has been the target for attack because it has seemed overcomplicated and has been made still more difficult by a confusion of theories. But the poets faced a confused and increasingly complicated world, and it was not always possible to express in simple terms the welter of their experiences.

One of the most daring attempts to summarize the fluctuating aspects of the modern scene was made by Hart Crane, who did not live to complete the synthesis. Crane was born July 21, 1899, in Garrettsville, Ohio, and published his first poem at sixteen. He was unhappy in childhood, self-driven in youth, and self-doomed in manhood. In the year that his parents permanently separated, Crane left high school and found work in a print shop. The rest of his life was a succession of jobs—candy packer, shipyard riveter, reporter, advertising copy writer, manager of a tearoom—and between jobs he drank recklessly. His fits of drunkenness were accompanied by sexual irregularities; he suffered from the extremes of self-glory and guilt. Escaping to Europe and Mexico, sharpening his sensibilities and blunting his faculties, he grew more and more unstable. In his thirty-third year he resolved to return to America and responsibilities. But he never fulfilled his resolution. On April 26, 1932, he jumped from a northbound steamer in the Gulf of Mexico.

Because of the difficulties of his language, it is not always easy to enjoy Crane's work. The difficulties do not arise from a lack of ideas, but, on the contrary, from an overcrowding of them, from a piling up of emotional and pictorial effects. Crane's images are bewildering because he departed from the usual method of image making. He discarded the logical progress of an idea, and substituted a set of wide-ranging associations. Instead of being single, the ideas came in clusters; instead of being closely related and quickly recognizable, they divided themselves with strange variety. One figure set off another until an entire chain of metaphors was ignited. Thus Crane's poetry is one in which the thought progresses in wild leaps over sudden gaps. It is expansive and, at the same time, explosive.

The early poems are particularly obscure because of the mixture of metaphors, oblique references, and broken syntax. The theme, as Allen Tate pointed out in his foreword to Crane's WHITE BUILDINGS, "never appears in explicit statement. . . . The logical meaning can never be derived, but the poetical meaning is a direct intuition."

Crane was seeking a centralizing theme. In THE BRIDGE, finished in his thirty-first year, he almost found it. THE BRIDGE attempts to express the "Myth of America" by uniting national figures, history, early legends, and modern inventions. Crane's symbols for a gigantically expansive America are the Brooklyn Bridge, the airplane, the subway train. "Unless poetry can absorb the machine," he wrote, "acclimatize it as naturally and casually as trees, cattle, galleons, castles, and all other human associations of the past, then poetry has failed of its full contemporary function."

Writing about THE RIVER, one section of THE BRIDGE, Crane declared that the subway was "a figurative, psychological vehicle for transporting the reader to the Middle West." THE RIVER begins with "an intentional burlesque on the cultural confusion of the present —a great conglomeration of noises analogous to the strident impression of a fast express rushing by":

> Stick your patent name on a signboard
> brother—all over—going west—young man
> Tintex—Japalac—Certain-teed Overalls ads
> and land sakes! under the new playbill ripped
> in the guaranteed corner—see Bert Williams—what?
> Minstrels when you steal a chicken just
> save me the wing, for it isn't
> Erie it ain't for miles around a
> Mazda—and the telegraphic night coming on . . .

But soon the jazz tempo slackens, the noises blend into a quiet flow of sound, the rhythm settles down to "a steady pedestrian gait," and the reader is carried into interior after interior, "all of it funneled by the Mississippi." The river of steel develops into the "Father of Waters."

The River

> Down, down—born pioneers in time's despite,
> Grimed tributaries to an ancient flow—
> They win no frontier by their wayward plight,
> But drift in stillness, as from Jordan's brow.

You will not hear it as the sea; even stone
Is not more hushed by gravity . . . But slow,
As loth to take more tribute—sliding prone
Like one whose eyes were buried long ago

The River, spreading, flows—and spends your dream
What are you, lost within this tideless spell?
You are your father's father, and the stream—
A liquid theme that floating niggers swell.

Damp tonnage and alluvial march of days—
Nights turbid, vascular with silted shale
And roots surrendered down of moraine clays:
The Mississippi drinks the farthest dale.

O quarrying passion, undertowed sunlight!
The basalt surface drags a jungle grace
Ochreous and lynx-barred in lengthening might;
Patience! and you shall reach the biding place!

Over De Soto's bones the freighted floors
Throb past the City storied of three thrones.
Down two more turns the Mississippi pours
(Anon tall ironsides up from salt lagoons)

And flows within itself, heaps itself free.
All fades but one thin skyline 'round . . . Ahead
No embrace opens but the stinging sea;
The River lifts itself from its long bed,

Poised wholly on its dream, a mustard glow,
Tortured with history, its one will—flow!
—The Passion spreads in wide tongues, choked and slow
Meeting the Gulf, hosannas silently below.

from THE BRIDGE

The Broken Tower

The bell-rope that gathers God at dawn
Dispatches me as though I dropped down the knell
Of a spent day—to wander the cathedral lawn
From pit to crucifix, feet chill on steps from hell.

Have you not heard, have you not seen that corps
Of shadows in the tower, whose shoulders sway
Antiphonal carillons launched before
The stars are caught and hived in the sun's ray?

The bells, I say, the bells break down their tower;
And swing I know not where. Their tongues engrave
Membrane through marrow, my long-scattered score
Of broken intervals. . . . And I, their sexton slave!

Oval encyclicals in canyons heaping
The impasse high with choir. Banked voices slain!
Pagodas, campaniles with reveilles outleaping—
O terraced echoes prostrate on the plain! . . .

And so it was I entered the broken world
To trace the visionary company of love, its voice
An instant in the wind (I know not whither hurled)
But not for long to hold each desperate choice.

My word I poured. But was it cognate, scored
Of that tribunal monarch of the air
Whose thigh embronzes earth, strikes crystal Word
In wounds pledged once to hope—cleft to despair?

The steep encroachments of my blood left me
No answer (could blood hold such a lofty tower
As flings the question true?)—or is it she
Whose sweet mortality stirs latent power?—

And through whose pulse I hear, counting the strokes
My veins recall and add, revived and sure
The angelus of wars my chest evokes:
What I hold healed, original now, and pure . . .

And builds, within, a tower that is not stone
(Not stone can jacket heaven)—but slip
Of pebbles—visible wings of silence sown
In azure circles, widening as they dip

The matrix of the heart, lift down the eye
That shrines the quiet lake and swells a tower . . .
The commodious, tall decorum of that sky
Unseals her earth, and lifts love in its shower.

Designed as an epic, THE BRIDGE is actually a series of loosely connected lyrics. Crane's last work tended toward a simplification and a clearer structure. At the time of his death he was preparing for publication a volume to be called KEY WEST. ROYAL PALM, richly figurative yet controlled, indicates the order which the poet was attempting to make out of inner chaos.

Royal Palm

Green rustlings, more-than-regal charities
Drift coolly from that tower of whispered light.
Amid the noontide's blazed asperities
I watched the sun's most gracious anchorite

Climb up as by communings, year on year
Uneaten of the earth or aught earth holds,
And the gray trunk, that's elephantine, rear
Its frondings sighing in aethereal folds.

Forever fruitless, and beyond that yield
Of sweat the jungle presses with hot love
And tendril till our deathward breath is sealed—
It grazes the horizons, launched above

Mortality—ascending emerald-bright,
A fountain at salute, a crown in view—
Unshackled, casual of its azured height,
As though it soared suchwise through heaven too.

LÉONIE ADAMS

[1899–   ]

AT NINETEEN Léonie Adams announced her faith in the imaginative vision. In APRIL MORTALITY, her first published poem, she wrote:

With all the drifting race of men
  Thou also art begot to mourn
That she is crucified again,
  The lonely Beauty yet unborn.

And if thou dreamest to have won
  Some touch of her in permanence,
'Tis the old cheating of the sun,
  The intricate lovely play of sense.

That vision sustained her; it strengthened one of the least spectacular but finest sensitivities of the period.

Léonie Adams was born December 9, 1899, in Brooklyn, New York, and was raised with unusual strictness. She had not been allowed to travel on the subway until she went to Barnard, and then, although she was eighteen, her father accompanied her. After getting her degree from Barnard, Miss Adams received a Guggenheim Fellowship, lived abroad for two years, and returned to teach at New York University and later at Sarah Lawrence College. She married the critic, William Troy, and, after teaching at Bennington, returned to New York.

Although there are few surface changes in Miss Adams' verse, her poetry shows the growth of a shy wonder into an intense and semi-devotional lyricism. It is suggested even in her early stanzas:

I watched the hills drink the last color of light,
All shapes grow bright and wane on the pale air,
Till down the traitorous east there came the night,
And swept the circle of my seeing bare.

Descriptions that seem most candid take on uncommon emphasis in Miss Adams' lyrics. A rarefied atmosphere surrounds her delicate perceptions; even the richly detailed picture of a country scene is uplifted by a spirit that transcends personality.

Country Summer

Now the rich cherry whose sleek wood
And top with silver petals traced,
Like a strict box its gems encased,
Has spilt from out that cunning lid,
All in an innocent green round,
Those melting rubies which it hid;
With moss ripe-strawberry-encrusted,
So birds get half, and minds lapse merry
To taste that deep-red, lark's-bite berry,
And blackcap-bloom is yellow-dusted.

The wren that thieved it in the eaves
A trailer of the rose could catch
To her poor droopy sloven thatch,
And side by side with the wren's brood—
O lovely time of beggars' luck—
Opens the quaint and hairy bud;
And full and golden is the yield
Of cows that never have to house,
But all night nibble under boughs,
Or cool their sides in the moist field.

Into the rooms flow meadow airs,
The warm farm-baking smell blows round;
Inside and out, and sky and ground
Are much the same; the wishing star,
Hesperus, kind and early-born,
Is risen only finger-far.
All stars stand close in summer air,
And tremble, and look mild as amber;
When wicks are lighted in the chamber
You might say stars were settling there.

Now straightening from the flowery hay,
Down the still light the mowers look;
Or turn, because their dreaming shook,
And they waked half to other days,
When left alone in yellow-stubble
The rusty-coated mare would graze.
Yet thick the lazy dreams are born,
Another thought can come to mind,
But like the shivering of the wind,
Morning and evening in the corn.

Without being imitative, Léonie Adams suggests Vaughan (see page 487) and the seventeenth-century metaphysical poets. She records with almost religious ecstasy the changing shapes of earth, the fluid seasons, the twilit revelations of a "blue which sucks whole planets in." The mood is mystical in which all matter is "sanctified, dipped in a gold stain."

Sundown

This is the time lean woods shall spend
A steeped-up twilight, and the pale evening drink,
And the perilous roe, the leaper to the west brink,
Trembling and bright, to the caverned cloud descend.

Now shall you see pent oak gone gusty and frantic,
Stooped with dry weeping, ruinously unloosing
The sparse disheveled leaf, or reared and tossing
A dreary scarecrow bough in funeral antic.

Aye, tatter you and rend,
Oak heart, to your profession mourning; not obscure
The outcome, not crepuscular; on the deep floor,
Sable and gold match lusters and contend.

And rags of shrouding will not muffle the slain.
This is the immortal extinction, the priceless wound
Not to be staunched. The live gold leaks beyond,
And matter's sanctified, dipped in a gold stain.

The best of her previous work, together with hitherto uncollected pieces, appeared in POEMS: A SELECTION in 1954. It was a small volume but penetrating in its intensity. Delicate in texture and quiet in tone, it contained some of the finest lyrics of the period.

OGDEN NASH

[1903–   ]

IT SEEMS incredible that a new form of light verse should have been invented, perfected, and ruined by one man as late as the first third of the twentieth century, but that feat was accomplished by Ogden Nash. Nash's haphazard measures, impossible rhymes, and slightly lunatic manner delighted his readers and deceived his imitators, who attempted to achieve, without success, Nash's dizzy blend of sense and nonsense. No one but Nash was able to put such point into such seemingly pointless off-rhymes as:

He who is ridden by a conscience
Worries about a lot of nonscience.

and:

Poor girls with nothing to their names but a compromising letter
or two can get rich and joyous
From a brief trip to their loyous.

and:

Many an infant that screams like a calliope
Could be soothed by a little attention to its diope.

and:

The wasp and all his numerous family
I look upon as a major calamily.
He throws open his nest with prodigality,
But I distrust his waspitality.

It is little wonder that when the brightest jewels from Nash's six volumes were assembled in THE FACE IS FAMILIAR, the collection became known as THE GOLDEN TRASHERY OF OGDEN NASHERY.

Very Like a Whale

One thing that literature would be greatly the better for
Would be a more restricted employment by authors of simile and
metaphor.
Authors of all races, be they Greeks, Romans, Teutons or Celts,
Can't seem just to say that anything is the thing it is but have to go
out of their way to say that it is like something else.
What does it mean when we are told
That the Assyrian came down like a wolf on the fold?
In the first place, George Gordon Byron had had enough experience
To know that it probably wasn't just one Assyrian, it was a *lot* of
Assyrians.
However, as too many arguments are apt to induce apoplexy and
thus hinder longevity,
We'll let it pass as one Assyrian for the sake of brevity.

Now then, this particular Assyrian, the one whose cohorts were gleaming in purple and gold,
Just what does the poet mean when he says he came down like a wolf on the fold?
In heaven and earth more than is dreamed of in our philosophy there are a great many things,
But I don't imagine that among them there is a wolf with purple and gold cohorts or purple and gold anythings.
No, no, Lord Byron, before I'll believe that this Assyrian was actually like a wolf I must have some kind of proof;
Did he run on all fours and did he have a hairy tail and a big red mouth and big white teeth and did he say Woof woof woof?
Frankly I think it very unlikely, and all you were entitled to say, at the very most,
Was that the Assyrian cohorts came down like a lot of Assyrian cohorts about to destroy the Hebrew host.
But that wasn't fancy enough for Lord Byron, oh dear me, no, he had to invent a lot of figures of speech and then interpolate them,
With the result that whenever you mention Old Testament soldiers to people they say Oh yes, they're the ones that a lot of wolves dressed up in gold and purple ate them.
That's the kind of thing that's being done all the time by poets, from Homer to Tennyson;
They're always comparing ladies to lilies and veal to venison,
And they always say things like that the snow is a white blanket after a winter storm.
Oh it is, is it, all right then, you sleep under a six-inch blanket of snow and I'll sleep under a half-inch blanket of unpoetical blanket material and we'll see which one keeps warm,
And after that maybe you'll begin to comprehend dimly
What I mean by too much metaphor and simile.

Ogden Nash was born August 6, 1903, in Rye, New York. His schooling was fitful. At eighteen he entered Harvard, but left after a year. He spent another year at St. George's School in Rhode Island where, he says, he wrecked his nervous system carving lamb for fourteen-year-olds. He became a bond salesman, and sold one bond —to his grandmother; he wrote slogans for cards and advertising matter for publishers. He joined the staff of THE NEW YORKER, left it for free lancing and Hollywood, and published his first book, not perceived that a new tempo as well as a new manner had been added inaccurately entitled HARD LINES, at twenty-seven. It was immediately to "social verse," and that no one since W. S. Gilbert had tossed pun, rhyme, and reason about with such brilliance. A trickster, Nash was also an innovator.

Kind of an Ode to Duty

O Duty,
Why hast thou not the visage of a sweetie or a cutie?
Why glitter thy spectacles so ominously?
Why art thou clad so abominously?
Why art thou so different from Venus
And why do thou and I have so few interests mutually in common
    between us?
Why art thou fifty per cent martyr
And fifty-one per cent Tartar?

Why is it thy unfortunate wont
To try to attract people by calling on them either to leave undone
    the deeds they like, or to do the deeds they don't?
Why art thou so like an April post-mortem
Or something that died in the ortumn?
Above all, why dost thou continue to hound me?
Why art thou always albatrossly hanging around me?

Thou so ubiquitous,
And I so iniquitous.
I seem to be the one person in the world thou art perpetually
    preaching at who or to who;
Whatever looks like fun, there art thou standing between me and it,
    calling you-hoo.
O Duty, Duty!
How noble a man should I be hadst thou the visage of a sweetie or
    a cutie!
But as it is thou art so much forbiddinger than a Wodehouse hero's
    forbiddingest aunt
That in the words of the poet, When Duty whispers low, Thou must,
    this erstwhile youth replies, I just can't.

Seemingly irresponsible, Nash's verse is often as purposeful as it is original. Beneath the wild mispronunciations, there are witty pronouncements on a variety of topics; Nash's soft questions do not turn away wrath, and his nonsense has a way of turning into criticism.

MERRILL MOORE

[1903–1957]

A PSYCHIATRIST, authority on alcoholism, author of some twenty-five medical papers, including the idyllic SYPHILIS AND SASSAFRAS, Merrill Moore published eight volumes and several pamphlets of sonnets before his fiftieth year. At twenty-four he had written about nine thousand sonnets; at thirty-five he published a volume starkly entitled M, accurately indicating that the book contained one thousand pages of sonnets. Moore himself did not know exactly how many sonnets he composed during a busy life, but a rough estimate accounts for a total between sixty and seventy thousand—more sonnets than have been produced by all the leading sonneteers who ever wrote in English.

If Moore's sonnets intimidate the reader with sheer bulk, they charm with their unpredictability, their superb casualness. In rapid-fire succession they present a genre picture, an abnormal case history, a reasoned meditation, a mad dream, a compact drama, and chaos in fourteen lines.

Warning to One

Death is the strongest of all living things,
And when it happens do not look in the eyes
For a dead fire or a lack-luster there;
But listen for the words that fall from lips
Or do not fall. Silence is not death;
It merely means that one who is conserving breath
Is not concerned with tattle and small quips.

Watch the quick fingers and the way they move
During unguarded moments—words of love
And love's caresses may be cold as ice,
And cold the glitter of engagement rings.
Death is the sword that hangs on a single hair;
And that thin tenuous hair is no more than love,
And yours is the silly head it hangs above.

Born September 11, 1903, in Columbia, Tennessee, Merrill Moore was educated at Nashville. He attended Vanderbilt University, where he was one of the youngest members of the group known as The Fugitives, and was graduated at twenty-one. He supported himself by teaching in night school and at a Negro university. At twenty-five he received his M.D. degree, interned in Nashville, moved to Boston, where he joined the Harvard Medical School, became neurologist at the Boston City Hospital, and built up a large practice as specialist in nervous and mental diseases. The titles of his later volumes have a certain significance: CLINICAL SONNETS, ILLEGITIMATE SONNETS, and CASE RECORD FROM A SONNETORIUM.

Moore was never able to give his work that finish which means final perfection; it was easier for him to write a new poem than revise an old one. He was known to improvise a sonnet and dictate it to a soundscriber, which he carried in his car, during a change of traffic lights. Moore's sonnets range the world for their themes, from the clinic to a contemplation of the farthest nebula, from the fantasies of the unconscious to love poems which mingle passion and raillery.

The Noise That Time Makes

That noise that Time makes in passing by
Is very slight but even you can hear it
Having not necessarily to be near it,
Needing only the slightest will to try!

Hold the receiver of a telephone
To your ear when no one is talking on the line
And what may at first sound to you like the whine
Of wind over distant wires is Time's own
Garments brushing against a windy cloud.

That same noise again but not so well
Can be heard by taking a large cockle shell
From the sand and holding it against your head;
Then you can hear Time's footsteps as they pass
Over the earth brushing the eternal grass.

W. H. AUDEN

[1907–   ]

After the First World War, poetry in England suffered a sudden decrease in vitality. During the conflict many of the brilliant young men—Rupert Brooke, Wilfred Owen, Edward Thomas, Charles Hamilton Sorley, Isaac Rosenberg, among others—were killed before they achieved their full utterance. Those who returned could not take up their work where they had left it. Some of them suffered physically from shell shock; others were psychologically shocked out of their former heartiness and confident way of life.

Seeking reassurance as well as refuge, many of the English poets turned to the consoling countryside. But another generation, faced with another war, repudiated the tradition-loving Georgians. They could not be comforted by bucolics in a falsely pastoral setting. Unlike their immediate predecessors, the young men of the 1930s were willing to confront the darker side of life, the exhausted soil and exploited labor, the spiritual emptiness and economic bankruptcy. The "postwar poets," led by W. H. Auden and Stephen Spender, sounded a call to action. They turned away from nostalgic thoughts of an idealized past to grapple with the difficult present; they sought to bring poetry out of a world of shadows into the full light of general life. Their impact might be compared to that of Wordsworth and Coleridge. They, too, restored vitality to English poetry; they recovered ground lost by their immediate predecessors. They reestablished the former activity of language; they went farther, extending the poetic vocabulary along new scientific and intellectual frontiers.

Wystan Hugh Auden, the most brilliant of the "postwar" group, expressed more fully than his contemporaries a sick world. "What do you think about England, this country of ours where nobody is well?" he asked in 1932 at the beginning of THE ORATORS, and the note was maintained to reflect a time of agonized insecurity and isolation. Born February 21, 1907, in York, England, Auden was educated at Christ Church, Oxford, and became a teacher. For five years he taught in a boys' school at Malvern. In his late twenties he joined a film unit; at thirty-one he came to America and took out citizenship papers. In the United States he alternated between various universities and Hollywood.

Auden's early poetry is restlessly experimental, influenced by the echnique of T. S. Eliot (see page 1149), Wilfred Owen (see page 1173), and Gerard Manley Hopkins (see page 977). Hopkins' breathless tempo, his blend of alliteration and concealed rhyme, his very accents, are heard in such lines as:

> Which of you waking early and watching daybreak
> Will not hasten in heart, handsome, aware of wonder
> At light unleashed, advancing, a leader of movement,
> Breaking like surf on turf on road and roof . . .

Many of Auden's brilliant early effects are both gained and obscured by his easy virtuosity, by a continual play of private references and remote allusions. At thirty, Auden suddenly clarified his style without sacrificing emotional intensity. Still protesting against a world sick of old standards, distrustful of new values, and in love with death, Auden emphasized a new lyricism, a romantic reaction against conventional romanticism. The note is heard in:

> Lay your sleeping head, my love,
> Human on my faithless arm;

and, more extensively, in the quietly poignant LOOK, STRANGER.

Look, Stranger

Look, stranger, at this island now
The leaping light for your delight discovers,
Stand stable here
And silent be,
That through the channels of the ear
May wander like a river
The swaying sound of the sea.

Here at the small field's ending pause
Where the chalk wall falls to the foam, and its tall ledges
Oppose the pluck
And knock of the tide,
And the shingle scrambles after the suck-
ing surf, and the gull lodges
A moment on its sheer side.

Far off like floating seeds the ships
Diverge on urgent voluntary errands;
And the full view
Indeed may enter
And move in memory as now these clouds do,
That pass the harbor mirror
And all the summer through the water saunter.

The most unpredictable as well as the most provocative writer of his generation, Auden at thirty-four had written two travel books, five volumes of verse—one of them, THE DOUBLE MAN, a seventeen-hundred-line chain of couplets as epigrammatic as Pope's—compiled two anthologies, and collaborated on two plays. More than most of his fellows, Auden speaks as the multiple man. LAW, SAY THE GARDENERS, IS THE SUN, a triumph over impertinence, unites the dexterous craftsman and the smiling iconoclast, the sensitive lover and the supple wit.

Law, Say the Gardeners, Is the Sun

Law, say the gardeners, is the sun,
Law is the one
All gardeners obey
Tomorrow, yesterday, today.

Law is the wisdom of the old
The impotent grandfathers shrilly scold;
The grandchildren put out a treble tongue,
Law is the senses of the young.

Law, says the priest with a priestly look,
Expounding to an unpriestly people,
Law is the words in my priestly book,
Law is my pulpit and my steeple.

Law, says the judge as he looks down his nose,
Speaking clearly and most severely,
Law is as I've told you before,
Law is as you know I suppose,
Law is but let me explain it once more,
Law is The Law.

Yet law-abiding scholars write;
Law is neither wrong nor right,
Law is only crimes
Punished by places and by times,
Law is the clothes men wear
Anytime, anywhere,
Law is Good-morning and Good-night.

Others say, Law is our Fate;
Others say, Law is our State;
Others say, others say
Law is no more,
Law is gone away.

And always the loud angry crowd
Very angry and very loud
Law is We,
And always the soft idiot softly Me.

If we, dear, know we know no more
Than they about the law,
If I no more than you
Know what we should and should not do
Except that all agree
Gladly or miserably
That the law is
And that all know this,
If therefore thinking it absurd
To identify Law with some other word,
Unlike so many men
I cannot say Law is again,
No more than they can we suppress
The universal wish to guess
Or slip out of our own position
Into an unconcerned condition.

Although I can at least confine
Your vanity and mine
To stating timidly
A timid similarity,
We shall boast anyway:
Like love I say.

Like love we dont know where or why
Like love we cant compel or fly
Like love we often weep
Like love we seldom keep.

Although Auden often alternates between a confused symbolism and a hard-bitten, hard-biting plain speech, the best of his poetry proceeds neither from the coterie nor the music-hall mind which prompted the trifling "popular" rhymes in competition with light-verse writers and singers of "blues." Auden is most distinguished when he is most divided; his work is all the more affecting because it is a record of ambivalence. His hesitations between tradition and revolution communicate not only a sense of painful bewilderment but also of estrangement. Yet Auden moves toward affirmation. He progresses from the strange torment of the early LETTER TO A WOUND to the hope of brotherhood ("We must love one another or die") and understanding companionship ("Teach the free man how to praise"). It is a hope that culminates in the obituary poem written shortly after the death of Yeats (see page 1035), a poem that is an estimate and a prayer as well as an elegy.

In Memory of W. B. Yeats

1

He disappeared in the dead of winter:
The brooks were frozen, the airports almost deserted,
And snow disfigured the public statues;
The mercury sank in the mouth of the dying day.
O all the instruments agree
The day of his death was a dark cold day.

Far from his illness
The wolves ran on through the evergreen forests,
The peasant river was untempted by the fashionable quays;
By mourning tongues
The death of the poet was kept from his poems.

But for him it was his last afternoon as himself,
An afternoon of nurses and rumors;
The provinces of his body revolted,

The squares of his mind were empty,
Silence invaded the suburbs,
The current of his feeling failed: he became his admirers.

Now he is scattered among a hundred cities
And wholly given over to unfamiliar affections;
To find his happiness in another kind of wood
And be punished under a foreign code of conscience.
The words of a dead man
Are modified in the guts of the living.

But in the importance and noise of tomorrow
When the brokers are roaring like beasts on the floor of the Bourse,
And the poor have the sufferings to which they are fairly accustomed,
And each in the cell of himself is almost convinced of his freedom;
A few thousand will think of this day
As one thinks of a day when one did something slightly unusual.

O all the instruments agree
The day of his death was a dark cold day.

2

You were silly like us: your gift survived it all;
The parish of rich women, physical decay,
Yourself; mad Ireland hurt you into poetry.
Now Ireland has her madness and her weather still,
For poetry makes nothing happen: it survives
In the valley of its saying where executives
Would never want to tamper; it flows south
From ranches of isolation and the busy griefs,
Raw towns that we believe and die in; it survives,
A way of happening, a mouth.

3

Earth, receive an honored guest;
William Yeats is laid to rest:
Let the Irish vessel lie
Emptied of its poetry.

Time that is intolerant
Of the brave and innocent,
And indifferent in a week
To a beautiful physique,

Worships language and forgives
Everyone by whom it lives;
Pardons cowardice, conceit,
Lays its honors at their feet.

Time that with this strange excuse
Pardoned Kipling and his views,
And will pardon Paul Claudel,
Pardons him for writing well.

In the nightmare of the dark
All the dogs of Europe bark,
And the living nations wait,
Each sequestered in its hate;

Intellectual disgrace
Stares from every human face,
And the seas of pity lie
Locked and frozen in each eye.

Follow, poet, follow right
To the bottom of the night,
With your unconstraining voice
Still persuade us to rejoice;

With the farming of a verse
Make a vineyard of the curse,
Sing of human unsuccess
In a rapture of distress;

In the deserts of the heart
Let the healing fountain start,
In the prison of his days
Teach the free man how to praise.

Auden's later work exhibits a human warmth and a humility barely suggested by the dazzle of his early cerebrations. Many of the images in his COLLECTED POEMS and in some of the poems in NONES may seem chill and even ominous, full of a "menacing mutter," but they show new depths of feeling. Auden's erudition and inventiveness have joined to display a sense of rich reserve and an intensified communication.

Musée des Beaux Arts

About suffering they were never wrong,
The Old Masters: how well they understood
Its human position; how it takes place
While someone else is eating or opening a window or just walking
dully along;
How, when the aged are reverently, passionately waiting
For the miraculous birth, there always must be
Children who did not specially want it to happen, skating
On a pond at the edge of the wood:
They never forgot
That even the dreadful martyrdom must run its course
Anyhow in a corner, some untidy spot
Where the dogs go on with their doggy life and the torturer's horse
Scratches its innocent behind on a tree.

In Brueghel's *Icarus,* for instance: how everything turns away
Quite leisurely from the disaster; the ploughman may
Have heard the splash, the forsaken cry,
But for him it was not an important failure; the sun shone
As it had to on the white legs disappearing into the green
Water; and the expensive delicate ship that must have seen
Something amazing, a boy falling out of the sky,
Had somewhere to get to and sailed calmly on.

THEODORE ROETHKE

[1908–1963]

A SUBTLE artisan whom Dylan Thomas considered the most original of the younger poets, Theodore Roethke was born May 25, 1908, in Saginaw, Michigan. Educated in his native state and at Harvard, Roethke became a teacher; his connection with various colleges brought him from one extreme of the country to the other, from Lafayette College, Penn State, and Bennington to the University of Washington.

Roethke was slow to publish. His first volume, OPEN HOUSE, did not appear until he was thirty-three. By the time he had reached his mid-forties, he was the author of four distinguished volumes, one of which, THE WAKING, had been awarded the Pulitzer Prize in 1953. He also wrote stories and satires, as well as poems for children, under the pseudonym of Winterset Rethberg.

His poetry underwent a gradual but pronounced series of changes, developing from forthright lyrics of recognizable people and places through loose autobiographical reminiscences to surrealist, or supra-rational, explorations. Much of Roethke's poetry accomplishes a release of the unconscious mind, stressing odd but illuminating figments of memory and imagination. While the surface is often puzzling, the melodic line is as simple as a nursery rhyme, composed of a child's words remembered and heightened in maturity. The half-mocking, half-mournful humor suggests the music of Prokofiev and the drawings of Paul Klee. Referring to the first part of THE LOST SON, Roethke wrote: " 'The Flight' is just what it says it is: a terrified running away—with alternate periods of hallucinatory waiting (the voices, etcetera); the protagonist so geared-up, so over-alive, that he is hunting, like a primitive, for some animistic suggestion, some clue to existence from the sub-human. These he sees and yet does not see; they are almost tail-flicks from another world, seen out of the corner of the eye. In a sense he goes in and out of rationality: he hangs in the balance between the human and the animal."

The Flight

At Woodlawn I heard the dead cry:
I was lulled by the slamming of iron,
A slow drip over stones,
Toads brooding in wells.
All the leaves stuck out their tongues;
I shook the softening chalk of my bones,
Saying,
Snail, snail, glister me forward,
Bird, soft-sigh me home,
Worm, be with me.
This is my hard time.

Fished in an old wound,
The soft pond of repose;
Nothing nibbled my line,
Not even the minnows came.

Sat in an empty house
Watching shadows crawl,
Scratching.
There was one fly.

Voice, come out of the silence.
Say something.
Appear in the form of a spider
Or a moth beating the curtain.

Tell me:
Which is the way I take;
Out of what door do I go,
Where and to whom?

Dark hollows said, lee to the wind,
The moon said, back of an eel,
The salt said, look by the sea,
Your tears are not enough praise,
You will find no comfort here,
In the kingdom of bang and blab.

Running lightly over spongy ground,
Past the pasture of flat stones,
The three elms,
The sheep strewn on a field,
Over a rickety bridge
Toward the quick-water, wrinkling and rippling.

Hunting along the rivers,
Down among the rubbish, the bug-riddled foliage,
By the muddy pond-edge, by the bog-holes,
By the shrunken lake, hunting, in the heat of summer.

The shape of a rat?
It's bigger than that.
It's less than a leg
And more than a nose,
Just under the water
It usually goes.

Is it soft like a mouse?
Can it wrinkle its nose?
Could it come in the house
On the tips of its toes?

Take the skin of a cat
And the back of an eel,
Then roll them in grease,—
That's the way it would feel.

It's sleek as an otter
With wide webby toes
Just under the water
It usually goes.

from THE LOST SON

Roethke's later poems are less backward-seeking but fully as intuitional as the earlier verse. Semi-obscurity gives way to connotative clarity, and eerie sensibilities are disciplined without losing their boldness. The love poems combine light play and sensuousness; they radiate ecstasy as their physical exultations blend with spiritual exaltation.

Poem

I knew a woman, lovely in her bones,
When small birds sighed, she would sigh back at them;
Ah, when she moved, she moved more ways than one.
The shapes a bright container can contain!
Of her choice virtues only gods should speak,
Or English poets who grew up on Greek
(I'd have them sing in chorus, cheek to cheek.)

How well her wishes went! She stroked my chin,
She taught me Turn, and Counter-turn, and Stand;
She taught me Touch, that undulant white skin:
I nibbled meekly from her proffered hand;
She was the sickle; I, poor I, the rake,
Coming behind her for her pretty sake
(But what prodigious mowing we did make.)

Love likes a gander, and adores a goose:
Her full lips pursed, the errant note to seize;
She played it quick, she played it light and loose;
My eyes, they dazzled at her flowing knees;
Her several parts could keep a pure repose,
Or one hip quiver with a mobile nose
(She moved in circles, and those circles moved.)

Let seed be grass, and grass turn into hay:
I'm martyr to a motion not my own;
What's freedom for? To know eternity.
I swear she cast a shadow white as stone.
But who would count eternity in days?
These old bones live to learn her wanton ways:
(I measure time by how a body sways.)

STEPHEN SPENDER

[1909–   ]

At TWENTY-NINE, just before the outbreak of the Second World War, Stephen Spender wrote: "The violence of the times we are living in, the necessity of sweeping and general and immediate action, tend to dwarf the experience of the individual." Before that he had written: "Surely the point at which modern poetry becomes revolutionary is the point where it tries to define truths which are related to the world around us: to politics and economics. It is revolutionary because it has retired altogether from the attempt to find satisfaction in the 'possible worlds' of mythology: it is back in the world which surrounds us."

Stephen Spender was nine years old when the First World War ended and thirty when the Second World War began. Born February 28, 1909, near London, he spent his youth in the nervous uncertainties of a false peace, in the long tension between two wars. But Spender, unlike many of his fellows, did not fear his times. He refused to retreat, to isolate himself in a hermetically sealed art. He was particularly insistent that poetry should reaffirm its power and responsibility, accept the world of the airplane and the radio, speak to living men about the living age. "Drink from here energy," Spender insisted, pointing to a world of violent action, "as from the electric charge of a battery." And with energy Spender called for compassion. How could we ever doubt the common heart of humanity he asked, how could it be

. . . That works, money, interest, building could ever hide
The palpable and obvious love of man!

Less obscure, more certain of his symbols than Auden, Spender writes with a passion emphasized by quietness. His technique is assured without being exciting, but his tone is moving. His vein of "lyrical speculation," wrote the critic David Daiches, "produces poetry which can hold its own with anything produced in the century." AN ELEMENTARY SCHOOL CLASSROOM IN A SLUM is not an attempt to escape hard actuality and "find satisfaction in the 'possible worlds' of mythology." Rather it is a contrast between the "possible worlds" of poetry, as exemplified by Shakespeare, and beauty, symbolized by pictures of travel, and the grim world of politics and economics "which surrounds us."

An Elementary School Classroom in a Slum

Far far from gusty waves, these children's faces.
Like rootless weeds the torn hair round their paleness.
The tall girl with her weighed-down head. The paper-
seeming boy with rat's eyes. The stunted unlucky heir
Of twisted bones, reciting a father's gnarled disease,
His lesson from his desk. At back of the dim class,
One unnoted, sweet and young: his eyes live in a dream
Of squirrels' game, in tree room, other than this.

On sour cream walls, donations. Shakespeare's head
Cloudless at dawn, civilized dome riding all cities.
Belled, flowery, Tyrolese valley. Open-handed map
Awarding the world its world. And yet, for these
Children, these windows, not this world, are world,
Where all their future's painted with a fog,
A narrow street sealed in with a lead sky,
Far, far from rivers, capes, and stars of words.

Surely Shakespeare is wicked, the map a bad example
With ships and sun and love tempting them to steal—
For lives that slyly turn in their cramped holes
From fog to endless night? On their slag heap, these children
Wear skins peeped through by bones and spectacles of steel
With mended glass, like bottle bits on stones.
All of their time and space and foggy slum
So blot their maps with slums as big as doom.

Unless, governor, teacher, inspector, visitor,
This map becomes their window and these windows
That open on their lives like crouching tombs
Break, O break open, till they break the town

And show the children to the fields and all their world
Azure on their sands, to let their tongues
Run naked into books, the white and green leaves open
The history theirs whose language is the sun.

Without being didactic Spender is essentially an interpreter of baffled but onward-struggling men; with all its modern imagery his is a poetry prompted by a moral sense. The depths of his moral convictions are sounded in the lines beginning "I think continually of those who were truly great." In one of the noblest rhapsodies of the period, Spender praises the pioneers, the unsung fighters, firebringers, children of the sun. In a lyrical ODE (see page 976) O'Shaughnessy celebrated the poets who built up the world's great cities:

One man with a dream, at pleasure,
  Shall go forth and conquer a crown;
And three with a new song's measure
  Can trample an empire down.

Spender extends the implication. He exalts "those who in their lives fought for life, who," he says in a triumphant coda:

. . . wore at their hearts the fire's center.
Born of the sun they traveled a short while towards the sun,
And left the vivid air signed with their honor.

Such lines have an almost Shakespearean eloquence. They are authoritative; most of all, they are noble.

I Think Continually of Those

I think continually of those who were truly great.
Who, from the womb, remembered the soul's history
Through corridors of light where the hours are suns,
Endless and singing. Whose lovely ambition
Was that their lips, still touched with fire,
Should tell of the spirit clothed from head to foot in song.
And who hoarded from the spring branches
The desires falling across their bodies like blossoms.

What is precious is never to forget
The essential delight of the blood drawn from ageless springs
Breaking through rocks in worlds before our earth.
Never to deny its pleasure in the simple morning light
Nor its grave evening demand for love.
Never to allow gradually the traffic to smother
With noise and fog the flowering of the spirit.

Near the snow, near the sun, in the highest fields
See how these names are fêted by the waving grass,
And by the streamers of white cloud,
And whispers of wind in the listening sky;
The names of those who in their lives fought for life,
Who wore at their hearts the fire's center.
Born of the sun they traveled a short while towards the sun,
And left the vivid air signed with their honor.

In a time of darkness and confusion, poetry again expresses the flowering of the spirit of a greater humanity, of dreamers and workers, the yea sayers stubbornly "bringing light to life," leaving "the vivid air signed with their honor."

ELIZABETH BISHOP

[1911–]

PRESSED for a statement of writing principles embodying her theory of poetry, Elizabeth Bishop replied: "No matter what theories one may have, I doubt very much that they are in one's mind at the moment of writing a poem or that there is even a physical possibility that they could be. Theories can only be based on interpretations of other poets' poems, or one's own in retrospect, or wishful thinking." Elizabeth Bishop's poetry has challenged and withstood analysis because of its peculiar fusion of free whimsicality and intellectual control.

She was born February 8, 1911, in Worcester, Massachusetts, was graduated from Vassar College, and traveled widely. After she received a Fellowship for her volume, NORTH AND SOUTH, she was, for a while, Consultant in Poetry to the Library of Congress. Her origin and long sojourns in the South may account for the distinctive color of her images which combine tropical floridity with New England severity. "The Fish," a miniature Moby Dick, is an excellent example of her sharp scrutiny and soaring imagination.

The Fish

I caught a tremendous fish
and held him beside the boat
half out of water, with my hook
fast in a corner of his mouth.
He didn't fight.
He hadn't fought at all.
He hung a grunting weight,
battered and venerable
and homely. Here and there
his brown skin hung in strips
like ancient wall-paper,
and its pattern of darker brown
was like wall-paper:
shapes like full-blown roses
stained and lost through age.
He was speckled with barnacles,
fine rosettes of lime,
and infested
with tiny white sea-lice,
and underneath two or three
rags of green weed hung down.
While his gills were breathing in
the terrible oxygen
—the frightening gills
fresh and crisp with blood,
that can cut so badly—
I thought of the coarse white flesh
packed in like feathers,
the big bones and the little bones,
the dramatic reds and blacks
of his shiny entrails,
and the pink swim-bladder
like a big peony.
I looked into his eyes
which were far larger than mine
but shallower, and yellowed,

the irises backed and packed
with tarnished tinfoil
seen through the lenses
of old scratched isinglass.
They shifted a little, but not
to return my stare.
—It was more like the tipping
of an object toward the light.
I admired his sullen face,
the mechanism of his jaw,
and then I saw
that from his lower lip
—if you could call it a lip—
grim, wet, and weapon-like,
hung five old pieces of fish-line,
or four and a wire leader
with the swivel still attached,
with all their five big hooks
grown firmly in his mouth.
A green line, frayed at the end
where he broke it, two heavier lines,
and a fine black thread
still crimped from the strain and snap
when it broke and he got away.
Like medals with their ribbons
frayed and wavering,
a five-haired beard of wisdom
trailing from his aching jaw.
I stared and stared
and victory filled up
the little rented boat,
from the pool of bilge
where oil had spread a rainbow
around the rusted engine
to the bailer rusted orange,
the sun-cracked thwarts,
the oarlocks on their strings,
the gunnels—until everything
was rainbow, rainbow, rainbow!
And I let the fish go.

KARL SHAPIRO

[1913-]

A POET deeply disturbed by the dilemmas of his day but who regarded them with unfailing wit, Karl Shapiro was born November 10, 1913, in Baltimore, Maryland. He attended the University of Virginia and Johns Hopkins University, was inducted into the Army and, during the Second World War, was sent overseas as a sergeant. For three years (1942–1945) he served in the South Pacific, and it was there that his first three books were put together. One of them, V-LETTER, won the Pulitzer Prize in 1945; another, ESSAY ON RHYME, was a remarkable feat of erudition, written by a soldier thousands of miles from any library. After the war he acted as Consultant in Poetry at the Library of Congress, was editor of the magazine POETRY, and taught creative writing.

The early poems vibrate with hatred of injustice and resentment against the stereotyped sentiments which Shapiro felt had misled his generation. "Certainly our contemporary man should feel divested of the stock attitudes of the last generation, the stance of the political intellectual, the proletarian, the expert, the salesman, the world-traveler, the pundit-poet." But, for all his indignation, Shapiro is neither a pessimist nor an evangelist. His irony is bitter but compassionate; he can regard pain with a kind of wounded whimsicality.

The Leg

Among the iodoform, in twilight-sleep,
What have I lost? he first inquires,
Peers in the middle distance where a pain,
Ghost of a nurse, hazily moves, and day,
Her blinding presence pressing in his eyes
And now his ears. They are handling him
With rubber hands. He wants to get up.

One day beside some flowers near his nose
He will be thinking, *When will I look at it?*
And pain, still in the middle distance, will reply

At what? and he will know it's gone,
O where! and begin to tremble and cry.
He will begin to cry as a child cries
Whose puppy is mangled under a screaming wheel.

Later, as if deliberately, his fingers
Begin to explore the stump. He learns a shape
That is comfortable and tucked in like a sock.
This has a sense of humor, this can despise
The finest surgical limb, the dignity of limping,
The nonsense of wheel-chairs. Now he smiles to the wall:
The amputation becomes an acquisition.

For the leg is wondering where he is (all is not lost)
And surely he has a duty to the leg;
He is its injury, the leg is his orphan,
He must cultivate the mind of the leg,
Pray for the part that is missing, pray for peace
In the image of man, pray, pray for its safety,
And after a little it will die quietly.

The body, what is it, Father, but a sign
To love the force that grows us, to give back
What in Thy palm is senselessness and mud?
Knead, knead the substance of our understanding
Which must be beautiful in flesh to walk,
That if Thou take me angrily in hand
And hurl me to the shark, I shall not die!

COLLECTED POEMS, published when Shapiro was forty, shows a considerable advance in range and persuasion. The idiom is simpler, the tone sharper, the emotion more frankly personal. "Buick" is typical of the poet's happier mood, an example of how the mechanical material of the modern world is lifted until it attains the pitch of ecstasy.

Buick

As a sloop with a sweep of immaculate wing on her delicate spine
And a keel as steel as a root that holds in the sea as she leans,
Leaning and laughing, my warm-hearted beauty, you ride, you ride,
You tack on the curves with parabola speed and a kiss of goodbye,
Like a thoroughbred sloop, my new high-spirited spirit, my kiss.

As my foot suggests that you leap in the air with your hips of a girl,
My finger that praises your wheel and announces your voices of song,
Flouncing your skirts, you blueness of joy, you flirt of politeness,
You leap, you intelligence, essence of wheelness with silvery nose,
And your platinum clocks of excitement stir like the hairs of a fern.

But how alien you are from the booming belts of your birth and the smoke
Where you turned on the stinging lathes of Detroit and Lansing at night
And shrieked at the torch in your secret parts and the amorous tests,
But now with your eyes that enter the future of roads you forget;
You are all instinct with your phosphorous glow and your streaking hair.

And now when we stop it is not as the bird from the shell that I leave
Of the leathery pilot who steps from his bird with a sneer of delight,
And not as the ignorant beast do you squat and watch me depart,
But with exquisite breathing you smile, with satisfaction of love,
And I touch you again as you tick in the silence and settle in sleep.

MURIEL RUKEYSER

[1913–   ]

MURIEL RUKEYSER is one of the younger poets who uses the material of modern life without self-consciousness. For her a truck rumbling along in the dark before dawn is a more natural prelude to sunrise than the lark at heaven's gate; the airplane is a more rousing if more ominous symbol of man's longing for freedom than the traditional flight of released doves. Her images rise from the tension and terror of the contemporary scene.

Born December 15, 1913, in New York City, Muriel Rukeyser attended Vassar and Columbia, became a statistician, and worked her way through a ground-course at Roosevelt Aviation School. The varied experiences were embodied in her first book, THEORY OF FLIGHT, published when she was twenty-two. By her mid-thirties she was the author of six more volumes of poetry, the most notable being BEAST IN VIEW and ORPHEUS, as well as a biography of the scientist Willard Gibbs.

Complex but rarely obscure, Muriel Rukeyser's poems are characterized by their abrupt change of mood and action, by their interpenetration of music and meaning, most of all by their rousing and sometimes runaway fervor. It is difficult to tell where the unconscious propulsion ends and the conscious artist begins. "My own experience," she wrote, "is that the work on a poem 'surfaces' several times, with new submergence after each rising. The 'idea' for a poem may come as an image thrown against memory, as a sound of words that sets off a traveling of sound and meaning, as a curve of emotion (a form) plotted by certain crises of events or image or sound, or as a title which evokes a sense of inner relations." Whatever the genesis of her work, the result is a poetry which is introspective but socially conscious, highly individualized and passionately affirmative.

Effort at Speech Between Two People

Speak to me.   Take my hand.   What are you now?
I will tell you all.   I will conceal nothing.
When I was three, a little child read a story about a rabbit
who died, in the story, and I crawled under a chair:
a pink rabbit: it was my birthday, and a candle
burnt a sore spot on my finger, and I was told to be happy.

Oh, grow to know me.   I am not happy.   I will be open.
Now I am thinking of white sails against a sky like music,
like glad horns blowing, and birds tilting, and an arm about me.
There was one I loved, who wanted to live, sailing.

Speak to me.   Take my hand.   What are you now?
When I was nine, I was fruitily sentimental,
fluid: and my widowed aunt played Chopin,
and I bent my head on the painted woodwork, and wept.
I want now to be close to you.   I would
link the minutes of my days close, somehow, to your days.

I am not happy.   I will be open.
I have liked lamps in evening corners, and quiet poems.
There has been fear in my life.   Sometimes I speculate
On what a tragedy his life was, really.

Take my hand.   Fist my mind in your hand.   What are you
  now?
When I was fourteen, I had dreams of suicide,
and I stood at a steep window, at sunset, hoping toward death:
if the light had not melted clouds and plains to beauty,
if light had not transformed that day, I would have leapt.
I am unhappy.   I am lonely.   Speak to me.

I will be open.   I think he never loved me:
he loved the bright beaches, the little lips of foam
that ride small waves, he loved the veer of gulls:
he said with a gay mouth: I love you.   Grow to know me.

What are you now?   If we could touch one another,
if these our separate entities could come to grips,
clenched like a Chinese puzzle . . . yesterday
I stood in a crowded street that was live with people,
and no one spoke a word, and the morning shone.
Everyone silent, moving. . . . Take my hand.   Speak to me.

HENRY REED

[1914-   ]

MAKING the routine event seem remarkable and giving classic legends contemporary significance, Henry Reed fashioned an idiom, alternately playful and poignant, out of incongruities. He was born in 1914 in Birmingham, England, and was educated at the University there. During World War II he was in the Army and conscribed out of it into the Foreign Office. After the armistice he spent much of his time broadcasting on books and films, writing radio scripts on extended themes—his five-part "Ishmael" is a set of lyrical variations on Melville's MOBY DICK—as well as a study of Thomas Hardy.

Reed established himself as another poet who marked a return to lucidity. The return was not, however, merely a reaction. Reed did not hark back to the standard stereotypes of the Georgians and the glib rhetoric of the Edwardians. He learned from Eliot and Auden without imitating them. In "Lessons of the War," for example, Reed juxtaposes the matter-of-fact instructions of the manual of arms and the indescribable beauty of spring with delicacy and sardonic humor.

Lessons of the War

NAMING OF PARTS

Today we have naming of parts. Yesterday,
We had daily cleaning. And tomorrow morning,
We shall have what to do after firing. But today,
Today we have naming of parts. Japonica
Glistens like coral in all of the neighbouring gardens,
    And today we have naming of parts.

This is the lower sling swivel. And this
Is the upper sling swivel, whose use you will see,
When you are given your slings. And this is the piling swivel,
Which in your case you have not got. The branches
Hold in the gardens their silent, eloquent gestures,
    Which in our case we have not got.

This is the safety-catch, which is always released
With an easy flick of the thumb. And please do not let me
See anyone using his finger. You can do it quite easy
If you have any strength in your thumb. The blossoms
Are fragile and motionless, never letting anyone see
    Any of them using their finger.

And this you can see is the bolt. The purpose of this
Is to open the breech, as you see. We can slide it
Rapidly backwards and forwards: we call this
Easing the spring. And rapidly backwards and forwards
The early bees are assaulting and fumbling the flowers:
    They call it easing the Spring.

They call it easing the Spring: it is perfectly easy
If you have any strength in your thumb: like the bolt,
And the breech, and the cocking-piece, and the point of
        balance,
Which in our case we have not got; and the almond-blossom
Silent in all of the gardens and the bees going backwards and
        forwards,
    For today we have naming of parts.

DYLAN THOMAS

[1914–1953]

THE most spectacularly effusive poet of the period, Dylan Thomas, was born in Carmarthenshire, Wales, October 27, 1914. After a catch-as-can education, he tried journalism, gave it up, and earned a living by writing film scripts and reading poetry. PORTRAIT OF THE ARTIST AS A YOUNG DOG was a slightly disguised autobiography written at twenty-five. His first book, however, was put together at twenty and was entitled 18 POEMS, which, with subsequent poems and short stories, was published in America in 1939 as THE WORLD I BREATHE. A later collection, IN COUNTRY SLEEP, appeared in 1952. A comprehensive COLLECTED POEMS was issued in 1953.

Thomas's vocabulary is both sensuous and violent. His lines leap and shout and all but leave the printed page in an excess of abandon. The words often bewildered those unaccustomed to such onrushing syllables and seemingly inchoate images. But the imagery establishes a logic of its own; interlocking phrases, echoing sounds, and balanced repetitions reveal designs which are not only intricate but fascinating. Strong emotion is always evinced; the words have the power of incantation and evoke an indefinite but individual magic. Thomas identifies himself with the elemental forces of nature—"the force that through the green fuse drives the flower drives my green age; that blasts the root is my destroyer." Although Thomas's poetry is intuitive rather than deliberate, its passion is so genuine, its spirit so persuasive, that few readers can resist it.

The Hand That Signed the Paper Felled a City

The hand that signed the paper felled a city;
Five sovereign fingers taxed the breath,
Doubled the globe of dead and halved a country;
These five kings did a king to death.

The mighty hand leads to a sloping shoulder,
The finger joints are cramped with chalk;
A goose's quill has put an end to murder
That put an end to talk.

The hand that signed the treaty bred a fever,
And famine grew, and locusts came;
Great is the hand that holds dominion over
Man by a scribbled name.

The five kings count the dead but do not soften
The crusted wound nor pat the brow;
A hand rules pity as a hand rules heaven;
Hands have no tears to flow.

At thirty-five Thomas described himself as "old, small, dark, intelligent, and daring-doting-dotting eyed . . . balding and toothlessing." During his third visit to the United States, where he attracted large audiences with his resonant and almost incantatory readings, he expected to confer with Igor Stravinsky concerning plans for an opera similar to his pageant-play UNDER MILK WOOD. Parties given for him in New York were particularly convivial—Thomas was a large and steady drinker—but the festivities were followed by a sudden collapse. He died of a virulent brain disease on November 9, 1953, a few days after his thirty-ninth birthday.

Much of Thomas's work was autobiographical to an unusual degree. "Fern Hill," a joyful picture of summer on the boy's Welsh farm, is not only nostalgic but spontaneous with a blithe love for all earthy luxuriance. The air Thomas breathed was taut with wonder; he took part in the tumult of living with a child's rich and irresponsible enjoyment.

Fern Hill

Now as I was young and easy under the apple boughs
About the lilting house and happy as the grass was green,
    The night above the dingle starry,
        Time let me hail and climb
    Golden in the heydays of his eyes,
  And honored among wagons I was prince of the apple towns
  And once below a time I lordly had the trees and leaves
        Trail with daisies and barley
    Down the rivers of the windfall light.

  And as I was green and carefree, famous among the barns
  About the happy yard and singing as the farm was home,

In the sun that is young once only,
Time let me play and be
Golden in the mercy of his means,
And green and golden I was huntsman and herdsman, the calves
Sang to my horn, the foxes on the hills barked clear and cold,
And the sabbath rang slowly
In the pebbles of the holy streams.

All the sun long it was running, it was lovely, the hay-
Fields high as the house, the tunes from the chimneys, it was air
And playing, lovely and watery
And fire green as grass.
And nightly under the simple stars
As I rode to sleep the owls were bearing the farm away,
All the moon long I heard, blessed among stables, the nightjars
Flying with the ricks, and horses
Flashing into the dark.

And then to awake, and the farm, like a wanderer white
With the dew, come back, the cock on his shoulder: it was all
Shining, it was Adam and maiden,
The sky gathered again
And the sun grew round that very day.
So it must have been after the birth of the simple light
In the first, spinning place, the spellbound horses walking warm
Out of the whinnying green stable
On to the fields of praise.

And honored among foxes and pheasants by the gay house
Under the new-made clouds and happy as the heart was long
In the sun born over and over,
I ran my heedless ways,
My wishes raced through the house-high hay
And nothing I cared, at my sky blue trades, that time allows
In all his tuneful turning so few and such morning songs
Before the children green and golden
Follow him out of grace.

Nothing I cared, in the lamb white days, that time would take me
Up to the swallow-thronged loft by the shadow of my hand,
In the moon that is always rising,
Nor that riding to sleep
I should hear him fly with the high fields

And wake to the farm forever fled from the childless land.
Oh as I was young and easy in the mercy of his means,
    Time held me green and dying
  Though I sang in my chains like the sea.

ROBERT LOWELL

[1917–]

ACCLAIMED by his colleagues as the most provocative and powerful poet who had appeared in America for years, Robert Traill Spence Lowell was a Puritan Lowell in revolt. He was born March 1, 1917, in Boston, Massachusetts, attended Harvard and Kenyon College, where he taught briefly, and Louisiana State University. Although he attempted to enlist in the Army in 1943, he was rejected; when he was drafted, he refused to serve on the grounds that the bombing of civilians was unprincipled murder. As a conscientious objector, he served five months in a Federal prison.

Like James Russell Lowell, his great-grandfather's brother, and Amy Lowell, a distant cousin, Robert Lowell was a nonconformer. LORD WEARY'S CASTLE, which won the Pulitzer Prize in 1946, is full of an impassioned exasperation. His hatred of what New England had become is intensified by his concept of what it was and what it could be. The poetry develops into a muffled, tortured outcry against the corruption of the times, the voicing of a need to find some faith in a world torn between frivolity and failure. "The poems understand the world as a conflict of opposites," wrote Randall Jarrell in *The Nation*. "In this struggle one opposite is . . . the inertia of the complacent self, the satisfied persistence in evil that is damnation. Into this realm of necessity, the poems push everything that is closed, turned inward, that blinds or binds: the Old Law, imperialism, militarism, capitalism, Calvinism, Authority, the Father, the 'proper Bostonians,' the rich who will 'do everything for the poor except get off their backs.' But struggling within this like leaven, is everything that is free or open, that grows or is willing to change: here is the generosity or willingness or openness that is itself salvation. . . . This is the realm of freedom, of the Grace that has replaced the Law, of the perfect liberator whom the poet calls Christ."

Where the Rainbow Ends

I saw the sky descending, black and white,
Not blue, on Boston where the winters wore
The skulls to jack-o'-lanterns on the slates,
And Hunger's skin-and-bone retrievers tore
The chickadee and shrike. The thorn tree waits
Its victim and tonight
The worms will eat the deadwood to the foot
Of Ararat: the scythers, Time and Death,
Helmed locusts, move upon the tree of breath;
The wild ingrafted olive and the root

Are withered, and a winter drifts to where
The Pepperpot, ironic rainbow, spans
Charles River and its scales of scorched-earth miles
I saw my city in the Scales, the pans
Of judgment rising and descending. Piles
Of dead leaves char the air—
And I am a red arrow on this graph
Of Revelations. Every dove is sold.
The Chapel's sharp-shinned eagle shifts its hold
On serpent-Time, the rainbow's epitaph.

In Boston serpents whistle at the cold.
The victim climbs the altar steps and sings:
"Hosannah to the lion, lamb, and beast
Who fans the furnace-face of IS with wings:
I breathe the ether of my marriage feast."
At the high altar, gold
And a fair cloth. I kneel and the wings beat
My cheek. What can the dove of Jesus give
You now but wisdom, exile? Stand and live,
The dove has brought an olive branch to eat.

As a Plane Tree by the Water

Darkness has called to darkness, and disgrace
Elbows about our windows in this planned
Babel of Boston where our money talks
And multiplies the darkness of a land

Of preparation where the Virgin walks
And roses spiral her enamelled face
Or fall to splinters on unwatered streets.
Our Lady of Babylon, go by, go by,
I was once the apple of your eye;
Flies, flies are on the plane tree, on the streets.

The flies, the flies, the flies of Babylon
Buzz in my ear-drums while the devil's long
Dirge of the people detonates the hour
For floating cities where his golden tongue
Enchants the masons of the Babel Tower
To raise tomorrow's city to the sun
That never sets upon these hell-fire streets
Of Boston, where the sunlight is a sword
Striking at the withholder of the Lord:
Flies, flies are on the plane tree, on the streets.

Flies strike the miraculous waters of the iced
Atlantic and the eyes of Bernadette
Who saw Our Lady standing in the cave
At Massabielle, saw her so squarely that
Her vision put out reason's eyes. The grave
Is open-mouthed and swallowed up in Christ.
O walls of Jericho! And all the streets
To our Atlantic wall are singing: "Sing,
Sing for the resurrection of the King."
Flies, flies are on the plane tree, on the streets.

MAY SWENSON

[1919–]

In the 1940s another generation of poets reacted against emotional expansiveness and devoted itself to intellectual austerities. Many of the younger writers seemed to regard a poem not only as an act of self-analysis but, since most of them were critics and teachers, as a verbal expression created mainly to be dissected. Scorning popularity, they sought for singularity; distrusting the romantic attitude, they found a dry, flat utterance which turned personal experience into an erudite, brilliant, but depersonalized reportage.

Within a decade the pendulum had swung back toward a poetry which had warmth, ardor, and even passion as its motivating force. Among the poets whose work proceeded from physical delight and spiritual stress was May Swenson. She was born May 28, 1919, in Logan, Utah, of Mormon parents. The first of ten children, she was educated at Utah State Agricultural College, where her father taught Mechanical Engineering. After finishing college, she came to New York, worked as a trade-journal writer, author's assistant, secretary, and dictaphone operator. She followed the policy of saving part of her salary until she had enough for a few months away from work. Her first collection, ANOTHER ANIMAL, was published as part of a series entitled POETS OF TODAY.

Strange without being strained, May Swenson's work is completely itself; it stems from no other poet. Its images are odd but exact—she speaks of a sky "cobbled with clouds," of a bird's eyes as "seeds in a quartered apple," of a lion's head "heavy with heraldic curls," of the "knuckled fist of the heart," of love as "a rain of diamonds in the mind," of the sea "champing" upon small stones "like Demosthenes' mouth, whose many stumblings make him suave." The idiom is strictly contemporary in its blending of intelligence and intuition; if comparisons are demanded, one might say that this is the kind of poetry Emily Dickinson might have written had she read D. H. Lawrence.

Evolution

the stone
would like to be
Alive like me

the rooted tree
longs to be Free

the mute beast
envies my fate
Articulate

on this ball
half dark
half light
i walk Upright
i lie Prone
within the night

beautiful each Shape
to see
wonderful each Thing
to name
here a stone
there a tree
here a river
there a Flame

marvelous to Stroke
the patient beasts
within their yoke

how i Yearn
for the lion
in his den
though he spurn
the touch of men

the longing
that i know
is in the Stone also
it must be
the same that rises
in the Tree
the longing
in the Lion's call
speaks for all

o to Endure
like the stone
sufficient
to itself alone

or Reincarnate
like the tree
be born each spring
to greenery

or like the lion
without law
to roam the Wild
on velvet paw

but if walking i meet
a Creature like me
on the street
two-legged
with human face
to recognize
is to embrace

wonders pale
beauties dim
during my delight
with Him

an Evolution
strange
two tongues Touch
exchange
a Feast unknown
to stone
or tree or beast

At first sight some of the poems seem a set of descriptive and typographical distortions. But the lines are arranged so that they are read more slowly, with due regard for weight and emphasis, while the unusual descriptions transform the actual world into a world of magic. "Poetry," wrote May Swenson, "must do more than interpret the particulars of experience of the poet's own generation and environment. It must also speak to and for every age, past and future. Its material should be such that a savage would have found it familiar, and such that Neo-Man a thousand years from now may say, 'Yes, I have felt this too.' . . . The fact that our present civilization seems sealed and smothered in synthetic wrappings makes it only the more imperative for poetry to insist with all its strength on uttering the elemental." The poetry lives up to the program. Here are intensities of observation and heightened sensitivities which flare into images of pure vision.

Feel Like a Bird

feel like A Bird
understand
he has no hand

instead A Wing
close-lapped
mysterious thing

in sleeveless coat
he halves The Air
skipping there
like water-licked boat

lands on star-toes
finger-beak in
feather-pocket
finds no coin

in neat head like
seeds in A Quartered
Apple eyes join
sniping at opposites
stereoscope The Scene
Before

close to floor giddy
no arms to fling
A Third Sail
spreads for calm
his tail

hand better
than A Wing?
to gather A Heap
to count
to clasp A Mate?

or leap
lone-free and mount
on muffled shoulders
to span A Fate?

RICHARD WILBUR

[1921–]

ONE of the most intellectual yet one of the most persuasive poets of his generation, Richard Wilbur was born March 1, 1921, in New York City. He was educated at Amherst College and Harvard University, leaving to serve overseas two years in Italy, France, and Germany. He returned to teach, first at Wellesley, later at Harvard. At thirty-two he was awarded the Prix de Rome. Meanwhile, he had published two volumes, THE BEAUTIFUL CHANGES and CEREMONY AND OTHER POEMS.

Wilbur's outstanding quality is his dexterous use of form and depth of feeling, complex in matter and straightforward in emotion. Challenging and, at the same time, charming, his lines are strengthened by a half-concealed force; he accomplishes difficult effects with a minimum of strain and a maximum of precision. Wilbur can take the most commonplace subject matter—a potato, a washline, the daily newspaper—and make the reader see with wonder, as though for the first time, the objects of the poet's contemplation. Without being a perfectionist, Wilbur's lines attain an almost perfect organization. Commenting on the limitations of strict poetic forms, Wilbur wrote: "Subtle variation is unrecognizable without the pre-existence of a norm. . . . Form, in slowing and complicating the writing process, calls out the poet's full talents, and thereby insures a greater care and cleverness in the choice and disposition of words. In general, I would say that limitation makes for power: the strength of the genie comes of his being confined in a bottle."

Potato

An underground grower, blind and a common brown;
Got a misshapen look, it's nudged where it could;
Simple as soil yet crowded as earth with all.

Cut open raw, it looses a cool clean stench,
Mineral acid seeping from pores of prest meal;
It is like breaching a strangely refreshing tomb:

Therein the taste of first stones, the hands of dead slaves,
Waters men drank in the earliest frightful woods,
Flint chips, and peat, and the cinders of buried camps.

Scrubbed under faucet water the planet skin
Polishes yellow, but tears to the plain insides;
Parching, the white's blue-hearted like hungry hands.

All of the cold dark kitchens, and war-frozen gray
Evening at window; I remember so many
Peeling potatoes quietly into chipt pails.

"It was potatoes saved us, they kept us alive."
Then they had something to say akin to praise
For the mean earth-apples, too common to cherish or steal.

Times being hard, the Sikh and the Senegalese,
Hobo and Okie, the body of Jesus the Jew,
Vestigial virtues, are eaten; we shall survive.

After the Last Bulletins

After the last bulletins the windows darken
And the whole city founders easily and deep,
Sliding on all its pillows
To the thronged Atlantis of personal sleep,

And the wind rises. The wind rises and bowls
The day's litter of news in the alleys. Trash
Tears itself on the railings,
Soars and falls with a soft crash,

Tumbles and soars again. In empty lots
Our journals spiral in a fierce noyade
Of all we thought to think,
Or caught in corners cramp and wad

And twist our words. And some from gutters flail
Their tatters at the tired patrolman's feet
Like all that fisted snow
That cried beside his long retreat

Damn you! damn you! to the emperor's horses' heels.
Oh none too soon through the air white and dry
Will the clear announcer's voice
Beat like a dove, and you and I

From the heart's anarch and responsible town
Rise by the subway-mouth to life again,
Bearing the morning papers,
And cross the park where saintlike men,

White and absorbed, with stick and bag remove
The litter of the night, and footsteps rouse
With confident morning sound
The songbirds in the public boughs.

The poems written since the publication of Wilbur's first two books have an increasing wit, a freshness of language and vitality of thought. He accomplishes, said Louise Bogan, "an ease of pace, a seemingly effortless advance to a resolute conclusion. . . . Wilbur's gift of fitting the poetic pattern to the material involves all sorts of delicate adjustments of the outward senses to the inner ear." Proof of such commendation can be found in many instances, notably in a poem written in Rome in 1954, "Love Calls Us to the Things of This World," which takes its title from St. Augustine.

Love Calls Us to the Things of This World

The eyes open to a cry of pulleys,
And spirited from sleep, the astounded soul
Hangs for a moment bodiless and simple
As false dawn.
                    Outside the open window
The morning air is all awash with angels.

Some are in bed-sheets, some are in blouses,
Some are in smocks: but truly there they are.
Now they are rising together in calm swells
Of halcyon feeling, filling whatever they wear
With the deep joy of their impersonal breathing;

Now they are flying in place, conveying
The terrible speed of their omnipresence, moving
And staying like white water; and now of a sudden
They swoon down into so rapt a quiet
That nobody seems to be there.
                                        The soul shrinks

From all that it is about to remember,
From the punctual rape of every blessed day,
And cries,
            "Oh, let there be nothing on earth but laundry,
Nothing but rosy hands in the rising steam
And clear dances done in the sight of heaven."

Yet, as the sun acknowledges
With a warm look the world's hunks and colors,
The soul descends once more in bitter love
To accept the waking body, saying now
In a changed voice as the man yawns and rises,

"Bring them down from their ruddy gallows;
Let there be clean linen for the backs of thieves;
Let lovers go fresh and sweet to be undone,
And the heaviest nuns walk in a pure floating
Of dark habits,
                    keeping their difficult balance."

ACKNOWLEDGMENTS

Leonie Adams. For the selections from HIGH FALCON AND OTHER POEMS by Leonie Adams.

Brandt and Brandt, Inc. For "The Mountain Whippoorwill" from BALLADS AND POEMS, published by Farrar & Rinehart, Inc., copyright, 1925, by Stephen Vincent Benét; "O Sweet Spontaneous Earth" and "Somewhere I Have Never Travelled" from COLLECTED POEMS OF E. E. CUMMINGS, published by Harcourt, Brace and Company, copyright, 1923, 1925, 1931, 1935, 1938, by E. E. Cummings, copyright, 1926, by Boni & Liveright; "Pity Me Not" from THE HARP WEAVER AND OTHER POEMS, published by Harper & Brothers, copyright, 1920, 1921, 1922, 1923, by Edna St. Vincent Millay; "Dirge Without Music" from SECOND APRIL, published by Harper & Brothers, copyright, 1921, by Edna St. Vincent Millay; "On Hearing a Symphony of Beethoven" and "To Jesus on His Birthday" from THE BUCK IN THE SNOW, published by Harper & Brothers, copyright, 1928, by Edna St. Vincent Millay; selections from THE SELECTED POEMS OF CONRAD AIKEN.

Jonathan Cape, Ltd. For the selections from COMPLETE POEMS OF W. H. DAVIES, reprinted by permission of the publishers and Mrs. H. M. Davies.

The Clarendon Press (Oxford). For the selections from THE SHORTER POEMS OF ROBERT BRIDGES.

Dodd, Mead & Company, Inc. For "Jesse James" from GOLDEN FLEECE by William Rose Benét, copyright, 1935, by Dodd, Mead & Company, Inc.; "The Great Lover" and "The Soldier" from COLLECTED POEMS OF RUPERT BROOKE, copyright, 1915, by Dodd, Mead & Company, Inc.; "A Prayer in Darkness" and "Elegy in a Country Churchyard" from COLLECTED POEMS OF G. K. CHESTERTON, copyright by Dodd, Mead & Company, Inc.

Doubleday & Company, Inc. For "The Flight" from THE LOST SON AND OTHER POEMS by Theodore Roethke. Copyright 1947 by The University of the South, reprinted by permission of Doubleday &

Company, Inc.; "I Knew a Woman" from WORDS FOR THE WIND: THE COLLECTED VERSE OF THEODORE ROETHKE, reprinted by permission of Doubleday & Company, Inc.

Grove Press, Inc. For "Lethe" from SELECTED POEMS OF H. D., published by Grove Press, Inc., copyright © 1957 by Norman Holmes Pearson.

Harcourt, Brace & World, Inc. For "The Love Song of J. Alfred Prufrock" from COLLECTED POEMS 1909–1962 by T. S. Eliot, copyright, 1936, by Harcourt, Brace & World, Inc., © 1963, 1964, by T. S. Eliot; "Losers" from SMOKE AND STEEL by Carl Sandburg, copyright, 1920, by Harcourt, Brace & World, Inc., copyright, 1948, by Carl Sandburg; "The People Will Live On" from THE PEOPLE, YES by Carl Sandburg, copyright, 1936, by Harcourt, Brace & World, Inc., © 1964 by Carl Sandburg, all of which are reprinted by permission of the publishers; "Lessons of the War" from A MAP OF VERONA AND OTHER POEMS, copyright, 1947, by Henry Reed; "Where the Rainbow Ends" and "As a Plane Tree by the Water" by Robert Lowell from LORD WEARY'S CASTLE, copyright, 1944, 1946, by Robert Lowell; "Potato" by Richard Wilbur from THE BEAUTIFUL CHANGES AND OTHER POEMS, copyright, 1947, by Richard Wilbur; "After the Last Bulletins" and "Love Calls Us to the Things of This World" by Richard Wilbur from THINGS OF THIS WORLD, © 1956, by Richard Wilbur, all of which are reprinted by permission of Harcourt, Brace & World, Inc.

Holt, Rinehart and Winston, Inc. For the selections from THE COMPLETE POEMS OF ROBERT FROST. Copyright 1916, 1921, 1923, 1928, 1930, 1939 by Holt, Rinehart and Winston, Inc. Copyright 1936, 1942 by Robert Frost. Copyright renewed 1944, 1951, © 1956 by Robert Frost. Copyright renewed © 1964 by Lesley Frost Ballantine. Reprinted by permission of Holt, Rinehart and Winston, Inc.; CORNHUSKERS by Carl Sandburg. Copyright 1918 by Holt, Rinehart and Winston, Inc. Copyright renewed 1946 by Carl Sandburg. Reprinted by permission of Holt, Rinehart and Winston, Inc.; COMPLETE POEMS by A. E. Housman. Copyright 1922 by Holt, Rinehart and Winston, Inc. Copyright renewed 1950 by Barclays Bank, Ltd. Reprinted by permission of Holt, Rinehart and Winston, Inc.

Houghton Mifflin Company. For the selections from POEMS 1924–1933 by Archibald MacLeish; MEN, WOMEN AND GHOSTS by Amy Lowell; THE COMPLETE POEMS OF JOHN GREENLEAF WHITTIER, THE COMPLETE POEMS OF HENRY WADSWORTH LONGFELLOW, THE COMPLETE

POEMS OF RALPH WALDO EMERSON, "The Fish" from NORTH AND SOUTH by Elizabeth Bishop, all of which are used by permission of, and by arrangement with, the publishers, Houghton Mifflin Company.

Nannine Joseph. For the selections from COLLECTED AND NEW POEMS by Mark Van Doren, published by Hill and Wang, © 1963.

Alfred A. Knopf, Inc. For "The Assassination," copyright 1947 by Robert Hillyer. Reprinted from PATTERN FOR A DAY by Robert Hillyer, by permission of Alfred A. Knopf, Inc.; "Down to the Puritan Marrow of My Bones" and "Velvet Shoes," copyright 1921 by Alfred A. Knopf, Inc. Renewed 1949 by William Rose Benét. Reprinted from COLLECTED POEMS by Elinor Wylie, by permission of Alfred A. Knopf, Inc.; "Peter Quince at the Clavier," copyright 1923, 1951 by Wallace Stevens. Reprinted from COLLECTED POEMS OF WALLACE STEVENS by permission of Alfred A. Knopf, Inc.; "The Poems of Our Climate," copyright 1942 by Wallace Stevens. Reprinted from COLLECTED POEMS OF WALLACE STEVENS by permission of Alfred A. Knopf, Inc.; "Piazza Piece" and "Lady Lost," copyright 1927 by Alfred A. Knopf, Inc. Renewed © 1955 by John Crowe Ransom. Reprinted from SELECTED POEMS by John Crowe Ransom, by permission of Alfred A. Knopf, Inc.; "Let No Charitable Hope," copyright 1923 by Alfred A. Knopf, Inc. Renewed © 1960 by Edwina Rubenstein. Reprinted from COLLECTED POEMS by Elinor Wylie, by permission of Alfred A. Knopf, Inc.

Little, Brown and Company. For the selections from the POEMS OF EMILY DICKINSON, edited by Martha Dickinson Bianchi and Alfred Leete Hampson, and from THE FACE IS FAMILIAR by Ogden Nash, all of which are reprinted by special permission of Little, Brown and Company.

Liveright Publishing Corporation. For the selections from THE COLLECTED POEMS OF HART CRANE. By permission of Liveright Publishers, N. Y. Copyright © R, 1961, by Liveright Publishing Corporation and for "Hymen" from THE COLLECTED POEMS OF H. D.

Monica McCall. For "Effort at Speech Between Two People" from THEORY OF FLIGHT by Muriel Rukeyser, published by Yale University Press.

David McKay Co., Inc. For Frank Ernest Hill's translation of "The Nun's Priest's Tale" from THE CANTERBURY TALES by Geoffrey Chaucer.

The Macmillan Company. For "What Are Years" from COLLECTED POEMS by Marianne Moore. Copyright 1941 by Marianne Moore;

"On Distrust of Merits" from COLLECTED POEMS by Marianne Moore, copyright 1944 by Marianne Moore; "Mr. Flood's Party" from COLLECTED POEMS by Edwin Arlington Robinson, copyright 1921 by Edwin Arlington Robinson, renewed 1949 by Ruth Nivison; "Tomorrow" from POEMS by John Masefield. Copyright 1916, 1944 by John Masefield, all of which are reprinted with permission of The Macmillan Company; "Sea Fever" from POEMS by John Masefield, copyright 1912 by The Macmillan Company, renewed 1940 by John Masefield; "The Daniel Jazz" from COLLECTED POEMS by Vachel Lindsay, copyright 1920 by The Macmillan Company, renewed 1948 by Elizabeth C. Lindsay; "I Shall Not Care" from COLLECTED POEMS by Sara Teasdale. Copyright 1915 by The Macmillan Company, renewed 1943 by Mamie T. Wheless; "Let It Be Forgotten" from COLLECTED POEMS by Sara Teasdale; copyright 1920 by The Macmillan Company, renewed 1948 by Mamie T. Wheless; "The Coffin Worm" from A MAD LADY'S GARLAND by Ruth Pitter, copyright 1935 by The Macmillan Company, renewed © 1963 by John Masefield; "The Lake Isle of Innisfree" from COLLECTED POEMS by William Butler Yeats, copyright 1906 by The Macmillan Company, renewed 1938 by William Butler Yeats; "Leda and the Swan" and "Among School Children" from COLLECTED POEMS by William Butler Yeats, copyright 1928 by The Macmillan Company, renewed 1956 by Georgie Yeats; "An Irish Airman Foresees His Death" from COLLECTED POEMS by William Butler Yeats, copyright 1919 by The Macmillan Company, renewed 1946 by Bertha Georgie Yeats; "Eve" and "Time, You Old Gypsy Man" from COLLECTED POEMS by Ralph Hodgson, copyright 1917 by The Macmillan Company, renewed 1945 by Ralph Hodgson, all of which are reprinted by permission of the publisher.

Ellen C. Masters. For the selections from SPOON RIVER ANTHOLOGY by Edgar Lee Masters, published by The Macmillan Company.

New Directions. For "The Hand That Signed the Paper Felled a City" from THE WORLD I BREATHE by Dylan Thomas, copyright 1946, by New Directions; "Fern Hill" from COLLECTED POEMS by Dylan Thomas, copyright 1953 and published by New Directions; "The Ballad of the Goodly Fere" from PERSONAE OF EZRA POUND; "Canto I" from CANTOS OF EZRA POUND, copyright 1949 by Ezra Pound and published by New Directions; "Tract" and "The Hounded Lovers" by William Carlos Williams.

Oxford University Press. For the selections from THE POEMS OF GERARD MANLEY HOPKINS, reprinted by permission of the publishers.

Random House. For "Musée des Beaux Arts," "Law, Say the Gardeners" and "In Memory of W. B. Yeats" (ANOTHER TIME), by W. H. Auden, copyright 1940 by W. H. Auden, reprinted from THE COLLECTED POETRY OF W. H. AUDEN by permission of Random House, Inc.; "Look, Stranger" (ON THIS ISLAND), by W. H. Auden, copyright 1937 by W. H. Auden, reprinted from THE COLLECTED POETRY OF W. H. AUDEN by permission of Random House, Inc.; "The Leg" (V-LETTER AND OTHER POEMS), by Karl Shapiro, copyright 1944 by Karl Shapiro, reprinted from POEMS 1940–1953, by Karl Shapiro by permission of Random House, Inc.; "Buick" (PERSON, PLACE AND THING), by Karl Shapiro, copyright 1941 by Karl Shapiro, reprinted from POEMS 1940–1953, by Karl Shapiro, by permission of Random House, Inc.; "Post Mortem" (ROAN STALLION, TAMAR, AND OTHER POEMS), by Robinson Jeffers, copyright 1925 and renewed 1953 by Robinson Jeffers, reprinted from THE SELECTED POETRY OF ROBINSON JEFFERS by permission of Random House, Inc.; "To the Stone-Cutters" (ROAN STALLION, TAMAR, AND OTHER POEMS), by Robinson Jeffers, copyright 1924 and renewed 1951 by Robinson Jeffers, reprinted from THE SELECTED POETRY OF ROBINSON JEFFERS by permission of Random House, Inc.; "An Elementary School Classroom" (RUINS AND VISIONS, POEMS 1934–1942) by Stephen Spender, copyright 1942 by Stephen Spender, reprinted from COLLECTED POEMS 1928–1953 by Stephen Spender by permission of Random House, Inc.; "I Think Continually of Those" (POEMS BY STEPHEN SPENDER), copyright 1934 and renewed © 1961 by Stephen Spender, reprinted from COLLECTED POEMS 1928–1953 by Stephen Spender by permission of Random House, Inc.

St. Martin's Press, Inc. For "Silver Wedding" from COLLECTED POEMS by Ralph Hodgson.

The Society of Authors. For the selections from COLLECTED POEMS and PEACOCK PIE by Walter de la Mare.

Charles Scribner's Sons. For the selections from THE CHILDREN OF THE NIGHT and THE TOWN DOWN THE RIVER by Edwin Arlington Robinson; POEMS by George Santayana; the translation of Chaucer's BALLADE OF GOOD COUNSEL from THE MAN BEHIND THE BOOK by Henry Van Dyke; "Feel Like a Bird" and "Evolution," copyright 1949, 1954, by May Swenson, reprinted from POETS OF TODAY and used by permission of the publishers, Charles Scribner's Sons.

Shapiro, Bernstein & Company. For the original version of "Casey Jones."

Henry A. Stickney and William W. Mathewson. For the selection from THE POEMS OF TRUMBULL STICKNEY.

The Viking Press, Inc. For the selections from THE COLLECTED POEMS OF D. H. LAWRENCE, copyright, 1929, by Jonathan Cape and Harrison Smith, Inc. By permission of The Viking Press, Inc.

A. Watkins, Inc. For "Still Falls the Rain" by Edith Sitwell.

GENERAL INDEX

[NOTE: Small capitals are used for titles of literary works. Large capitals are used for quoted authors. Roman type indicates persons mentioned in passing. All italic numerals refer to actual quotation, roman numerals to passing mention.]

INDEX OF FIRST LINES

About the Author

Born in New York City, Louis Untermeyer has been in the forefront of various cultural movements since his youth. An outstanding poet, critic and biographer, he is also America's best-known and most creative anthologist. His experiences have been reflected in more than eighty works, including *Makers of the Modern World,* a biographical survey of the great minds and talents of the past hundred years; *A Treasury of Laughter; The Britannica Library of Great American Writing,* a comprehensive two-volume survey; *The Golden Treasury of Children's Literature,* an eighteen-volume series in collaboration with his wife; *Lives of the Poets,* the story of one thousand years of English and American poetry; *Modern American Poetry* and *Modern British Poetry,* which have long been standard textbooks; and *The Letters of Robert Frost to Louis Untermeyer.*

He has had a multiple career. He has served as poet in residence at half a dozen universities, gave the Henry Ward Beecher lectures at Amherst, was Phi Beta Kappa poet at Harvard, and received the Gold Medal of the Poetry Society of America for services to poetry. During World War II he was Senior Editor in the Office of War Information as well as Editor of the Armed Services Editions. For some fourteen years after the war he supervised the cultural division of a leading record company. In 1961 he was appointed Consultant in Poetry for a two-year term at the Library of Congress. In the same year he was sent by the State Department to India, where he represented the United States at a series of literary conferences. In 1963, the State Department sent him to Japan for a series of summer seminars that he conducted in Kyoto, Tokyo, and other cities. In the United States, he has long been a familiar figure on the lecture platform, on radio, and on television.

Except when his commitments take him elsewhere, he spends his time at home in a 220-year-old farmhouse in Connecticut with his wife, Bryna Ivens, formerly fiction editor of *Seventeen* Magazine, three unusually large cats and one exceptionally small dog.